Wo(men) and Bears

The Gifts of Nature, Culture and Gender Revisited

Wo(men) and Bears
The Gifts of Nature, Culture and Gender Revisited

EDITED BY KAARINA KAILO

INANNA PUBLICATIONS AND EDUCATION INC.
TORONTO, CANADA

Published in Canada by
Inanna Publications and Education Inc.
210 Founders College, York University
4700 Keele Street, Toronto, Ontario M3J 1P3
Telephone: (416) 736-5356 Fax (416) 736-5765
Email: inanna@yorku.ca
Website: www.yorku.ca/inanna

Cover Design/Interior Design: Luciana Ricciutelli
Cover Artwork: Irma Heiskanen, "Karhun Enki (Bear Spirit)," 2005.

Printed and Bound in Canada.

Library and Archives Canada Cataloguing in Publication:

 Wo(men) and bears : the gifts of nature, culture and gender revisited / edited by Kaarina Kailo

Includes bibliographical references.
ISBN 978-0-9782233-6-6

1. Bears – Folklore. 2. Women – Folklore. 3. Human-animal relationships – Folklore. 4. Ecofeminism – Folklore. I. Kailo, Kaarina, 1951-

GR730.B4W64 2008   398'.369978   C2008-902591-1

*Dedicated to my friends and Care Bears, Ella Saganash and
Catherine Frye, and to my dear sister, Anne. You all passed away too young,
too soon, too suddenly. Under the Great Bear, in the light of the Moon,
I look up, and I know you are here, somewhere, near …*

Contents

KAARINA KAILO

Giving Back – Acknowledgements

This book goes back a long way to the 1990s when I still lived in Canada, where I spent 17 years as a Ph.D. student, landed immigrant, and women's studies scholar. Apart from such "official" biographical labels, persistent, recurrent, and strong dreams of Bear—which finally I had to begin interpreting and understanding—led me even further North to paths that some inner compass and an academic "research topic" prompted me to follow. I ended up spending nine years as an "adopted" member—not the traditional white anthropologist but rather an ecospiritually-oriented feminist—of a Cree family in Montreal. The "chance" encounter with a neighbour, the single mother of nine children from Waswanipi, changed my life in more ways than the pursuit of an academic career might have led me to expect.

Initially I was interested in doing research on the affinities I perceived between Native Canadian and Finnish modern/traditional life at the interface of urban and bush values. I visited numerous reservations, particularly in the Toronto-Montreal-Chicoutimi area (having also held my first assistant professor position at the University of Quebec, Chicoutimi) and further up in James Bay, from Ouje-Bougamou and Mistissini to Waswanipi. The focus of my planned study changed radically, however, as I integrated into First Nations communities of Mohawks, Crees, Abenakis, and Montagnais—to mention just some of the groups whose people I befriended—when I decided I could not treat my closest friends in Canada as "research objects." I was privileged to share the daily life of the members of Ella Saganash's extended family where I received everything but a textbook, academic introduction to modern Cree life. I wish to thank Ella and the community she brought together in her home, for her, and their, friendship as well as the experiences that significantly deepened my understanding of all aspects of life.

I cherish the memories of the rough-hewn, stone-hard bearskin that Ella left one day at my house. This was a taking of turns in gift-giving between Finland and Waswanipi that also answered a wish I had long held to own a bearskin of my own, a marker, I felt, of my passion for bear research. The hard lump of dark Bear fur stood rigid, like a corpse, in my closet for several years as I tried to learn how it should be treated. How might I transform it into the soft, furry presence I had dreamt of, instead of it remaining in my closet, a frozen fantasy and reminder of my inability to practice the traditional art of preparing skins. After many failed attempts, I travelled with Ella (and my bearskin!) to Quebec City and further, to visit her friends and relatives who might help bring the stiff corpse to "life." We ended up staying on Rue Ursula in Quebec City and I thought this was a good sign. But it would take a few more frustrating months before the Cree hunter materialized who released me from my years of frustration. I think Bear has been something of a trickster in my life. It has played tricks on my wits, my creativity, my patience, my grasp of things and values that I previously took for granted or never needed to question. It taught me a tough lesson—the necessity of learning to let go—not only to give and give back, but also to receive without a sense of indebtedness.

Finally, after too much waiting and disappointment, I decided that I did not need a bearskin. To hell with it. Bear was something deeper, inside me, in my relationship with Nature and my Indigenous friends, my Finnishness, my grandfather who killed a bear to save a man's life, and who instilled the love of bears in me with his exciting, ecofriendly stories, in Kouvola, the land of "Kouvo," meaning Bear. I did not need the skin because Bear was my cosmic co-dependent and more powerful in my imagination than any rough touch could ever become once out of the closet. I let go of my desire for the bearskin and was told by an Anishnabe, Ojibway acquaintance, and by a Dene bear man, that women were not to lie on such skins because they would give her too much power. Too much? I thought I needed more, not less power.

Suddenly things shifted. Out of the blue, I received one fully treated and soft bearskin and then two more landed in my lap, like feathers floating down from the Great Bear, with no effort on my part. Later, when I returned to Finland, I was approached by a man who wanted to get rid of his bearskin—was I interested? The Bears now hold a place of honour at my summer cottage near Kouvola, and in my home in Jääli, Finland. They have been used as Bears in the Bear Ceremonials that have been recently reintroduced in Finland, in events organized among others by the Four Winds organization. My Bearskin partners have thus participated in efforts to revive old ecologically sustainable traditions through dramatic performances in different parts of Finland. Bear has a wonderful sense of humour. It comes out of the closet when it is ready. Not before.

Thank you, Bear. And thank you, Ella. You passed away much too soon. Much was left unsaid and undone. But the work, the research for a more ecologically, socially, biologically, ethnoculturally, and economically sane world continues to keep me busy.

I also thank Carole Brazeau who was a student in my Cultural Studies course, and who completed a project in her Abenaki community near Ottawa regarding women and bears, thus introducing me to modern varieties of the ancient motif, or story, or performance, or ... sacred law. I cannot retell the stories she collected and shared with me for I have not managed to be in contact with the Abenaki community in order to get their permission to do so. Once again, I have learned the lesson of "letting go"; this time it was easier. Nevertheless, as a scholar, it was frustrating to learn that the valuable, tape-recorded material collected by Carole was lost. Bear taught me another lesson: Bear cannot be captured. Some thing are not meant to be recorded, stored in archives or reference libraries. Perhaps the stories were meant to remain in the Abenaki community.

I thank the many Montagnais, Mohawk, Micmac, Anishnaabe, Tlingit, and Cree friends who introduced me to the sweatlodge, or the Lakota *inipi*, and the lesser known aspects of newly resurrected, partly old, partly new, healing practices. As we crawled on all fours into the *inipi*, imitating bears, I was given the opportunity to learn about Bear in yet another way. Most importantly, I was asked to share my own cultural knowledge regarding saunas, healing practices, bearlore, and the like. In this way, we shared with each other the gift of our knowledges. This prompted me to find out more about my own Finnish culture, and thus be able to give back what the Indigenous communities in Canada had so generously given me. Most importantly, perhaps, through this experience I learned about a different kind of "exchange"—not one based on getting back the equivalent or more than what I gave (the exchange economy). Although then I did not have a word for this, I know realize I was taught the art of the gift or "give-back" economy and worldview where needs are satisfied, and human beings are valued, not for the sake of trade, but rather simply for the experience, pleasure, and satisfaction of giving unconditionally.

I wish to thank Genevieve Vaughan, who started the international network Feminists for a Gift Economy, where I had more of these soul-lifting experiences working toward a better world with Indigenous, European, North American, Asian, African, and many other women from near and afar. Genevieve introduced me to the notion of the "gift economy," which immediately struck a familiar chord. With much encouragement from Genevieve in all kinds of ways, I developed the notion of a "gift imaginary," and began applying it to my deepening research on women, Bear, and the symbolic systems and structures of my own people.

Apart from the Saganash family, I have lived with another Indigenous family in Europe, that of the Sami writer and activist Kirsti Paltto in Utsjoki, her Finnish husband Eino Kuokkanen, and their many friends in the Northernmost municipality in Finland/Samiland. I thank Kirsti and the others for sharing with me their many stories ranging from Kirsti's two-headed women to the story of Rásstos, given to this anthology. The relationship with Sami scholar Rauna Kuokkanen started from my visit to her family, and I had a chance to get her funding to work as my assistant in the Women's studies program, introducing her at the same time to Native studies in Montreal.

I also send thankful thoughts in the direction of the star constellation, Ursus Arctos, the Great Bear. I am sure that is where you look down on the Earth and its follies, Catherine Frye, my bear friend, bear soul mate. More lessons of letting go in my life. Not only did I lose Ella but also Catherine, the spiritually-oriented filmmaker with whom we were planning a documentary on women and bears. It is not surprising, if hard to explain, that this anthology on wo(men) and Bears has taken many years to materialize. It seems that Bear was again at it, creating one obstacle after another—personal, academic, financial, and mysterious—to forestall the publication of this book. The project began in the 1990s when I first took an interest in the Bear Ceremonial and began collecting articles for the book with Sima Aprahamian. Already then, as an advocate of ecofeminism, I was distressed about the fate of Grizzlies, the narrowing of their living space in the North, and all of what that signified mythically and in terms of human-animal-planetary history. Now that the ice is melting from under the very feet of the Arctic Polar Bear, I feel there is even more urgency for us humans to take responsibility for our anthropocentrism, our short-sighted economic plunder of the Earth's resources, our irresponsible actions advancing global climate change.

I thank the women in the women's movements and political circles to which I belong. I thank particularly Irma Heiskanen with whom, among others, we initiated and founded the Finnish Ecopsychology Association in 2001. Irma has supported my research into the erotic, cosmic, spiritual, and material adventures of Bearwomen and has provided me with many great insights, generously sharing her own Bear dreams and academic materials on Bear.

I also thank my students at Simone de Beauvoir Institute, Montreal, Canada, and in Oulu, Finland, who have had to "grin and bear it" as I subjected them to smaller or bigger doses of Bear in my courses on Nordicity, Indigenous women and Bears, and other related Northern themes to do with violence and healing. Writing journals or essays on the texts we studied together, they have brought many insights to Bear on my research. In this regard, I also thank Helga Reischl, whose dissertation on The Woman Who Married the Bear I co-supervised for Humboldt University, Berlin between 2000-2004. Having read numerous versions of her work-in-progress, I was introduced to her rich analysis and knowledge regarding the topic in which we shared a deep interest. I believe our mutual Bear dialogue benefited both of us, in different ways, advancing the course of research into the neglected dimensions of an important religious-cultural and ecological topic.

There are many more people I should acknowledge but I limit myself to the bearpeople most central to the "project" of unearthing traces of Bear. Ulla Ryum, a member of the Feminist for a Gift network, whom I met at the Women's University, Kvinneuniversitet in Løten, Norway, gave me much more than an academic interview. Our discussions about Bear and Inuit spirituality have continued on and off. Satu Marit Natunen, known in Finland and Samiland for her art featuring women with bears, wolves, and other animals, gave me of her time and insights and agreed to be part of a videotaping of bearwomen. I also recognize the now deceased Åke Hultkranz, the great "old" man of Studies on Native Peoples whom I met in Helsinki, at a conference on sauna, sweatlodge, and the Japanese furo. Prof. Hultkrantz kindly commented on my research, supported it with a genuinely positive attitude, and gave me useful hints for sources I had not considered. It was uplifting also to meet with Scott Momaday during his visit to a conference at the University of Helsinki. Although our conversation was brief, it gave me direction and an internal sense of balance. That is Bear in action. Juha Nirkko, of Suomen

Kirjallisuuden Seura (SKS), the Finnish Literature Society, provided archival help when I searched the vast records for evidence of the Bear Ceremonials and related motifs at this treasure-house of Finnish literature.

I would like to give back to all of the scholars, artists, and writers who agreed to send material for this anthology. I had engaged in stimulating conversations about Bear with Chris Trott while we both worked at Concordia University. I have recognized the role of Sima Aprahamian, my colleague from Simone de Beauvoir Institute, who was initially my co-editor for this anthology. Once again, thanks for the efforts we made together before my departure to Finland interrupted our rich collaboration. Jürgen Kremer has likewise commented on my research, and on my own article in this collection, and provided useful suggestions for improving it.

I extend my heartfelt thanks also to Angela Miles who showed her commitment to the gift paradigm when giving very concrete and detailed feedback on many intercultural/postcolonial issues of the anthology, contributing invaluable comments regarding the introduction.

Luciana Ricciutelli, Editor-in-Chief of Inanna Publications and Education Inc., also merits words of recognition and a big bear hug. Inanna has taken the risk of putting out a book that transgresses academic genre conventions with its mix of essays, poetry, artwork, and academic articles. The book will give headaches to librarians: where should it be placed, which shelf, what category? Luciana first expressed interest in publishing the book in our chance encounter in Kampala, Uganda—perhaps another incidence of Bear up to her tricks—when we found ourselves sitting next to each other, both of us taking a break from the Women's World Conference in 2004. During that leisurely moment, I told her of my manuscript, and here we are. Bear works in mysterious ways. I thank Luciana for her skilfull editing of the contributions to this anthology and for offering solid advice for the book's improvement and final shape.

Finally, my thanks go to my family—Seppo, my teddy-bearish husband, and our dog, Hulda, who are my daily bearadise, a place of solace, balance, adjustment to the hardships and losses of life, a space of rejuvenation and rebirth.

Of course, Bear will have the last word on where the Gifts come from and where they go. Mainstream research and the academy are deeply embedded in colonial practices and ideologies. Courage is needed to transform academe and point it in more humane and ecoresponsible directions. In this regard my thanks go also to the expert on Sami "give-back" philosophies, Rauna Kuokkanen. Our years of collaboration and student-supervisor relations have yielded many mind-altering debates about white mythology, epistemic violence, and the denial of the Gifts of Native cultures in academic circles. Rauna is today Assistant Professor in the Department of Political Studies/Aboriginal Studies at the University of Toronto, and formerly Dean of the Sami University College in Kautokeino, Norway. Her name is that of the maiden of Spring in Sami storytelling traditions, Ravna. As Jürgen Kremer notes in his article in this anthology, Ravna is also, perhaps unknown to herself, linked to Bear for it is this maiden of Spring who wakes the Bear and thus participates in the ritual of life renewal. Or maybe she knows this only too well. Rauna translated her mother, Kirsti Paltto's story of Rásstos, She-bear, for this collection.

Finally, it is customary to give recognition to the Finnish Academy that has provided me with funding at different stages of my academic life. Most recently, in 2007-08, I was appointed Senior Researcher with the project "Trauma and Healing in Northern Native and non-Native women's Fiction." Although the focus of the research project is a comparative study of the themes of violence and healing in women's writings in the North, this anthology has also benefited from the research and my discovery of new materials and contributors for this anthology. *Giitu. Kiitos.* Thank you. *Megweetch.* A woman is not born a woman, she is made into one, notes Simone de Beauvoir. Nor are women born Bears, but under the threat of global climate change, they may well need to revert to their ancient role as Bear spouses, presiding over the rituals of rebirth and renewal.

Preface

> Between the ... "encoded" eye and reflexive knowledge there is a middle
> region which liberates order itself.
>
> —Michel Foucault (1973: xxi)

This collection of articles has been in the birthing and delivery process for several
linear and cyclical years. It has also had several "triggers." One of the catalysts was
an informal discussion between myself and Kaarina Kailo at Simone de Beauvoir
Institute, Concordia University. We were discussing the way in which anthropology and western science at their early phase ended up producing or reinforcing
a dichotomous way of looking at Nature and Culture. Much of anthropology
has, in fact, been about the way in which western cultures relate to these much-
debated concepts. For example, Claude Levi-Strauss, one of the leading theorists
in anthropology, has devoted four volumes of his *Mythologiques* (1964-1969) to
the relationship between Nature and Culture. The first volume of *Mythologiques*
published in 1964 was about the passage from Nature into Culture symbolically
represented through the *Raw and the Cooked*. The second volume published in
1966 continued the theme through a focus on *From Honey to Ashes*. The 1968
volume on the origins of table manners continued the theme of Nature/Culture.
The last volume is the final product: *Man* (Levi-Stauss 1971). Some of the
dominant themes in Levi-Straussian and modernist anthropology since Lewis
Henry Morgan have been (1) kinship as a category which is about both Nature
and Culture; (2) incest prohibition setting distinctions between the in-group and
categories with whom one could have intercourse; (3) totemism as a system of
classification involving a relationship between a human group and a non-human
category; (4) the raw and the cooked; (5) types of organization; (6) modes of
obtaining a livelihood; (7) ecology (MacCormack and Strathern 1990). Marilyn
Strathern, in her book *After Nature* (1992), recognizes that the study of kinship
has played a significant role in the making of anthropology itself: "The concept
of kinship as a set of principles by which people organized their fundamental
relations epitomized the anthropological capacity to describe cultural production
on the one hand and the way people made collective and social life known to
themselves on the other" (MacCormak and Strathern 1990: 46).

Following our informal discussions Kaarina invited me in the spring of 1995 to be a guest lecturer in one of her advanced Women's Studies classes on Women and Culture. The topic that I had chosen in the context of folk and fairytales was Armenian stories about women running away with bears. I read these stories as attempts to transgress Nature and Culture and discovered that Kaarina had also been interested in bear symbolism and bearlore for quite a long period of time. In other words, we were both concerned with "kinship relations" from the point of view not of neutral (= male-defined) social contracts, but of bears and women. We were both aware that kinship is symbolic in the sense of David Schneider's now classic book *American Kinship* (1968), and the subsequent studies by Carol Delaney (1991) and others.

We decided to organize either a mini-conference or forum to bring together storytellers and scholars of bear narratives. Our first step was co-organizing a session entitled "Transgressing Nature/Culture/Gender: Women and Bears" at the 1997 Canadian Anthropology and Society Association meeting in St. Johns, Newfoundland, where the focus was on stories or narratives that involve bears and women. Such stories, we argued, can be viewed as challenges to the very categories of Nature, Culture, and Gender. Western science and many scholars believe these categories are primal differential categories of socio-religious organization. We believe, beyond that particular issue, that wo(men) and bear stories present epistemic, philosophical, and socio-political challenges to contemporary thought.

The starting position of our session was that two decades had passed since the 1977 meeting of the Association of Social Anthropologists in Swansea that led to the collection of articles edited by Carol MacCormack and Marilyn Strathern entitled *Nature, Culture and Gender* (1990). The starting point in MacCormack and Strathern was to show, through ethnographic data, that Nature, Culture, and Gender are analytic categories or constructs and that their representations are about human interaction. In this collection, these categories and their transgressions are analyzed by questioning the very division of human and animal as such taken-for-granted differential categories. Many cultures have and continue to consider bears as half-human and half-animal, and have much more flexible and fluid boundaries for a variety of phenomena (dreams/reality, history/story, truth/fiction, etc.). We wished to broaden the possible range of interpretations and the social significance of stories about women and bears through case studies and hybrid narrative modes of approaching the question. The very category of gender had to be questioned as the centrally relevant one as in many ancient bear hunting cultures, bear feasts or ceremonials served to blur not just gender-related, but other types of dualistic distinctions rather than reinforce them. In our experience, the very study of kinship relations bears the stamp of euro, andro, and cognicentric biases. As many Indigenous thinkers and "practitioners" have shown, kinship relations in their very broadest framework involve *all* our relations, the entire ecosystem. Hence the need to deconstruct the hierarchically ordered and dualistic "bearlore" that may well tell us more about patriarchal, androcentric scholarship than about the bear as a widely-spread pre-Christian cosmological trope.

This project began as a close collaboration between Kaarina Kailo and myself. We decided, however, to retain this preface as separate from the introduction because in the process of collecting the materials for the anthology, Kaarina moved back to Finland, accepting a university position as Chair of Women's Studies and Multiculturalism at Oulu University in 1999, which ultimately hindered our ongoing collaboration. The neo-liberal restructuring at both the Canadian and Finnish universities also had its negative effects by downsizing much of the material and immaterial resources for Women's Studies, finally slowing down this project, due, as well, to our increased workload as Women's Studies educators.

While we initially conceived of the book and collected submissions together, in the end Kaarina shouldered the major responsibility for editing the book and writing the introduction. She undertook the analysis and organization of the materials received, and the overall vision of the book is of her making. The book has changed quite a bit over the years and now bears the mark of recent issues—globalization and the increasing need for ecosocial sustainability, all themes which Kaarina has taken into account in updating, for example her own piece. In 2001, Kaarina also joined the international research and activist network, Feminists for a Gift Economy; the values regarding gift circulation and an ecosocial justice have come to mark her vision for the book.

This preface attests to the role I have had in different stages of our collaboration, contacting the contributors and being part of the initial planning of the anthology. We both wish to thank all the participants for their patience with this project. We recognize gratefully some seed funding received from Concordia University's General Research Fund towards this research. And we thank our families for support during these many years of "bearing and grinning" with us.

References

Delaney. Carol. 1991. *The Seed and the Soil.* Berkeley: University of California Press.

Foucault. Michel. 1973. *The Order of Things.* New York: Vintage Books.

Levi-Strauss. Claude. 1964. *Mythologiques I: The Raw and the Cooked.* New York: Harper and Raw.

Levi-Strauss. Claude. 1966. *Mythologiques II: Du Miel aux cendres.* Paris: Plon.

Levi-Strauss. Claude. 1968. *Mythologiques III: L'origine des manières de table.* Paris: Plon.

Levi-Strauss. Claude. 1971. *Mythologiques IV: L'homme.* Paris: Plon.

MacCormack. Carol and Marilyn Strathern, eds. 1990. *Nature, Culture, and Gender.* Cambridge: Cambridge University Press.

Schneider, David. 1968. *American Kinship.* Chicago: Chicago University Press.

Strathern, Marilyn. 1992. *After Nature.* Cambridge: Cambridge University Press.

The spirit of Bear is awakening
The Heart Hears
with some Strange Ear

—Irma Heiskanen

"Bear and Bride," 1996.
Photographers: Ritva Kovalainen and Sanni Seppo

The Girl Who Married the Bear

As told by Maria Johns (to Catherine McClellan)*

Once there was a little girl.... And she used to pick berries in the summer. Every summer she would go with her family, and they would pick berries and dry them. When she used to go with her women folk on the trail, they would see bear droppings on the trail. In the old days the girls had to be careful about bear droppings. They shouldn't walk over it. Men could walk over it, but young girls had to walk around it. But this girl always did jump over it and kick it. She kept seeing it all around her. She did this from childhood.

When she was quite big, they were going camping. They were going to dry fish. They went out picking berries. She was just a young girl. She went out and was picking with her mothers and aunts and sisters. She saw some bear droppings. She said all kinds of words to it and kicked it and jumped over it.

While they were all coming home, they were all carrying baskets of berries. The girl saw some nice berries and stopped to get them. The others went ahead. When she had picked the berries and was starting to get up, her berries all spilled out of her basket. She leaned down and was picking them off the ground.

Soon she saw a young man. He was very good looking. She had never seen him before. He had red paint on his face. He stopped and talked to her. He said: "Those berries you are picking are no good. They are all full of dirt. Let's go up a little ways and fill your basket up. There are some good berries growing there. I'll walk home with you. You needn't be afraid!"...

After they had gotten the basket half full of berries, the man said, "There is another bunch of berries up there a little ways. We'll pick them too."

When they had picked them all, he said, "It's time to eat. You must be hungry." He made a fire....

They cooked gopher, quite a lot of it, and they ate some. Then the man said, "It's too late to go home now. We'll go home tomorrow. It's summer, and there's no need to fix a big camp."

So they stayed there. When they went to bed, he said, "Don't lift your head in the morning and look at me, even if you wake up before I do."

So they went to bed.

Next morning they woke up. The man said to her, "We might as well go. We'll just eat that cold gopher. We needn't make a fire. They we'll go pick some berries. Let's get a basket full."

All the time the girl kept talking about her mother and father. All the time she wanted to go home, and she kept talking about it.

He said, "Don't be afraid, I'm going home with you."

Then he slapped her right on top of her head, and he put a circle around the girl's head the way the sun goes [clockwise]. He did this so she would forget. Then she forgot. She didn't talk about her home any more.

Then they left again. He said, "You're all right. I'll go home with you."

Then after this, she forgot all about going home. She just went around with him picking berries. Everytime they camped, it seemed like a month to her, but it was really only a day. They started in May. They kept travelling and going.

Finally she recognized a place. It looked like a place that she and her family used to dry meat. Then he stopped there at the timberline and slapped. And he made a circle sunwise [on her head], and another on the ground where she was sitting. He said, "Wait here. I am going hunting gophers. We have no meat. Wait 'til I come back."...Then he came back with the gophers. They kept travelling. Late in the evening they made camp and cooked.

Next morning they got up again, and it was getting near fall. It was getting late. And she came to her senses and knew it. It was cold. He said, "It's time to make camp. We must make a home." He started making a home. He was digging a den. She knew he was a bear then.

He got quite a way digging the den, then he said, "Go get some balsam boughs and brush." Then she went and got some. She broke the branches from as high as she could. She brought the bundle.

He said, "That brush is no good. You left a mark, and the people will see it and know we were here. We can't use that. We can't stay here."

So they left. They went up to the head of a valley. She knew her brothers used to go there to hunt and to eat bear. In the spring they took the dogs there, and they hunted bears in April. They would send the dogs into the bear den long ago, and then the bear would come out. That's where her brothers used to go. She knew it.

He said, "We'll make camp." He dug a den and sent her out again. "Get some brush that is just lying on the ground—not from up high. No one will see where you get it, and it will be covered with snow."

She got it from the ground and brought it to him, but she bent the branches up high too. So she let them hang down so her brothers would know. And she rubbed sand all over herself—all over her body and limbs. And then she rubbed the trees all around, so that the dogs would find where she had left her scent. Then she went to the den with her bundle of brush. She brought it.

Just when the man was digging, he looked like a bear. This was the only time. The rest of the time he seemed like a human being. The girl didn't know how else to stay alive, so she stayed with him as long as he was good to her.

6

"This is better." he said, when she brought back the brush. Then he brushed up and fixed the place. After he fixed the den, they left.

They went hunting gophers for winter. She never saw him do it. She always sat around when he was hunting gophers. He dug them up like a grizzly bear, and he didn't want her to see it. He never showed her where he kept the gophers.

Nearly every day they hunted gophers and picked berries. It was quite late in the year. He was just like a human to her.

It was October. It was really late in the fall. He said, "Well, I guess we'll go home now. We have enough food and berries. We'll go down."

So they went home. Really they went into the den. They stayed there and slept. They woke up once a month and got up to eat. They kept doing it and going back to bed. Every month it seemed like another morning, just like another day. They never really went outside. It just seemed like it.

Soon the girl found that she was carrying a baby. She had two little babies—one was a girl, and one was a boy. She had them in February in the den. This is when bears have their cubs. She had hers then.

The bear used to sing in the night. When she woke up, she would hear him. The bear became like a doctor [shaman] when he started living with the woman. It just came upon him like a doctor. He sang the song twice. She heard it the first time. The second time the bear made a sound, "*Wuf! Wuf!*" And she woke up.

"You're my wife, and I am going to leave soon. It looks like your brothers are going to come up here soon, before the snow is gone. I want you to know that I am going to do something bad. I am going to fight back!"

"Don't do it!" she said. They are my brothers. If you really love me, you'll love them too. Don't kill them. Let them kill you! If you really love me, don't fight! You have treated me good. Why did you live with me, if you are going to kill them?"

"Well, all right," he said, "I won't fight, but I want you to know what will happen."

His canines looked like swords to her. "These are what I fight with," he said. They looked like knives to her. She kept pleading.

"Don't do anything. I'll still have my children if they kill you!" She knew he was a bear then. She really knew.

They went to sleep. She woke again. He was singing again.

"It's true," he said. "They are coming close. If they do kill me, I want them to give you my skull—my head, and and my tail. Tell them to give them to you. Wherever they kill me, build a big fire, and burn my head and tail and sing this song while the head is burning. Sing it until they are all burnt up!"

So they ate and went to bed, and another month went by. They didn't sleep the whole month. He kept waking up. "It's coming close," he said. "I can't sleep well. It's getting to be bare ground. Look out and see if the snow is melted in front of the den."

She looked and there was mud and sand. She grabbed some and made it into a ball and rubbed it all over herself. It was full of her scent. She rolled it down the hill. The dogs could smell it. She came in and said, "There is bare ground all over in some places."

He asked her why she had made the marks. "Why? Why? Why? They'll find us easy."

After they had slept for half a month, they woke, and he was singing again. "This is the last one," he said. "You'll not hear me again. Any time the dogs are coming to the door. They are close. Well, I'll fight back! I am going to do something back!"

His wife said, "You know they are my brothers! Don't do it! Who will look after my children if you kill them? You must think of the kids. My brothers will help me. If my brothers hunt you, let them be!"

Then they went to bed for just a little while. "I can't sleep good, but we'll try," he said.

Next morning he said, "Well, it's close! It's close! Wake up!"

Just when they were getting up, they heard a noise. "The dogs are barking. Well," he said, "I'll leave. Where are my knives? I want them!"

He took them down. She saw him putting in his teeth. He was a big bear. She pleaded with him. "Please don't fight. If you wanted me, why did you go this far? Just think of the kids. Don't hurt my brothers!"

When he went, he shook hands and said, "You are not going to see me again!"

He went out and growled. He slapped something back into the den. It was a pet dog, a little bear dog.

When he threw the dog in, she grabbed it and shoved it back in the brush under the nest. She put the dog there to hide it. She sat on it and kept it there so it couldn't get out. She wanted to keep it there for a reason.

For a long time there was no noise. She went out of the den. She heard her brothers below. They had already killed the bear. She felt bad, and she sat down. She found an arrow and one side of a glove. She picked it up, and all of the arrows. Finally she fitted the little dog with a string around his back. She tied the arrows and the glove into a bundle. She put them all on the little dog, and he ran to his masters.

The boys were down there dressing the bear. They knew the dog. They noticed the bundle and took it off. "It's funny," they said. "No one in a bear den would tie this on!" They talked about it. They decided to send the youngest brother up to the den. In those days a younger brother could talk to his sister, but an older brother couldn't.

The older brothers said to the youngest brother. "We lost our sister a year ago in May. Something could have happened. A bear might have taken her away. You are the youngest brother. Don't be afraid. There is nothing up there but her. You go and see if she is there. Find out!"

He went. She was sitting there crying. The boy came up. She was sitting and crying. She cried when she saw him. She said, "You boys killed your brother-in-law! I went with him last May. You killed him, but tell the others to save me the skull and the tail. Leave it there for me. When you get home, tell mother to sew a dress for me so I can go home. Sew a dress for the girl, and pants and a shirt for the boy. And moccasins. And tell her to come and see me."

He left and got down there and told his brothers, "This is my sister [up there]. She wants the head and tail."

They did this, and they went home. They told their mother. She got busy and sewed. She had a dress and moccasins and clothes for the children. The next day she went up there. She came to the place. They dressed the little kids. Then they went down to where the bear was killed. The boys had left a big fire. She burned the head and tail. Then she sang until all was ashes.

Then they went home, but she didn't go right home. She said. "Get the boys to build a house. I can't come right in [to the main camp]. It will be quite a while. The boys can build a camp right away."

She stayed there a long while. Towards fall she came and stayed with her mother. All winter. The kids grew. Next spring the boys [her brothers] wanted her to act like a bear. They wanted to play with her. They had killed a female bear that had cubs, one male and one female. They wanted their sister to put on the hide and to act like a bear. They fixed little arrows. They pestered her to play with them, and they wanted her two little children to play too. She didn't want it.

She told her mother, "I can't do it! Once I do it, I will turn into a bear. I'm half there already. Hair is already showing on my arms and legs. It is quite long."

If she had stayed there with her bear husband another summer, she would have turned into a bear. "If I put on bear hide, I'll turn into one," she said.

They kept telling her to play. Then the boys sneaked up. They threw the hides over her and the little ones. Then she walked off on four legs, and she shook herself just like a bear. It just happened. She was a grizzly bear. She couldn't do a thing. She had to fight against the arrows. She killed them all off, even her mother. But she didn't kill her youngest brother, not him. She couldn't help it. Tears were running down her face.

Then she went on her own. She had her two little cubs with her.

That's why they claim that long ago a bear is partly human. That is why you never eat grizzly bear meat. Now people eat black bear meat, but they still don't eat grizzly meat, because grizzlies are half human.

Maria Johns was born probably some time between 1860 and 1870. Maria belonged to the tuq'wedi *[or decitan] sib, and she traced her ancestry ultimately to the coastal Tlingit town of Angoon.... Maria volunteered the bear story [to researcher Catherine McClellan] on the morning of July 16, 1948.*

From The Girl Who Married the Bear: A Masterpiece of Oral Tradition, *Catherine McClellan, Gatineau: Canadian Museum of Civilization, 1970, pp. 28-33. © Canadian Museum of Civilization. Reprinted with permission.*

Mari Redkin, "Karhun kans(s)a [With Bear People]," pastels, 2007. Private Collection.

KAARINA KAILO

Introduction

In order to perpetuate itself, every oppression must corrupt or distort those various sources of power within the culture of the oppressed that can provide energy for change.

—Audre Lorde (1984: 55)

Global climate change, the threats to the survival of countless plant and animal species, and the increasing storms around the world have finally begun to command worldwide attention. Bears and bees, which feature prominently in world mythology as supreme embodiments of world renewal have become symbols of the threats to our ecological survival. According to one report, "the still-puzzling phenomenon of disappearing honey bees that scientists call 'Colony Collapse Disorder' has been reported in 35 states, five Canadian provinces, a dozen European countries, China, Taiwan, Guatemala, Brazil, and Ukraine" (Howe 2008). I wish to begin by contextualizing this ecocritical and ecomythologica/historical anthology in terms of the threats to bears and bees, among other species, threats that represent this collection's most urgent ethical background.

Steve Kroft (2008) finds that "Bees are the unsung heroes of the food chain, crucial to the production of one third of the foods we eat." Considered in ancient times the messengers of the gods and goddesses due to honey's mysterious healing and nourishing properties, bees today, with a 33 percent disappearance rate in North America to date, are having a significant impact on the pollination of a wide variety of crops (Howe 2008), and on honey production—a favourite food for bears. Polar bears are also at risk as global warming causes catastrophic environmental change in the Arctic. "Because the bears are deeply dependent on the sea ice for their survival, they stand to become the first mammals in the world to lose 100 percent of their habitat to global warming" (Centre for Biological Diversity 2005), causing "polar bears to become extinct by the end of century" (Eilperin 2004: A13). Researchers have noted that bears in Manitoba, Canada "have been losing weight … if the weight loss continues, most females in the population will be below the minimum threshold needed for successful reproduction" (Mittelstaedt 2008: A9). Grizzly bears, too, face the prospect of extinction. A review of grizzly bear populations in Canada designated over 60 percent of grizzly bears as either vulnerable or threatened, and they are no longer found in 99 percent of their former habitat in the lower 48 states and Mexico (Columbia Mountains Institute of Applied Ecology 1999), caused in large part by humans' encroachment of their habitat (and development, such as oil and gas drilling). Is all this Earth's warning signal, the proverbial canary in the coal mine for the planet? At the very least it speaks to the pressing need for greater ecological responsibility and care.

In light of the empirical observations and environmental concerns of many Indigenous[1] peoples (e.g. Helander and Mustonen 2004), what do we make of the alarming ways nature is changing and of the many other disturbing "seasonal freaks" that scientists list as the consequence of the climate change almost daily? As Indigenous thinkers, ecophilosophers, and ecofeminists, among many other academics and activists, have noted, humans have become so alienated from nature and ecological balance that solutions to the ecocrises are now sought from within the very same approaches and paradigms that have caused or contributed to the problems: a mechanical worldview and trust in profit-driven measures and innovations—the staple of the unbridled market economy or the exchange economy criticized by feminists of all backgrounds (Abrahams 2007; Adelkarim-Chikh 2007; Antrobus 2007; Armstrong 1995; Benally 2007; Eikjok 2000; Jimenez 2007; Kuokkanen 2008; Kuokkanen and Riihijärvi 2006; LaDuke 1997; Mies and Shiva 1993; Trask 2007). Although many useful tools have no doubt been invented for tackling the ecological problems, the dominant ethos of neoconservative politics of accumulation, the greed and creed of limitless growth in a world of finite resources, continues to water down their impact. Without a critical mass of people recognizing the role played by utilitarian and production-rationalistic attitudes in environmental destruction and loss of diversity, the psychosocial root causes of ecological destruction remain unrecognized and unfocused. This book takes issue particularly with the consequences of the mastery over nature that informs the dominant eurocentric worldview, patriarchal attitudes, and relations with nature, characterized by a lack of respect for the inherent rights of *all* living beings.

As a case in point, this anthology explores the many-sided, multidimensional status and role of Bear in the human imaginary through ancient and modern worldviews. This includes Indigenous epistemes of balance and cultures of "giveback" in their various manifestations (Bopp 1984; Caffyn 1992; Colorado 1988; Eikjok and Birkeland 2004; Kailo 2003, 2004; Kuokkanen 2007; LaDuke 1997; Länsman 2004; Lowe 2001; Nahani 1993; Scholtmeijer 2004; Verrall 1991; Wheeler 1992). Myths contain and transmit vital knowledge including ecological wisdom related to survival. In this regard, reclaiming and circulating ecomythologies—my term for myths expressing respectful human/animal relations, with their time-tested environmental, sustainable rationality and wisdom, represent some of the many necessary means of bringing about collective transformation. Ecopsychology, ecofeminism, ecocriticism (literary ecology),[2] and other related fields are of increasing importance for the future, since they seek solutions to the crises through changes in human behaviour and values, not only through market mechanisms. As bears are threatened by the loss of their habitat,[3] it is civilized and rational rather than "flaky" to evoke the once powerful, even divine Bear Goddess/King of the Forest, and other spirit beings guarding the Earth, the dethroning of which from many cultural narratives epitomizes the devaluation of not only animals but of many other life forms.

This anthology is a collection of articles, poetry, art, and fiction that focus on the mythological, academic, ethnographic, aesthetic, and socio-historic relations between wo(men) and Bear/s,[4] by contributors from many cultures and disciplinary backgrounds. The anthology presents a variety of viewpoints on an archaic and modern story, legend, or historical fragment that has had wide circulation across time and space. "The Girl Who Married the Bear" is an ancient narrative with numerous cross-cultural variants and fragments that can be found throughout the world. The book brings these perspectives together not only because the story is a recurrent element of a cross-cultural women's ecomythological genealogy, but also because it sheds light precisely on the importance of honouring bees, bears, birds, and other beings associated with sustainability and the renewal of life on Earth.

The widely circulated narratives of wo(men) and Bear/s carry traces of shifts in worldview that are of ethnocultural and gendered relevance and that speak to the different stance humans have historically taken toward the environment and their own communities/community members. The variants in the stories point to suppressed or marginalized worldviews based among other things on gift and "give-back" economies.[5]

The theoretical approach in which I ground the anthology consists in bringing together traditional and contemporary Indigenous and non-Indigenous views and interpretations on the theme of wo(men) and Bear/s. As editor, I emphasize the need for new ecologically and biologically, culturally and economically sustainable research methods. As diversity, not only of method but of theoretical approaches themselves is a key value and goal, I am pleased to include diverse—Northern, Central and Mediterranean, Armenian, Canadian, Dene, Ojibway, Tlingit, Tagish, Tsimshian, Inuit, Cree, Sami, Finnish, Evenk (Finno-Ugric), and German—perspectives on the chosen theme.

The stories of wo(men) and Bear/s hold many vestiges of a life-respecting and sustaining logic, that of the gift paradigm, which may serve to unite Indigenous and non-Indigenous people concerned about the planet's future and other ethical issues. By honouring diverse cultural practices and beliefs surrounding the bear narrative and its context, I hope to contribute, at the same time, to the kind of paradigm shift that sees value in sustainable diversity, rather than monoculture—an academic blueprint for collective well-being. Where the neoconservative profit-oriented ethos of monoculture (Shiva 1993) seeks profit through homogenous mass products and cultures, the ethos of diversity does the opposite: it values diversity of species and culture not only as an end in itself but also as a means for collective, global survival. The gift paradigm on which many of the texts in this anthology comment, implicitly or explicitly, can help guide us back towards the ecomythologies that patriarchal fundamentalisms have, in the course of history, replaced and suppressed with more ecophobic narratives. These bear narratives are important for they bring tidings from many parts of the world of a saner worldview, one of interdependence rather than the glorification of autonomous individuality. The gift paradigm is a promising matrix for respectful intercultural conversations. For while it remains more intact in Indigenous cultures, the logic persists even in "modern" cultures which deny it and have largely lost their pre-Christian gift-circulating ways, for example in the care work of most women beyond the essentialized and sentimental politics of patriarchal mothering.

The politics of cultural appropriation and asymmetrical, imperialistic "borrowing" from Indigenous peoples have received much attention in women's and cultural studies, particularly in Canada. Hopefully, with this awareness, sharing becomes truly egalitarian. I have sought to create a space for respectful and fruitful intercultural sharing, although I realize how challenging it remains in light of the systemic ethocentrism and racism that still prevails in the research community. Assumptions have been made that the Finns must have appropriated the bearlore and even the Bear ceremonial from the Sami or other Indigenous peoples of the North. In fact, the Finns (like the Sami) have even today a rich body of folktales, poems, and other materials attesting to the central importance of the Bear ceremonial and related cultural practices with vestiges of the Bear rituals and Bear-honouring worldview still found in the nineteenth century. The Irish, the Armenians, Greeks, and many other cultures, which have long lost most of their pre-patriarchal Indigenous heritage, also have echoes of comparable narratives from their Indigenous past. After the debates on cultural appropriation—themselves of course timely and necessary—we might now focus on what those of us committed to a sustainable future have in common, beyond the common enemy: the master identity and any politics of power-over. The multidisciplinary, cross-genre approach attempted in this book role-models a kind of hemispheric cross-talk across cultural politics of difference, or as I call it (based on my Finnish background and self-reflective ethos), a politics of af-finn-ities (Kailo 1997a, 1997b), aimed at creating more solid intercultural bridges through the sharing of life-celebrating ecomythologies/narratives/histories.

It is important to stress, from the very start, that the gift paradigm unifying many of the contributions does not represent a new politics of appropriating Indigenous philosophies or a new myth of global sisterhood, already exposed as a fallacy in the 1980s. Rather, advocates of the gift paradigm seek to create a sisterhood/brotherhood of re-sisters against the inhuman and ecophobic politics of neoliberalism or neoconservatism and it recognizes the intersectionalities of ethnicity, hetero/sexism, speciesism, and a host of other manifestations of "othering," rooted in the master identity (Plumwood 1993) and patriarchy (or whatever other terms have been used to refer to the politics of power over, or mastery over nature, women, and vulnerable populations).

To examine myths of wo(men) and Bear/s allows us to consider the implications of reclaiming a genealogy and symbolic order based on inclusive interspecies notions of regeneration. Archaeologist, Marija Gimbutas (1989) has helped foreground the mythico-historical genealogy of goddesses within Old European agricultural societies, giving as one example the Vinca Culture, symbolized by the Bear Madonna with a Bear-son (116). Gimbutas claims that agricultural societies celebrating birth and the Great Goddess, as well as a matrilineal pattern of descent, were replaced over the course of history by waves of Indo-European patriarchal invaders. Although her theories have threatened dominant versions of history, and have been objects of many attacks, recently more studies have come to support her findings (Dergachev 2007). The story of the Vinca Bear Madonna has similarities to the story of the Greek Kallisto, which some regard as a kind of nomadic proto-type of the Bear Goddess in her endless free-floating, contingent variants (Gimbutas 1989; Reischl 2004). In the European context, the stories of women and Bear/s point to the overwriting, suppression, incorporation, and renaming of the Bear Goddess and her myths, accompanied by the subsequent demonization of those symbolic, political, familial, and religious sources of power traditionally associated with women and other icons of regeneration/reproduction. However, at a time when non-dualistic/non-essentializing paradigms are in vogue in women's studies, among other disciplines, scholars focused on antiquity are wise to avoid projecting on the distant past any naturalized assumptions of an unchanging sex/gender system. As feminist anthropological studies (e.g. pioneers MacCormack and Strathern 1980; Moore 1988; Sanday 1998, 1981) have amply revealed, although gender and sexuality have been central principles of social arrangements and power across time and space, patriarchy cannot be assumed to be universal. There is nothing to prove that *arch*-aic societies based on Bear totemism privileged a sexual or reproductive culture with male and female sexuality as a hierarchical polarity. As Lillian E. Doherty (2001) points out in her feminist revision of Greek and Roman narratives: "Hard as we may try, we can never completely divorce ourselves from the nexus of gendered meanings and practices in our own world, which their modern, adapted versions" (23). The classical and other myths tend to be "naturalized" into our gender system and reflect the ancient systems in and for which they were produced.

Through the study of the story, "The Girl Who Married the Bear," this book challenges the ideological first principles of heteronormativity but also the anthropocentric matrix that Butlerian "queer"[6] or "sexualities" politics, despite their "cutting" edge status within many women's studies circles, has failed to address (Butler 1990). In fact, revisiting these ancient stories of human/animal kinship relations permits us to speculate on and analyze the various transitions in status that the often bisexual or transgender gods and goddesses and their sacred animals (or "cosmic partners") underwent in the course of history.[7] For, whereas the collective attributes projected on the archaic "imaginary body" (Gatens 1991) consisted in life-honouring forms of "feminized" creativity, which included acceptance of death as a "natural" process within the cycle of life, the more historically recent male body politic is inextricably bound up with the defiance of death and a whole imaginary focused more on death and violence than a symbolic/imaginary order of regenerativity (Condren 2002). The imaginary of "the womb/tomb/bear's lair" has been gradually replaced by that of "the tomb" with the notion of "transcendence" and male-exclusive spirituality resulting in the devaluation of the Earth, matter, life, carnality, sexuality, animals, and women. Many scholars in this book also recognize the life-renewing matrix of bees, birds, bears, and divinities of motherhood that were linked with ancient rituals and symbols of regenerativity (Guilbault, Kailo, Paper, Heiskanen, Kremer most clearly).

Lewis Hyde (1983) has analyzed the notion of an Indigenous "return gift," called among the Maori a "nourishing *hau*," as interspecies feedback. Without the gestures of giving back, humans act through greed or arrogance of will and thus the cycle of human/animal interdependency is broken. The narratives of wo(men) and Bear/s are powerfully interruptive of such developments and values, since they represent a saner form of ecological interdependency. It is not literally the act of returning a bear's bones and skull to nature (a practice followed by many Indigenous and/or Northern cultures after a successful hunt) that causes game to be abundant. It is the very attitude of mutuality that ensures that the game, fish, or plants are not taken to the point of causing their extinction. David Rockwell claims in *Giving Voice to Bear* (1991) that the woman and bear story's popularity derives from its simple core: it addresses through a series of agonizing dilemmas two of the most fundamental and decisive issues of life: marriage and death (122). It is an understatement to note that these concepts take on a radically different meaning in the context of *arch*-aic Bear feasts and ceremonials where weddings and funerals are seen as two sides of a coin and where many taken-for-granted dualisms (compulsory anthropocentrism) do not apply (e.g., the dead and the living, humans and animals are not strict binary opposites). The further back we go in history, the less collective rituals reflect the naturalized western tenets of compulsory heteronormativity and the more they give us glimpses of a geography of elsewhere with socio-cosmic arrangements beyond eurocentric norms and comprehension. Indeed, the authors and researchers in this book imply that the reasons for the tales' remarkable persistence, elasticity, and appeal may reside in their being an age-old "human/animal interest story" that deals with profound existential and socio-cosmic issues (cf. Pratt 1987). Apart from the bear narrative, both Greek and Roman, as well as Indigenous, mythologies/histories contain references to a host of other types of human-animal marriages (Reischl 2004). On the other hand, the narrative variants in stories or myths revolving around marriage and/or death can also be seen as dramatizations of conflicting loyalties between different kinship systems, for example, one's maternal and paternal kin. On a yet deeper level, they are also artistic expressions of desire, the kinds of longings and yearnings that we need not, in the Freudian tradition, reduce to a sexuality understood as separate from spirituality.

This anthology attests to expressions of women's spirituality and shamanic relations with Bear and the Divine that offer alter-natives to how the religious and spiritual realms have come to be naturalized in patriarchal, institutionalized religions. Defining the mythic patterns that more accurately reflect the forms and realities of woman's historically and ethnoculturally contingent experiences is, of course, also an important concern of feminist literary criticism. The analysis of the worldview in which the stories of wo(men) and Bear/s are embedded, in the vast literature on the topic of the Bear ceremonial, has been restricted mostly to white mainstream points of view. This has prevented scholars from seeing in the stories deeper layers and levels of discursive complexity and dimensions of interest to women. Thus, this anthology aims at creating new thinking and storytelling spaces related to the context of Bear ceremonials with more gender- and ethnosensitive approaches and respect for Indigenous peoples' own interpretations of the narrative and practices to do with the worldview of "give back" (i.e., articles on the meaning of Bear by Sami scholar Elina Helander-Renvall; comments on Bear by Sami artist Satu Maarit Natunen, Tsimshian Patricia Vickers, Anishnaabe Wacoquaakmik; drama by Greenland Innu Ulla Ryum; poetry by Cree Louise Bernice Halfe; and fiction by Sami writer Kristi Paltto). The aim is not to re-romantize the Indigenous, woman, other (Trinh 1989), but to create a more balanced theoretical groundwork for the epistemic, academic, and ecomythological conversation between Indigenous and non-Indigenous academics and writers who are differently situated on the continuum of "tradition," assimilation, resistance, and cultural renewal (Dion-Buffalo and Mohawk 1992; Colorado 1988) regarding eurocentric hegemonic discourses (cf. Jürgen Kremer's chart regarding recovered Indigenous consciousness in this volume). As Kremer's article probes in depth the issues of cultural appropriation, the preconditions of a responsible intercultural conversation, and the avoidance of cultural projections, I refer readers to his "*Bear*ing Obligations." Although Christian patriarchy has colonized women and helped suppress and overwrite the Bear-woman stories among other cultural items, non-Indigenous women must address their collusion with the kind of nationalism that has hurt Indigenous populations. Thus, prior to engaging in the pre-Christian legacies of my own culture, I have also addressed the issues of Finnish colonial impingements against the Sami (e.g. Helander and Kailo 1998).

The Gift Gaze and Imaginary

The organizing principle and approach in this anthology is what I call the "gift gaze,"[8] in alignment with the ecological ethos and worldview of many past agricultural and/or hunting societies. In gift-based societies people were (and in some cases still are) related to their physical and natural surroundings through a particular land ethic, through genealogies, oral tradition, and complex rituals aimed at social bonds, ecological balance, and sustainability. The gift paradigm is not restricted to Indigenous cultures, but as we will see, has broad cross-cultural affinities with women's ways of sustaining life, women's practices of the gift logic. Nor is it a way of sentimentalizing or romanticizing the mothering function of sex/gender systems where this life-sustaining culture of biological and cultural reproduction has been pitted, dualistically and hierarchically, against the more valued social fatherhood and the logic of exchange.

The theoretical stance in this volume accords with Sandra Harding's (1994) view that eurocentrism in its numerous forms is a "a set of institutional, societal, and civilizational arrangements for distributing economic, social, and political resources" (13). Civilizational or philosophic eurocentrism occurs when the beliefs and practices at issue are held by entire "civilizations" over large periods of history. This kind of bias is the most difficult to identify because it structures and gives meaning to such apparently seamless expanses of history, common sense, and daily life that it is hard for members of such "civilizations" even to imagine taking a position that is outside the prevailing norm. Harding lists as examples "the scientific worldview," "the modern worldview," or the Judeo-Christian, Judaic, Islamic worldview. The very notion of totemism today—humans' animal ancestors or half-animal/half-human kinship structures—defy the naturalized assumptions of the western socio-economic and moral universe. The challenge for gender and ethnosensitive research is to yet better articulate the situated nature of knowledge-production and academic research denied by the conventional masculated/white view, and to work through the implications that this understanding of styles of knowing has for "objectivity," relativism, rationality, and reflexivity. Also, it is necessary to recognize that for Indigenous North Americans (and the Sami[9] Indigenous people living in Europe), what has often been at risk with cultural appropriation is the loss or weakening of self-representation (Battiste 2000; Churchill 1992; Dandie 1990; Hirvonen 1996: Lutz 1990, 1993, 1995: Maracle 1989). But, as Vine Deloria Jr. (1999) notes: "No one is suggesting that Indians 'revert' to the old days or old ways. Rather we must be able to understand what those old days and ways really were and model our present actions and beliefs within that tradition" (16).

Gender, Culture, Species

Through the anthology's matrix of narratives—"furrytales" from the past and from the present (Kailo 1994)—we revisit at the same time the classic debate in anthropology and women's studies: the relationship between nature, culture, and gender. The authors move contemporary discussions within multidisciplinary cultural studies to yet another level of analysis since the focus on the intersections of gender, class, ethnicity, and other social variables rarely address epistemic (knowledge-related) differences of identity-formation and situatedness beyond the taken-for-granted eurocentric science and worldview. These alternative epistemes (Kuokkanen 2007), mostly unfocused within women's and queer/sexualities studies (among other fields), conceive of gender and nature in light of species, beyond compulsory heterosexuality and the either/or systems of eurocentric sexuality. The Bear stories are also about hybridity in another voice. They represent alternatives to postmodern discourses of hybrid states of the in-between, by recognizing the value of the human/animal kinship instead of the self-conceptions of cyberculture that have given us the anti-organic and alienating cyborgs (Haraway 1991; Kailo 2003).[10]

Beyond the Politics of Appropriation: Circulating Stories as Cross-Cultural Gifts

Some of the stories in this collection are not "stories" as separate from histories; they have to do with cultural protocol, ancestral laws, orally-transmitted knowledge about human/animal relations, and historical knowledge. The Indigenous contributions to this anthology acknowledge the vital importance of Indigenous epistemic styles and the way in which stories transmit culturally vital oral traditions and knowledge.

The art included in the book and interspersed between the poetry, essays, and articles includes depictions of the woman/bear theme by the Sami artist Satu Maarit Natunen, Helena Junttila, a Finn from Northern Finland, Indigenous artist Aleksandr Suvorov (of Finno-Ugric Udmurt background), Sami Elina Helander-Renvell, Finnish psychotherapist Irma Heiskanen, Edwina Goldstone from England, Canadians Karen Guilbault, and Maureen Enns who literally "ran away with grizzly bears" and lived with them in Kamchatka. Finnish cultural anthropologist and artist, Jenny Kangasvuo, from Northern Finland, allowed us to use a humorous drawing of a bear and woman on all fours, which was originally used to describe the women's movement.

It is important to heed and to be aware of different cultural protocols and copyrights regarding the telling and transmission of stories considered sacred and to respect cultural differences as to their meaning, including the roles they play in different communities. Some of the Finno-Ugric bear stories alluded to in the anthology are part of established collections from the nineteenth century and form an exception in this regard. As part of the same Finno-Ugric group of languages, Finns and Sami also share many cultural items and traditions, although only the latter are defined as Indigenous (according to World Council of Indigenous Peoples' definitions). The Finns, themselves colonized until 1917 (by Swedes and Russians), have formed their own independent nation, and hence do not qualify as politically Indigenous, although they have inhabited Northern Europe for thousands of years.[11]

As with women's socialization into a forced rather than consciously chosen gift labour, we need more nuanced ways of doing justice to the complexities of nature, culture, self, and "other." We need to imagine difference itself with a difference, without hierarchy and notions of superiority/inferiority. This also applies to literary genres. As Penny Petrone (1990) notes: "Western readers are prone to view non-Western literatures [and storytelling] in terms with which they are familiar, however irrelevant those may be to them" (4). Arnold Krupat (1993) believes that "an adequate ethnocriticism for Native American culture, history, and literature does not yet exist … [and] will only be achieved by means of complex interactions between a variety of Western discursive and analytic modes and a variety of non-Western modes of knowing and understanding" (43-44). Furthermore, many Indigenous scholars point out that oral stories are no less sophisticated and complex than written literatures and suggest that it is their degree of "conversivity" and orality that gives the works their power, depth, and vitality (Brill de Ramirez 1998).[12]

Instead of approaching orality in Indigenous literature from the point of view of a western critical discourse that emphasizes the distanced objectification of texts—thereby looking at orality as the object of a critical gaze—a conversive approach places the scholar ideally within the oral engagement as a "mutual participant" (Moore 1993: 371), one willing to give up his or her "sanctioned ignorance" (Spivak 1990). I look upon the latter as an expression, also, of the gift imaginary where the community-building social impact is placed above analytical action and classification as the relatively more privileged epistemic pursuits.[13]

The Structure and Contents of the Anthology

The structure and organization of the materials in this collection "transgress" academic base conventions to the extent that academic and "conversive" theory and storytelling are presented side by side. As Terry Eagleton (1995) has suggested, and as postmodernists recognize, the very distinctions between theory and autobiography, fiction and theory are themselves effects of govern/mentality, power-over relations, and institutional conventions. Science based on masculation (Vaughan 1997) raises artificial boundaries between disciplines and areas of study, with the aim of keeping them under epistemic control. Disciplines also have their internal ranking order and hierarchy. Postmodernism has joined ranks with Indigenous scholars who question the artificial separation of many fields and registers of knowledge and being that could contribute more by being merged and combined, or theorized together. Fiction and reality, history and story, are separated artificially to create hierarchies that benefit the ruling hegemonic class (Trinh 1989). History is reserved for the elites with literature, storytelling, and "culture" in the sense of ethnography being reserved to the "subaltern" (Spivak 1990) relegated to museums. Or else women's legitimate interest in matriarchies is *a priori* dismissed as "deluded," "unscientific" or in other ways "polluting" to academic credibility (the male monopoly on the past).

Making space for stories from another epistemic register, this book mixes poetry, fiction, drama, and hybrids of theory, biography, and Bear art with the academic itinerary. Artwork of women and Bear/s also serve to interrupt the academic trajectory, offering a visual resting place and maybe helping bring us, occasionally, back into the body, beyond the cognitive one-sidedness of academic endeavours. As many Indigenous scholars have taught, stories are not the opposite of Truth and History, Knowledge and Reality (Brant 1991; Helander and Kailo 1998; Trinh 1989). The master narratives, the Great patriarchal Histories are also stories, "his" stories and white mythologies. To separate art and politics as sharply as the western academy tends to do (Jensen 1993), is a symptom of the same controlling stance as the impetus to keep women and Bear/s apart, of "not mixing categories."[14]

We introduce this volume with Irma Heiskanen's poetic lines. The artwork of the Finnish psychotherapist, artist, and ecoactivist is featured on the cover of this book. Heiskanen's poem refers to another mode of gaining knowledge and connection: "hearing with another ear." In Heiskanen's own description of her art gracing the cover, the woman embracing Bear evokes the spiritual and cosmic yearnings that have an Arctic dimension and associations. They evoke the Northern twilight or winter period without light but without any of the negative connotations. In this mystified Northern darkness, there is another parallel universe/reality, one that is both familiar and uncanny, and approachable best through "defamiliarization." So, too, the reader needs to listen with "another ear" to the stories and writings in this book since many of them come to us from a mystical and mythical, and not only an academically investigated and verifiable, past. Alternatively, western-ers are likely to psychologize Bear and to propose the psychoanalytic view that stories come from within our Self, the unfettered, dynamic, expansive, forever shifting totality of our being, the dream world. For many Indigenous people in North America, spirits are real, not to be labelled simply as "manifestations of psychic reality" (see Allen 1986). We are dealing with a bare space of beeing that cultures try to verbalize and articulate through different epistemic styles. Dreams are the one frontier that humans have not yet managed to harness, control, and colonize.

The "Bear and Bride" photograph is taken by Ritva Kovalainen and Sanni Seppo, Finnish artists and photographers who have exhibited their work widely and over a long period. The photograph, taken from their 1997 book, *Tree People* (which provides a comprehensive picture of the traditional beliefs of ancestral Finns regarding trees and forests), evokes the origin story of the Finnish Bear Myth and the Bear Hunting Drama preserved in the so-called *Viitasaari* text.

This book opens with a classic/prototypical Athabascan Bear-woman version of "The Girl Who Married a Bear," variants of which have been collected among others by Catherine McClellan (1970) and Georgina Loucks (1985) in Canada, to provide a reference point for readers unfamiliar with the story. "The Story," as told by Maria Johns to McClellan, is taken from her book, *The Girl Who Married the Bear: A Masterpiece of Indian Oral Tradition* (1970), which documents her 1948 fieldwork and various versions of the story of the girl who married a bear among the Tlingit- and Athabascan-speaking Indians of southern Yukon Territory. Ida Calmagen, daughter of honoured storyteller, Mrs. Angela Sidney, gave permission to reprint Mrs. Sidney's previously published story, "The Girl and the Grizzly" (Cruikshank 1990), a Tagish variation of the classic story included later in this volume. Mrs. Sydney's version of the story foregrounds the fact that there is much more to the women and bear narratives than meet the eyes, even as recently as the 1970s when Mrs. Sydney's version of the story was recorded. The Finnish, Sami, and Norwegian stories also included in this book offer interesting examples of the wide variations in tone and spirit of the bear narrative, as do variants of the story discussed in articles focused on Sami, Armenian, Russian-Evenk, and Cree contexts. The "Veiled Bear" illustration by Edwina Goldstone refers to a Finno-Ugric (Viena Karelian) bearwoman story involving three brothers in their quest for wives and valuables; like the Sami story, it relates to the ecological life-oriented lessons transmitted by, in this case, the bearwife.

The cross-cultural narratives of women and Bear/s consist of various depictions of a voluntary union between the two, stories of abduction, even rape, and finally, moral allegories of respectful human/animal pacts, and which do not always necessarily present the female protagonists in positive light. This may well attest to the Christianization and patriarchal influence on the narratives and myths, which resulted in the shift toward the woman- and nature-denigrating ethos of patriarchal religions (a form of "pollution" linked with women's menstruation). Rather than analyze the two "classic" types of stories of women and Bear/s, I leave them as a gift to the readers, to interpret as they wish. At the same time, the anthology provides theoretical and practical guidelines on the genealogy and changes that the narratives have undergone as tools of socialization, and also methods and approaches that might better help make sense of them.

The poems included in this book serve to highlight the theme of the anthology through other than academic styles. Isabella Colalillo Katz provides the anthology's most dystopian vision of "bear-adise" in the mythical past and future. Her poem, "She Bear," shows the she-bear's two faces as Goddess of Death, Kali, and the bringer of new life—a radical post-nuclear spinner of the "coil of rebirth." She-Bear's mothering song stirs the flesh of new humans and provides hope against hope in the landscape of the ultimate ecological crises (beyond the insufficient rhetorical measures taken by governments to address flooding, food price hikes, climate change and other ecosocial crises). Colalillo-Katz's eco-critical poem sketches the outlines of the reader's own gaze into the nuclear core of the heart of darkness, evoking the consequences of ecologically and socially short-sighted attitudes, lifting them above any recognizable time-space context. Her poem has, despite its historically ambiguous "gaze" affinities with Susan Bright's dramatization of the fate of polar bears as mere objects of a callous, consumerist tourist gaze in her poem, "Bear Watch." The art work and poems in the anthology share a common horizon in terms of their themes but leave much space for divergent ecocritical approaches and for personal interpretation.

Karen Guilbault is a Canadian artist/poet and "bearwoman" living in British Columbia. Much of her art is focused on sacred animals, particularly the love affair between women and Bear/s. Her paintings, some of which are reproduced in this book, are accompanied by poems honouring the ancient-modern relationship. Guilbault's art in this book serves to give visual, artistic expression to the widely-shared beliefs and observations about Bear as healer, fierce and protective defender of her cubs, icon of rebirth, and a crucial link in the chain of bees, snakes, and nocturnal symbols of death and "other modes of seeing"—the owl. Bear epitomizes in her feminine form the birth-death cycle of nature. She also evokes the shamanistic dream-dimension of hibernation beyond the natural sciences approach with its scientific/rationalistic rather than imaginative and aesthetic focus. Guilbault's art has perhaps been influenced by First Nations' bear stories, but they also reflect a wider cultural knowledge of Bear narratives among Greeks and Roman for example, as well as other world mythologies. Most importantly, however, "Myrna's Vision" evokes the repertoire of mythic associations and symbols associated with Bear—death, rebirth, suffering, healing, wisdom. Feathered serpents in the artwork accompanying the poem challenge the strict dualisms and boundaries of the "rational" ego and combine with the other elements of the poem to create the ursine paradox: the ancient serpent sign of pharmakon refers both to medicine, remedies, healing and, in contrast, to poison. In "Backbend," the artist links Bear with a fall into "polar thoughts" where opposites melt away. She honours Bear with a poetic language that combines the spiritual, the sexual, the cosmic, the physical, the geographic, the real, the imaginary.

Guilbault's poem, "Bare on Bear," allows us to consider how we might apply the gift philosophy also to art. Instead of approaching aesthetics merely through the rationalistic method of classifying, analyzing, dissecting, and using institutional power to canonize normative interpretive conventions, the gift perspective on poetry/art enters the realm of the imaginary in the spirit of affinity, infinity, and ecological be-longing. It may mean experiencing the bare depths of the unnameable, the ineffable, the numinous. Paradoxically Guilbault's art helps make more visible what in Bear aesthetic is ultimately approachable only through metaphors or symbols.

For Hyde (1983), "The fruit of the creative spirit is the work of art itself, and if there is a first-fruits ritual for artists, it must either be the willing waste of art in which one is happy to labor all day with no hope of production, nothing to sell, nothing to show off, just fish thrown back into the sea as soon as they are caught or else, when there is a product, it must be this thing we have already seen, the dedication of the work back toward its origins" (148). It may well be that "if the artist is gifted, the gift increases in its passage through the self. The artist makes something higher than what he [sic] has been given, and this, the finished work, is the third gift, the one offered to the world in general or directed back specifically to the 'clan and homeland of an earlier gift'" (1983: 191). In his approach that might be called implicitly ecocritical, he stresses that "We nourish the spirit by disbursing our gifts, not by capitalizing upon them ... the artist who is nourishing *hau* is not self-aggrandizing, self-assertive, or self-conscious, he [sic] is, rather, self-squandering, self-abnegating and self-forgetful.... No art is sunk in the self, but rather, in art the self becomes self-forgetful in order to meet the demands of the thing seen and the thing being made" (193). Ecocriticism is often interpreted and defined as an approach that leads to an enhanced eco and ethnosensitive stance regarding our relations with nature (Buell 2001; Garrard 2005: 139-140). It is a matter for debate whether images "appropriating" Indigenous figures and mixing them with other shared cultural themes and goddesses meets the goal of an eco and ethnosensitive stance. I suggest, however, that approaching art that converses across boundaries in the spirit of the gift yields a different outcome than the approach rooted in a master imaginary. An exploitative attitude of appropriation is, then, qualitatively different from the kind of cultural borrowing that serves to enhance connection and social, ecofriendly ties. An appropriate ecocritical method to apply to the artwork in this book by Helander-Renvall, Heiskanen, Natunen, Junttila, Enns, and Guilbault is no doubt the recognition of a logic according to which art in the nourishing mode feeds without the creative source becoming depleted, the mystery or appeal of creative forces being that they increase as they are used, releasing the regenerative flow in both the onlooker/reader and the artist. In its bare (economically unpolluted) forms, art can serve as an invisible umbilical cord creating the webs of belonging that are the best antidote against Durkheim's *anomie* (1893), self-estrangement and the many dysfunctions resulting from the corporate worldview, its rat race and endless competition over dwindling resources.

Hibernation, as Guilbault suggests, is as necessary for our replenishment and creativity as "reason," logic, and the "waking consciousness." Bear serves as a guide in this dimension of being, as the articles by Helander-Renvall, Paper, and Heiskanen also point out. This condition is necessary if the formula "being is round" (Bachelard 1969) helps us recognize the *arch*-aic power of other than the *archi*-rational modes of relating. The fear of alternative epistemic approaches and ways of "beingknowing," the obsession with the orthodox scientific methods, prevents us from developing our full-rounded and deeply regenerative human potential, blocking rather than facilitating that which leads to inventions, beyond profit innovation. It is all the more important to foreground this dimension of creativity since the neoliberal obsession with innovation fails to grasp the dynamics of creativity that cannot be controlled and harnessed to the needs of the market without losing their very source of "innovation." Those approaching creativity through the master imaginary or exchange economy often dismiss the very metaphors through which gift-oriented people try to express their psychic reality; Bachelard's "round being," Jung's mystical symbols (see Kailo 1990), and other attempts at circumscribing the unspeakable and "unnameable" are mocked as "transcendental spinach" or violently denied. They do, for all that, refer to dimensions of art and literature that cannot be scientifically captured, defined, and measured. Roman Jakobson (1960) refers to the communicative function aimed at creating a sense of social bonding or connection as "the phatic function"; I believe that the symbolic word/image matrix of women and Bear/s in this anthology may well represent such artistic outreach. Those denying the existence or validity of dimensions of being they have not experienced are like embryos that would deny, if they could, any reality outside of the womb. The same attitude applies to eurocentric scholars who deny the Indigenous experiences and realities of the spiritual that they are unable to imagine, experience, or believe in.

Many of the poems in this volume evoke the bond between women and Bear/s in ways that might be labelled as gynocentric and essentializing in the negative understanding of the concepts. Do they reinforce the sentimental and romantic myths of female closeness to nature rather than deconstructing the very binaries and gender constructs? Indeed, the western mapping of a gender hierarchy on the nature/culture distinction has been a significant root cause in the destruction of the biosphere and the denigration of women and Indigenous populations. Ecological salvation should not be sought in women or Indigenous peoples as reverse categories to be glorified (angels in the ecosystem); rather, the worldview and the social attributes coded as "feminine" need to be extended as the human norm and ideal to Eurocentric cultures while revisiting all hierarchical binaries.

Ulla Ryum's play, "Annanatsiat," about a shaman Grandmother-bear evokes another herstory of gender relations—those of Greenland Inuit women who challenge western assumptions of gender-specific behaviour in more than one way. Inuit Bearwomen as shamans, co-hunters joining men in the struggle for survival, are transmitters of Indigenous history, storytelling, beliefs, and values that defy any simplistic reduction to primitive magic or totemism. The play was originally published as a short story in Denmark in 2003 and performed as a play for the first time in Winnipeg, Canada in 2004. Ryum situates her play in the modern era and builds into it voices, sounds, and elements of the past that are provocative interventions in the realm of modernity. The gaze and sight are not the senses that dominate the play: rather, the reminiscences are filtered through mysterious animal and nature sounds and an inner gaze focused on a compass charting both the past and the present. The play reminds us of the female line of shamanism that continues to be ignored, downplayed, and trivialized in ethnographic literature. Storytellers from different generations meet to hear and tell in their turn the dying woman's story of her grandmother, Annanatsiat. The storyline traces the death of a father and hunter, and a girl's selection and initiation as Bear into the role of shaman, *angagok*. There is in the play no strict gender opposition regarding hunting or being Bear. Christopher Trott's article in this anthology argues that in Inuit culture the relationship between women and Bear/s is not articulated essentially through the categories of gender. In his view, from whom and in what context one receives one's name is much more critical. Indeed, in this play it is significant that the young girl receives her name from an *angagok* who sought to perpetuate her own life by circulating and passing on the name of one of her familiar spirits to the younger generation. Ryum's play reflects this very relationship between naming, culture, nature, species, and the hybrid relationship between bears and humans.

My brief conversation with Ryum,[15] which follows the play, provides the playwright's own "insider" understanding of women as Bear/s. The significance of her comments consists, among other things, in outlining the ways in which Greenland's Bearwomen challenge the western myth of female passivity and dependency, reminding us of the extent to which gender is a social construction.

Marie-Françoise Guédon's article, "Of Big Animals, Women and Shamans in Nabesna Country: A Tale of Assumed Identities," delivers a culture-specific and in-depth contextualization of women and Bear/s as part of a particular cultural worldview. Guédon's article consists of a description of the Alaskan field research that she began as early as 1970. Her article, complete with her field drawings, provides a challenge to many dominant beliefs about Indigenous life, gender, power, and women and Bear/s including taboos and how they function. Guédon lists the many taboos placed on women in connection with their relationship to Bear. Her description of how *enji* or power functions in Dene society echoes in some ways the meaning of the Finnish dynamistic concept *väki*, a form of dynamistic power charge linking ideas about women's, animals', and shamans' "energies" (Apo 1995; Stark-Arola 1998). Both concepts also have to do with the power of women's menstrual blood and its links with other social forms of influence—interpreted very differently depending on historical era of the group in question. The concept of *enji* challenges dominant eurocentric interpretations of hierarchical politics of subjugation—power-over—and implicitly refers back to life-oriented societies' belief in the sacredness of menstruation in the social imaginary. Guédon establishes links between menstruation and *enji*, which has more to do with sacredness, danger, taking care of one's self, and taboo than pollution in its negative patriarchal interpretation. Now the imaginary female body and its physiological functions, like menstruation, are sources of social esteem, not the opposite, as in the eurocentric Christian view. Guédon discusses at length the different ways in which women and Bear/s bond through a kind of spirit-to-spirit kinship which she sees as demanding self-awareness and the ability to communicate, resonate, empathize, and link with others. Like Ulla Ryum, Guédon shows that western sex/gender systems do not fit Dene conceptions of nature, culture, species, and their non-hierarchical ordering.

Guédon stresses that the story, and Dene culture, defy the simplistic reductionism of nature versus culture. Although Guédon's interpretation of the story as a tool of socialization for girls suggests patriarchal, even Christian influences, the narrative has not lost its distinctive Indigenous understanding of hybrid species—the Big Ones are as cultured as "human" beings. The Big Ones also have families and kin, houses and leaders, shamans, and game animals, thereby making explicit the belief in animals as animal-individuals, an unheard-of notion in the western, ecophobic context. The Dene attitudes towards Bear also show, as does the article by Wacoquaakmik (Rodney Bobiwash), that bearlore is not just "lore:" in fact, the relationship between Indigenous communities and Bear/s continues to be sacred among many Indigenous people. As with the other articles dealing with Indigenous cultures, the article also points to gift giving as a social paradigm for creating social ties, including a mention of men who by giving away their possessions come close to a self-transformation of the kind women's bodily functions predispose them to. Guédon's article is a valuable description of the Denes' sex/gender/species system.[16]

The poem by Cree poet, Louise Bernice Halfe that follows, adds to this volume poetic reminiscences of Bearwomen that offer respectful representations of women Elders. Western feminists have in recent years exposed the extent to which elderly women are portrayed in pejorative terms as post-menopausal, no longer useful members of society. This is yet another espression of the exchange economy or master identity, a lens through which aging women are unproductive and deserve little, if any, dignity or respect once their reproductive roles are fulfilled. Unlike the silenced, marginalized elders of western communities, Indigenous women Elders continue to be appreciated and valued for their age-related wisdom, skills, experience, and social contributions. Halfe's "Medicine Bear" transcends the eurocentric stereotypes of Indigenous women by juxtaposing references to traditional herbal knowledge and aspects of modern life as if they were mutually exclusive, which of course they are not. *Nōhkom's*, Medicine Bear's room is described vividly and concretely as that of a bear-like den with its carrot roots, yarrow camomile, rat-root, and *cácámosikan*. The body language and other gendered gestures of the Bearwoman evoke strength, independence, and a gendered style that is beyond early western constructions of female vacuity, frailty, passivity, vulnerability, western stereotypes of femininity that have fortunately begun to disappear. The image of the brown labouring bear, *Nōhkom*, the medicine woman alone in her attic den smoking "slim cigarettes," wearing the perfume of sage, sweetgrass, and earth medicine ties, is a combination of modernity and historical stereotypes. What the western mindset might perceive as a romanticized depiction of an Indigenous Elder merges with irony as Bear grandmother hums her medicine songs among her secrets and mysteries. It needs to be said that on the other hand, the strong Indigenous woman is a stereotype that needs to be undone: the "strength" of the women in communities with a colonial past marked by substance abuse and violence, does not necessarily make women strong—rather, the circumstances leave them with few alternatives. More importantly, one should analyze and make visible the circumstances, the institutional, structural and political realities that force women to rely on their legendary Northern strength.

Patricia Vickers' "The Princess and the Bears" deals with Bear within the Indigenous territories that are not geographically far removed from Guédon's Dene fieldwork. Vickers situates the story of her people, for which she has ensured a particular culturally-appropriate First Nations copyright, in the current social conditions of Tsimshian peoples on the coast of Northwest British Columbia. Within Tsimshian, Nisga'a and Gitxsan law, *ayaawux*, the individual who retells the story must have permission from the owners of the story. The writing of this story on the woman and the Bear has the permission of the current "speaker" for the House of Gitsees, Mr. Andrew Tait. What Lewis Hyde (1983) writes about the difference between gift-based and exchange-oriented societies may help us understand Vickers' description of the First Nations copyright. Hyde (1983) writes: "First-fruits rituals protect the spirit of the gift by making evident the true structure of our relationship to the sources of our wealth. The salmon are not subject to the will of the Indians; the imagination is not subject to the will of the artist. To accept the fruits of these things as gifts is to acknowledge that we are not their owners or masters, that we are, if anything, their servants, their ministers" (144). In a similar vein, the Indigenous sense of copyright includes a spiritual dimension that has to do with teachings and sacred knowledge that belongs to all, for the benefit of the community, even if one respects the custodian of a story by recognizing he or she has its "copyright" or transmission power.

The sacred story that Vickers provides as her cultural gift is intricately woven with the numerous events of cultural oppression and Indigenous peoples' forced adaptation to European lifestyles. The sacred story teaches eurocenric peoples in particular about the different roles stories/storytelling play in some Indigenous communities. Although the social conditions that she describes leave much to be desired, the power of her people's ancestral law, *ayaawx*, remains. Intimately connected to the *ayaawx* is, according to Vickers, the *adaawx* (history of en-counters with supernatural beings to increase individual and collective power in a community) in what is now known as "story" format. The most obvious lesson provided by Vickers is the power of respecting the "owner of a story," something that power-derived patent or copyright laws protect in a purely utilitarian and commercial sense in the western world. In Vickers's culture, ownership is part of the spiritual worldview in which profit-seeking and individual property-rights have traditionally no honour, in stark contrast with the neo-liberal creed of today's capitalistic worldview (e.g. LaDuke 1997; Kuokkanen 2007). Many details of "The Princess and the Bears" story bring to mind motifs in European folklore, although their cultural status is clearly different. In the European context they are transmitted and read mostly to children as fairytales, whereas the Tsimshian storyteller performs them in a cultural context where they have an important social function and meaning.

Kira Van Deusen's article, "Women and Bears: Indigenous Udegei and Ulchi Traditions of the Russian Far East," takes us to another part of the world with strong oral traditions reflecting the lasting bonds between women and Bear/s. The article is based on the author's conversations with Valentina Kyalundzyuga, an Udegei scholar and storyteller in the Russian Far East, who provides a folk or insider (emic) point of view on cultural practices. Van Deusen's fieldwork has borne thought-provoking results in this and her other research (Van Deusen 2001) that allow scholars to expand their gender-sensitive understanding of shamanism. By revealing the way in which female shamanism and healing functions, Van Deusen exposes the imaginative limitations of the "white male gaze." Van Deusen tells us that Indigenous women, among whom shamanism is still practiced, continue to tell and dramatize the story about women marrying or becoming Bear/s. She notes that consciously or not, Indigenous storytellers always select their tales with specific regard for their listeners. She thus foregrounds the performative, contex-tual, and conversive function of stories that do not have uniform meaning but acquire their significance from the interaction of the narrator and the person(s) to whom the story is told.

The neglect, and the ensuing consequences, of woman-specific shamanism are discussed in Van Deusen's research in ways that challenge early anthropological biases. The Indigenous people she describes have strong traditions of storytell-ing and shamanism, in which women and Bear/s play important roles. One of the functions of stories or myths is to serve as the means of integrating spiritual knowledge into everyday life. Many of the details van Deusen reports challenge western assumptions about species distinctions and relations. Van Deusen's article speaks to women's role in today's cultural and political life as evidence of a long tradition of respect for female wisdom as evidenced in stories. On another note, Van Deusen describes how communism has impacted on cultural practices, in some cases in a more serious way than what Christianity managed to do to them. This view is confirmed by Wacoquaakmik's essay in this volume. While Van Deusen's piece does not deal explicitly with the gift, or gift giving, the contributions in this book highlight different dimensions of the life-oriented societies where women "marry" different types of power animals, and offer alternative envisionings to the sex/gender/species system. Thus they create a dialogical space for each other, producing an accumulative effect regarding new research questions and insights. A recurrent theme, linked with gift economies, is the reference again to a particular life force that is seen in Bearwomen, which overrides all social constructs.

The story by Kirsti Paltto's—one of the Sami's most celebrated writers and activists—called "Rásstos," evokes a well-known mythic character ("Runtamuš"), a woman shape-shifting into a Bear and a guide/teacher of ecological ways of living. The story brings back to life, in the modern context, an ancient Sami legend regarding a Bearwoman who entices men to stay with her. On one level, the story's significance for this collection lies in its political challenge of gender role reversal to help us revisit stereotypes even within Bear narratives and myths. It reminds us that many cross-cultural myth complexes have in the course of history been reduced to a few dominant and fixed narratives although the main protagonist has a shifting gender depending on the cultural context (the Russian's and Samis' male Cinderella, for example). Rásstos, too, is now a female bear attracting men to embrace her "life style" in what might be referred to as a parallel reality. In Paltto's story the focus is not gender alone, however, but the slippery slope of human/animal affinities. In archeological and other studies of wo(men) and Bear/s, there are few stories of Men Who Marry Bears. Helga Reischl (2004) locates these stories in Southeastern Europe noting that, "Kephalos of Attica also marries a she-bear" (174). Among Finno-Ugric peoples, from the Sami to the Finns and the Viena Karelians, there are numerous versions of the bearwoman story involving men marrying she-bears (cf. Goldstone's illustration). On the other hand, this could be Sami women's challenge to some currents within feminism that are bent on excluding men from the victim discourse. Paltto's story may suggest that it is men who need to be encouraged to enter the "bear's den," a site of healing hibernation where the ego enters the realm of a broader psycho-cosmisc Self—or in Indigenous, and in this case, Sami terms, the Spirit Realm—beyond the politics of competitive masculation and mastery over nature. Such "hibernation" beyond the myths of masculinity could help men recognize the reality of our interdependency beyond western illusions of autonomy and rationality (which conceal the reliance of the individual on communal gifts and gifts of mothering and nature's riches).

Sima Aprahamian's article, "Running Away With Bears: Armenian Women Transcending Patriarchy," focuses on unexamined assumptions about "universal" definitions of "femininity" and "masculinity," but also provides female readers with pre-Christian female role models and stories. Defining women in relation to male desire has taken place under all "isms" from communism and socialism to capitalism. Furthermore, Aprahamian's piece provides knowledge about women's power beyond male fantasies and control, something that feminist spiritual writings are also disseminating in order to empower women and facilitate the broadening of the spectrum of possible representations of femininity and gender/species. According to Aprahamian, Bear stories, although still told in Armenia, have been excluded or banned from official Armenian folk collections giving us a clue as to their tabooed power, and showing that the politics of representation have colluded with other forces in trying to keep women, nature, and Bears apart (suppression of women's history). Aprahamian bases her argument on the fact that the women she interviewed claim the protagonist of the stories was not ravished or abducted but rather, willingly ran away with the Bears. This contrasts with the narratives telling of bears raping and abducting women, which many see as patriarchal interventions into a gynocentric narrative genealogy (e.g. Pratt 1987).

Aprahamian's analysis of women and Bear/s marries the politics of resistance to the voice of marginalized groups. Her article provides a clear case of revealing how myths, far from being just stories, are made to function as tools of socialization and discourses consolidating a given social order. Colonization and attempts at genocide overlap partially with attempts at mythic gynecide: the destruction of knowledge regarding women's ancient cultures. In fact, she suggests that it is dangerous to keep women and Bear/s apart. Aprahamian suggests that it is by allowing them to "marry" that Armenian women have managed to rise up in arms against the combined colonization of women, animals, and Armenians. Implicitly, Aprahamian evokes another kind of a social contract, one not imposed by dominant men. Her article also reflects the extent to which woman-positive, matriarchal myths and worldviews have been overwritten. It may thus contribute to the recovery of the voice of the Bear religion and Bear cults, the traces of which are lost in many parts of the world. Aprahamian's project is thus part of the movement to bring about a radical shift of paradigms, in Armenia, in Canada, and within the androcentric traditions of anthropology.

Celine Leduc's poem, which follows, celebrates the interspecies blood-bond that Karen Guilbault's art evoked in her imagination. It is intriguing that Leduc came up with the poem about the "blood bond" even before reading about blood rituals or the cyclical worldview of ancient bear-hunting societies. I leave open the roots of such imagery, merely recognizing that it seems to touch a deep core among many women. Leduc implicitly challenges the Christian view of paradise and its "covenant," maybe seeking to empower women to return to the state before the fall—the fall into patriarchy—through their imaginations.

The articles in this volume by male scholars reveal that men do not need to and indeed, in many cases, do not all identify with the patriarchal stance of masculated science or the hierarchies, competitiveness, exclusionary politics and other attributes linked with male socialization. Men need not abuse their greater political, religious, and other privileges and power. Jürgen Kremer and Wacoquaakmik (Rodney Bobiwash) embody and model a non-violent, non-hierarchical, and as Vaughan (1997) calls it "non-masculated," male identity. Wacoquaakmik models the Ojibway male scholar as the subject rather than object of bearlore. Kremer for his part openly advocates a self-reflective and ethical stance addressing his own implication in a colonial scholarly genealogy and its "sins of the past." Trott and Paper likewise reflect a sensitivity to the Indigenous point of view, having both also interacted closely and respectfully with the First Nations peoples they have written about.

Kremer's article, "*Bear*ing Obligations," "uses an epistemology of recovering Indigenous consciousness to explore his scholarly obligations." The format of Kremer's article is more than an abstract critique of the eurocentric approaches in that it reflects his commitment to act on his theories, "to walk his talk." His contribution transgresses standard academic genres and represents an effort to embody theories, to model their rootedness in our physical being beyond the disassociation he believes is caused by reified abstractions and monocausal thinking. Kremer outlines the epistemological framework that he uses by contrasting two major discourses: modernity and its critiques versus Indigenous thought—the process of decolonization. This part-autobiographical account describes his travel to the European Arctic North in a way that contrasts with stereotypical and in part normative anthropological theorizing; for him, far from being a process of data collection, it has been "a process of knowledge 'trade' situated within an ancient history of such exchanges." Part of this investigation is his conscious exploration of the meaning of Bear in old Germanic traditions. He explores the story's significance for the relationship between Indigenous peoples and peoples participating in the eurocentered discourses lacking in balanced relations. The analysis is not only situated historically; Kremer also pays attention to the story's gendered dimensions, pointing to its significance for renewing and reintroducing ecologically responsible "nurturing conversations." Kremer believes that an early undestanding of the role of bear was associated with what he calls a participatory lifeway with the ancestral she-bear as a provider, as well as a signficant connection to shamanic practices. Kremer recognizes the risks of the bold inferences that are made on the basis of contemporary Indigenous people still practising Bear ceremonials, but implies that moving on to more culturally situated and specific beingknowing is facilitated when eurocentered scholars regain their own ancestral memories, rituals, traditions, and other ecosocially relevant knowledge base. Kremer's chart for the different positions that he adopts from Indigenous theorists, Dion-Buffalo and Mohawk (1994) of Indigenous assimilated/recovered consciousness and "the third way" offers a useful comparison of different attitudes toward modernity. I find Kremer's chart a welcome alternative to "us/them" dualistic theories regarding minority/majority relations.

The article is rich in establishing new connections and links regarding cross-Atlantic rituals, shamanic beliefs, and representations of ecocentric cultures. As Kremer points out, stories in the participatory mode are not primarily evidential but "injunctive": they are guidelines for narrative and ceremonial participation in a culturally-specific way, at a specific time and place. The piece brings ethical, lyrical, and academic perspectives together to highlight the importance of the worldview that forms the backdrop for the Bear ceremonial in Eurasia as an expression of the striving for balance. Furthermore, Kremer's contribution consists in his (re)discovery of a rock carving in Bohuslän, Sweden, which he compares to the Mexican voladores. He relates both to an ancient cyclical calendar and the ceremonies held in relation to the "turning of the ages."

Susan Bright's "Bear Watch" is a clearly eco-critical prose poem that has the tactile and sensuous quality of the climes it seeks to render palpable, tangible, and symbolically present. The polar bear of her poem grins and bears with the onslaught of white civilization "colder and harsher than any arctic climes." The polar bear voices the dysfunctional "progress" of civilization as the spectre of Halloween-clad children, evoking death rather than fertility rites, artificial hibernation technology as hideous monster mothers. The image of the tourists gazing through glass terrain vehicles with credit cards to pay for a look at the bear embody the modern tourist gaze, the techniques for objectifying bears as targets of nostalgia shootings. The polar bear, in this interpretation, is the mirror image of the lost tourist-self of modern humans, and no longer the religious symbol evoking awe, respect, responsibility, and rituals of give-back.

Christopher Trott's article on "The Gender of the Bear: Bear Symbolism and the Third Sex among the Inuit" also focuses on the forbidden, taboo relationship between wo(men) and Bear/s. Much of the scholarship on the people focuses on the Inuit view that strict boundaries are needed between entities (including those of sacred/profane distinction) to ensure economically and socially viable arrangements. Various models of gender relations among the Inuit have also been proposed that suggest either a two-gender or three-gender framework. "The third sex," which Trott examines critically in his article, is a challenging concept in the western world which has long rooted its philosophies and values in an unexamined and unchallenged heterosexual myth of gender relations—one that has been dismantled and deconstructed increasingly within both anthropology, women's and sexualities studies, and cultural studies from scholars Judith Butler (1990) to Midnight Sun (1988). Within Inuit culture, a single person may have multiple genders that are reflected in their various names, which leads Trott to examine how gender is situationally defined. One of the effects of gender scripts deriving from the names given to children is the return of the ancestors to the living, something Guédon also describes as part of Dene cultural beliefs. For Trott, the Bear is essentially a taoistic cosmic actor and a species that cannot be reduced simplistically to a male/female or human/animal dualism. He argues that the story of wo(men) and Bear/s explores both the reality that women can transform into bears while at the same time maintaining that it is the women who must construct and maintain the boundary between them and humans. Trott challenges the notion put forward by Saladin d'Auglure (1980) of a "third sex" among the Inuit and that the symbolism of the Bear parallels such a conclusion. Indeed, he argues that given the ambiguities of gender in Inuit society, the gender of each person only becomes evident as men and women construct and demonstrate their gender through the practical activities they perform and undertake.[17] Trott cites an intriguing if isolated example of a sex/gender/species system where gender identity is related to the give-back or give-away-oriented worldview. Unlike the hierarchical western gender system where male identity is constructed above all in relation to a subaltern female gender and to property relations/accumulation: "The significance of marking a boy's first catch is that the boy has demonstrated his maleness and is thus in the position to give away his first game. Only when a girl produces her first child does she become 'fixed' as woman, and, parallel to the boy renouncing his first game, the girl must renounce her first child to the community through adoption."

In other words, Inuit sex/gender systems are not, like the Eurocentric ones, based on women being defined in relation to and inferior to male gender, but gender roles are more fluid and negotiable, and linked with similar responsibilities of "giving." The above seem cruel examples of renunciation, if one interprets such alternative social relations through the lens of western individualism, compulsory heteronormativity, and nuclear family values. However, in alternative communal social systems grounded in extended families and gift philosophies this is far from the case. Hyde (1983) quotes examples of Indigenous cultures that include "first-fruits rites" as part of a philosophy where the gifts provided by nature are eaten but parts of it are returned (27), or "given-back." Although his insights do not address the giving up of a child as one's personal property, they do help explicate the philosophy of "giving back." The ritual Trott describes likely expresses the same spirit of "giving back" that is also present in the narratives of women and Bear/s and the various rituals of returning the Bear skull back to its original home. Such practices reflect the belief that the objects of the ritual will remain plentiful if they are treated as gifts. Hyde (1983) notes that the first-fruits ceremony and its equivalents establish a gift relationship with nature, a formal give-and-take that acknowledges our participation in, and dependence upon it. Gift exchange brings with it, therefore, a built-in check on the destruction of its objects.

In conclusion, Trott claims that within Inuit ethnography, boundaries between the animal and the human, the living and the dead, male and female are not sharp: each of these polarities contains the other within it while simultaneously providing a passage between the two. It is this conceptual framework that leads to the series of cycles and transformations between each of these realms that are acted out in human and animal bodies and through rituals. Trott's conclusion about the links between sex and species among the Inuit contributes thus to the anthology's focus on the gift gaze on several levels and perspectives: in terms of gift practices, in terms of the taken-for-granted dualistic hierarchies at the root of western epistemologies and on the level of the first principles of social organization.

"The Warrior Way and the Bear: A Personal Narrative," by Wacoquaakmik (Rodney Bobiwash) is included in the book in honour of his memory and to acknowledge and to show appreciation for his activism in the Toronto First

Nations community. Wacoquaakmik passed away unexpectedly in the midst of this project. The piece is a personal narrative regarding the author's development of his own political philosophy as a warrior of the Bear Clan, and touches on family history, childhood memories, and meetings with the Mansi-Hanti Indigenous people of Russia. Wacoquaakmik presents his observations on how these influences and values have formed his worldview and how this relates to a warrior's duties within Anishnabek tradition. Finally, his reflections are offered from the point of view of Indigenous peoples' contemporary struggles for their rights. Interestingly, Wacoquaakmik alludes to the kinds of matriarchal societies in which men have not hesitated to honour and imitate maternal behaviour, like that of the She-Bear protecting her cubs. Among Indigenous societies, caring and self-defense or warrior behaviour are not oppositional categories as they tend to be in the eurocentric, armoured forms of masculinity. The Indigenous warrior model of masculinity described here comes close to the tenets of the gift rather than the master imaginary since the latter are characterized by asymmetrical and hierarchical gender relations. Wacoquaakmik's essay provides evidence for the thesis often presented by scholars studying matriarchies that indeed, patriarchy is no more a universal structure any more than matriarchies should be dismissed as a figment of a deluded ecofeminist imagination.[18] Wacoquaakmik juxtaposes thoughts and practices related to bears in modern-day warrior societies (from the Anishnabek Warrior Society to the Ogi-Gitchi-Da of Wisconsin) with the American Indian Movement embodying traditional Bear Clan notions of responsibility. He begins with a story about Grandmother Bear that accounts for the inability of sky children to return home to the sky world. The story is followed by references to important events in Anishnabek history and a description of the responsibilities given to different clans such as the Crane Clan People and Bear Clans. We learn that Bears hold the oldest medicine within their bundles—the knowledge of which herbs and plants can be used to treat which ailments. The first responsibility, however, of the Bear Clan is justice; Bears are responsible in council meetings to ensure that all voices are heard fairly and then to see that the common will is carried out. Finally, as warriors, Bears defend the perimeter of the community. The story of his experiences among the Finno-Ugric Mansi-Hanti Indigenous people of Russia reveals the fact that Bear rituals are not a thing of the distant past but have continued to be practiced even in recent history, although the political machinery in places like Russia often oppose them in brutal ways.

Wacoquaakmik's essay contains important information about the continued imposition of western values on Indigenous peoples. At the same time, the article provides a cross-culturally important interpretative horizon for considering the differences between male and female attitudes towards "nature/culture" within a culture where no such sharp, reified distinctions exist. Wacoquaakmik reminds us that the western militaristic male mystique does not apply to all cultures, that the term "warrior" need not imply aggressive impulses. Representations of Bear/s and men as bears do not assume the same exaggerated, sharply differential form as they often do among men in patriarchal cultures.[19]

The relationship between the Bear and the "other" remains among Ojibway bearmen one of respect and positive identification, contrasting with the objectifying and anthropomorphizing stance of dominant, white bear hunters (whether academic and metaphoric or real). Wacoquaakmik provides challenges for men's studies as regards the construction of and culturally contingent expressions of "masculinity." Clearly the markers of maleness in western theory do not fit Wacoquaakmik's description of the ecosensitive and responsible warrior consciousness beyond the ethos of conquest and domination (even though this hegemonic form of masculinity should not be reified or turned into a reductive stereotype).[20]

Kari Sallamaa's "Chant of the Bear," as well as the poem contained within Jürgen Kremer's article, are the only poems in the anthology written by men. Considering the gendered theme of the book, it is of course tempting to tease out the "male theme" or manhood agenda (Vaughan 1997). If the focus on aggression, hunting, competition, the exchange economy, hierarchical and dualistic values, "power-over," mark the reductive, stereotypical male object relation, Sallamaa's poem bears little witness to such a gender script/worldview. Sallamaa reveals his erudition as to bearlore through his reference to the "chains of gold" tying the bear to his father in heaven. There are, in fact, stories in the North (particularly Finland and among the Mansi-Hanti (Voguls) where Bear descends on the Earth in a carriage, and is lifted back on golden chains. There is a similarity here with Ugrian and Algonquian Celestial Bear Who also Comes Down to Earth. The Finno-Ugric Mansi also have an origin myth of a She-Bear pleading with her father in heaven to let her descend on the Earth (Kannisto 1958). Sallamaa's poem does not enact the objectifying stance that often characterizes male writers' attitudes towards animals from Ernest Hemingway to Gary Snyder (see Snyder [1990]; Shepard and Sanders 1985). The bear is not an object or trophy but a revered singer of a kinship chant uniting generations of beings—a clear element of the many varieties of Finno-Ugric gift economies. The grand theme and chant may well refer to the shamanistic understanding of the universe where singing, chanting, *galein* is prior to speech and the logocentric worldview—in the female voice. Séamas Ó Catháin (1995) likewise evokes the importance of singing, rhythm, and memory for the Bear ceremonial, something that is also a particularly strong distinguishing mark of Finnish-Carelian hunting drama. The Finnish word *kieli* has a double meaning, referring to a literally salty tongue, as well as a more abstract reference to language (as in the idiom "mother tongue"), which is lost in translation. Sallamaa's use of this word in his poem suggests that the mythical Primal Mother Goddess prepared the language, with all its salt, taste, meanings, and greatness.

Having met Jordan Paper in Canada in the framework of a conference on Women and Spirituality at York University in 1996, and recalling his writings on women and Bear, I invited him to contribute to this anthology. I also shared ideas with him regarding the affinities between women's menstrual rituals, the sauna, and the sweatlodge.[21] Paper brings together both experiential and academic viewpoints regarding his life-long research on spiritual topics as they relate to

Bear, particularly in the Anishnaabe culture that he is most familiar with. Paper honours Bear by including the Bear Song he was given during his soul travels, and by integrating information about the spiritual experiences that led him to his research topic. The epiphany he had experienced not only "brought to fruition his functional spiritual life," but led to his later writings and research. Paper brings to the anthology knowledge and insights about Bear rituals and related cultural phenomena that lend credence and legitimacy to many of the tentative and more academically-grounded theses presented in this anthology. While much of the research on matriarchal cultures of life has been challenged and questioned Paper's research, in contrast, adds weight to the arguments many scholars from Gimbutas (1989) to Makilam (1996) have made regarding several interconnecting signs of life-oriented cultures. They include vagina-shaped caves, positive representations of vulvas, diamonds, decorative symbols, nurturing animals (Bear, bison) and pictographs—rock paintings describing other central, cultural items of "feminine" or ursine nature.

Paper also helps make the case for the centrality within Indigenous cultures of gift economies, both past and present, contrasting with the stance that reduces spiritual rituals and practices to mere economic interests or displaced symbolic violence (e.g. Bourdieu 1997). Like many other contributors in this anthology, Paper describes the kinds of gift-giving practices that have the creation of social bonds as their purpose.

Echoing Finnish, Sami, and many other cultural Bear traditions, Paper's description of the rituals of honouring the feminized She-bear centres on the dynamics of give-back and respect marking the Bear rituals among the Ojibway. Paper supports the view presented in the anthology that western literature is often misleading in its analysis of spiritual rituals because it is hierarchical and monotheistic. He questions the interpretation of theriomorphic spirits as a kind of "Master" of the species, doubting that such a view reflects the assumptions of people embracing a *non*-monotheistic outlook. Paper argues that for Indigenous people, at least the ones he has familiarized himself with, the concept of a master of anything could not exist. Hence, their respect is due to each and every bear on encountering Her as the spirit, Bear, not to any "Master" of the Bear. Animals that provide food are utterly natural, Paper points out. Thus there is no notion of their being subject to anything, let alone an overarching spirit. More important, these cultures are often egalitarian, and leadership is a matter of a community voluntarily accepting leadership for specific tasks, while allowing anyone to opt out if they so desire. Paper's article gives also implicit recognition to feminist viewpoints regarding non-monotheistic forms of spirituality and the sacred. Lending support also to my own research on the affinities between menstrual rites, the Finnish sauna, the Bear's den, and other symbolic containers of death and rebirth, Paper elaborates on the Anishnaabe Spirit Lodge. In some of the Anishnaabe traditions, menarche is called "Becoming Bear."

Paper's analysis of the gendered division of "Bear labour" commands attention. He reports that those with a special relationship to She-bear, having Bear power, are frequently healers, unless their visions are of the ferocious aspect of Bear. In that particular case, Bear gives people warrior power. Does the Spirit Bear divide women into healers and men into warriors, or is this the projection of the contingent sex/gender system of recent Ojibway societies (by both the Ojibway and western scholars)? Paper's article also brings Guédon's description of the meaning of power among the Dene into an interesting cross-cultural focus. His take on Bear stresses Her meaning as pre-eminent spirit for healing, one having the ability to provide life-force, to visit a recently dead human, and bring the corpse back to life. For Paper, Bear is quite simply Earth in Her living terrestrial form. Paper's article also creates a bridge to Elina Helander-Renvall's description of the role of dreams in Sami culture, and of her own Bear dreams. Paper claims, with a relationship such as the one involving Bear, one can merge in various ways with the spirit, but it is a spiritual, not a physical merging.

My own research and theory, "From the Unbearable Bond to the Gift Imaginary: Archaic Bear Ceremonials Revisited," elaborates on my vision for this book and contains more detailed examinations of the gift economy/imaginary and other key concepts that have guided the structure and selection of materials for this anthology. Apart from presenting the theoretical background of the collection, it describes the multidisciplinary ecocritical/ecofeminist, religious, and Indigenous studies approaches from which I have drawn insights.[22] I analyze the narratives of wo(men) and Bear/s by contrasting two gendered and ethnocultural paradigms—the gift gaze/imaginary and the master imaginary. I highlight Bear ceremonial feasts, and the traces of ecosocially sustainable societies linked with them from a gender-sensitive "gift" perspective. Focusing on the Finno-Ugric and other Northern contexts, I discuss how the two logics are co-present, yet embedded in different gender-related worldviews (life and death-oriented cultures). I elaborate on the different assumptions scholars project on the evidence of Bear religions and concerning human nature, economic issues, spirituality, the function of rituals, human/animal as well as gender relations. My goal is to help lift the veil on the repressed, suppressed, and/or forbidden contact between women and Bears on the many levels in which it epitomizes ecological attitudes. The stories have been approached by many scholars merely as reflections of pre-patriarchal societies' moral regulation and gender socialization, as primitive fear management and/or as vestiges of totemic rules and taboos. The motivation for my own piece, as well as for the entire anthology, is to ask new questions of the *arch*-aic materials, and to foreground the submerged gift economy perspectives.

The tales of wo(men) and Bear/s present challenges not only regarding taken-for-granted sex/gender systems but all oppositional pairings ordered as hierarchical and dichotomous thought patterns and practices. I suggest that in many parts of the world ancient bear hunting and/or life-oriented societies celebrated fluid, hybrid human/animal relations and that bears with their hybrid, shifting and fluid identity (male, female, human, animal) represent a more challenging "first principle" than even gender beyond patriarchal binaries (mind/body, nature/culture, spirit/matter, woman/man, animal/human, primitive/civilized). I also suggest that the associated concepts, menstruation, the moon, the cyclical world order, bees, serpents, the bear's lair, the sweatlodge or sauna, the power of fe/male sexuality, and the forbidden eye contact between women and Bear/s partake of a matrix that has become a complex of negative taboos within Judeo-Christian thinking and practices. They involve reversals of Goddess-related values, practices, and ways of ordering life.

Sami scholar Elina Helander-Renvall adds original and fresh perspectives on women and Bear/s with her article, "'Váisi', the Sacred Wild: Transformation and Dreaming in the Sami Cultural Context." On the broadest level, her goal is to contribute to discussions on Indigenous and western ways of knowing and being, all of which relates to our understanding of nature-culture-species and a host of other cultural categories. The article contributes new material and knowledge about the Sami worldview and relations with Bear on many levels that have previously remained unfocused: the specificities of traditional Sami female spirituality, the role of personal and collective dreaming in Indigenous cultures like the Sami, and the special status of Bear as a power animal that challenges the strict boundaries of the dichotomies human versus animal. Helander-Renvall elaborates on Sami female spirituality with its "expanded and inward ways of knowing" by analyzing one of her own dreams about Bear that she recorded and reflected upon over a period of time and as part of a series of dreams. Helander-Renvall draws attention to the ontological status of dreams as having a social character with regard to relations between humans and non-humans, analyzing her own Bear dream as revealing the social character of the space between nature and society. Similar to the findings of Guédon's field research among the Dene, she claims that in Sami culture there are animals and spirits who at least in some situations are considered to be more powerful than humans. Clearly, Helander-Renvall is not referring only to physical strength, but endows Bear with traditionally "human" attributes such as extensive knowledge and the ability to understand speech. How would western science relate to such unscientific claims? My suggestion is that we listen to them with the other ear, as evidence of other styles of knowing that have their own rationale and logic.

Finally, Helander-Renvall foregrounds dreaming as an important, and unrecognized, dimension of shamanism and of the Sami concept of the sacred.[23] She points out the scarcity of texts available about the dreams of the Sami people and underlines that "by narrowing the spaces for important cultural elements, we reduce our ability to know things about the world we live in." Citing nineteenth-century scholars of the Bear ceremonial, Helander-Renvall tells us that, "an individual's power is believed to reflect his or her reciprocity, both with supernatural creatures, and with other humans." Accepting the validity of this view for her own culture, Helander-Renvall gives the example of "reindeer-luck" that those who honour the powers of nature are blessed with. In order for Sami reindeer herders to be successful with their herding activities, they have to show respect to the land and the spirits dwelling on the hunting grounds. Here Helander-Renvall provides further evidence for the claim often made in this book that utilitarian attitudes towards nature are not universal but rather expressions of the materialistic ethos of industrialized western peoples among others.

Helander-Renvall also focuses on how mythic discourse helps people in their daily activities and empowers them to take up particular directions in life. Taking her own dream as an example, she points to the ways in which dreams can allow people to transform and to become capable of adopting the bear-like gaze. Although the scholarship on discourses of gender power, particularly in the field of women's and cultural studies, is extensive and full of complexity, involving the intersectional and overlapping dimensions of power abuses, Helander-Renvall provides a vantage-point for the continued analysis of this key concept that involves literally eccentric dimensions (in the positive sense of the term referring to "out of the center" [Daly 1978]). Contrary to the often individual focus of the analyses of power and identity, she exposes the ways in which empowerment of Sami women is both a personal and a collective process of social transformation, with ecopolitical consequences. Helander-Renvall claims that Sami dreamers bring the self, their world, and their experience into public view, not in a dogmatic and static way but with the aim of giving rise to new, collectively-formulated cultural narratives. This challenges any simplistic notion of the stability and conservatism of storytelling and their modes of transmission. The public sharing of dreams is also here related to goals that go beyond mere entertainment. What Helander-Renvall tells us about the communal function of dreams challenges the Freudian, Jungian, and other hegemonic theories of dream interpretation and comes close to North American studies on the role of dreams in Indigenous communal life (see, for example, Trigger 1990). To what extent these kinds of dream sessions are ongoing practices in Sami communities, Helander-Renvall does not tell us. Most importantly, from the point of view of the gift paradigm, Helander-Renvall elaborates on a vision of life that is in relatively stark contrast to the taken-for-granted norms of the *homo-economicus* and of the exchange economy with its attempts to reduce all social rituals to the pursuit of economic interest and materialist accumulation. The ecofeminist conception of subjectivity as signification in process, permanently forming and reforming itself in collision with the social totality, is based in a materialism that defies the limits of bourgeois epistemology. Helander-Renvall's article lends weight to many of the arguments and theories presented in the book. She supports at the same time Satu Maarit Natunen's comments about Bearwomen not necessarily embracing the sex/gender/species systems of their societies' male members, her view about the role of alder juice in the Bear ritual, and the power of Sami mythic animals.

Overall, the Sami contributions in this volume can be summed up as follows: colonization and Christian patriarchy have failed to fully stamp out many central aspects of the traditional Sami worldview and spiritual practices. Rather than mirroring the persistence of "primitive" customs, they call for a deeper deconstruction also of white mythology, and the dominant discourses of eco and gynophobic power. Clearly, Indigenous cultures, at least on the level of the worldview that scholars introduce us to, continue to relate to nature in the kinds

39

of ways that would significantly improve our chances for planetary responsibility and a more sustainable future. Ecopolitics demands much more than a balance among competing interests and stake(stock)holders. The bodies of all species are under attack from capitalist patriarchal institutions.

"Dreaming, Bear Spirit, and Finno-Ugric Women's Handicrafts" is the article that Irma Heiskanen from Muurame, Finland, sent to accompany her drawing of the woman and Bear on the cover of this anthology. The article is a description of Heiskanen's personal dreams of the Spirit of Bear as well as her subsequent academic journey to the worldview and seasonal activities of Finno-Ugric women. Heiskanen's special contribution is how she has linked separate strands of research on Finno-Ugric women's handicrafts in terms of their life-cycle symbolism and art, and her final speculation about their role in Arctic dramas of world renewal. Heiskanen's article reinforces the more theoretical research of Séamas Ó Catháin (1995), and the scholars in the anthology that find evidence for a similar matrix of woman-bear-snake-bird-bee symbolism at the heart of matricentric, pagan, and/or gift circulating cultures of life (or whatever scholars might call the historical context in which such symbols of regenerativity played a key role).

Heiskanen also draws gender-sensitive interpretations out of Permian bronze casts and ornaments from various Finno-Ugric "cultures of life" that express their imaginary of regenerativity in many symbols including women's handicrafts. She draws on the insights of other scholars in the field while adding to them a new, more inclusive interpretation. Heiskanen has been researching traditional Indigenous ecological knowledge and applying it also to the Finnish context (see Heiskanen and Kailo 2006). She points out that early Permian casts depict the same kind of symbolic relationship between birds, the goddess, Bear/s, and other animals as those found in some of the key figures and ornaments of the ancient European Vinca culture. Heiskanen reconstructs through Finno-Ugric ornaments depicted on handicrafts how women renewed and strengthened their relationship with the creative forces of Nature. The ornaments reveal, in her view, the central meaning of the Cosmic and Earthly Bear/First mother, a one-time nexus of Finno-Ugric women's identity. She argues that the ornaments point to and embody the connections between the cycles of Star Constellations and the fertile cycles of women and Bear/s. Heiskanen has also been led by her research to associate the prehistorical rod and spike distaff, the helical movement of fingers caused by threading, the helical force of the sun during seasons, the spinning of stars in the nightly sky and finally, the weaving principle of Mother Nature.

An abstracted multilayered vagina in the form of a rhombus, a tree of life pointing in four directions, and birds represented on women's headscarves and clothing are some of the examples that Heiskanen finds depicting women as the co-source and contributors of Creation. It is as if the emotional and music-like experience of interconnectedness were transmitted through the figures, colours, and patterns in order to protect and to strengthen the nurturing ties between all forms of creation. However, Heiskanen's particular focus on the dynamic symbolism of the ornaments in women's handicrafts adds an important dimension to findings in the other articles. What Heiskanen writes about the protective power of ornaments that are designed to enhance the cycles of growth and fertility brings to mind Kira van Deusen's (2001) work on Indigenous women's shamanism, which she claims is reflected in their embroidery serving to ward off the evil eye. With these kinds of insights we are delving more deeply into uncharted territories regarding the particular expressions of female shamanism, which have remained invisible to less gender-sensitive scholars, and which are related to the Bear religion. As regards Heiskanen's strong dreams of Bear, it is intriguing that many of the scholars in this anthology have been motivated in their research by such "unorthodox" contacts and visions in their noctural psyche (or spirit?) (e.g. Guilbault, Paper, and Helander).

Suvorov's bronze cast, "Udmurtia 1996" reproduces and epitomizes in my view the matrix of regeneration and balance that is a central aspect of the worldview of the gift economies. Suvorov's bronze figure combining the earthly or chtonic bear, the woman-as-a-world tree, and an ambiguous creature with wings encapsulates the key signifiers of the ancient Finno-Ugric worldview, but with a modern and localized culture-specific and artistic interpretation. Sukorov's art is most appropriate for this anthology as it epitomizes the ecologically and culturally sustainable and empowering potential of ethnocultural revival and the revisiting of a culture's Pagan-Christian repertoire of myths and symbols. In Suvorov's case, ancient symbols have contributed to reshaping the values of contemporary civilization, and draw on the power of ancient matriculture. His art bears striking affinities with Udmurt and other Finno-Ugric, Permian art where the human and the animal realms are combined in hybrid forms and are often connected with the universal theme of the world tree (that Heiskanen refers to in her article).[24] The combination of woman, bird wings, and bear, plus the Christian linen cloth draped over the woman's arms in Suvorov's cast suggest the co-existence, partnership, of realms held to be irreconciliable or opposite, earth and sky, woman and nature, Pagan and Christian. I believe that these figures can also be seen as symbols of the gift paradigm where all creatures together represent the interconnections of various animate life forms.

My conversation with Sami artist, Satu Marit Natunen, "'Baiki'… The Place Where Your Heart Is," held in 1998, offers an Indigenous woman's modern views on women and Bear/s. Natunen challenges the trust male anthropologists place in social contracts and suggests that women may well not have accepted their prescribed behaviours, such as avoiding a direct gaze at Bear. Natunen believes that despite the taboos, they "looked" anyway, whatever such a resisting gaze implies. Natunen thus provides a most thought-provoking interpretation of the Bear-woman union, one that refers to the possibility of a stronger human woman-centered race.

My prayer, "Honeypaws in Heaven" is a playful take on "Our Father in Heaven," suggesting that this Christian prayer consists of an appropriative rewriting and overwriting of Bearlore and Bear songs in which Bear was addressed as the Queen of Heaven and Earth. Collections of Bearlore in Finland (Honko, Timonen, Branch and Bosley 1993) contain numerous Bear prayers which call to mind aspects of "Our Father in Heaven," although the latter focuses, like Christian culture in general, on the primacy of male gods, divine sons, and [a masculated] Heaven over goddesses, animals, and divine relations between mothers and daughters. During my research of Finnish Bear poems and prayers, I realized that the rebirth drama of the Bear is in many ways very similar to the resurrection story of Christ on the Cross (Kuusi and Honko 1983: 33-42, among others have elaborated on this).

Finally, the book concludes with a "testament" by artist Maureen Enns, a woman who literally ran away with Bears. Maureen Enns's message from Grizzlyland bridges the myth of women and Bear/s and the reality of contemporary adventurous women who have chosen to abandon society for bears. Her example challenges any view according to which myths are the opposite of "reality." Her words attest to the persistence of love affairs between women and Bears, and remind us that Bears are not just metaphors and projection screens for academics alienated from their inner animal. For her, Bears have their own intrinsic value that needs to be protected and defended, in practice, not theory. She has immortalized her own love for Bears and their rights in her rich artistic depictions of her cohabitation with Bear. In her most recent messages, she has raised concerns about grizzlies becoming or in some cases already being an endangered species and evokes the ecological issues that concern all the contributors in this volume.

The essays, articles, poetry and artwork included in the book each tell their story of the continuing power that bears or Bear exert on the fe/male imaginary and imagination. The gaze between wo(men) and Bear/s, then, is only "unbearable" to those who wish to sever this deep connection, deep ecology, deep feminism. To many modern women, their forebears are transmitters of a form of ecospirituality that is needed in today's dysfunctional global village where consumerism does not succeed in filling the existential void. Ownership of the past is to a great extent ownership of the future. History/herstory and ecomythology are a particular form of power and knowledge involving the manipulation of academic and political resources and serving to ensure the dominance of certain groups. A better integrated and contextualized theory can thus provide a better basis for alliances around a host of ecological, economic, and social issues. This book is thus not only about wo(men) and Bear/s, but on a metalevel, it is about what makes us human: reclaiming our subject positions on a "great chain of being," beyond self-destructive human-centrism and scientific paradigms that collude with the current ecophobic ethos.

[1]There are different criteria used by scholars to refer to the first and colonized inhabitants of the Americas and other continents. In Canada it is customary to refer to First Nations people, in Australia to Aboriginal people, while the specific tribal names are preferred by all (Cree, Dene, etc.). As a general reference I have opted to use the term Indigenous except when the specific context makes it more appropriate to resort to other terms.

[2] Camilo Gomides (2006) defines ecocriticism as "the field of enquiry that analyzes and promotes works of art which raise moral questions about human interactions with nature, while also motivating audiences to live within a limit that will be binding over generations" (16). For me, the essential defining features of ecocritical texts consist in how they help question and challenge the hiearchical dualisms of mind/body, spirit/matter, nature/culture, male/female, civilized/primitive, which are the psychological core of the master consciousness in its alienation from modes of interconnectedness and self-other continuity.

[3] There are more and more studies proving that the Arctic's climate change with a noticeable warming trend is affecting polar bears where, it is said, people and animals are experiencing the warmest air temperatures in four centuries. See, for example, Canadian Museum of Nature <www.nature.ca/education>.

[4] I spell Bear with the capital "B" to evoke her/his Divine/Cosmic status whereas bears, included in "Bear/s" contains also a reference to bears as a species with different (also secular or devalued) meanings and roles. I use the phrase "wo(men) and Bears" to refer to the stories in general because although the primary version of the story is about women and Bear/s, there are a few versions where it is a male figure that marries a She-bear. I use the phrase "women and Bear/s" to refer in these instances specifically to the role of women in the stories.

[5] See <www.gift-economy.org> and <www.akademieHAGIA.org> for elaborations on the gift paradigm, and gift and "give-back" economies.

[6] By "queer" I refer to the concept made famous by Judith Butler (1990) where she exposed the heteronormative matrix of western sexuality, addressing how dualistic and reductive sexual representations create reality by their sheer repetitiveness. Queer has come to refer to the more general deconstruction of sexual and other binaries, but it does not as a rule question anthropocentrism.

[7] In Finnish folk poetry, for example, many gods have female names which can utterly confuse scholars. Are they "mistakes of transcription" or should we revisit the assumption of strict male/female binaries? Shepard and Sanders (1985) refer to the non-paired representation and remote location of the bear as suggesting an "androgynous principle of creativity even more fundamental than that of the polarity of masculine and feminine" (189).

[8] Since 2001 I have belonged to a international alliance of women activists established by Genevieve Vaughan called "Feminists for a Gift Economy" where in addition to our activism, we explore theories of the gift as an alternative to the current hard-core neoliberal values. I coined the concept of the "gift gaze" in my effort to find an alternative to the male gaze; however, I discovered later that the concept, together with the "exchange gaze," had been formulated by Vaughan in an unpublished manuscript, "Epistemology and Gender: Knowledge as Gratitude," now available on her web page as *Homo Donans* (2007). I have been greatly inspired by Vaughan's writings on the gift, and elaborate on her work in my article in this volume.

[9] The Sami are Indigenous people living in Europe; due to colonization they have been split by the national borders of Sweden, Norway, Finland, and Russia. For

postcolonial writings on the Sami, see for example Helander and Kailo (1998) and Kuokkanen (2007).

[10]For those wary of tales of animal love, it may be necessary to point out that the marriage of wo(men) and Bear/s should not be interpreted literally as promoting interspecies sex, but is best understood as a symbolic dramatization of pacts of interdependency between humans and animals (totemism) and other modern Indigenous covenants of mutuality.

[11]In Finland, the Sami are formally recognized as Indigenous people. However, "Finland still treats the Sami people as a national linguistic minority rather than an Indigenous people and ignores the special relationship the Sami people enjoys with its surrounding environment and natural resources, livelihoods, legal systems and traditions, giving the false impression that legal protection of linguistic rights alone is sufficient for the Saami people to be able to maintain its culture" (Wessendorf 2005). According to the Finnish *Constitution* the Sami, as Indigenous people, have the right to maintain and develop their own languages and culture and to use their own language in court and before authorities. To date, Finland has not ratified ILO convention no. 169 nor have Sami land rights in Finland been resolved.

[12]I am aware that the role of story performance, issues of genre classification, and interpretations of beliefs and archaic worldviews are approached very differently by Indigenous nations in their diversity. Many academic Samis have found it offensive to think that they would not embrace the same academic discourses as mainstream scholars. Like white scholars, Indigenous scholars adopt different attitudes, styles, and discourses for different purposes. Hence we need to approach the systemic, epistemic and resource-related otherness of women and Indigenous people through a politics of non-hierarchical, non-dualistic difference.

[13]As worldviews, ontologies, cosmologies, systems of knowledge and values are dynamic and constantly evolving in time and space, so it remains impossible to define an Indigenous *episteme*, or even more specifically, a Sami, Salish, or Maori episteme, to use the concept posited and reworked by Sami scholar, Rauna Kuokkanen (2007). However, although culturally distinct in many ways, Indigenous people believe that they share certain fundamental perceptions particularly as they relate to the human relationship with the natural world. This is also noted by Danielle Sanders (1985): "Although each tribe is different because of tribal structure and geography, there are prevailing basic, consistent values and attitudes held by American Indians that transcend and cut across tribes as well as across reservations and urban areas" (82). Finally, the focus on the gift in this anthology does not serve to deny that all epistemologies also contain their shadow side, as the very etymologies of the word "gift" suggest (poison/remedy) (Vaughan 1997).

[14]However, although my research involves deconstructing and re-aligning such separated domains of study as folklore and literature, it also tries to facilitate the creation of a new body of material on aesthetics and the alternative gynocentric imaginary in the largest sense of the word. The ostensive strength and test of

appropriate intercultural methods is their value for suggesting ever more culture-sensitive ways of reading Indigenous and non-Indigenous stories that go beyond those in this anthology. These stories are not meant to exemplify ultimate ideals of one gender and ethnosensitive method or approach, but represent a collection of different approaches defying the "male gaze" as an academic politics of "power over." I find Rauna Kuokkanen's (2007) thesis particularly useful for grasping the complexities of ethnosensitive, anti-racist approaches that recognize difference, but differently, beyond new forms of dualism or ways of shunning responsibility.

[15]The brief conversation was held at the feminist university of Løten, Norway, in 2001, and does not directly reflect the contents of the play.

[16]Guédon has represented the Dene views as they are held by most members of the group she lived with. I trust, however, that Guédon and all other contributors to this book welcome any feedback on the interpretations given, so we might collectively enlarge our understanding of each other's cultural traditions and epistemic systems.

[17]It would be challenging to apply the theories of Judith Butler (1990) to the Inuit sex/gender system where the repetition of particular gender-related gestures and their performative societal role constitute gender instead of gender being reducible simplistically to biology.

[18]See Leahy (1998) for a thorough critical assessment of ecofeminist positions.

[19]Bear poetry and fiction by Scott Momaday is a case in point; Bear is the spirit of the wilderness, not a target for shooting sprees.

[20]Sadly, Wacoquaakmik (Rodney Bobiwash) cannot continue this debate with us as he passed away suddenly in the midst of this project. Much loved and appreciated, and well-recognized for his activism in Indigenous circles and regarding human rights in a broader context, Wacoquaakmik, or Rodney, was very much himself the positive warrior Bear he is writing about. His contribution to this book remains then a gift from a Indigenous man embodying the best of an Indigenous culture based on the circulation of Gifts and "social capital." Thank you!

[21]All Indigenous nations have had their own linguistic terms for this kind of a spiritual ritual such as the Lakota (Siouan) word *inipi* and the Anishnaabe (Ojibway) word, *madodoswun*, which literally means "spirit lodge." Jordan Paper pointed out, in the process of dialogues regarding this book, that although virtually all First Nations people use the term "sweat lodge," the term itself is in essence demeaning. He explained that the terminology came about as the result of an explicit denial by Christian missionaries that there was any religious element to this Indigenous spiritual practice. Had it been recognized for what it is, then it would have been illegal in Canada and the U.S. along with all other Indigenous religious practices. Since Indigenous religion is now legal in the U.S. and not illegal in Canada, Paper considers it time that spiritual practices be recognized for what they are, hence, his preference for the Anishnaabe term, "spirit lodge." When referring generally to this Indigenous spiritual ritual, I use the general "sweatlodge" for lack of a better term, and because it was commonly used among the First Nations communities I

frequented in Canada during 1991-97. I do so with the utmost respect, however, for linguistic and ethnocultural specificity, and recognize the problem of naming. I am grateful to anyone providing me with information for a more appropriate general term to refer to these practices, as well as for nation-specific concepts.

[22]My background in comparative literature which combines semiotics, cultural studies, Marxist criticism, psychoanalytic theory, and hermeneutics in part explains my multidisciplinary approach; my political activism and grass-roots experience has allowed me to apply my theories in practice. I have co-founded an association on ecopsychology and traditional ecological knowledge with Irma Heiskanen through which we reintroduce marginalized ecofriendly rituals rooted in our Finnish culture; I have also co-founded an association providing assistance to migrant women suffering from gendered violence in addition to my membership in local and international women's, peace, and pro-democracy networks. I mention this because ecofeminists are often accused of wasting energy on goddess worship rather than political action. The claim is mostly unfounded as regards activist-witches like Starhawk, to name just one, but it continues to characterize the competitive politics of labelling and misnaming even within women's studies.

[23]I consider the belittlement of dream interpretation to be part of the fear and suppression of our "nature" and agree that dreams are paths towards a deeper self-knowledge and self-presence beyond the empty recipes of consumer identities. The Self as Bear is a bridge to the other in his or her multiple manifestations and to the dream reality where we cannot avoid truths about ourselves. As Finnish poet Helena Anhava says: "Dreams don't fool us. They know us."

[24]Eero Autio in *Eagles, Elks and Bears: Permian Bronze Art* (2000) has published intriguing elements of rock art and archaic artefacts that closely resemble Sukorov's combined woman, bear, winged hybrid being and world tree. Such composite figures have been interpreted in a variety of ways that cannot be reduced to the matrix of regenerativity that I foreground in this book. The view is common, however, that the ancient bronze figures evoke the three dimensions of an ancient worldview in its three layers (the underworld, the middle world of the living, and the world of ancestors and spirits) (Autio 2000: 157).

References

Abrahams, Yvette. 2007. "The Khoekhoe Free Economy: A Model for the Gift." *Women and the Gift Economy: A Radically Different Worldview is Possible.* Ed. Genevieve Vaughan. Toronto: Inanna Publications and Education. 217-222.

Adelkarim-Chikh, Rabia. 2007. "Solidary Economics: Women's Banking Networks in Senegal." *Women and the Gift Economy: A Radically Different Worldview is Possible.* Ed. Genevieve Vaughan. Toronto: Inanna Publications and Education. 238-241.

Antrobus, Peggy. 2007. "The Gift Economy in the Caribbean: The Gift and the

Wind." *Women and the Gift Economy: A Radically Different Worldview is Possible.* Ed. Genevieve Vaughan. Toronto: Inanna Publications and Education. 230-235.

Apo, Satu. *Naisen väki: tutkimuksia suomalaisten kansan omaisesta kulttuurista ja ajattelusta (Woman's Väki: Studies on Finnish Folk Culture and Thought).* Helsinki: Hanki ja Jää, l995.

Armstrong, Jeannette. 1995. "International Covenants: A New World Order? Indigenous Women Address the World." *Our Future, Our Responsibility. United Nations Fourth World Conference on Women.*

Autio, Eero. 2000. *Kotkat, hirvet, karhut. Permiläistä pronssitaidetta (Eagles, Elks, Bears: Permian Bronze Art).* Jyväskylä: Ateena Oy.

Bachelard, Gaston. 1969. *The Poetics of Space.* 1958. Boston: Beacon Press.

Battiste, Marie, ed. 2000: *Reclaiming Indigenous Voice and Vision.* Vancouver: University of British Columbia Press.

Benally, Louise. 2007. "Big Mountain Black Mesa: The Beauty Way." *Women and the Gift Economy: A Radically Different Worldview is Possible.* Ed. Genevieve Vaughan. Toronto: Inanna Publications and Education. 154-157.

Bopp, Judie. 1984. *The Sacred Tree.* Lethbridge, AB: Four Worlds Development Press.

Bourdieu, Pierre. 1997. "Selections from the Logic of Practice." *The Logic of the Gift. Toward an Ethic of Generosity.* Ed. Alan D. Schrift. New York: Routledge. 34-45.

Brant, Beth 1991. "This is History." *Food and Spirits.* Vancouver: Press Gang Publishers.

Brill de Ramirez, Susan Berry. 1998. *Contemporary American Indian Literatures and the Oral Tradition.* Tucson: University of Arizona Press.

Buell, Lawrence. 2001. *Writing for an Endangered World: Literature, Culture, and the Environment in the U.S. and Beyond.* Cambridge: Harvard University Press.

Butler, Judith. 1990. *Gender Trouble: Feminism and the Subversion of Identity.* New York: Routledge.

Caffyn, Kelley, ed. 1992. *Give Back: First Nations Perspectives on Cultural Practice.* North Vancouver: Gallerie Publications.

Caldwell, Richard. 1989. *The Origin of Gods: A Psychoanalytic Study of Greek Theogonic Myth.* New York: Oxford University Press.

Centre for Biological Diversity. 2005. "Polar Bear." Online: <http://www.biologicaldiversity.org.pecies/mammals/polar_bear/index.html>. Accesed March 23, 2008.

Churchill, Ward. 1992. "A Little Matter of Genocide: Native American Spirituality and New Age Hucksterism." *Fantasies of the Master Race: Literature, Cinema and the Colonization of American Indians.* Eds. Ward Churchill and M. Annette Jaimes. Monroe, ME: Common Courage Press. 10-20.

Colorado, Pamela. 1988. "Bridging Native and Western Science." *Convergence* 21 (2/3): 49-67.

Columbia Mountains Institute of Applied Ecology. 1999. "Grizzly Bear Information Sheet." Online: <http://www.cmiae.org/grizzlyinfo.htm>. Accessed March 23, 2008.

Condren, Mary. 2002. *The Serpent and the Goddess: Women, Religion and Power in Celtic Ireland*. 1989. Dublin: New Island Books.

Cruikshank, Julie, ed. 1990. *Life Lived like a Story: Life Stories of Three Yukon Native Elders*. In collaboration with Angela Sidney, Kitty Smith, and Annie Ned. Vancouver: University of British Columbia Press.

Daly, Mary. 1978. *Gyn/ecology: The Metaethics of Radical Feminism*. Boston: Beacon Press.

Dandie, Allyson. 1990. "Native People Must Start Telling Their Own Stories." *The Leader Post* April 19: B6.

Deloria, Vine Jr. 1999. *Spirit and Reason. The Vine Deloria Jr. Reader* Ed. Barbara Deloria, Kristen Foehner, and Sam Scinta. Golden, CO: Fulcrum.

Dergachev, V. A. 2007. *O skipetrakh, o loshadiakh, o voine. Etiudy v zashchitu migratsionnoi kontseptsii M. Gimbutas (About Scepters, Horses, and War: Sketches in Defence of Migrational Conception by M. Gimbutas)*. SPB: Nestor-istoriia.

Dion-Buffalo, Yvonne and John C. Mohawk. 1994. "Thoughts From an Autochtonous Center." *Akwe:kon Journal* 9 (4) (Winter): 16-22.

Doherty, Lillian E. 2001. *Gender and the Interpretation of Classical Myth*. London: G. Duckworth and Co. Ltd.

Dodson Gray, Elizabeth. 1982. *Patriarchy as a Conceptual Trap*. Wellesley, Mass.: Roundtable Press.

Durkheim, Emily. 1964. *The Division of Labor in Society*. 1893. New York: Free Press.

Eagleton, Terry. 1995. *Literary Theory: An Introduction*. 1983. London: Blackwell.

Eikjok, Jorun. 2000."Indigenous Women in the North: The Struggle for Rights and Feminism." *International Work Group for Indigenous Affairs* 3 (July-August-September): 38-41.

Eikjok, Jorunn and Inger Birkeland. 2004. "Natur, kjönn og kultur: om behovet for dokumentasjon av samisk naturforståelse i et kjönnsperspektiv. (Nature, Gender and Culture: The Need for the Documentation of the Sami Understanding of Nature and Gender)." *Samiske landsskapsstudier. Rapport fra et arbeidsseminar* Diedut 5: 58-71.

Eilperin, Juliet. 2004. "Study says polar bears could face extinction: Warming shrinks sea ice mammals depend on." *Washington Post* November 9: A13.

Gatens, Moira. 1991. "A Critique of the Sex/Gender Distinction." *A Reader in Feminist Knowledge*. Ed. Sneja Gunew. London: Routledge. 139-157.

Garrard, Greg. 2005. *Ecocriticism*. London: Routledge.

Gaard, Greta. 1993. "Ecofeminism and Native American Cultures: Pushing the Limits of Cultural Imperialism." *Ecofeminism, Women, Animals, Nature*. Philadelphia: Temple University Press. 295-321.

Gimbutas, Marija. 1989. *The Language of the Goddess*. San Francisco: Harper and Row.

Glotfelty, Cheryll and Harold Fromm. 1996. *The Ecocriticism Reader. Landmarks in Literary Ecology*. Athens and London: the University of Georgia Press.

Godbout, Jacques T. 1998. *The World of the Gift*. With Alain Caillé. Trans. by Donald Winkler. Montreal: McGill-Queen's University Press.

Goettner-Abendroth, Heide. 2007. "Matriarchal Society and the Gift Paradigm: Motherliness as an Ethical Principle." *Women and the Gift Economy: A Radically Different Worldview is Possible*. Ed. Genevieve Vaughan. Toronto: Inanna Publications and Education. 99-107.

Gomides, Camilo. 2006. "Putting a New Definition of Ecocriticism to the Test: The Case of the *Burning Season*, a Film (Mal)Adaption." *ISLE* 13 (1): 3-16.

Grant, Agnes. 1988. *Native Literature in the Curriculum: Selected Papers from the 1986 Mokkakit Conference*. Vancouver: Mokkakit Indian Education Research Association.

Gunn, Paula Allen. 1986. *The Sacred Hoop: Recovering the Feminine in American Indian Traditions*. Boston: Beacon Press.

Haraway, Donna. 1991. "A Cyborg Manifesto: Science, Technology, and Socialist-Feminism in the Late Twentieth Century." *Simians, Cyborgs and Women: The Reinvention of Nature*. London: Free Enterprise Association Books. 149-83.

Harding, Sandra. 1994. "Is Science Multicultural? Challenges, Resources, Opportunities, Uncertainties." *Configurations* (2): 301-330.

Heiskanen, Irma and Kaarina Kailo, eds. 2006. *Ekopsykologia ja perinnetieto. Polkuja eheyteen. (Ecopsychology and Traditional Ecological Knowledge: Paths Towards Wholeness)*. Helsinki: Greenspot.

Helander, Elina and Kaarina Kailo. 1998. *No Beginning, No End: The Sami Speak Up*. Edmonton: The Canadian Circumpolar Institute/Nordic Sami Institute, Kautokeino.

Helander, Elina and Tero Mustonen, eds. 2004. *Snowscapes. Dreamscapes. Snowchange Book on Community Voices of Change*. Tampere: Tampere Polytechnic, 2004.

Hirvonen, Vuokko. 1996. "Research Ethics and Sami People: From a Woman's Point of View." *Awakened Voice: The Return of Sami Knowledge*. Ed. Elina Helander. Nordic Sami Institute. Diedut 4. 7-12.

Honko, Lauri, Senni Timonen, Michael Branch and Keith Bosley. 1993. *The Great Bear: A Thematic Anthology of Oral Poetry in the Finno-Ugric Languages*. Pieksämäki: Suomen Kirjallisuuden Seura.

Howe, Linda Moulton. 2008, April 10. "Honeybee Collapse Now Worse on West Coast." Online: <http://www.earthfiles.com>. Accessed March 23, 2008.

Hyde, Lewis. 1983. *The Gift: Imagination and the Erotic Life of Property*. 1979. New York: Vintage Books.

Jakobson, Roman. 1960. "Linguistics and Poetics." *Style in Language*. Ed. T. Sebeok. Cambridge, MA: MIT Press. 350-377.

Jensen, Doreen. "Art History." 1993. *First Nations Perspectives On Cultural Practice: essays*. Ed. Kelley, Caffyn. North Vancouver: Gallerie Women Artists' Monographs Gallerie Publications. 64-69.

Jimenez, Maria. 2007. "Gift Giving Across Borders." *Women and the Gift Economy:*

A Radically Different Worldview is Possible. Ed. Genevieve Vaughan. Toronto: Inanna Publications and Education. 222-230.

Kailo, Kaarina. 2004. "Gift and Give-Back Economies: Cultural Sensitivity and Gender Awareness as Social Capital in the North." Second Northern Research Forum Open Meeting, Northern Veche, Veliky Novgorod, Northwest Russia, 19-22 September.

Kailo, Kaarina. 2003. "Cyber/Ecofeminism: From Violence and Monoculture Towards Eco-social Sustainability." Paper presented Gender and Power in the New Europe, the 5th European Feminist Research Conference August 20-76. 24, Lund University, Sweden.www.5thfeminist.lu.se/filer/paper_803.pdf. 32-44.

Kailo, Kaarina. 1997a. "Hemispheric Cross-Talk: Women Collaborating on Storytelling." *Northern Parallels: 4th Circumpolar Universities Cooperation Conference Proceedings.* Eds. Shauna McLarnon and Douglas Nord. Prince George: University of Northern British Columbia. 102-116.

Kailo, Kaarina. 1997b. "The She-Bear: Circumpolar Mother of Spiritual Feminism." *Canadian Woman Studies/les cahiers de la femme* 17 (1): 48-52.

Kailo, Kaarina. 1994. "Furry Tales of the North: A Feminist Interpretation." *Simone de Beauvoir Institute Bulletin/Bulletin de l'Institut Simone de Beauvoir* 12 (2): 104-133.

Kailo, Kaarina. 1990. *The Short Fiction of Nathaniel Hawthorne and Gérard de Nerval: A Study in Post-Jungian Aesthetics.* Diss. University of Toronto.

Kannisto, Artturi. 1958. *Wogulische Volksdichtung. IV: Bärenlieder. Mémoires de la Societé Finno-Ugrienne.* 114.

Kheel, Marti. 1995. "Licence to Kill: An Ecofeminist Critique of the Hunter's Discourse." *Women and Animals: Feminist Theoretical Explorations.* Eds. Carol J. Adams and Josephine Donovan. Durham: Duke University Press. 85-126.

Kremer, Jürgen. 1997. "Shamanic Inquiry as Recovery of Indigenous Mind. Toward an Egalitarian Exchange of Knowledge." *Curare* 13: 127-142.

Kroft, Steve. 2008, January 24. "What's wrong with the Bees? The mysterious disappearance of bees." Online: CBC News <www.cbcnews.com/stories/2007/10/25/60 minutes/main3407762.shtml> Accessed March 28, 2008.

Krupat, Arnold. 1993. *New Voices in Native American Literary Criticism.* Washington: Smithsonian Institute.

Kuokkanen, Rauna. 2008. "Sami Higher Education and Research: Toward Building a Vision for Future." *Indigenous Peoples: Self-Determination, Knowledge, Indigeneity.* Ed. Henry Minde. Netherlands: Eburon Delft. 267-287.

Kuokkanen, Rauna. 2007. *Reshaping the University: Responsibility, Indigenous Epistemes, and the Logic of the Gift.* Vancouver: University of British Columbia Press.

Kuokkanen, Rauna and Marja Riihijärvi. 2006. "Suttesája – From a Sacred Sami Site and Natural Spring to a Water Bottling Plant? The Effects of Colonization in Northern Europe." *Echoes from the Poisoned Well: Global Memories of Environmental Injustice.* Eds. Sylvia Hood Washington, Paul C. Rosler and Heather Goodall. Lanham, MD: Lexicon Books. 30-40.

Kuusi, Matti and Lauri Honko. 1983. *Sejd och saga. Den finskan forndiktens historia (Narratives and Tales: The History of Ancient Finnish Poetry)*. 1963. En översättning av Suomen kirjallisuus.

LaDuke, Winona. 1997. "Voices from White Earth: Gaa-waabaabiganikaag." *People, Land and Community*. Ed. Hildegarde Hannum. New Haven: Yale Univesity Press. 22-38.

Länsman, Anna-Siiri. 2004. *Väärtisuhteet Lapin matkailussa. Kulttuurianalyysi suomalaisten ja saamelaisten kohtaamisessa (Exchange Relations Within Lapland Tourism: A Cultural Analysis of Encounters Between Finns and Samis)*. Inari: Kustannus Puntsi,

Leahy, Terry. 1998. *What is Ecofeminism? Different Positions within Ecofeminism*. University of Newcastle, Australia. 1-53. www.octapod.org.

Lorde, Audre. 1984. *Sister Outsider*. New York: Crossing Press, 1984.

Loucks, Georgina. 1985. "The Girls and the Bear Facts: A Cross-Cultural Comparison." *The Canadian Journal of Native Studies* 5 (2): 218-239.

Lowe, Lana. 2001. "Caring for the Land, Caring for the People: The Role of Canadian Resource Managers in the Realization of Aboriginal Rights." *Dispatches from the Cold Seas: Indigenous Views on Self-Governance, Ecology and Identity*. Eds. Curtis Rattray and Tero Mustonen. Tampere Polytechnic Publications Ser. C, Study Materials 3. 11-30.

Lutz, Helmut. 1995. "Confronting Cultural Imperialism: First Nations People are Combating Continued Cultural Theft." *Multiculturalism in North America and Europe: Social Practices, Literary Visions*. Eds. Hans Braun and Wolfgang Klooss. Trier: Wissenschaftlicher Verlag Trier. 132-51.

Lutz, Helmut. 1993. "Robbed Graves, White Shamanism, and Stolen Stories: (Re?)Appropriation of Native Cultures." *Kulturen in Kontakt (Cultures in Contact)*. Ed. Sigrid Markmann. Hamburg: Verlag Kovac. 245 258.

Lutz, Helmut. "Cultural Appropriation as a Process of Displacing Peoples and History." *Canadian Journal of Native Studies* 10 (2) (1990): 167-182.

MacCormack, Carol and Strathern, Marilyn, eds. 1980. *Nature, Culture and Gender*. Cambridge: Cambridge University Press.

Makilam.1999. *Symbols and Magic in the Arts of Kabyle Women*. Tr. Elizabeth Corp. from the French, Signes et rituels magiques des femmes kabyles. Edisud, Aix-en-Provence. www.makilam.com

Maracle, Lee. 1996. *I Am Woman: A Native Perspective on Sociology and Feminism*. Vancouver: Press Gang.

Maracle, Lee. 1989. "Moving Over." *Trivia: A Journal of Ideas* 14 (Spring): 9-12.

Mauss, Marcel. 1923/1924. "Essai sur le don: Forme et raison de l'échange dans les sociétés archaïques." *L'Annee Sociologique* 30-186.

McClellan, Catharine. 1970. *The Girl Who Married the Bear: A Masterpiece of Indian Oral Tradition*. Ottawa: National Museums of Canada.

Messer-Davidow, Ellen. 1987. "The Philosophical Bases of Feminist Literary Criticisms." *New Literary History* 19: 65-103.

Midnight Sun. 1988. "Sex/Gender Systems in Native North America." *Living the Spirit: A Gay American Anthology.* Coordinating Ed. Will Roscoe. New York: St. Martin's Press. 16-23.

Miedzian Myriam. 1991. *Boys Will be Boys: Breaking the Link Between Masculinity and Violence.* New York: Doubleday.

Mies, Maria And Vandana Shiva. 1993. *Ecofeminism.* London: Zed Books, 1993.

Mittelstaedt, Martin. 2008. "Manitoba recognizes the threat to polar bears." *The Globe and Mail* February 8: A9.

Moore, David. 1993. "Myth, History, and Identity in Silko and Young Bear. *"New Voices in Native American Literary Criticism.* Ed. Arnold Krupat. Washington: Smithsonian Institute. 370-95.

Moore, Henrietta L. 1988. *Feminism and Anthropology.* Oxford: Polity Press.

Nahani, Phoebe. 1993. "Thoughts on Aboriginal Knowledge." *Social Sciences in the North.* Eds. Louis-Jacques Dorais and Ludger Müller-Wille. Ste.-Foy, QC: International Arctic Social Sciences Association. 23-31.

Ó Catháin, Séamas. 1995. *The Festival of Brigit: Celtic Goddess and Holy Woman.* Dublin: Dundalgan Press.

Olsen, Mel. 1996. "The Sami Bear." *Baiki* 5: 6.

Petrone, Penny. 1990. *Native Literature in Canada: From Oral Tradition to the Present.* Toronto: Oxford University Press.

Plumwood, Val. 2003. "Feminisma y ecología: ¿Artemisa versus Gaia? (Feminism and Ecology:Artemis versus Gaia?)." *Mujeres y Ecología: Historia, Pensamiento, Sociedad.* Coords. Maria Luisa Cavana, Alicia Puleo, and Cristina Segura. Madrid: Asociación Cultural Al-Mudayna. Colección LAYA. 53-107.

Pratt, Annis. 1987. "Affairs with Bears: Some Notes Towards Feminist Archetypal Hypotheses for Canadian Literature." Ed. Barbara Godard. *Gynocritics/la Gynocritique.* Toronto: ECW Press. 102-122.

Reischl, Helga. 2004. "Who is Kallisto? Semiotic and Discursive Comparisons of Texts about Bears, Women, and Wolves." Unpublished dissertation. Humboldt University Berlin, Germany.

Rockwell, David. 1991. *Giving Voice to Bear.* Niwot, CO: Roberts Rinehart Publishers.

Saladin d'Auglure. 1980. "Nanuk Super-Mâle: L'ours blanc dans l'espace imaginaire et le temps social des inuits de l'arctique canadien." *Etudes mongoles* 11: 63-94.

Sanders, Danielle. 1985. "Cultural Conflicts. An Important Factor in the Academic Failures of American Indian Students. *Journal of Multicultural Counseling and Development.* 15 (2): 81-90.

Schmidt, Eva. 1989. "Bear Cult and Mythology of the Northern Ob-Ugrians." Eds. M. Hoppal and Juha Pentikäinen. *Uralic Mythology and Folklore.* Budapest/Helsinki: Ethnological Uralica. 220-223.

Scholtmeijer, Marian. 2004. "The Listening World: First Nations Women Writers and the Environment." *This Elusive Land: Women and the Canadian Environment.* Eds. Melody Hessing, Rebecca Raglon, and Catriona Sandilands. Vancouver:

University of British Columbia Press.

Shepard, Paul and Barry Sanders. 1985. *The Sacred Paw: The Bear in Nature, Myth and Literature.* New York: Viking Penguin. Sidney, Angela. 1977. "The Woman and the Grizzly." *My Stories Are My Wealth.* As told to Julie Cruikshank. Whitehorse: Council for Yukon Indians.

Shiva, Vandana. 1993. *Monocultures of the Mind: Perspectives on Biodiversity and Biotechnology.* London: Zed Books.

Snyder, Gary. l990. *Practice of the Wild.* San Francisco: North Point Press.

Stark-Arola, Laura. 1998. *Magic, Body and Social Order: The Construction of Gender Through Women's Private Rituals in Traditional Finland.* Tampere: Tammer-Paino, Suomen Kirjallisuuden Seura, Studia Fennica Folkloristica 5.

Spivak, Gayatri. 1990. *The Post-Colonial Critic: Interviews, Strategies, Dialogues.* Ed. Sarah Harasym. Routledge: New York and London.

Stasiulis, Daina. 1993. "'Authentic Voice': Anti-Racist Politics in Canadian Feminist Publishing and Literary Production." *Feminism and the Politics of Difference.* Eds. Sneja Gunew and Anna Yeatman. Halifax: Fernwood, 1993. 11-19.

Strathern, Marilyn. 1992. *After Nature.* Cambridge: Cambridge University Press.

Trask, Mililani. 2007. "Indigenous Women and Traditional Knowledge: Reciprocity is the Way of Balance." *Women and the Gift Economy: A Radically Different Worldview is Possible.* Ed. Genevieve Vaughan. Toronto: Inanna Publications and Education. 293-301.

Trigger, Bruce. 1990. *The Huron Farmers of the North: The Individual and Society.* 1969. Revised ed. New York: Holt, Rinehart and Winston.

Trinh, T. Minh-ha. 1989. *Woman, Native, Other: Writing, Post-Coloniality and Feminism.* Bloomington: University of Indiana Press.

Van Deusen, Kira. 2001. *The Fling Tiger: Women Shamans and Storytellers of the Amur.* Montreal, McGill-Queen's Native and Northern Series.

Vaughan, Genevieve, ed. 2007. *Women and the Gift Economy: A Radically Different Worldview is Possible.* Toronto: Inanna Publications and Education.

Vaughan, Genevieve. 1997. *For-Giving: A Feminist Criticism of Exchange.* Austin: Plain View Press.

Verrall, Catherine. 1991. *Resource Reading List.* 2nd ed. Toronto: Canadian Alliance in Solidarity with the Native Peoples.

Wessendort, Kathrin, ed. 2005. "An Indigenous Parliament? Realities and Perspectives in Russian and the Circumpolar North." International Work Group for Indigenous Affairs. No. 116.

Wheeler, Jordan. 1992. "Voice." *Aboriginal Voices: Amerindian, Inuit, and Sami Theater.* Eds. Per K. Brask and William Morgan. Baltimore: John Hopkins University Press. 37-43.

Edwina Goldstone, the "Veiled Bear" of the Viena Karelian fairytale, "Three Trees, Tree Sons." From Vienan Satuja (Fairy Tales from Viena Karelia), *Ed. Markku Nieminen. Helsinki: Suomalaisen kirjallisuuden seura, 2004. Reprinted with permission.*

A Sami Bear Story

Three brothers had an only sister who was so hated by her brothers that she had to take refuge in the wilds. When exhausted, she finally comes across a bear's den, she enters it to have some rest. A bear comes to the same lair and, on closer acquaintance, he weds her and begets a son by her.

After a while when the bear has become old and his son is grown up, the bear is said to have informed his wife that, on account of his great age, he can no longer live, but wishes to go out on the first snow in the autumn, so as to enable her three brothers to see his tracks and then "ring him in" and kill him. Although his wife tries in every way to prevent him from doing this, the bear does not let himself be persuaded, but does as he has said, so that the three brothers can "ring him in" when seeing his footprints. Then the bear asks to have a piece of brass attached to his forehead, for this sign would distinguish him from other bears and also prevent his own son who had now left him from killing him.

After a deep fall of snow, the three brothers go out together to fell the bear, whom before that they have been "ringing in." Then the bear asks his wife if all the three brothers had been equally spiteful to her, and she answers that her two eldest brothers had been more spiteful than the younger who had been somewhat more clement. When the brothers come to the lair, the bear turns out and attacks the eldest brother, bites him and injures him rather severely, and he himself returns uninjured to his lair. When the second brother comes, the bear runs against him in the same manner and injures him in the very same way and then he returns to his lair. Then he orders his wife to get hold of him round his waist. When she has done so, he walks out of his lair on his hind-legs carrying her; then she orders her youngest brother to shoot him, which he does.

The wife then sits down some distance away, covers her face, as if she has not the heart to see the bear being shot and flayed, but still she watches with one eye....[1] When the three brothers have felled the bear and all the meat has been put in the cauldron to be boiled, the son arrives and the brothers tell him that they have shot a strange animal with a piece of brass attached to his forehead. He says that it was his father, who had been marked with such a piece of brass and he says that he has therefore a right to an equal share in the bear with them. When they keep on refusing to give him this, the son threatens to wake up his father, and then he takes a rod and saying the words "my father, arise!" ... [and] he beats the skin with it. Then the meat in the cauldron begins to boil so violently that it looks as though it wants to rise up out of the cauldron and so they are forced to give him an equal share.[2]

From Carl-Martin Edsman, "The Story of the Bear Wife in Nordic Tradition," Ethnos 21 (1-2) (1956): 36-54. Reprinted with permission from the Institute for Language and Folklore, Uppsala Landsmåls-och Folkminnesarkiv (ULMA) (Archives of Dialect and Folklore)1118.3, pg. 13. Collector: Einar Granberg. Informant: Kristina Wik.

[1]"This is the origin of the old custom that no woman may see the bear of the men dealing with the bear, unless she has her face covered and is looking through a brass ring" (Edsman 1956: 47)

[2]Edsman adds: "This is said to be the origin of the following custom ... when the bear has been felled, the hunters immediately drag him out of his lair and beat him with with twigs or soft rods. From this come the proverb: "beat a bear with twigs. The fact that the bear hunters as well as all the implements used in the capture of the bear must be adorned with brass chains and rings has its origin in the piece of brass attached to the bear's forehead.... As for the ceremonial used, the woman is said to have been instructed by the bear, and that she passed on the instructions to her brothers and told them that the ceremonial was necessary if they wished to overpower such a fierce animal as the bear: thus everything has been handed down to the Lapps by tradition, and therefore they have been all the more anxious to preserve and practice such customs as were prescribed by the bear himself, as they believed that far from being able to overpower him, they would be overpowered and injured by him, if they failed to keep the rules of the old custom" (48).

Editor's Note: The word Lapp was often used to refer to the Sami in early anthropology and ethnography; today the Indigenous people of Northern Europe are referred to as Sami to distinguish them from the inhabitants of Lapland (*lappilaiset*) who include both Finns and Samis. Matti Sarmela notes that Edsman's analysis of the bear bride story and its relationship to the Bear festival is based on a narrative recorded in the 1750s (see Sarmela, "Bear in Human Environment," <www.kotikone.fi/matti.sarmela/bear.html>).

KAREN GUILBAULT

Astride the Bear

Jubilant!
Arms outflung in victory
I ride the bear
who tolerates my gripping thighs
my shrieks of glee
I tame the beast
I paint him all colors
I ride him as they do
a sacred elephant
feeling his weighty presence
beneath me
his laborious strength
a mountain under me
as I perch upon him
like a butterfly

Backbend

his icicled fur
reflects the shimmering colors
of the Northern Lights
laying down upon him
I arch like a rainbow
backwards I fall
into bear
polar thoughts
as brittle as icce
glisten in my mind
I melt his fierceness away
with my warm
woman body

ISABELLA COLALILLO KATZ

The She Bear

for Kaarina Kailo

1
the She Bear opened wide her mouth
and swallowed up the coral sun

cool rain swept through lilac shadows
dazed birds screeched the sorrow of dying forests

the chatter of votive birches
the heartbeats of trees
wailed in the ravaged lands

behind me
a dirge of windy voices
before me
hollow eyes
scattered in anguish

the moon wove frantic signals
to the domain of Guardians
but time did not relent

and this is how creation was shattered
and this is how time became nuclear
this is how Earth was laid bare
in the breath and ice of fire

nothing left to feel
nothing left nothing to learn
nothing to remember
the ghostly rain a blur of fitful shadows

2
the She Bear slept for a hundred thousand days
nourishing the sunglow in her silver womb
Kali danced the Dance of Time
commanding the Dream
waiting for the She Bear to awaken
for her birthing time to deliver
a new race

3
in time the rain dissolved
the sobbing moon
lifted her arms to the wounded sky
gazing and longing

4
the She Bear in her dreaming cave
spun the coil of re-birth
her great belly pushed and heaved
shattering the weight of cosmic silence

her brown eyes flickered on barren landscapes

her sighs woke buds and streams
her mothering song stirred the flesh of new humans
those sweet tendrils of hope
those fresh fractals of love

her gaze
still gazing
her brightness
a breath of love

Jenny Kangasvuo, "Bear Shadow," ink drawing on paper, 20 x 20 cm, 2003

Helena Junttila, "Bear Lisa," oil on canvas, 105 x 65 cm, 1999.
Jenny and Antti Wihuri Foundation/Art Museum of Rovaniemi, Finland.

ULLA RYUM

Annanatsiat

A journey through the landscapes for sounds and voices—a play for four human bodies in movement developed from a story.

ADA: an old dying woman in a bed
NAQUA: a young nurse or socialworker
OLD STORYTELLER: a woman dressed in everyday clothes, *anoraq*
YOUNG STORYTELLER: a woman dressed in fancy modern clothes,
                                wearing some traditional amulets

(sounds from all kinds of streaming water, wind, birds, animals, human laughter, barking dogs)

Old Storyteller: It had been three years, or perhaps closer to ten years, or maybe just one single long day, since she had last passed this shallow little place in the river. She noticed that the water ran in the right direction, towards the south.

Young Storyteller: For her north was the natural culmination, the expected conclusion to the globe. The ice-cap at the top toward the north hold the landscapes and the waters and the clouds in place, each in their own rhythm.

Old Storyteller: Maybe it hold even the sky—and, as long as the water ran from north to south, she could understand her own life and the lives of her relatives.

Ada: Each have their job. Nothing is without meaning, no nothing.

Young Storyteller: Yes, yes, in keeping their settlement livable and everyone alive, and in all recent times hers had been to secure for her community insight into the unknown—into the incomprehensible.

Ada: No no inconceivable … inconceivable … inconceiv—

63

Old Storyteller: She saw her life slide past her in the gushing water. The time her father and older brothers had followed the tracks of a polar bear long out on to the sea ice. She had followed them together with her grandmother, and when the hunters had spotted the bear her grandmother had pulled her up on to a rock from which they had watched the three figures until they were no bigger than dried peas.

Young Storyteller: Peas!

Ada: Yes, dried peas.

Old Storyteller: Ada and her grandmother checked on two grouse snares, but they vere empty, and now they sat up on the rock again and stared out over the unending white expanse.

Ada: (trying to get her legs out of the bed) My eyes burned from looking out at the whiteness and perhaps I fell asleep, yes …

Young Storyteller: She woke in any case when her grandmother suddenly turned towards her and said in a voice she hadn't heard before that she no longer had a father.

Old Storyteller: You don't have a father any more!

(Naqua places Ada in her bed again)

Naqua: Don't try now. The doctors said you should rest.

Old Storyteller: Frightened, she pulled off her hood to hear more, and her grandmother, with tears running down her cheeks, had sternly told her to pull her hood back up, for now she was the one who must help her brothers. You must take care of your self.

Ada: My father fell down between two ice floes, they hadn't heard that the ice was about to break up. My grandmother saw him fly away. (sits up in the bed) Then she began to rock from side to side and it was only after I had taken hold of her arm and had let her slide down from the rock that I was able to drag her home with me.

Old Storyteller: It went very slowly, for the grandmother had wanted to sit down the whole time, and strange sounds, half human weeping and half animal scream, from time to time came out of her mouth.

Young Storyteller: You must not say that, you must not say that sort of thing! My brothers, my brothers where are they? My brothers and she had slung her arms around her grandmother's body to keep her there. Her grandmother had become much lighter, almost the dry little shadow of a human.

Ada: Just wanted to know if her brothers had also disappeared, but the grandmother could only tell of the vision she must have had, for Ada understood that no human eye could see so far.

Old Storyteller: She could still remember the intense fear that had seized her then. She could still feel the air stiffen with cold around them and now she heard her own voice whisper, as it did then—

Ada: "Now we will die, grandmother, we will die now, you must come with me. Listen the raven already waits for us." And somehow I managed to bring her up to our settlement, where everyone came running out to see what was causing the strange sounds.

(Ada wails and howls and Naqua leaves her chair, puts her book away and comes closer to Ada's bed)

Naqua: What are you trying to say? Are you in pain? Please be calm now and lay down. You have to understand that I have an examination tomorrow. I must have peace to prepare.

Young Storyteller: Later the two brothers came home with the polar bear and their father's harpoon and fishing line. He had disappeared between two ice floes when the ice suddenly broke up.

Old Storyteller: They hadn't noticed that the wind had shifted while they were following the polar bear. And then he suddenly disappeared. They had looked for him, but in vain.

Ada: They killed the bear.

Young Storyteller: It is a very long story …

Old Storyteller: It is important.

Ada: They brought down the bear, a young female, when it strangely enough returned the same way—it wasn't us who killed her, it was him, it was him.

Old Storyteller: The two brothers killed the bear.

Ada: No, it was my father. He asked the bear to go back and be killed.

Old Storyteller: They laid his sleeping skin and summer anorak under a pile of flat stones, and laid the bear next to it, protected by stones, so the ravens couldn't peck at it. They removed all the entrails and laid the heart and the liver in an ice pocket higher up on the slope. We always do this.

Young Storyteller: Not any longer, we are modern people. We have got electricity.

Old Storyteller: And what then ... does it help with grief? Stay with the story ... Then her grandmother crawled into the furthest corner of the tent where she sat and grieved for many days, and each time Ada saw the now very old woman sitting there and rocking from side to side in the faint light of the fat-burning lamp, she grew cold from an unexplainable fear and hurried to set the food at her grandmother's feet and go outside again into the light and the wind. The others felt the same way and no one said a word to each other about the dead father, whose possessions they had laid under the flat stones, just as they would have done if his body had also been there.

Young Storyteller: What is wrong with electricity?

Old Storyteller: Nothing. Perhaps a wrong time.

Ada: Wrong time, yes. Wrong time.

Old Storyteller: At night they skinned the bear and laid our father's fishing line and harpoons on top of the stones. They hoped that the grandmother would return to them again from her journey of grief, for she could make them all new pants and *kamiks* of the bear's skin.

Ada: And who should we listen to? She was the one who saw and knew.

Naqua: Are you dreaming? Try to sleep ... Are you thirsty?

(Ada wants to get out of the bed. Fights with Naqua)

Old Storyteller: She could still remember her fear that the grandmother wouldn't want to return from the dead, and she understood that she couldn't manage until her Grandmother came back to them by herself. She had pulled her hands and arms inside her anorak and had almost not been able to feel them.

Young Storyteller: Then she had, just like now, stuck her hands up in her armpits, and bit by bit she felt the warmth spreading. She counted on her fingers inside the warmth, and figured that she must be about as old now as her grandmother had been then.

(Ada succeeds in climbing out of her bed and falls on the floor. She is fighting, laughing and swearing, sitting on the floor)

Ada: Let me go! I want to go home! I want to go home!

Naqua: (tries to help Ada up) You will die then.

Ada: Yes, I want to go home now. Help me to go home! Help me!

(the two storytellers have turned their back to Ada and Naqua)

Naqua: I can't help you to escape. I could lose my job. You will come home when you are better.

Ada: Now I know, your name is Naqua? I remember you.

Naqua: I remember you too. Your family were Angaqoqs. I was a child. My family called for you to help us.

Ada: Yes, it was me and my brothers. No hunt. You were starving.

Naqua: (to the two storytellers) Help me get her to bed again.

(Young Storyteller comes and together they get Ada to bed)

Ada: Don't use what you know to stop me. I know what I know. Real knowledges do not fight each other. They help each other create survival, yes.

Naqua: Forgive me. I am listening to you, but I am paid to help you here. You need rest and good food. You were starving and half dead when they found you. You can't live alone any longer. Your house is not good enough.

Ada: I want to die…

Naqua: You live too far away from others.

Ada: I want to go home.

Naqua: You were starving!

Ada: I want to go home! I want to be alone!

Naqua: Then eat your food and rest.

Ada: I can't. I am too tired. I want to leave this place. Go to the sea … perhaps. To go home.

(Naqua kisses Ada and pulls her chair closer to the bed)

(sounds of air, water, wind, and birds)

Ada: Why will you not help me to go home? Have all my people died? I want to go to my place and sit down there.

Naqua: But here you can't just walk out and find a place to sit like they did before. It is not like home here. People here would be so scared to find your body. Here they want old people to get better. Anyway, I am told to take care of you, so you don't scare anybody.

Young Storyteller: Her father and her two brothers and above all her grandmother had all been angaqoqs. Ada herself was also trained as a midwife. And they all helped people who asked for their help. But her grandmother had seen the accident in a vision without being able to intervene. And she had not been able to tell them what they all should do.

Old Storyteller: She just sat there and was in another place and let these terrible sounds come out between her teeth.

Young Storyteller: And her father couldn't have helped himself. Ada never felt that it had been the right time for her father to die. She felt he should have lived. Died some other time.

Old Storyteller: But when is it the right time?

Ada: Life can be full of wrong times, or full of fear of loss, of being left, of dying.

Old Storyteller: She remembered suddenly that on the beach she had grabbed her grandmother and screamed into her face, "How do you know, how do you know that he is dead?" And Ada hadn't been able to see any signs of life in the grandmother other than her thousand wrinkles and the dark holes where her eyes used to be. "Look at me, look at me! "How do you know?" she had repeated and repeated until the grandmother had hissed in her direction in an unsettling voice, "I saw him disappear, disappear, disappear and the bear's blood followed him out over the edge. Now they both are swimming. Understand that I saw him disappear." She remembered that she had held both her hands over her ears. Didn't want to hear the terrible voice.

Young Storyteller: But the voice also lived inside of her.

Ada: My voice. I can't hear it any longer

(sounds of birds, water and wind)

Young Storyteller: After her grandmother had been with the dead for three days, she returned and got up, a little stiff in the legs from sitting and rocking for so long, and asked for the dead bear's liver and heart. She asked for the skin and everyone was so relieved that they began to laugh, small hiccoughing gasps of laughter, which just as easily could have been from fear.

(drumming from far away)

Old Storyteller: But the ancient dried up woman tottered outside and had them lay the frozen liver and heart on the table stone. Then her grandmother had called to her: "Bring your ulo with you for now we are sharing the gifts from the bear.

Young Storyteller: She didn't dare do anything other but obey, and her mother and smaller siblings had stood in a frightened cluster and continued their work with the stiff frozen clumps. It was a difficult job but at last everything was cut up.

Ada: We all received our share, but not before our grandmother had called me in close to her and, shaking with fear, I came closer.

Old Storyteller: "You will eat first. You have the bear's name now. Eat your liver and your heart."

Young Storyteller: Her two older brothers had squatted down, surprised, and had waited to eat their pieces. She had felt that she would choke, but the grandmother's coal black eye sockets had burned through her, and she had eaten and felt that she must stand up. Something inside her had forced her to get up and look out over the others' heads.

Old Storyteller: While she had stood there her grandmother took her father's first *Tikut* out of her hood; she shortened the strap it hung on and added the girl's own amulets to each side.

Ada: … and I saw that my grandmother had given it to me and she said that I should hang it around my neck. Yes …

Young Storyteller: Involuntarily she had glanced at her two older brothers and noticed their confusion, but their grandmother had shared the father's other things between them and their jealousy was lessened.

Ada: They received our father's dancing strap and his fishing tools, so it was easier for them to accept that I had the right to his first Tikut and his bone knife.

Old Storyteller: She carries this bear's name and will always bring us food, together with you, so we all can survive this winter as well as the next.

Young Storyteller: And no one had dared to say anything.

Old Storyteller: "I will teach you what you should know, and your father's helping spirit will help you, and you shall call for your own." Then her grandmother had given her a little leather bag in which there were especially powerful things, which she should use when necessary.

Ada, Young Storyteller and Old Storyteller: That afternoon everything changed. I must have been around nine years old. I followed my grandmother and my two older brothers. I fished and set snares, and learned to hunt from a kayak.

Old Storyteller: Sometimes she had helped her mother with her younger siblings, but it was no longer her work to live the mother's life, and she was happy and proud when she caught her first speckled seal.

(Ada has a violent fit of coughing ... she is very tired now and the two storytellers and Naqua move closer to the bed. They are all inside a "light spot." The rest of the stage is dark.)

(Sometimes the sounds of barking dogs and wind come up)

Old Storyteller: There was much in that time she didn't wish to talk about. And there were times when she had not wanted to be an Angaqoq. But her grandmother had always nudged her back into the story those times when she had wanted to hide herself or let others take over the telling of her life.

Ada: *Annanatsiat*, who tells us?

Old Storyteller: We do it ourselves and don't ask anymore.

Ada: But who tells me? I want to know anyway.

Old Storyteller: You do yourself. No one else can tell your story. You are only yourself and you are the only one who knows it. You will see and understand everything else around you, and others will see what they see.

(Ada coughs violently again and Naqua holds her in her arms)

Young Storyteller: She didn't understand, but continued her many tasks without feeling anything special. She followed the half-faded path her grandmother and the many others already dead in her family had walked.

Old Storyteller: Now and then her grandmother had told her about "all the others before us." Names totally unknown and strange to her, some of them with an eerie tone of ruin and oblivion…

Young Storyteller: … "dark names" her grandmother called them. They had never made it up to the stars.

Old Storyteller: Some other names were filled with light and joy and when she heard them named, or met someone who bore the name, then the room was always lit up by it.

Ada: There are all the stars, and they hear everything you are thinking.

Old Storyteller: She thought of her grandmother and could already make out the first stars in the southern sky. When she was a child, she always believed that her grandmother was two hundred years old.

Young Storyteller: Her grandmother had been dead for more than two generations, and now she felt that being two hundred years old no longer had the same great meaning.

Naqua: I understood as she sat and followed the streaming water in the late afternoon light that for a long time she had been ready for new lives, and that is just what it is. No more, no less.

Ada: I am here. Here now.

Naqua: It has become colder where you are sitting and watching the silver running water. Soon the sun will disappear behind the bluish hills in the west and you know that you must make a decision. It will be a cold and clear night, and you will freeze to death before the first morning light calls life back around you.

Ada: Yes, I am here now. I am hearing … (wind and water, barking dogs) *Ay ay aya*

Naqua: You are singing a song for your children, for the living and for the two who are dead. You are singing for the children's father, who has disappeared on the sea in his kayak.

Ada: *Ay ay aya ut imar itisok Ay aya ay*

Naqua: And you are singing for your many grandchildren, whose names you have filled with strength and knowledge.

Ada: Yes, I am here *immaqa singuagtortutut aya ay ay aya*

Naqua: And you are singing for your siblings and for your parents, for all the dead who will soon bid you welcome out in the great starry room.

Old Storyteller: Where she sat she could see the clearest of all the stars in the southern sky, the one called Nelarsik. She knew that it was her grandmother who called to her. So this was the night she would wander over the rainbow and join the others.

Young Storyteller: It filled her with peace and joy to see one star after another rise and find its place.

Ada: *Niruak nipaitsok – ay ay aya*

Naqua: You are still warm and grateful for the sun, which has all day warmed the rock you are leaning against. Maybe you fall asleep for a moment. You wake up and think you can hear your youngest grandchild crying.

Ada*: Aya ayayayayay aya mikisok sarfaipok*

Naqua: You gave her your own polar bear name, and carved a little *Tikut* out of a bear bone for her. You wanted to pass the *Angaqoq* gift to the little girl?

Ada: *Aya ayayayayay aya mikisok sarfaipok*

Old Storyteller: The child's mother was not pleased about the name, but your son, Ada … do you remember that? He wanted it that way.

Young Storyteller: And the little girl already showed many abilities and would follow her brothers in school, so she could help them all later.

Ada: *Tulugag – tulugag*

Naqua: A raven flies over your head and soars against the sky in large irregular circles. You can no longer hear the little girl's crying. She is probably hungry. It is that time now you know. The last rays of sun disappear and the crystal blue sky closes in over the earth. You don't notice the cold rising. You are dreaming about your two youngest children who got that foreign disease and died in your arms before the youngest could even walk.

Ada: *ay ay aya kujassutigssakaka unga*

Naqua: Now you are holding them close in your arms. You can feel them warm there. Two small soft living creatures.

Young Storyteller: Do you feel them?

Naqua: They are here to collect you. They are here and you are on your way.

Ada: Yes, I am coming with you. Listen! Can you hear the water singing for us and the stones answering? The earth is singing for us and the mountains are answering now.

Old Storyteller: The night sings…

Young Storyteller: …and we answer.

Naqua: Yes, we answer

Ada: Yes, I answer. *ay ay aya aya aya ay ay ay aya*

(the light fades out around the dead Ada and the other three walk slowly towards the audience; they stay beside each other)

Old Storyteller: Her dead body was never found in the snow. This wasn't that unusual for that time.

Young Storyteller: I heard this story for the first time a few years ago when I visited Tassilaaq, East Greenland, where it was told to me by an old woman …

Old Storyteller: …Who also knew why my grandmother's father was likely sent as a seventeen-year-old to Copenhagen …

Naqua: …Where he died nine years later of tuberculosis and was buried under his new Christian name.

(the light fades out, sound of distant laughter, barking dogs, wind, water, birds)

END

Translated by Emily Warne

Note: some words in kalatdlisut:

Tikut	the hour hand (to show the spiritual direction inside yourself)
Annanatsiat	grandmother
Immaqa singuagtortutut	maybe in a dream
Nelarsik	the name for the star Vega in the constellation Lyra in East Greenland
Niruak nipaitsok	a quiet (silent) night
Mikisok sarfaipok	"little one who floats with the stream"
Tulugag	Raven
Kujassutigssakaka unga	"I have a lot to thank for 'that foreign disease' measles"

ULLA RYUM AND KAARINA KAILO

A Conversation About Women and Bears

Kaarina: Ulla, what does the bear and the motif of the woman and the bear mean to you?

Ulla: It is not a motif. It is a spiritual reality and has been so in my life since the name Ulla was given to me at birth. Ulla means little bear, "Ursula." In kalatlisut it is "Nakuuku." All the stories I have heard about polar, brown, or grizzly bears were about the lack of fear. I should never be afraid of them, which does not mean arousing them needlessly. They will never appear in your dreams because they will never hurt you in dreams. They are close relatives, you see (Grandmother Bear).

Kaarina: Do you think a special relationship with women and bears exists? I am thinking of the European cosmology and the persistence of the stories throughout the North.

Ulla: In the Inuit way, this knowledge was not spoken about, loudly. We don't fear polar bears although we do always warn children. They know how to protect themselves against hungry bears. The way a polar bear lives and takes care of cubs is the only way to survive. This knowledge is around. The way they hunt seals is the way they are furious—like women who struggle for survival. In the old days women knew that they could not depend on their husbands, something that has changed. The husbands were often killed by bears, in the ice or whatever, and the women had to survive with the little kids alone. They had to take the old and the kids in the *umiaq*, or big boat, and sail out. It was the women's responsibility to go down the stream south where they might sell the boats. I am talking about this sailing-out in the big *umiaq* to the southern point of Greenland, where these women with children and sometimes old people, landed and where they all survived by selling the boat.

Two years ago when I was visiting my family-place in Eastern Greenland, they told me more private things about value: a *umiaq* was at that time sold for four rows of pearls. Coming from the northeast Greenland meant that one was very well-known as builder of *umiaq* and *kayaq* with skins from seals, polar bears, and walruses that they had with them. I just got that knowledge, which actually is new—because the old lady (my far-away relatives) asked if I had 12 rows of pearls, and my answer was "yes"; and she was very pleased because then I was rich. Then she told me that they all survived and that all the fertile women who had lost their husbands tried to get pregnant during the coming winter. They had to stay in the South with the plan of returning North one and a half years later. The sailing North would take five times as long as sailing South because they had to fight the stream and ice, but as she said, "women normally cope better with going against the stream and ice. They just find the right way to survive." And there you have a very big pot of Bear-women-knowledge, just knowing how to survive.

It was quite tough. It was women's business to choose a man when the husband died, to choose a new one and maybe start in a new place. They made the decision about the new partner. There were a few bearwomen among them, from the families of *angogok*. It was normal that women had this role of a*ngagok* but it was the men's role that was given more value according to western patriarchal Christianity. Europeans educated the women from *angogok* families as midwives. Now many have repressed this bear-knowledge. The Inuit women were not afraid of their strength. They have self-esteem, they are not afraid to act their roles, act out their male strength.

Kaarina: What do you see as the core aspects of the woman-bear relationship?

Ulla: The marriage of woman and the bear … its meaning is really what its meaning is to you. That is the meaning. Listen to the bear, what it is saying, the bodysoul. For western women it is very important to trust the knowledge they already have, to trust the soul knowledge of the bearwoman. Women can be the strong ones; they often are. Men often need the bearwoman to reassure them that they as men are also bears. Women are so strong and that scares men. Men know that so they must pretend that this is not the case. Fear of women's bear. We must support each other as women to trust this bear inside ourselves. The bear is linked with self-confidence.

This conversation took place during the meeting of the World Wise Women at the Norwegian Kvinneuniversitet, Loten, July 19, 2001. The conversation was continued via email in May 2002.

MARIE-FRANÇOISE GUÉDON

Of Big Animals, Women and Shamans in Nabesna Country

A Tale of Assumed Identities

Alaska 1969. I was just entering the wilderness I had yearned to explore since my childhood. I was going to spend several months in the little Athapaskan Indian village of Tetlin, nestled in the forest and swamp-covered valley of the Nabesna river, at the Alaskan-Yukon border. I came armed with definite notions and principles. Together with the course work for my Ph.D. in anthropology, I had recently completed field work among the Inuit of New Quebec, where animals are game, men are hunters, women are submitted to taboos, and shamans are masters of spirits. That much I had encountered as well in ethnographic material on European and Siberian peoples.

From the perspective of my Athapaskan hosts, the Upper Tanana or Nabesna t'ani (shortened here to Nabesna), however, I urgently needed re-education, if for no other reason than to prevent me from destroying the fragile equilibrium between the human and the non-human inhabitants of this part of the world. I did not realize the extent or the manner of this education until much later. For the moment, I was still reeling from a quasi-ecstatic wonder engendered by the fullness and richness of the Alaskan landscape, symbolized and summarized by its most famous inhabitants, whether grizzly, brown, or black. My education began, as it does with Athapaskan children, with stories. Among these, the tale of the girl who married the bear was one of the most frequently told. As I was slowly but surely socialized by my new mentors, the wilderness transformed around me, together with its inhabitants. For the Athapaskan Aboriginal, or Dene people (in Alaska, Yukon, Denedah, Nunavut) the "big ones," " those who walk in the hills," "they who stand upright," "the brown ones," "the black ones," "grandfathers," are a "real" presence. As is shown by this litany of circumlocutions designating them, it is not proper to designate them by their name, especially when one is a woman. The ursine ones, whose Dene common name simply means "animal," share their territory with human beings, compete for the same food, including fish, roots, and berries, sleep in house-like dens, raise and educate their young in families that stay together, and their babies' cry is identical to that of human babies. "Too much like us, too close, that's why we don't eat them," warns a Nabesna woman from Tetlin, echoing her neighbours. "It's like the story says," remarks another woman from the same village, "this kind once married with us, wolf too, this

77

Chistochina Valley (All drawings by Marie Françoise Guédon).

kind is *enji*…. That's why we don't say its name." Yet, in daily life, whether in the woods or in the camp, Nabesna women have to think and talk often about their big and furry "grandparents" who remain a source of concrete preoccupation, the object of ritual prescriptions, and the focus of intense emotions including fear, admiration, and even gratitude.

Women and Ritual Taboos

All my informants agree on the following point: women are not supposed to tell stories about these animals, though they do so anyway—older women can take liberties, especially when men are not present. These stories are *enji* to women. This avoidance rule is broad, applying as it does not only to the animal's name but also to touching its meat, fur, and body parts, and extends even to not being allowed to look at it. Such ritual avoidance may stem from the general set of taboos and ritual prescriptions to which Nabesna women, from puberty to menopause, are subjected. As I followed and made my way into Nabesna society, I was gently but firmly instructed as to the correct behaviour expected from girls and women. Such behaviour is especially restrictive during menstruation, during the first months after reaching puberty, as well as during and after childbirth. A young woman, upon reaching puberty goes through a lengthy ritual retreat that may last up to one year, but ideally for at least three months. She is isolated in a little hut in the woods, or behind a curtain in the common cabin. For most of the day she remains quietly seated on the ground, with folded legs. She wears

Women hunting near Buffalo Lake.

red thread around her wrists and ankles, sometimes her knees and elbows as well as around the joints of her fingers. She cannot scratch herself except with a little stick. Her lips cannot touch water and she thus drinks sparingly—luke-warm water—through a straw made of a hollow swan bone. She eats little, never fresh meat or fresh berries, only dried food. On those rare occasions when she is escorted outside, early in the morning or late at night, she wears a special hooded and fringed hat to prevent her from looking at the horizon or, worse, at the sun. She sleeps little, on dark pillows (to keep her hair black even in old age) and she is coaxed not to smile or speak (to preserve the beauty of a small mouth with puckered lips). She is treated to lectures on morality by her older female relatives, the only people allowed to visit her and she is given repetitive tasks: taking needles off a spruce branch for instance. She is also taught how to sew, to make moccasins, and to embroider skin. At the end of her ordeal, she will be washed, dressed, combed, and ritually re-taught how to speak and how to eat. Later on each month, until menopause, during her "bleeding times," she, like all "properly" trained women, will follow similar restrictions. During these days, she cannot hunt or fish; she has to sleep apart from the rest of the family and eat from her own bowl; she cannot walk on the same trail as men, step over men, men's clothing, tools or weapons, over a threshold, path or stream; she cannot attend shamanic rituals; and she cannot touch the meat or the body of fur-bearing animals. After menopause, older women are theoretically no longer obligated to obey the taboos and prescriptions followed by younger women. I was presented those prescriptions—which I was supposed to follow given my gender, my age, and my situation in the community—as necessary for the well-being of my children to come, for my own health, as well as for the protection of the men of the village, in short, women are *enji.*

In earlier anthropological literature, such taboos and limitations were perceived to reflect women's low status among Dene, recalling traditional European fear and shame surrounding women's bodies. The term *enji* was then translated as "impure"; but this and other similar terms used in other Northern Dene languages and communities are not so simply understood. The term *enji* corresponds to the Eastern Dene term *inkonze* or *ink'on* (Dogrib), to the central Dene or Denetha *ech'inte* (Goulet 1998: 64), to the Koyukon *hoklani.* These terms apply also to shamans, the local healers, or, in Dene terms, the "sleep-doctors" or "dreamers." The Nabesna term, *enji,* was at first translated by my anglophone informants as "taboo," or "danger," or "take care." What is shared by women, by "dreamers," and by their big four-legged furry relatives is a complex notion that does not correspond to our understanding of "impurity" but has more to do with sacredness. Linking (or separating) women, carnivorous animals of various kinds, and shamans, among other beings, the term primarily denotes power of a spiritual or psychic nature, hence the connotation of danger. When women are said to be *enji,* they are judged "powerful." The English term "power" is itself a popular translation in both anthropological discussions and Aboriginal circles for a series of notions that are complex and embedded in a specific cultural context. For women, this power has its primary focal point in menstrual blood. Jean-Guy Goulet (1998), talking about the Dene-Tha women, notes:

> In many native societies menstrual blood is seen as detrimental to successful hunting. In these societies, "menstrual blood is not thought of as polluting but as clashing with a man's power(s)" (Irvin 1994: 177). Joan Ryan (1995: 29) uses the term "endanger" rather than "contamination" to refer to a "woman's power to affect men's ability to hunt, thus endangering the survival of the group." (95)

These remarks apply to the Nabesna people as well. The potential presence of menstrual blood means that fertile women cannot always attend community rituals, but it does not prevent them from becoming shamans. Blood may even become a shamanic tool/medium. It is then seen as a potent ally or "medicine." In daily life, female shamans are, in the end, as respected as their male counterparts (Guédon 1988, 17-18, note 5). Yet menstrual blood is not the only expression of this power. Human milk and the saliva of both menstruating women and babies, among other substances, also carry similar injunctions.

The power emanating from menstrual blood and from other substances from female or infant origin, seems to clash with those of the animal world, partly because it is considered akin to animal powers (see Testart 1996 and Guédon 2005: 173-135 for an elaboration of this idea). It is not lethal to men, but to men's ability to hunt. It reaches its full expression when dealing with the world of spiritual powers and game animals, especially those animals considered spiritually powerful, such as It-Who-Walks-in-the-Hills.

The Story of She Who Married the Big One

Whenever I enquire about the reasons for or foundations of the special relationship between women and He-Who-Stands-Upright, the habitual answer is an allusion to a well-known myth. From one end of the Dene country to another, Dene versions of the story of the girl who married one of the Big-Ones are repeated to children and adults alike. It is clearly one of the most important texts in the Dene repertoire of stories. In her book *The Girl Who Married the Bear*, Catherine McClellan (1970) has presented several versions of this story as told among the Southern Yukon Indian peoples. Similar versions were taught to me in Tetlin, Tanacross, and Northway, with comments on the appropriate behaviour of the heroine. In all versions, the girl attracts the attention of He-Who-Stands-Upright by insulting his kind, and is tricked by him in the guise of a young attractive hunter who kidnaps her but later turns into a kind and loyal lover and husband. When the girl's brothers, led by the youngest of them, approach the couple's den, the noble beast, upon the prayer of his wife to spare her brothers, lets himself be killed. The woman, now the mother of several cubs, manages to save her children, to bring them back to the human community, and eventually to get at least some of them to assume human shape. But, in most versions, her daughter will fail the test of her confrontation with the male youth of the village during her puberty ritual confinement; the mother and the daughter will either die or turn back into animals and flee into the woods.

The story in question can be heard, like all myths, at various levels. Its usual conclusion points to a direct and concrete level of interpretations: "And this is how we know how to treat the Animal when we kill it." More precisely, men telling the story are likely to refer to these kinds of conclusions while women offer a different ending: "And this is why the Big Animal now protects women. Because it married us. We cannot eat this kind." It would indeed be unthinkable for women to eat the flesh of one who was once a husband and who died for the sake of his human family.

The myth concerns a girl, her relationship with a male beast, and therefore may also have to do with sexuality. Sexuality is a touchy subject among the Dene. Among the Nabesna, one does not talk about it to the members of one's clan or to relatives on the mother's side. Sexual topics are broached with cross-cousins (potential partners or mates) and paternal relatives. Yet, past puberty, sexuality is no longer problematic as it is neither sinful nor dangerous in itself. Furthermore, a lover or husband, belonging as they do to the father's side, call for a friendly, open, equal-to-equal partnership very different from the authoritarian hierarchical relationships on the clan or maternal side. The story thus has indirectly to do with gender relations and definitions. In Dene society, men and women share the same essential nature, the same positions on the moral and spiritual levels (gender is an aspect that can be chosen by the baby after conception and before birth). Daily tasks separate the genders, men being more inclined to hunt big game and go on long trips, while women, at least those able to bear and mother children, will remain closer to the camp and do some small game hunting together with skin preparation, sewing of clothing, tent manufacture, and food preservation (though men as well as women do the cooking). It is also the women's responsibility to manage, pack, and transport the tent and camp materials, as well as to pack meat back from the site of a kill. (Packing demands a great deal of strength and energy; women are not perceived as physically weak.) Women usually pick berries and dig roots but everybody, male or female, is involved in fishing. However, in the 1970s, and, long before, according to the women's stories, the best hunters in the three largest Nabesna villages were older women (see illustration woman hunting in Big Tetlin Hill). Though these women did not hunt carnivorous game (the powerful ones), even less the Big Ones, they successfully hunted birds and small mammals as well as moose and caribou. Among men, it was not considered abnormal to learn how to dress skin and sew moccasins.

It is to be noted that at the linguistic level, there is no distinction between "he" and "she"; so gender is indicated when necessary by adding the terms meaning "male" or "female."[1] Moreover, at the personal level, the general belief in the possibility of reincarnation, still very much alive and showing no sign of decline, results in the presentation of one's individuality or self in non-gendered terms. This is because one can change from one sex to the next as one is reborn, and can choose one's sexual identity at the moment of conception (some say birth); one's gender is therefore not part of one's "soul," only of one's body (Guédon 1988: 17, n.5).

At the social level, observers, including missionaries, have not agreed on the status of women in Dene society. My own observations not only among the Nabesna but also in neighbouring villages, as well as in Northern British Columbia and the Yukon, led me to think that this status varies, but that generally speaking Dene women work hard but are full members of their community with a strong voice in communal affairs and the economy of the family. According to traditions, however, they are supposed to retreat and hide when strangers of any kind arrive. This is what the girl in the story should have done. Used as a teaching device, this myth does not add to existing knowledge, among the Nabesna or the Dene, about sexuality or gender relations.

A more promising level of interpretation of the myth arises from the marriage motif. Taken literally, it could have to do with the founding of a lineage or clan, with an animal ancestor.[2] In the Nabesna valley, it is to be stressed, the story belongs to everybody and directly addresses not just one clan but the structure of clan organization and its consequences on interpersonal relationships. In Alaska, the Yukon, and parts of British Columbia, Dene society is constructed on matrilineal exogamous clans; one must marry someone from another clan. To marry too close, that is a kin within one's "side" or clan is incest. To marry a stranger leads to the severing of kin connections on the mother's or on the father's side, depending on the new domicile of the couple. The ideal marriage among the Nabesna, (observed in 75 percent of the cases) is with someone belonging to the father's side or clan. Father's clan or not, one marries a partner who, not being from one's side, belongs to the side of potential enemies, following several of my informants' expression: "One marries the people against whom one fights." That is to say one's husband or wife belongs to a clan that might become the enemy. Even in daily life, a married woman must constantly choose which side she will assist and help with food or materials. She respectfully recognizes her allegiance to her family of origin, including her sisters whose children she addresses in the same terms as her own, and her brothers who, as maternal uncles, watch over the education and behaviour of the sons of their clans. Yet she cannot negate her attachment to the husband who is also her partner and her friend—that is, "a person with whom you can talk about everything." The myth marks the tensions provoked daily by those contradictory responsibilities and which are further expressed and enhanced by war stories where women become pawns and actors accused of betraying sometimes one side, sometimes another side of the kinship equation. The myth, however, concludes decisively, if painfully, by the primacy of blood kin and clan over husband and alliance kin, brothers taking precedence over husband.[3] But this husband is not human; it has fur and claws and a snout. This set of elements marks him (in Claude Lévi-Strauss's terms) as someone who is too far, rather than too close, to be acceptable as a partner. The rule of exogamy must be followed neither too loosely (too close) nor too precisely (too far), but as just right. For this transgression of the rule of the "just right," the young mother of the story will suffer tragic consequences. Not only does she lose her husband, but her children will remain "a bit wild" and the young she-cub will be harassed by the young men of the camp which she will then attack, upon which she and her mother will be driven away from human society.

Yet what if the myth is not to be interpreted, but rather lived. The outcome of the story shifts from abstract morality to experience or direct knowing. In my informants' terms: "Be polite to the animals, and stay around [human] people," or again: "I told you that story so you know what to do"; i.e., when you meet people, human or otherwise. In my own experience, this means facing the wilderness not as a lonely place with wild dangers, but as a place inhabited by real beings, that is animal-people. In spite of the tragic tone of the story, women gain something from this encounter with wilderness: they gain a protector. They also gain the possibility of a new relationship with the world different from that defined from within the confines of the human community. Men and women gain the possibility of defining themselves in relation with, or by contrast with, the non-human world, in a quasi-cultural differentiation. There, too, implicit rules guide one's relationship with the non-human world. Too distant, one cannot gain the power necessary for the survival of the community; too close and one loses one's humanity without any reward/benefit for the community. Men, as hunters, have well-defined relationships with animals, including the Big One. Women have to refuse this "hunting" relationship with the animals at least during their child-bearing years. They are not

Woman hunting in Big Tetlin Hill.

free to consider all animals as game.

There is a masculine version of the myth of the Big One, where a male hunter meets in the woods and marries a beautiful woman who reveals herself to be You-Know-What when she gets sleepy in the Fall. It is the hero who gets killed by his wife for betraying her with another girl during the Winter Solstice feasts. Men who told me the story concluded: "this is how we learned about what to do when one kills a big animal." However, women telling the same story more often conclude: "And this is how men know not to 'bother' [aggress or betray] their wives. If they do they will be attacked same as in the story." The pact of non-aggression and protection is here reaffirmed. Why this privileged relationship?

Ceremonial Animals

The fact that the term *enji* also applies to certain animals, and in general to nature as a whole, that is, nature taken in the Dene sense as the non-human world, indicates that female power plays on the same level and in the same field as Nature. All dealings with animals whether as game and source of food, or as neighbours, or as spiritual partners in what is called shamanism, have to cope with the fact that these beings are persons and have spirits. Among these "persons," there are some that are especially potent. Many animals are set apart from others because they are considered spiritually powerful. Indeed, according to the stories, the Big Animal is not the only inhabitant of the forest marked for power. Wolf, wolverine, lynx, fox, otter, and groundhog, among others, are all beings of high standing.[4] More powerful than human beings, all these animals are endowed with spiritual components similar to those of human beings, including a soul that separates from the body at death, and a spirit which, echoing the body, can leave during dreams, can travel, and can communicate with other beings. These animal beings are described as spiritually sensitive, and easily insulted, if not vengeful. Dealings with them are ritualized. Among these powerful beings, those who hibernate occupy

Women on the trap line near Big Tetlin Lake in April, in brush shelter.

a special place. Not only do they sleep close to the earth, a source of shamanic powers, they sleep for a long time and dream for equally long periods. Such animals, like shamans, are considered even trickier than the others, calling therefore for stringent rules of behaviour. Their shamanic-like powers are alluded to in the mythological cycle of Yamangtechai, "he who went around the earth"; also know as the Mariner or the Traveller or Big Beaver. Yamangtechai, helped by Mouse Woman, herself a powerful being, clashed with He-Who-Walks-in-the-Hills. Both opponents brought to the fight a formidable set of shamanic powers and allies; in the end they agreed that they were both very strong. The Big Beast let the hero marry his daughters, then ascended into the sky, turning into a sun-like figure. Faced with beings of such power, human beings must offer ritual gestures to appease the animals they want to hunt as well as earn their respect, and therefore their participation in the hunting game. Among the Nabesna people, both men and women hunt. The prevalent feeling, however, is that men are better suited to hunting and trapping the more powerful animals, if only because it is easier for them to keep away from children. Men can even afford to hunt, kill, and eat the "Big Animal," provided they do it ritually, away from the camp or village, with all the ceremonies and honours due to a great warrior, a rich person, or a being of power whose death requires a proper funeral. All Big Ones, whether grizzly, brown, or black were formerly hunted with a spear, face-to-face, a practice found in many parts of the Dene territory (including Kolchan, Tanaina, and Atna peoples).

A Big One who had killed a human being was pursued, killed, and then treated as a high-ranking guest to a potlatch or funerary feast given in its memory. Men can eat the meat of both the Black one and the Brown one. Women do not even approach the carcass and remain in the village while men assemble somewhere

Eating blueberries in Tetlin.

in the woods to ceremonially partake of the feast. In return, the Big One will not attack women, at least when it knows they are women, hence the advice I was often given: "If you meet the One-You-Know, lift up your skirt, may be it'll be ashamed." The animal is also capable of directly protecting women who are attacked by a man, including one's husband. It will also avenge a wife whose husband is "fooling around with another woman." The usual punishment for a transgression against a woman by a man is for him to be attacked by the Big One. A similar fate awaits a man if he comes in contact, real or symbolic, with menstrual blood; for instance, a hunter whose weapon, clothing, or moccasins have been touched by a woman, even his wife, during her menstruation or by a girl during the periods following the onset of puberty.

Some theorize that the smell of blood is what attracts the Big One. Many more explain that the animal is extremely sensitive to variations in spiritual power. Some affirm that it is a corollary expression of the protection granted women by the Big Animal. A hunter who would attack or rape a woman or worse, a girl ritually isolated in her puberty lodge, would be immediately set upon by the Grand Fathers. I note here that comments by women led me to think that menstrual blood may correspond to the blood shed by women in other circumstances, in childbirth for instance, but also when they are victims of violence.

I have heard many stories by women who encountered "Someone" face-to-face in the woods and solved the threat by addressing themselves directly to the beast: "Grandfather, I have three children to feed. I need those berries to feed them. Let me go." "Grandfather, my poor children need me, get out of my way." "Grandfather, I am alone here, a poor woman, you have plenty, be good to me and my family. I just came here to find food." This kind of connection is specific to the Big Animal, and marks it apart from other spiritually powerful animals, as far as the women are concerned. At this juncture, it would be easy to accommodate the classic opposition between Nature and Culture, and to complete the structural equation with a corresponding opposition between The Big Ones and Human beings, women standing as the mediating element between the two sides, hence their problematic and therefore ritual position. Nature is to Culture what the Big Animal is to Man; woman is involved in both Nature and Culture. This equation, however, does not hold for the Dene for several reasons. In the Dene context, as far as I can reconstruct it, the Big Ones, whether Black or Brown, are not part of a Nature opposed to a Human culture. According to all definitions of culture, or the equivalent notions, used locally, the Big Ones are in their own ways as "cultured" as human beings. They have families and kin, houses and leaders. They are treated by men as warriors and enemies in addition to being game animals. They even have their own shamans. The women are clear in their statements: "The Big Animals are 'too close' rather than too far."

Shamanic Powers

For the Nabesna or the Dene people, the human communities are scattered in an immense world inhabited by non-human beings. It is not a bad world intent on destroying humans. Neither is it a benign order. Instead, it is one in which human and other beings share a common neighbourhood maintained by a fragile equilibrium where goodwill sometimes transcends the boundaries between species or kinds. Dene shamanism is built on the encounter between the animals, whether in their concrete, or spiritual (or dream) form, and the human beings they have chosen to assist. The first hint of such calling is usually given in dreams, when the animal contacts the mind of the would-be shaman or "dreamer."

Since everyone is able to dream, in the Nabesna version of shamanism, every one is somehow involved in shamanic practice: "Everybody is a sleep-doctor." The assistance or help of the animal person or "animal people" results in certain powers, psychic or miraculous, which have mostly to do with healing, hunting, or communicating. The reception of such power, together with a song, and eventual prescriptions and teachings are concretized in an object, often part of the animal, or a fragment of the substance corresponding to the being who is now "that of which it is dreamed," that is the tutelary animal or being of the shaman. Human beings are not the only beings endowed with those kinds of powers. Animals may manifest them as well, though they do not need the assistance of other animals to do so. The Dene dreamers do not seem to use the Big Animal more or less frequently than others as an auxiliary. Whether grizzly or black, the Big Animal is not singled out as a more potent source of power than other animals. Besides, even the powerful animals like wolf, wolverine, or the other carnivorous animals, are not listed more often than other beings whether animals, birds or others as the dream-animals of the "sleep-doctors."

The way Nabesna people use the term power corresponds closely to what is found in other Dene groups. June Helm (1994), in collaboration with Thomas Vital, one of her informants, has attempted to define power, or *ink'on*, according to the Fort Rae people. She writes:

In Vital's usage, the signification of *ink'on* is protean. According to the context, the word *ink'on* denotes a human being who is powerful, an other-than-human being that is powerful, and a powerfulness itself. The last sense appears to be the encompassing conception. But *ink'on* is not free floating. It is lodged in, comes from, is exercised by some being (or possibly a natural phenomenon). In this sense, in order to delimit it as an instance or an attribute, it is better to think of "a power" or "a powerfulness" rather than as "power" unqualified by an article. (77)

What then is shamanic power in Nabesna terms? Unlike *mana*, Dene shamanic power is a specific power, given by a being with whom the recipient is linked by close mind-to-mind or spirit-to-spirit association which demands both self-awareness and the concomitant ability to communicate, resonate, empathize, and link with others. The Big Animal is exemplary because it is both fully present to itself, and linked with the other inhabitants of the world. As one of my Nabesna informants phrased it: "In that place [its den] it hears everything that is said in the world, because the roots let it know what's going on. It's like a giant telephone and it dreams for a long time and knows what others are doing. It dreams in the earth, and the earth is *enji*."

Women's Power

If, as is assumed, women are subjected to ritual prescriptions in order to protect the community—and hunting activities—from the uncontrolled power of women's blood, other justifications, just as explicit, emerge from the women's comments and attitudes. First of all, these prescriptions are part of a wide array of measures aimed at protecting children. This is why menstruation, pregnancy, and lactation are so often the object of such rituals. Children would otherwise be exposed to nightmares, illness, and other consequences of having been in contact with the non-human world, including "wanting to go back." The newborn are kept inside for several weeks before being exposed to the outdoors: "They come from outside; they have to get used to being here." Babies, like sick people, are kept in a closed room with curtains or screens preventing them from even seeing outside. Curtains are always drawn at night across windows. Young children, pregnant women, or fertile women, should not be exposed to violent scenes, intense emotions, or prolonged mourning.

Intense fear is also to be avoided. Corpses, human or animal, should be kept away from young people. The interactions with animal beings and other shamanic powers is to be ritualized or avoided until one grows stronger spiritually. The protection of the fetus or the baby extends to the future mother so that a pregnant woman is advised to stay away from killing, especially those animals that are "too close to us" or "too much like us." One can snare rabbits but one should not interfere with a mother animal with calf or young. For similar reasons, war and shamanic duels are kept on the male side and subjected to a number of rituals to avoid the contamination of women. That the protection of babies is intended is indicated by the fact that infertile women are not affected by these restrictions.

For the same reason, fresh kills are left a certain distance from the camp. Careful trappers and hunters will stop before entering the village to shed their non-human smell and influence. If a fur-bearing animal is to be brought back, the hunter, weapons,

Baby sleeping in hammock, Tanacross.

knives, and the game itself will be exposed to the smoke of a fire. Smoke is a human product; its smell keeps away bad spirits and harmful influences.

According to my informants and mentors, I was also to follow the discipline imposed on women in order to protect and improve myself, my physical appearance, and my health: "In these days, you learn easily." "What you do then, it stays with you. If you sleep on white pillow, you will get white hair later." During puberty, pregnancy, and menstruation, girls and women are considered open, easily influenced, ready to be shaped, taught, and to dream. "This is a good time to change, to learn things, to stop smoking." Men, who do not have access to this spontaneous and periodical occasion to change, were pitied by some of my oldest informants. However, when a man has lost or won a great deal of money, or has given away his possessions during a potlatch or a funerary feast, or when he has killed a Big One, he is then asked to follow a similar ritual retreat as a girl reaching puberty. At the edge of a new life, he too is given the ability to change himself.

In terms of ritual or symbolic representations, the Nabesna, like most of their Dene neighbours, are remarkably restrained. However, the ritual sequence of the retreat and return of the girls reaching puberty, similar to that of a person who goes on a quest for dream or power, cannot be interpreted as corresponding to the classic death and rebirth theme so dear to Mircéa Eliade (1968). The retreat and the puberty retreat hut, corner, or hole, are never associated with a kind of death, symbolic or otherwise. Instead, the only metaphor one encounters is that of a womb. (Again the hut does not *represent* a womb. It is a womb-like structure; it is not symbolic but actual.) One is taken out of the womb at the end as one who has undergone a second gestation and must therefore be re-taught "just like a little baby." A womb, in Dene terms, is a place where one can transform and where one is able to move in and out of the human world.

Typically, for Dene people, the earth is not spoken of as mother, not even in symbolic terms. In spite of the position of the person undergoing the ritual retreat, seated in quasi-fetal position on the ground, and in spite of the earth being considered one of the most powerful sources of shamanic power, the earth remains a location rather than a personalized actor in the ritual play. One is to be reborn, not from the earth but from the world. The power inherent in femaleness and expressed in female menstrual blood is in the end not different in nature from that of the animals and the "dreamers." It is rooted in the concrete experience of life and body. It functions, like shamanic powers and animal powers, in terms of transformations and communications, by-passing normal channels, feeding on the web of connections potentially linking a sentient being to other sentient beings. It paradoxically brings babies and weak or weakened spirits into contact with powers too strong for them, while allowing them to come into the human world. It is, like shamanic power, an opening into the non-human side of things. It is not totally antagonistic to the animals (and menstrual blood can be used by some shamans in their rituals). Rather, it attracts the attention of the animals. It is not perceived as something as controlled as shamanic power, but even shamanic power has its drawbacks and its backlashes and can result, according to local beliefs, in catastrophic murders and mayhem, something the

Women and children on a blueberry picking expedition, Big Tetlin Hill.

women cannot afford. If power is about communicating, in a psychic-like nature or transcendence, potentially linking all sentient beings, it engenders its own moral response appropriate to a world where nothing is private. It seems to me that the closer one is to the animals, the more urgent the need to distinguish between them and human beings.

Among the Nabesna, women view with suspicion powers and other shamanic gifts which bring their recipient too far from the human realm, linking them to the animals and imperilling their humanity. ("Do not watch the Northern lights so much, they used to take that 'girl' away. These girls listen to the wolf too much; forget the family.") Similarly, Julie Cruikshank (1983) working with Yukon Indian women around Whitehorse noticed that while her female informants were likely to introduce a story or a myth in their response to her questions, they were also more intent than men to emphasize the necessity for the heroines to come back home rather than court the animal powers to the point of losing their human identity. Julie Cruikshank noted the difference between the stories describing encounters between human beings and animals or spirits as told by women, and the same stories told by men with male protagonists. In those stories, men often identify with the animal that will become their tutelary to the point where they physically transform into the animal form before coming back, if they come back, with a new name, a new song, and new powers. In the female version of the stories, the women do not let themselves be so absorbed into the animal form. They prefer the use of human qualities such as intelligence, judgment, and knowledge, which allow them to come back to their own community and to validate collective human knowledge, thereby preserving their belonging to their own human community (Cruikshank 1983: 16-17).

I recognized the same emphasis in Tetlin, where women take on the responsibility to feed a fragile humanity, or even more specifically the human characteristics of their communities, and to preserve their own capacity to do so (Guédon 1994). *Primum vivere*, but it is not enough to survive. The life worth living is one where one keeps and develops one's own humanness in the midst of an immense non-human world, hence the repeated admonition I received about the need to know—and teach—how to sew and embroider one's clothes, how to dress skin and meat, how to speak properly, how to sit and walk properly.

The story of the girl who married You-Know-Whom, taught me that as a woman, or as a human being, one has to come back to the human camp. One may be changed, transformed, endowed with gifts or simply with madness, but the full meaning of the encounter with Grand-Father and the other powerful beings is gained only when the story is told to other members of one's own species, the knowledge shared and the songs learned.

It is not only to keep children from illnesses and nightmares that one keeps the spirits and animals away from the human camp. In a world surrounded by non-human beings and powers, one must respectfully and consciously take care to protect what is human in human beings. When the boundaries become too blurred, they have to be emphasized clearly through ritual and other means. Sha-

Woman gathering blueberries, Tetlin Hill.

manic activities do provide for such boundaries by identifying transitions between human and non-human sides. These take place in concrete encounters experienced by individuals rather than according to a taxonomy or hierarchy of entities.

The Structure of Power

Analysing the underlying symbolic structure of shamanic practices among the Tungus of Siberia, Roberte Hamayon (1998) discovered it was built on a direct reference to the kinship system whereby the shaman who sought the gift of meat from the animals had to symbolically become their in-law, hence the frequent references to the shaman's—and the spirit's—sexual identity. Among the Dene, no such references are used. If the dreamer's—that is the shaman's—practices are predicated on the establishment of a particular relationship with the animals, this relationship is not metaphorically constructed on kinship. Neither is it related to sexuality. In any case, the animals "of whom one dreams" are rarely identified as male or female. Instead, the Nabesna people refer to a re-enactment of an ancient mythical theme replayed in a different key.

Raven may be the prototypical model of the shaman as he exemplifies the workings of shamanic power: He thinks and it happens. Raven is the source of its own power. For human shamans, however, power is going to imply a relationship with others. This relationship is exemplified in the Travellers's mythological cycle, the stories of Yamangtechai. The early mythical world was not suited to humankind. There was a time where animals were really big; they hunted, pursued, and ate human beings. Yamangtechai, He-Who-Went-Around-the-World, initiated the reversal of that first situation. The hero, one of the first and the greatest human shamans, fought against these giant animals, the meat-eating rabbit with its razor-sharp tail, the cannibalistic wolverine, the monstrous eagle, and all the others. The hero vanquished them all and ascribed to them their present size and status as game for human hunters. By so doing he reversed the situation of human beings from the hunted to hunters. Yet the animals retain some of their early power as evidenced by the fact they are still dangerous, by their shamanic skills, and by the awe they induce in those who meet them in dreams. Furthermore, the gift they may bestow on those who thereby become dreamers or shamans is often linked with the ancestral character, or the events related in the myths told about them.

In Dene terms, the reverse of hunting, that is a human being killing animals, is an animal who stalks and kills human beings. Neither situation allows for the development of a shamanic relationship. When one is called by an animal person, by means of dreams and other encounters, to acquire certain powers, one must shed both the stance of the hunter and the stances of the hunted. When attention is paid to the details of the acquisition by the hero of those shamanic powers allowing him to survive his adventure and to transform the animals, the story of Yamongtechai can be understood as a model of that third alternative. Befriending the animals is one of the prerequisites for meeting them in person. Shamanic power starts with a cease-fire: an interpersonal meeting of minds between two individual beings both outside their habitual roles and cultures: "When you want to meet animals, when they come in dreams, you go outside [in the forest], take only a little bit of dry meat, dry fish, really dead. No gun. Maybe it comes." A hunter cannot acquire animal power from those he, or she, is killing. Another kind of event leading to dreams about an animal or to the acquisition of shamanic power is developing one's interest in a particular animal through observation and closeness.[5] Most tellingly, assisting a mother animal while she is giving birth is a sure way to acquire power from that animal.

Women of childbearing age restrict their hunting in order to protect their children and their own procreative capacities. Neither hunted nor hunter, they are open to an invitation which paradoxically may take them too far from their responsibilities. They can accept the shamanic call but must then carefully manage their relationship with the non-human world.

The Notion of Spirit and the Notion of Animal People

Contrary to the notion of shamanic spirit popularized by Mircéa Eliade (1968), the Nabesna spirits or *yeg* are expressions rather than sources of power. The *yeg* is not separate from the animal; rather, it is an extension of its being. Animals and other beings are not powerful because they have spirit. According to the Dene, they are involved in spiritual processes because they are powerful. Power, whether shamanic power, animal power, or woman power, does not arise from a spiritual realm separated from the profane world. It springs from a concrete being.

Animals and natural phenomena associating with human beings in order to offer them shamanic powers communicate with them as people. It would be erroneous to say that so-and-so has such an animal as spirit helper or such an animal spirit as guardian; the relationship between a person and the "being of which it is dreamed" is established between two individual concrete beings, rather than between a human and a spirit, albeit in an animal form. Instead, these two beings use their spirit, or dreaming mind, that is that part of themselves which can dream and leave the body, in order to meet and communicate (Guédon 2005: 118-123). Similarly, in the second part of her book on Dogrib prophets, June Helm (1994) clearly questions with the help of her Dogrib collaborator (Vital Thomas) the relationship between a human being seeking power and the animal granting it:

> To use the term *spirit* in reference to an attribute of an animal or its species or in fact any kind of nonhuman entity did not register. Whether an animal comes to a human being in its own form or in human guise, it is the actual animal-being that is there and speaking; no incorporeal essence or metaphysical entity, generic or individualized, is involved. That there are one-to-one interactions and relationships between human beings and real animal-beings came out when Vital strove to answer the question, "Can a man have more than one *ink'on*?" "Yes," he replied "There are thousands and thousands of animals, foxes, wolves, dogs, bears." There is no shortage of animals-individuals who may choose to be *ink'on* to some one human individual. Yet in some of the accounts the animal imposes strictures on the treatment of its entire kind. (77-78)

Athapaskanists seem to be aware of the problem even when they use the usual expression "spirit helper" to translate the native term. For instance, by providing the native term and its literal translation, Robert McKennan (1965) indicates the extent to which we, the anthropologists, may gloss over the Dene concepts, while still accessing something of their original meaning. "In these dreams, the neophyte's spirit travelled extensively and acquired an animal helper, or spirit, called *yitsotci* ('the animal to whom he sleeps')" (78-79). The Chandalar, therefore, like the Nabesna, prefer speaking in terms of "animal helper" rather than spirit, but the native expression sends the speaker back to "that of which one dreams." Similarly, Patrick Moore and Angela Wheelock (1990), writing about the Dene Dhaa, go from one translation to the next, from "animal spirit" to "animal people" and "spirit beings" to simply "animal" in the same paragraph to designate the same entities (xvii-xviii).

It seems therefore appropriate to consider the possibility for Northern Dene in general of a shamanic relationship built on the encounter with a concrete animal or being rather than on a more or less abstract spiritual entity. The fact that one meets the animal in dreams, i.e., in its spirit form, is a sign of power rather than the expression of a spiritual essence (Guédon 2005: 302-318). In this encounter, the animal exhibits a complex identity, being at once an individual (with a certain personality and life experience), the member of a group or family located precisely in a territory shared with other animals and beings (with ecological as well as moral interactions), and the representative of a species. At this third level, it is linked to all other beings of its kind as well as to its mythical counterpart, that is to these figures belonging to "the times when animals spoke like us" and whose stories are used as references to explain their present behaviour and influence on human beings. Yet this third level is integrated with the others; all three levels are active when one meets an animal whether in dream, or in the woods.

In the symbolic systems offered by contemporary neo-shamanistic practices, each animal or spirit helper is introduced as the symbolic expression of psychological or spiritual qualities and abilities. Such a system is alien to the Nabesna and other Dene worlds. The beings one meets in the forest are not symbols or expressions of a sacred but separate universe. Neither are they completely alien. Instead they are neighbours. Each of them is obligated to establish and defend their identity, yet all are bound by the fact that they "think" and therefore communicate with and to the others. After searching for months for traces of a systematic symbolic system where each animal would have its place and characteristic aspects, I had to conclude that such a system would violate Nabesna norms of conduct and representations. The Big Animal is more than a symbolic reference to a myth; it is not the representation of a spiritual force. It is met in the flesh (Guédon 2005: 528-529). Without the intellectual distance provided by formal symbolic connotations, however, it is more difficult to verbalize one's understanding.

Though my experience of the Nabesna way of life is very limited, what I have been able to access has challenged most of my initial assumptions about the relationship between human beings and animals. This is a world where wilderness is not opposed to civilization, since domestication never took place (dogs are not so much domesticated as "half-humanized" according to stories), and where animals are not only game but also neighbours and partners. This is a society where both men and women—in spite of the latter bearing children—hunt and meet the animals in their own space, a sacred space. This is a space where shamans are dreamers who encounter not entities appearing as animals, but rather animals who have the power to transform themselves into dream beings. This is a culture where rituals are not meant to be explained but rather to be experienced, where there is little distance between the human side and the non-human side of things. There is also less room for words.

Anthropologists like myself are taught to talk. We do transform our observations and experiences into writings, but writing culture aside, speaking about culture is what we do best, and we concentrate on what people can verbalise for us. It is therefore not easy to access, or to account for experiences that lie beyond or besides words.

Twenty years after my first encounters with the Subarctic forest, when I meet the Big One, I no longer see it as a symbol of wilderness or savagery, neither does it evoke masculinity or darkness. It does not represent strength or power. Instead,

95

there is no distance between the animal and the power emanating from it. I have the feeling that its power comes from it being fully what it is. It does not symbolise anything but itself. I remember "my" first Brown One, in the cage of a zoo. Taller than I was, sitting on its behind, it gave me a cursory glance, letting me know that it knew I was there, then went back to its own interest, totally intent on examining, petal by petal, a dandelion flower it held in its paw. I perceived a contradiction between such a human gesture in such a non-human beast. But then I did not know I was human. For the Northern woman who, walking in the woods, hears a cub cry and feels in response the milk rising in her nipples, the recognition of her kinship with the wild child flows together with the acknowledgment of her duty toward her human kin. In that tension awareness is created. There would be no power for her without such awareness.

The illustrations in this article, originally published in Marie-Françoise Guédon, Le rêve et la forêt *(2006), are reproduced courtesy of Les Presses de l'Université Laval, Québec.*

[1]This creates interesting difficulties for the translation into English of aboriginal myths where the gender of animals, spirits and other protagonists is often not indicated. Even Raven, the hero of the origin myth for the Nabesna and their neighbours, starts out with a rather ambiguous gender, and only later becomes male.

[2]This is not uncommon among the Dene—one of the Nabesna clans is indirectly associated with the Big Animal, among the Tsimshian a similar story is told as a clan or crest origin story.

[3]See Catherine McClellan (1970) for a detailed analysis of several versions of this myth among the Yukon Denes.

[4]This is the case also in other cultural contexts and our understanding of Bear ceremonialism would improve with our consideration of other animal ceremonials. See, for instance, *Rites de chasse des peuples sibériens* by Evelyne Lot-Falk (1953) and closer to us, *Wolverine Myths and Visions: Dene Traditions from Northern Alberta* by Patrick Moore and Angela Wheelock (1990).

[5]See also the many stories of people acquiring power from an animal they either spared or saved from danger. Though many animal tutelaries impose a taboo on killing them to their human partner, many such partnerships allow the hunter to kill them more easily.

References

Cruikshank, Julie. 1998. *The Social Life of Stories: Narrative and Knowledge in the Yukon Territory*. Vancouver: University of British Columbia Press.
Cruikshank, Julie. 1983. *The Stolen Women: Female Journeys in Tagish and Tutchone*. Ottawa: National Museums of Canada.

Cruikshank, Julie. 1979. *Athapaskan Women: Lives and Legends.* Ottawa: National Museums of Canada.

Eliade, Mircéa. 1968. *Le chamanisme et les techniques archaïques de l'extase.* 2nd ed. Paris: Payot.

Goulet, Jean-Guy A. 1998. *Ways of Knowing: Experience, Knowledge, and Power Among the Dene-Tha.* Vancouver: University of British Columbia Press.

Guédon, Marie Françoise. 2005. *Le rêve et la forêt: Histoire de chamanes nabesna.* Sainte Foy, QC: Les Presses de l'Université Laval.

Guédon, Marie Françoise. 1994. "La femme et le pouvoir dans les pratiques chamaniques des Amérindiens de l'Alaska et du Nord-Ouest canadien." *Femmes et religions.* Ed. D. Veillette. Sainte Foy, QC: Les Presses de l'Université Laval.

Guédon, Marie Françoise. 1988. Du rêve à l'ethnoraphie: Explorations sur le mode personnel du chamanisme nabesna." *Recherches Amérindiennes au Québec* 18 (2,3): 5-18.

Guédon, Marie Françoise. 1974. *People of Tetlin, Why Are You Singing?* Ottawa: National Museum of Man, National Museums of Canada.

Hamayon, Roberte. 1998. "Le sens de l'alliance religieuse: Mari d'esprits, femme de dieu." *Antropologie et Soociétes* 22 (12): 25-48.

Helm, June. 2000. *The People of Denendeh: Ethnohistory of the Indians of Canada's Northwest Territories.* Iowa City: University of Iowa City.

Helm, June. 1994. *Prophecy and Power Among the Dogrib Indians.* Lincoln, NE: University of Nebraska Press.

Helm, June. 1961. *The Lynx Point People: The Dynamics of a Northern Athapaskan Band.* Ottawa, Dept. of Northern Affairs and National Resources.

Lot-Falk, Evelyne. 1953. *Rites de chasse des peuples sibériens.* Paris: Payot.

McClellan, Catherine. 1970. *The Girl Who Married the Bear.* Publications in Ethnology, 2. Ottawa: National Museum of Canada.

McKennan, Robert. 1965. *The Chandalar Kutchin.* Arctic Institute of North America Technical Paper 17. Montreal: Arctic Institute of North America.

Moore, Patrick J. and Angela Wheelock, eds. 1990. *Wolverine Myths and Visions: Dene Traditions from Northern Alberta.* Lincoln, NE: University of Nebraska Press.

Testart, Alain. 1996. *Des mythes et des croyances: Esquisse d'une théorie générale.* Paris: Éditions de la Maison des sciences du l'homme.

Maureen Enns, "King of the Rockies," mixed media, canvas, painting, oil and acrylic, 1993.

LOUISE BERNICE HALFE

Nōhkom, Medicine Bear

A shuffling brown bear
snorting and puffing
ambles up the stairs.

In her den
covered wall to wall
herbs hang … carrot roots, yarrow
camomile, rat-root,
and *cācāmosikan.*

To the centre of the room she waddles
sits with one leg out, the other hugged close.
She bends over her roots and leaves
sniffs, snorts and tastes them
as he sorts them into piles.

She grinds the chosen few
on a small tire grater,
dust-devils settling into mole-hills.
Her large brown paws take a patch
of soft deer skin
and wraps her poultice
until hundreds of tiny bundle-chains
swing from the rafters.

The brown labouring bear
Nōhkom, the medicine woman
alone in her attic den
smoking slim cigarettes
wears the perfume of sage, sweetgrass
and earth medicine ties,

Nōhkom, the medicine bear
healer of troubled spirits,
A red kerchief on her head,
blonde-white braids hang below her breasts.
She hums her medicine songs
shuffling alone in her den where
no light penetrates, no secrets escape.

She bends and her skirt drapes
over her aged beaded moccasins.
She brushes the potions off her apron,
A long day's work complete
Nōhkom ambles down the stairs
sweeps her long skirt behind her
drapes her paws on the stair rails
leaves her dark den and its medicine powers
to work in silence.

"Nōkhom, Medicine Bear," by Louise Bernice Halfe, from the collection Bear Bones
& Feathers, *published by Coteau Books. Used by permission of the publisher.*

PATRICIA JUNE VICKERS

The Princess and the Bears

The Gitsees Bear *adaawx* (sacred story) transcends the current social conditions of Ts'msyen Indigenous peoples on the coast of Northwest British Columbia. The current social conditions are intricately interwoven with, and attributable to, the legacy of cultural oppression through the act of colonization.[1] These social conditions, including high unemployment, a high suicide rate, a decreasing number of the people who can speak the language, and the low number who graduate from high school, often appear overwhelming (Canada 1996); however, the power of our *ayaawx* (ancestral law) (Seguin 1984) remains. The *adaawx,* in what is now known as "sacred story" format, is intimately connected to the *ayaawx.*

The "Bear Mother" *adaawx,* recorded by William Beynon (Canadian Museum of Civilization 1990), is such an *adaawx,* one that, with variations, is also found in Nisga'a and Gitxsan territories. The story of the woman and the bears from the Gitsees Tribe is already recorded and available for the reader to appreciate in Marius Barbeau's collection (Canadian Museum of Civilization 1990). According to Ts'msyen, Nisga'a and Gitxsan *ayaawx,* the individual who retells the story must have permission from the owners of the story. The writing of this paper on the woman and the bears has the permission of the current "speaker" for the House of Gitsees, Mr. Andrew Tait.

This is a shortened version of the Princess and the Bears story:

The woman and the Bears is an *adaawx* (sacred story) about a beautiful princess, the daughter of a Sm'ooygyit (Chief), who remained unwed because her father was extremely particular about who should marry his daughter and had refused all suitors. One day she was permitted to go berry picking with other women from the village. Two significant events happened while she was on her day's excursion. The first was that she stepped in bear dung on the trail and became very angry, commenting on the stink of the bear excrement. The second event was when the berry picking was finished for the day; the packstrap of her berry basket broke three times on their journey home, detaining her so that she was behind and alone. Had the Princess noticed the chain of events, she would have realized that she was experiencing a succession of unusual circumstances. Not until the Bear prince, disguised as a human being, had led her back to his village did she realize that she was in an unusual place.

In the Bear village, she was taken to the Chief's house, placed on a woven marriage mat and told she was to marry the Chief's nephew, the handsome prince who had found her on the trail. At this point, Mouse Woman made herself known to the human princess. Mouse Woman takes pity on her and lets her know what she must do to be in favour with the Bear people.

Mouse Woman let the princess know that one day she would be rescued if she kept favour with the Bear people by being conscious of everything that she did. Once the princess had successfully passed all of the tests laid out for her by the Chief's household, she was well cared for and never alone. But the princess was lonely for her family and her home and especially for her youngest brother and her dog named Maesk.

Back in her home village, the villagers and the princess's family were grief-stricken. Her father had sent searchers out to find his daughter, for his *halaayts* (shaman, spiritual power) had seen the princess alive and being taken by the Bears. The father sent out his three oldest sons, one at a time, but none succeeded in finding the princess. In the meantime, the Bear prince knew that one day they would find them and he would be killed. He was very sad at this thought, for many of their village members had been killed and he had known that he must take the princess and leave the Bear village. So, while his wife was carrying their first child, the Bear prince had to carry her through treacherous mountains on the way to a den that was virtually unapproachable. The princess gave birth to twin sons. Now the Bear prince was very happy and he only transformed himself into a bear when he had to leave his wife and cubs to get their food.

The Bear prince had taken extra precautions by spreading Devil's Club around the area where he camped and where his family's home was. He loved his wife and sons and each day he grew sadder as he knew his time with his family was growing shorter. The princess did not give up hope of being found and she especially thought of her youngest brother and her dog, Maesk.

Back in her home village, her father had almost given up all hope of finding his daughter. He had called on his *halaayts* to try and locate his daughter and he had even called the *halaayt* from other tribes to assist them in locating the princess, without success. The youngest brother, whom the princess missed the most, now offered to find his sister. The older brothers ridiculed their youngest brother who was not yet an accomplished hunter, thinking him to be presumptuous. However, the Chief gave in and agreed that it was a good thing that he also be given the chance to search for his sister. And so the youngest brother set off with his father's best hunters, and with Maesk guiding them, to find his sister. The princess's dog quickly found her scent and at the perfect time the princess looked out from her cavern home to see her youngest brother and her dog on the hillside far below. She knew they could not see her from that great distance and so she made a ball from the snow and rolled it down toward her brother. Her dog quickly picked up his mistress's scent and her brother then knew that his sister was in the cavern on the hillside.

The Bear prince, knowing that his time had come, grew very sad and wept, telling his family he would be killed. After a long climb up the hillside, the princess's brother, with Maesk in the lead, reached the mountain ledge at the entrance of the cave. The Bear prince asked his brother-in-law to wait as he wished to sing his dirge song to pass on to his sons and to pass his powers on to his sons. The princess told her brother to do as her husband wished. The Bear prince took off the Bear garments his sons were wearing, making them human beings, and proclaimed that his sons would be the greatest hunters among their mother's people. He then turned to his brother-in-law and told him to be quick and kill him with his arrow. The brother-in-law did not want to kill the Bear prince but did as he was told and drew his bow, shooting to kill the Bear prince. It is true that the Bear prince's sons became the best hunters of the Tribe; they had the greatest knowledge of the bears and were the most successful bear hunters.

Adaawx and Alienation

Although time and colonialism has brought many changes to the Northwest coast of British Columbia, regardless of the changes, the *adaawx* remains a tangible thread that ties us to our ancestors. *Adaawx* offer a passageway to ancestral values and beliefs that instill the importance of the reciprocal relationship between the land, animals, humans, and the Creator. Christianity and generations of conditioning to accept the colonizers' beliefs have altered our interpretation and application of *adaawx*. Our *adaawx* has been forced into a storage box: the causes of such restriction still function in today's society, and can be traced back to oppressive colonial tactics such as the imposition of the residential schools system, in which children were removed from their communities and punished for speaking their language. Whether a particular child learned to adapt to the new culture and emerged with curious enthusiasm and remarkable courage, or whether the child was deeply traumatized from being treated inhumanely, the separation of the child from the community remains a fact. The separation of the child from family, tribe, and community over at least three generations has created alienation to greater and lesser degrees from ancestral teachings. Recovering the role of *adaawx* for teaching cultural protocol, decision-making, and meditation is one of the many tasks for those of us who are attempting to piece together the transformative principles of our ancestors' teachings.

Implications of Gitsees *Adaawx*

The *adaawx* of the Princess and the Bears offers numerous opportunities for teaching; however, with limited space in which to discuss this story, the focus of this paper will be on the ancestral principles that are intimately connected to the *adaawx*. These principles include, but are not restricted to: 1) family relationships; 2) respect; 3) relationship to the land; and 4) power both external and internal.

Family

There are four *Pdeex* (clans/tribes/crests) in the Ts'msyen nation: *Ganhada* (Raven Tribe), *Gisbutwada* (Killer Whale Tribe), *Laxgyibuu* (Wolf Tribe) and *Laxsgyiik* (Eagle Tribe) (see Campbell 2005). Ts'msyen society is matrilineal, with names and possessions being passed down through the *yaawk* (potlatch/feast). Both daughters and sons were and continue to be an asset to the family and clan. In this *adaawx*, we hear that it took the desire of the father and the will of the total of his sons to find his daughter. She was of importance to the family. The sons inherit their maternal uncle's chieftainship in Ts'msyen society, and the daughter's marriage can connect the House to wealth in other villages, nations, and clans, increasing territory access for the woman's family and *waap* (House group). In this particular *adaawx*, the outcome for the Gitsees people is increased power through a spiritual connection to the bear. The *adaawx* is intimately connected to language and social values and beliefs.

Respect

Loomsk (honour, respect) according to our *ayaawx* (law) is taught to the child by parents, grandparents, and maternal aunts and uncles. Once children come of age, they are weaned from the close direction of immediate family through *suwilsgüütk* (spiritual cleansing practice). *Suwilsgüütk* includes fasting, drinking a tea made from medicinal plants, prayer, and bathing in a stream. The ritual of spiritual cleansing is the main practice for keeping a clean heart and focused mind for the individual within a tribe.

In the *adaawx*, the princess is disrespectful toward the bears and the consequences are to live intimately with them and to marry the prince. By marrying and adding to their lineage she has paid her debt for her offence of disrespect.

The Land

Ts'msyen people believe that the land has a spirit and when we respect the land, the land in turn gives back to us and we increase our individual and collective power. Respecting the land includes remembering that everything has life and it is our responsibility to acknowledge that life and use it to benefit others (Gitksan and Wet'suwet'en Hereditary Chiefs 1992). When we learn this principle of respect for the land, the door opens to a relationship like the one between the Bear prince and the Devil's Club plant. The cleansing properties of this plant kept the *halaayts* (medicine people, or people who are trained to discern and use magical powers) from finding his cave. It is believed that the powers of the land exist today but there is a conflict between the teachings of the missionaries and respect for the land.

Power

Gatgyet is power that comes from the heart of the human being. It is believed that we are born with power and our family teaches us how to increase that power. How we use power is directly connected with our family and our community or the teachers who were most influential in our lives.

In the *adaawx*, the Bear prince knew how to use the land to assist him in hiding away from imminent danger. The Bear prince's family taught him how to use the power of the land to his advantage. The princess's family also had power from their ancestors and from the land, and eventually their combined power was able to assist them in locating their sister and reuniting her with family and community.

Conclusion

The power of the *adaawx* is not only in the telling, or passing on, but also in the family: clan, tribe, community, nation, and language that the *adaawx* rests in. Once the *adaawx* is removed from the people that it comes from, it is changed.

The skill of a storyteller lies in their understanding and practice of the *ayaawx*. For the *ayaawx*, people, land, and *adaawx* are connected with the same strand: the powers, both external and internal, are awakened by the relationship of the connection of the storyteller with the *adaawx*.

Our *adaawx* remain as a link to both the world of our ancestors and to strengthen our connection to our individual internal power and to the external power in the land and the *ayaawx*.

[1]The *Indian Act*, in which First Nations are defined as "wards of the Federal government," is a primary tool of cultural oppression.

References

Campbell, Kenneth, ed. 2005. *Persistence and Change: A History of the Tsimsyen Nation*. Prince Rupert, BC: The Tsimshian Chiefs and Matriarchs and School District 52.

Canada. 1996. *Report of the Royal Commission on Aboriginal Peoples: Gathering Strength. Volume 3*. Ottawa: Minister of Supply and Services Canada.

Canadian Museum of Civilization. 1990. *Totem Poles According to Crests and Topics*. Hull, Quebec: Canadian Museum of Civilization.

Gitksan and Wet'suwet'en Hereditary Chiefs. 1992. *The Spirit in the Land: Statements of the Gitksan and Wet'suwet'en Hereditary Chiefs in the Supreme Court of British Columbia 1987-1990*. Gabriola, BC: Reflections.

Seguiun, Margaret, ed. 1984. *The Tsimshian: Images of the Past; Views for the Present*. Vancouver: University of British Columbia Press.

Myrna's Vision

I swoon when bear slashes
my breast with razor claws
yet it is necessary
he holds me
while owl dives through the portal
in my belly
releasing coiled pain
unravelling the spiral of my past
Feathered serpents ascending
my body
stand guard at my heart

KIRA VAN DEUSEN

Women and Bears

Indigenous Udeghe and Ulchi Traditions
of the Russian Far East

A bear skull hangs on a pine tree beside a wooden house in Gvasyugi village, the Russian Far East. This is the home of Udeghe storyteller and folklorist, Valentina Kyalundzyuga.[1] Across the swift-rushing river a statue in the schoolyard honours one of Kyalundzyuga's relatives, the first Udeghe writer, Jansi Kimonko. In 1949, at the height of his powers, Kimonko was killed by a bear while hunting. The bear pulled off Kimonko's scalp, and then died of wounds the hunter inflicted. Because of Kimonko's tragic and untimely death, the people of the village carried out the ancient ceremony of accompanying the dead to *Buni*, the next world,[2] in spite of the fact that such shamanic ceremonies were strictly forbidden by the communist administration. Because he died "not his own death," he would not have been able to find *Buni* on his own.

When I first met Valentina Kyalundzyuga in 1993, she told me about the ceremony. She was a little girl at the time, and recalled that the people went far away up the river, to a place where the drum would not be heard from the village. Kimonko spoke to his family through the shaman; people gave him gifts of food and even money for the long road. Then the shaman took his soul, contained in a hay figure, on a long visionary journey into a distant mountain to the land of the dead. There she passed his soul on to members of his family who had died before him. Later another ceremony was held, in which the bear was "judged," and the skull was hung on the tree.[3]

Kimonko (1985) wrote about this second kind of ceremony, which took place in his childhood, before the Soviet era. A bear had killed a man, he says, and people then pursued and killed the bear. In the ceremony, a shaman translated the negotiations between bears and the hunter's brother, learning that this bear had attacked the man because he, in turn, had not obeyed the laws of the taiga. He had cursed the names of both bears and shamans. The people made an agreement that they would not break the laws in the future, and asked the bears not to touch the hunters (63-65).

The village of Gvasyugi is home to about 300 Indigenous Udeghe people who in all number only 2,000. The Udeghe live in a lush forest region, home to the Siberian tiger, and the healing ginseng plant. Today they live mostly on vegetables from their gardens and fish from the rivers, while during the Soviet era they hunted and fished in collectives. Villages like Gvasyugi were created, and the Udeghe, who had lived nomadically up until that time, were forced to settle in them. Related by language and cultural history to the Manchu and to other Indigenous peoples of Russia and China, for several centuries before the arrival of Russians the Udeghe traded valuable furs to the Chinese to the south.

North of Gvasyugi, on the Amur River lies the village of Bulava, home to many of the 2,500 Ulchi people, whose language and cultural heritage have much in common with those of the Udeghe. Both of these peoples have strong traditions of storytelling and shamanism, in which bears and human women play important roles. Story is the means of integrating spiritual knowledge into everyday life.

Today Indigenous people are a very small minority in the area. Their traditional lands are severely compromised by logging, industry, and a large influx of non-native population, and their culture compromised by the education of several generations in Russian-dominated Soviet schools. Communism has proved a much more pervasive cultural colonizer than the earlier attempts to convert native people to Christianity, which succeeded only superficially.

Until very recently there were no surviving Udeghe shamans,[4] and only a very few Ulchi. But other traditions persist, including that of powerful women like Kyalundzyuga who carry on the oral storytelling traditions, teach the children embroidery, carving, songs and dances, the use of healing plants, and respect for the bears and tigers of the taiga forest. Women like Kyalundzyuga are also administrators and political and ecological activists, leading their people in a time of crisis.[5] Women's overwhelming role in today's cultural and political life is evidence of a long tradition of respect for female wisdom, also reflected in their stories.

I first met Valentina Kyalundzyuga in Gvasyugi in 1993, and heard her stories there in 1995 and 1997 as well. In 1998 she came to Canada and performed at storytelling festivals in Vancouver and Whitehorse. She tells many magic tales with powerful heroines, active and wise, and sings a song which tells the story of Biatu, which is the name given to bears in Udeghe folklore.[6] In the performance Kyalundzyuga's niece, Nadezhda Kimonko, danced the part of the bear.

There was a girl who lived with her brother as husband and wife. Then one day when he was away she began calling the bear, Biatu. She sang to him, inviting him to her place. She prepared tasty food for the bear and he came to live with her. Later the brother came back and killed the bear. But by this time the woman was pregnant and she gave birth to two bear cubs. She was angry with her brother for killing Biatu, and left the children with him. She turned into a bear herself and disappeared into the forest.

The brother stayed with the children. When fall came the children found a den to sleep in. He settled them down, and left an embroidered robe behind to protect them and show that they had human parentage.[7] Nonetheless, when he came back in spring he found that the bear cubs had been killed by hunters. He found the hunters, and they offered him their sister as a wife so that he would not take revenge on them.

Jansi Kimonko's sister, Evdokia Batovna, or Auntie Dusia, was known as one of the most knowledgeable elders of the village, if a bit erratic and temperamental. Although she is now deceased, she was still doing divinations when I met her in 1993 and 1995. She offered to make me an herbal remedy so that I could get pregnant, even at the age of 50! When I asked for a story she told the tale summarized below—the only one she told me twice. This is no coincidence. Consciously or not, storytellers select their tales with specific regard for their listeners. Dusia sensed that I needed this story, and to have it repeated. Perhaps foreigners, potential readers of my books, needed this story. It also may be her personal favourite, as she certainly told it with gusto, laughing raucously between the gaps in her teeth as she told of the girl taking each of the three young men to her bed. I listened as she spoke in her own language, which I did not understand, feeling as if I were being borne along a great river, stopping here and there for episodes of the story. Later she translated it into Russian.

Using magic power, a sister tricks her brother into living with her as husband and wife. He senses that something is wrong but doesn't realize that the woman he met while searching for a wife is actually the sister he left behind. They give birth to a boy and a girl.

Gradually the man is forced to go further and further to find enough game to feed his family. One day while hunting near his childhood home he kills a moose. He has a sense that this may be his sister, realizing semi-consciously that he has married her. He sets his arrow up in such a way that it will strike the chest of a person who falls in that direction and goes home saying, "If the woman I married is my sister, this arrow will kill her."

The small son goes out and meets a bird who tells him that his parents are brother and sister. He relays this information to his father. Next morning his wife goes out to bring back the moose meat, and doesn't come back.

The man follows her tracks, and finds her, lying dead, killed in his trap beside the moose he had shot. He goes home, but does not enter the house and does not feed the children. At last he harnesses the two children to a sleigh and moves away from that place. One by one the children fall from exhaustion and are left by the wayside. The boy dies, but the girl is saved by a brown bear who takes her to his home.

The bear builds a special house for her, and she grows up under his protection. When she is old enough to marry, the bear attracts three hunters to the house, one after the other. He tests them until he finds one who is intelligent, strong, and fearless. Each of the three sleeps with the girl, but the first two are frightened when they hear the bear approach. The third one kills the bear and stays with the girl. The bear has left instructions that she must eat only certain parts of the meat, and the way to build a house using his bones.[8]

The Russian geographer and explorer V. K. Arseniev recorded several versions of this story in the early twentieth century. It is said that the girl who lived with the bear was the original ancestor of the Udeghe people. In Arseniev's versions the girl marries the bear, and her brother survives and marries a tiger (in Simonov 1998: 448-453). He later accidentally kills the bear while hunting.

Both Kyalundzyuga's and Dusia's stories tell of incest—a difficult subject for any society to deal with. Like most people, today's Udeghe also consider incest a great sin. According to their traditions, a person must not marry within his/her own patriarchal clan. In earlier times, however, marriage between an older sister and younger brother was the norm (Simonov 1998: 25). Udeghe myth says that a brother and sister were the only ones to survive a great flood, becoming the ancestors of the whole human race. Several stories tell of a girl who brings up a boy-child who is either orphaned or abandoned, and then marries him. These also refer to that tradition.

Many stories have to do with the difficulties of finding a suitable spouse from a different clan when distances were great, resources changeable, and people constantly on the move. Both male and female initiation stories often have to do with the search for a spouse. These stories are similar to tales of shamanic initiation, showing the difficulties involved in finding and coming to terms with one's spirit helpers. There must have been times when the search failed, and sisters lived with their brothers, their children becoming the carriers of the clan. Even when the structure of society and the interpretation of this relationship had changed, the ancient form was retained in story.

In both of these stories the children of incest are connected with bears. In Kyalundzyuga's song, the bear is the children's father. There are many tales in the Amur region of women marrying bears.[9] Sometimes the offspring are human with almost superhuman powers, other times they are bears, and sometimes the mother gives birth to one of each. The children of bears (and tigers) are always twins, whose sacred nature goes back to the time of creation. Nivkh elder Maria Pimgun told me that twins turn into bears after death.

Among the Ulchi people, twins and their mother are regarded as sacred. In 1995, Ulchi shamanism specialist Nadezhda Duvan told the following about the relationship between human twins and bears at a workshop in the U.S. "Twins are the children of a woman who has married in the animal kingdom," she said.

> The woman herself is a supernatural being, considered to be chosen by the Master of the Taiga.[10] First she has a dream that she is living with the bear, who is a protector of the tribe. The pregnant woman will begin to speak strangely and to sing special songs. She may lose her reason. Those around her see that she is carrying twins. When the birth begins she is taken to a special place, different from the usual birth hut in that it is decorated with wood streamers and images of bear paws. To aid the birth, the men play the bear's musical rhythms; how the bear walks, sits, eats, and cleans himself.[11] A female shaman, or an older woman if there is no shaman, sings a special song, which is later repeated at the twins' funerals and for the ceremonies a year later. The dances include special movements with the wood streamers, which are sacred objects, providing an entry into the world where we may

communicate with spirits. Twins and their mother receive special respect from hunters and children, and a special kind of burial, wrapped in white in a seated position.

Bears are also considered one of the two strongest helping spirits by Udeghe and Ulchi shamans—the other being the tiger. In stories where women marry tigers, their children become the founders of new clans. This usually happens when there is no human partner available. In one case the woman who married a tiger was the only survivor of an epidemic.[12] In the stories I have heard, there is no mention of incest, and the tiger's children always survive. Ulchi shaman Anga spoke of giving birth to tiger children who became her helping spirits, although she had no human children (Van Deusen 2001: 170-2). The fate of the bear children is more problematic. Some die, as in the story of Biatu. Kyalundzyuga says her story shows the wrongness of incest, but more importantly that the hunters should have respected the sign the man had left, allowing those children to live.

In Dusia's story the bear saves the girl's life and gives her a home until she grows up, at which point he finds her a husband, testing the young men until he finds one who prepares before he acts. Then the bear sacrifices his own life for the sake of the girl's future. At one point in Dusia's telling there was some ambiguity about whether the bear was the girl's father. The suitors suspected that the bear was the girl's husband, as indeed he was in the versions recorded by Arseniev (in Simonov 1998: 448-453).

The girl's human father was so distraught when he learned that he had been living with his sister that he killed his wife. She is now associated with the moose, another of the most powerful spiritual animals, a deity of the upper world. And as so often is the case, it was a child who delivered the news. In Siberian stories where a man has abused his wife, the child often heals the mother and then brings about a reconciliation. The fact that the child does this by telling a story to the father shows clearly the role of storytelling in healing families and speaking difficult truths. But incest seems to be even worse than abuse—even the child cannot reconcile it. In spite of this, the bear has a life force that guarantees survival.

Dusia's story explains the taboo against women eating bear meat except for certain parts.[13] Stories of women marrying bears also explain why women did not play a direct role in the Ulchi bear ceremony where the animal was raised in the home and then ritually killed to carry messages to the upper world, confirming that human beings were abiding by the laws of the taiga. Local people explain that a woman could not be expected to take part in killing her own children. But the ceremony cleared the channels by which animals killed by hunters for food and clothing may be reborn.

The Udeghe did not have this kind of ceremony, although they had the kind of ceremony described by Kimonko (1985) and Kyalundzyuga when we spoke in 1993. The fact that the Ulchi had the particular kind of bear ceremony described above can probably be explained by their proximity to the Nivkh and Ainu peoples of Sakhalin Island and the nearby mainland, who originated it.[14] However, both Udeghe and Ulchi had ceremonies for bears deliberately killed on a hunt, which involved giving gifts for the bear's spirit to take to the Master of the Taiga. The bones were collected and smoke-cured (Smolyak 1996: 125).

Nadezhda Duvan (1995) describes how the Ulchi bear ceremony was done:

People would catch a bear cub and keep it for two to three years in a special hut. The bear slept with the dogs, and came out to play and to be hand fed by the woman of the house. After three years they would kill the bear as a sacrifice to the masters of the taiga. Special dishes were carved with the image of a bear's head, and chains made with real links. Some of the dishes had the form of a dipper. Other dishes had the design of a dragon or snake—this is the sky god, the most powerful of all deities. People prepared many wood streamers from willow, alder, and bird cherry. These were used to cleanse the bear from evil spirits and allow new flesh to grow. When the people eat, the spirits of their deceased relatives are fed at the same time, and they are happy.

Two men would guide the bear on two chains around an ice hole in the river. It is a good omen if the bear takes a drink. Then they went along a corridor of poles with wood streamers on them, about one kilometre to the place called *arachu*, prepared for the killing. Women play special rhythms on a musical instrument made of a hollow log.[15] The women dance the part of the bear.

The men take the bear to the house of the person who is hosting the feast. The bear crosses the threshold three times—if he crosses with two paws it means he is not offended and wishes well to the family. Then they go back to the place of sacrifice. First they shoot three arrows in the air—to the earth, the sky, and the taiga, and then the last arrow to the bear's heart.

Mourning begins in the family. There are special rituals for taking off the skin—each male must touch the skin to get a blessing on his future success as a hunter. There is a big celebration with singing, feasting, and sports events. Afterward the bones are wrapped and placed in another special little house.

In 1937 the ceremony was to be hosted by Duvan's family. But at the last minute the authorities arrived. They "arrested" the bear and took him away on a steamship! In 1992, the people of Bulava revived the ceremony and carried it out in its entirety based on the memories of the elders. But there was so much sympathy for the cruelty to the bear that they decided in the future to carry out the ceremony without keeping and killing the bear (Duvan 1995).[16]

Why did Auntie Dusia want an outsider to hear the story of the bear who helped the little girl survive? In true shamanic storytelling style, she explained nothing. She just told the tale and let it do its own work. I cannot offer an insider's explanation, and can only add what I have seen for myself as an outsider. I believe the bear is dealing with the dark and difficult side of survival. The bear shows us the power of protection that resides in wildness and strength—the intelligence of the life force. Just as Dusia believed I could give birth at 50, it is never too late for a society to resurrect itself from spiritual, ecological, and social destruction. This life force runs especially strongly in women, and in cases of emergency overrides all social constructs.

Dusia seemed slightly outraged and mystified by the sister fooling her brother, although this may have been coyness on her part. I enjoyed the sister's willingness to sacrifice patriarchal morality for the sake of living with her brother, just as later she sacrificed her own life so that her children could live. And it is the girl-child who survives and carries on with the help of the bear. As we saw in the case of marriage with tigers, connection is made with the animal world when the clan must be preserved in a female line in this otherwise patriarchal society. In spite of the shift in the meaning of the marriage of brother and sister, the children of incest are still sacred.

The power of the bear in Udeghe and Ulchi society is rational and intelligent—the bear can be reasoned with through the proper ceremonials. Respecting contracts is an important part of bear ceremonies, keeping people in balance with nature. The bear protects women and children with a powerful life force that is stronger than the morality set up by society. Women and bears show us the wise and discriminating power of protection in wildness.

Portions of this article appear in The Flying Tiger: Women Shamans and Storytellers of the Amur *by Kira Van Deusen, published by McGill-Queen's University Press, 2001. Reprinted with permission of the publisher and author.*

[1]Valentina Kyalundzyuga has published collections of tales in Russian (1974) and English (1998) and is co-author of a scholarly Udeghe-Russian edition (Simonov 1998.)

[2]The ceremony is called *khanyaunya khuni* in Udeghe, and is also more widely known by its name in the neighbouring Nanai language as *kasa*. It is the highest form of shamanism in the Amur region. If souls are not properly seen off, they can cause problems for the living (Van Deusen 2001: 221-222).

[3]Related by Kyalundzyuga (1998). That skull is long gone now, and the one that hangs on the tree in Kyalundzyuga's yard is from a different bear, killed on a bear hunt.

[4]Adikhini, the last Udeghe shaman, died in 1997. Since about 2004, Vasily Dunkai (Udeghe) has been practicing in the village of Krasny Yar and Nadezhda Duvan (Ulchi) in Khabarovsk and Bulava.

[5]Valentina Kyalundzyuga retired in 1998 as head of Gvasyugi's village administration, a position she held for more than 30 years.

[6]Traditionally some stories can be either told or sung. In the past stories were only told at night, while people only sang during the day (Podmaskin cited in Simonov

1998: 56, 59). The story of Biatu can be found in Simonov (1998: 80-85).

[7]Embroidered designs representing protective spirits have the power to protect human beings from evil spirits (Van Deusen 2001, 1996a, 1996b).

[8]Using animal bones—bear, whale, stag, moose—is the most ancient form of Siberian house-building, showing human beings' intimate interdependence with the animal world.

[9]And other animals. I have heard Amur tales of women marrying bears, tigers, snakes, crows, fish, and puppies—and even a skull and an old discarded hunting bag. Further to the north the Indigenous Chukchi and Yupik people tell of women who marry whales and walrus. Kyalundzyuga (Van Deusen 2001: 32-33) tells of a man who married a seal. All these tales reflect the intimate relationship between a hunting people and the animals who sustain their lives. "Biatu" is unusual among the bear stories in that it is the girl who initiates the marriage.

[10]Often seen as a large bear (sometimes a tiger) who provides food and well-being for humans.

[11]The same rhythms are played at the bear ceremony described in this article.

[12]Told by Nanai writer Valentin Geiker (qtd. in Van Deusen 2001: 187-190).

[13]In earlier times this referred only to the bear killed by her brother, as happened in the story recorded by Arseniev (Simonov 1998: 448-453).

[14]Described in Campbell (1988: 147-55).

[15]The instrument is called *udyadyupu*. Other rhythms include "stopping at the lake" and "resting at the mountain pass," which represent stages on the bear's journey back to the land of the taiga people (Smolyak 1996: 125).

[16]Photos of the 1992 ceremonies can be found in Doeker-Mach (1993: 2).

References

Campbell, Joseph. 1988. *Historical Atlas of World Mythology. Vol. I. The Way of the Animal Powers.* New York: Harper and Row.

Doeker-Mach, Günther. 1993. *The Forgotten Peoples of Siberia.* Zürich: Scalo.

Duvan, Nadezhda. 1995. Workshop on Shamanism, Whidbey Island, Washington.

Kimonko, Jansi. 1985. *Tam, gde bezhit Sukpai (Where the Sukpai Runs).* Khabarovsk: Khabarovsk Book Publishers.

Kyalundzyuga, Valentina. 1998. *The Ice Mountain.* Vancouver: Udagan Books.

Kyalundzyuga, Valentina. 1974. *Dva solntse (Two Suns).* Khabarovsk: Khabarovsk Book Publishers.

Podmaskin, V. V. 1991. *Dukhovnaya kul'tura udegeitsev XIX-XXvv (Spiritual Culture of the Udegei in the Nineteenth-Twentieth Centuries).* Vladivostok: Izdatel'stvo dal'nevostochnogo universiteta.

Simonov, M. D., ed. 1998. *Fol'klor udegeitsev: Nimanku, telungu, ekhe. Pamyatniki fol'klora narodov Sibiri i dal'nego vostoka (Folklore of the Udegei: Nimanku, telungu, ekhe).* Novosibirsk: Nauka.

Smolyak, Anna. 1996. *Ul'chi: Khozyaistvo, kul'tura i byt v proshlom i nastoyas-*

hchem (The Ul'chi: Economy, Culture and Way of Life in the Past and Present). Moscow: Nauka.

Van Deusen, Kira. 2001. *The Flying Tiger: Women Shamans and Storytellers of the Amur*. Montreal. McGill-Queens University Press.

Van Deusen, Kira. 1997. "Ulchi Shamans." *Shaman* 5 (2): 155-64.

Van Deusen, Kira. 1996a. "The Flying Tiger: Aboriginal Women Shamans, Storytellers and Embroidery Artists in the Russian Far East." *Shaman* 4 (1-2): 45-78.

Van Deusen, Kira. 1996b. "Protection and Empowerment: Clothing Symbolism in the Amur River Region of the Russian Far East." *Braving the Cold: Continuity and Change in Arctic Clothing*. Eds. Cunera Buis and Jarich Oosten. Leiden, The Netherlands: National Museum of Ethnology. 149-168.

Helena Junttila, "She Bear," oil on canvas, 200 x 120 cm, 1997.
Jenny and Antti Wihuri Foundation/Art Museum of Rovaniemi, Finland.

KIRSTI PALTTO

Rásttos and Bear Woman

Rásttos walks out to get some firewood. He stops at the chopping block to look up at the slopes of Reatka Hill, covered by the first snow that had fallen the day before. He wanted to go to the mountains, he wanted to go far away, all the way to Seaibi Mountains where as a young man he had been trapped by the forest and the translucent bear. Trapped so powerfully that ever since then he had lived half of his life in the forest.

If he had the strength, nothing would hold him here! Nothing.

He goes back into the house, puts some more wood in the stove and sits down on a rocking chair looking up at Reatka Hill. The highest point of Seaibi Mountains ascends behind it. Up there are his children who do not want to become human and live within the narrowness of human life; who do not want the safe life but instead desire open space and soft moss upon which to fall asleep.

Rásttos smiles because today, the day of the first snow, is the day his oldest daughter Násttás comes to visit him. She who was born after that reindeer round-up when Rásttos was working for Liemmu.

It was late summer and reindeer herders were collecting reindeer so that they could mark the calves. On Nisu Hill a fence had been erected into which the female reindeer and their calves were to be driven. Liemmu and his two helpers had found a good-sized herd and they were chasing it toward the fence. They had got the herd nicely situated underneath the upper Seaibi Mountain when two reindeer with their calves escaped in the direction of Gáldu River. Liemmu ordered Rásttos to catch them but did not let him take a dog.

Rásttos rushed after the reindeer, running in an arc in order to get in front of them. Right before Gáranas Valley he managed to get the reindeer to turn around. The two female reindeer ran tamely along with their calves behind them and it seemed that at any moment they would be with the herd. But then what happened?! On a gently sloping knoll they fled again, this time in the direction of Lower Seaibi Mountain. Rásttos cursed Liemmu because he had sent him to chase such demented reindeer. Perhaps Liemmu had trained them in order to test his newest helper!

117

Rásttos ran in front of the two reindeer and persuaded them to turn and move in the right direction once more. This time he would not let the two rascals escape! He snapped a long branch from a tree and hurried from side to side in order to keep the reindeer turning away from the right track. But it did not help. Rásttos lost them again.

Let them go! Rásttos said, sitting on a root-stock. *Let Liemmu find his own reindeer.* He was not going to run after them any longer. The sun was already going down and he was still in the forest. He was thirsty but he could not see water anywhere. Rásttos peed, rolled a cigarette, and leaned against a pine tree. He was about to reach into his pocket to get some matches when something grabbed his wrist tightly.

Rásttos was shocked and was about to pull his hand away but the grip was too tight and it was hurting his hand. What the hell had grabbed him?

He got a fright when he saw what kind of hand had snatched his wrist. A broad paw like a bear but without any fur! A strong paw that could crush his hand into pieces.

Was he dreaming? Or was this thick pine forest haunted, with the autumn shadows growing longer beneath the trees? Rásttos again tried to shake his hand free, this time more carefully because every little movement hurt his hand. He felt a cold sweat running down his back and his whole body was shaking. He felt that something was standing behind the tree but he could not move to see what it was.

"Let me go," he whispered in a trembling voice.

The grip did not loosen. It was as if it was burnt onto his wrist.

Did he fall under that hand's spell? Or what really happened? It was something Rásttos could not explain to himself. After a long time, the grip finally loosened and his hand was freed. Rásttos rubbed his sore hand before he grabbed the matches and with shaky hands lit a cigarette. He was so bewildered that he did not even think to escape. He had a few puffs of his cigarette when a bear standing on its back legs appeared behind the tree. Rásttos suddenly regained his senses and realized that the bear was about to attack him. His cigarette flew to the ground as he sprinted off. He did not remember that one should not run away from an angry bear but rather stare into its eyes and roar as loudly as possible.

He did not get further than a few steps that the bear was standing in front of him. Rásttos fell onto his back on the ground and remembered that he had a knife with him. He grabbed it and summoned all his strength and bravery to stab the knife into the bear's chest if it attacked him.

The bear did not attack him. Gradually Rásttos gained courage enough to sit up and see whether the bear had gone away. His eyes opened wide and he felt dizzy when he saw the bear again. It was still standing on its back legs but it was no ordinary bear. No, this bear was translucent! It was the strangest animal that Rásttos had ever seen. Inside the shape of the bear there was a naked woman whose breasts were sticking out and whose lithe body shone. Long, black hair fell on her shoulders. And she was smiling! It was the warmest and most beautiful smile Rásttos had ever seen. Her eyes enchanted him.

The bear held out her hand to Rásttos, but it was no longer the hand of a bear. It was a small hand that radiated a strange warmth. Rásttos was reaching out to touch the small hand when he remembered the earlier grip. He turned his back to the bear. No, he was not going to hurt his hand again. He was going to mark reindeer calves, not lose his hand.

Rásttos checked the direction of Nisu Hill and started to run. He did not look back to see whether the bear had followed him or not. He did not raise his eyes to see if the bear would appear in front of him or somewhere else.

Rásttos waded across Gáldu River, drank from it and hurried ahead. But in walking heedlessly and in such a state of anxiety, he stumbled over a root and crashed to the ground on his stomach. His knee had hit a stone and was aching. He stood up grimacing and rubbed his knee where his pants had been torn. Why on earth had he ended up here, first to run after fidgety reindeer and then to fool around with a ghost bear? Rásttos swore and limped onward. He checked again to see if Nisu Hill was still in sight.

"Damn, it has disappeared," he cursed aloud. "Am I lost?"

He stopped to wipe the sweat away that was running down his face. This could not be real! It seemed that there was no point in trying to go anywhere before dawn, especially when hunger and fatigue were also wearing him down. And besides, he really was lost.

Rásttos limped over to sit on a fallen tree. He spotted a pine under which he could try to sleep, but before lying down he was at least going to have a smoke.

He smoked peacefully and was certain that the translucent bear had stopped chasing him. He stood up to arrange a spot to sleep for a few hours. As soon as he lay down, the ghost bear appeared again and approached him. Rásttos saw her stomach, belly button, and light-coloured tumescence. The wild smell of the bear's sweat blended with the smell of pinecones and crowberries.

I thought you were a ghost bear. And I thought of stabbing a knife into your heart. How much I would have lost if that thought became reality! The intentions of a scared person are so unpredictable. Especially when you meet something you have never experienced before.

What did this unusual animal want? She was smiling but did not come any closer. I must have fallen asleep and dreamt of the translucent bear licking my wounded knee and my aching wrist until the pain went away.

Rásttos sat on the fallen tree again. He had not been sleeping. Or had he been sleeping and woken up again? And why was his knee no longer painful? His wrist did not hurt either. He squatted on the tree, wasting time. He was cold, tired, and hungry. He was too tired even to eat the blueberries that surrounded him, ripe and blue.

Warm hands began to caress his stiff fingers and bade him to stand. The hands were guiding him somewhere. He followed without knowing if he was walking or being pulled. And then he was in a warm den, holding a bowl of hot broth. He emptied the bowl before he could see anything. The den was covered with warm moss. The translucent bear woman took the bowl, put it on the ground and came next to him. The woman no longer had the bear fur on; she was transformed into a human being and her warm body pressed against Rásttos like hot ashes. They embraced each other and rolled around the den. Happiness filled Rásttos's mind and body when they met in a deep pond, swinging there in a light boat, clashing into each other like a wave and a boat, like a rock and a snow storm, like sunny weather and a tempest.

He woke up with the first rays of sun. He noticed that he was lying beneath the same pine tree under which he had gone to sleep last night. He did not feel like going anywhere. The sky above the pines was clear. The forest was quiet and the wind had died down. He could smell the pinecones and the crow berries.

He looked at the place where he had been sleeping and saw the traces of two bodies on the moss.

At the round-up fence, Liemmu came to him with a big smile on his face and said carelessly, as if in passing: "You drove those two lost reindeer to the fence so well!"

Rásttos was going to tell Liemmu what had happened to him. But he was saying that the reindeer had arrived. How could that be? He had lost them!

"All the reindeer are by the fence now," Liemmu said happily. "Now we can let them rest so we can start slaughtering tomorrow."

Rásttos could not believe Liemmu. He walked over to his cousin to make sure what Liemmu was saying was true. His cousin was slaughtering a reindeer next to the fence.

"Are all the reindeer by the fence already?" Rásttos asked.

"Yes they are," answered his cousin. "In the morning Ovllá and Ande arrived with rest of the reindeer. And you brought the skittish female reindeer here last night."

I went to the cabin and lay down. My mind was full of thoughts and questions. Had the translucent bear woman driven the reindeer to the fence? They certainly did not come by themselves, that was for sure. Was it me? No, it could not have been. Why did Liemmu and the cousin claim that it was me who brought the reindeer?

At night I awoke as somebody was calling my name. I sat up and went outside to listen. The whole forest whistled and whispered, calling me to come. I walked and although it was dark I found the path. I walked until I was beside the same fallen tree I had been sitting on yesterday.

She came quietly and touched my hand first. She is a creature with hands like mine. This time I did not have to be dragged. I walked willingly into her den. There was a fire crackling in the fireplace. Again we swung on a light boat in a deep pond, clashing into each other.

The following day the old woman Juvssut, a member of Rásttos' *siida*, was watching him carefully. She saw the fleeting smile on his face and how his eyes were shining. Rásttos was happy and lively, moving and separating the reindeer better than ever before. What had he experienced on Seaibi Mountains? Could it be the same thing that her oldest brother Juoksa had many, many years ago?

Juoksa had been charmed by a strange bear and he had lived in a trance until he walked over the hills and was found drowned in Gáldu River. He had drowned himself, tied his hands and legs onto rocks in the bottom of the river. That was no joking matter, the old woman Juvssut thought as she recalled it. What would happen to Rásttos? Although Juoksa ... hmm ... had Rásttos after all been haunted/charmed? by the translucent bear? He had been a bit ... a bit insane. But Rásttos was not insane; everyone knew that. And in older times there were many men who had been with bear women, even women had been attracted to bear men.

Juvssut wanted to know how things were and if Rásttos needed any guidance. The translucent bear had her own specific smell that could be detected only by those who knew about her. Juvssut knew that smell. She slipped down to the fence where Rásttos was catching reindeer to be slaughtered. She approached him and did not need to sniff long to find that Rásttos had been with the translucent bear. Juvssut left the round-up fence but remained close by to guard him.

A woman, a real woman—that is what Rásttos needed. But where would he find one? He had never been with one. He was good looking enough and wealthy, too, but seemed to have some strange traits which made women hesitant. As if he had always been affected by the forest. If that was the case, then there was no way to help him, only to let him play with the bear woman until he came to his senses. But if he did not? What then?

She could not talk to Rásttos' old, crippled father. She could have talked to Rásttos' mother; she had been a woman with the skills of seeing. But Magga had died when Rásttos was only a little boy.

Those days people claimed to know everything. For them, the forest was no stranger place than a living room. There were no spirits and no invisibles. Everything had been explained to such an extent that Rásttos would end up being locked up if he told anybody of his experiences.

Just as well they do not know, sighed Juvssut. Rásttos was not deranged at all, far from it. It was difficult to find a smarter young man around here. It was not insanity if one could survive in the forest. And it was not insanity that Rásttos had met the bear woman.

The marking of the reindeer calves was long and arduous. So Rásttos did not have time to go up to the Seaibi Mountains again. He was bored and was not able to sleep properly. At night he could feel the bear woman's hands stroking his chest. He dreamed of the deep bond he felt when he was swaying with the bear woman. Was the bear woman calling him? Even if she was he could not go to her.

Winter arrived. I could not stay at home but walked over Reatka Hill. I reached the fallen tree and looked for bear tracks. There were no tracks and no sign of the bear woman. Was her den somewhere nearby? Could I find it?

I started to yoik; perhaps the bear woman could hear me. Gradually I raised my voice. But the forest was quiet. Only thrushes screeched on trees nearby.

Where was the bear woman? Had she abandoned me and left for other places to find other young men?

I became furious and clenched my fists. I had thought that the bear woman would be with me again. I felt anger. I felt the bear woman had betrayed me. I grabbed a branch from the ground and hit the trees with it, yelling and roaring like crazy. I crashed about until I calmed down and my fury was replaced by sorrow. A screaming loneliness filled me and I felt completely alone in the world. I had not felt this kind of sorrow since my mother's death. This time the sorrow seemed to be even deeper, drowning me.

I was drenched with sweat as I finally lay down feebly on the cold ground. I opened my arms and looked up at the sky where bright northern lights started to appear. My anger and sorrow had disappeared.

After a long while Rásttos sat up and forced himself to stand— it was not good to stay in the forest, lying on the ground. He had to leave, go back to his people and live there. It was a clear night with snow on the ground so it was easy to follow his previous tracks.

He arrived on Reatka Hill and set out towards the valley of Juniper River. Then he saw, or rather felt, that something was moving on his right side. He stopped.

The bear woman stood beside him and smiled! She came to Rásttos and licked his face. Rásttos stared back at her shining black eyes and his willpower drained away. He followed the bear as a tamed reindeer bull follows his owner. He did not look where they were going nor counted how many knolls they had crossed. Finally they arrived at the den that Rásttos recognized as the bear's winter den.

The woman took the bear fur away and stood in front of Rásttos, breathing spirits at him. He embraced the woman and lay down with her on the ground. They embraced each other once more, met in a deep bond on a light boat, swinging, clashing onto each other.

When I returned after three days, the old woman Juvssut ran towards me. I did not understand her behaviour but I did not push her away either because she had always been my neighbour. I had learned to respect and like her. I let her take me to her house.

"This is not good," the old woman said. "Do you understand what I'm talking about?"

"Of course it is good," I replied. "Don't be afraid. I live in the forest and with the forest."

Rásttos did not stay in the forest as Juvssut had worried. He went there but he always came back. One day he told her that he had conceived a beautiful girl bear cub who was now growing up in the bear's den in the forest. The old woman smiled and said: "You weren't meant for a human woman from the beginning."

And now I wait for you, Násttás, my bear daughter who wanders in the endless mountains, falling asleep on a soft moss and briskly running up the slopes of the Tail Mountains. Perhaps you also have found a young Sami man whose wrist you'll grab, whom you'll scare almost to death before showing him the same warmth your mother had; the same happiness and fulfilment that your mother and I found in her den.

In that way continues our life in the forest and with the forest. The life nobody knows. *Only us, you and me, my translucent bear woman.*

Translated from Sami by Rauna Kuokkanen and Philip Burgess.

Björn-Beret

A Norwegian Bear Story

There was a girl called "Bear-Beret" who had been captured by a bear. He took her into his den, and there she lived with him for some time. She had a child by the bear, too, and he took good care of her. Everyday a bowl of milk was put beside her. But one day the bowl was full of blood. Then the bear was shot, and she went back to the village again (Edsman 1956: 42).

From Carl-Martin Edsman, "The Story of the Bear Wife in Nordic Tradition," Ethnos 21 (1-2) (1956): 36-54. Reprinted with permission from the Institute for Language and Folklore, Uppsala Landsmåls-och Folkminnesarkiv (ULMA) (Archives of Dialect and Folklore)1118.3, pg. 13.

SIMA APRAHAMIAN

Running Away With Bears

Armenian Women Transcending Patriarchy

As an Armenian woman and one who has been engaged in anthropological (ethnographic) research to study Armenians in a variety of geographical regions (Lebanon, Armenia, and Canada), I have come across various versions of stories of women running away with bears. My personal interest in these stories stems from my own journey as an Armenian woman and anthropologist learning about Armenian gender identities. I became interested in the stories for several reasons. First, these stories were not part of canonized collections of folk and fairy tales.[1] Second, the stories challenged western Cartesian notions about nature, culture, and gender. And third, the Armenian concept and meaning given to the bear seemed ambiguous as the bear was and is still seen as an ancestor, a prey, a threat, and/or a trickster, and is often ridiculed and feared.

This article is an attempt to interpret Armenian stories about women running away with bears as "spaces" of resistance(s). Based on my fieldwork among Armenians in Lebanon, Armenia, and Montreal, I interpret Armenian stories of women and bears as reflecting the desire to know life outside of the constraints of Armenian culture and its patriarchal nature. My attempt to understand the meanings behind these particular bear stories also drew me to explore the notion of Armenianness, which is embedded in a conceptualization of the Nation as tragic and marked by an unrecognized genocide. My contribution to the theme of women and bears or women as bears is to situate this widely-spread motif in the context of Armenian women's attempts to organize themselves and to find their own "space" in their patriarchal, patrilineal, and patrilocal culture.

The Bear and its Meanings Among Armenians

In the lives of Northern peoples the bear is a pervasive theme. Cutting across the boundaries of Asia, North America, and Europe, the peoples of the North have had a curious relationship with the bear. Among the Ainu in Northern Japan, for instance, there is a dual relationship with the bear. The bear is both a "good" bear and a "rough" bear. Before starting a hunt, the Ainu used to follow a ritual involving a set of prayers addressed to various gods including the bear—the Kamui of Mountains—"the good bear," "which is synonymously referred to as *no-yuk*;

i.e., good-game" (Iromoto 1996: 297). Its opposite was *wen* or bad *kamui*, i.e., the rough, harmful bear, within the context of the actual hunt.

In Armenia, the bear, or *arch*, is a common presence in everyday discourse. The bear is the trickster, the forager, the hunter, the ancestor, the lover of honey, nuts, and fruits. Among the Armenians, the bear is perceived as human and not just "built somewhat like people" (Rockwell 1991: 2). Thus, although bears can be seen as threats and are feared, they are also protected, as indicated in the following report:

> Animals began to give trouble to residents as well. Thus, recently 25 residents of the village of Artsvanik asked the head of the regional administration of Siunik to allow them to hunt the bear and wild boar, which, according to them, get into their orchards and gardens and destroy crops. However, the senior expert for the State Inspectorate of the Ministry of Nature Protection for the Siunik region, Robert Mkrtchian, denied them this right, indicating that the given species of bears (the Caucasian brown bear) is entered in the Red Book and is protected by the state; the extermination of this species is punished by the law and a fine of 500,000 drams is stipulated. As for the damage, Mkrtchian advised the villagers to insure their crops as they do it in case of natural calamities. (Tapan 1998)

In Armenia the bear is not simply prey, as can be the case in different cultures, but rather has divine qualities:

> The bear had always been considered a beast of prey; it attacked people and the other animals. The God of the Earth punished it for that, cut off its head and threw its body into the sky with the words: "You cannot live on Earth, so live in the sky. If somebody gets lost on a dark night, let him/her find his/her way by your stars." And indeed, one can find one's way by these stars. There are four main stars, and they are located on the sides of a square. Two stars mark the bear's forelegs, and another two its hind legs. And in the middle, a little upwards, there is still another star, which is its neck. The stars have no individual names, they make a whole. (Shaman qtd. in Pentikainen 1996: 175)

In his ethnographic study of the Nagorno-Karabakh Armenians, Stephan Lisitzian (1981) points out that the bear was worshipped by the inhabitants. In the mountain slopes of Dizapayd there is a spring called "*archi aghpouyr*"—Bear Spring—that has become a shrine and a site of pilgrimage. According to Lisitzian,

> One summer day a bear comes out of the nearby woods. Feeling very thirsty, the bear starts to climb the mountain. Unable to continue because of the heat and fatigue, the bear starts licking the rocks and requests help from the heavens. The heavens answer by jettisoning water through the rocks, but

the bear is killed at the same time by lightning. The bear is buried under the cave near the top of the mountain. Pilgrims visit the site, pray, make bone fires, and sacrifice lambs. (57) [2]

In another ethnographic account from the Basin region in Armenia, Hagopian (1974) recorded the following story that shows that the bear is more "humane" than humans:

> Near the Karcloukh–Stonehead mountain top one could see huge stones and rocks resembling camels. The oral tradition tells us that a miserly, unsympathetic merchant and his caravan were passing via Basin to Karine. On the road they meet a pregnant bride who has gone into labour while taking bread to the fields. The helpless woman has fallen on the road with pain. The caravan passes by not only without providing any assistance to the woman, but also making fun of her. Just at the moment when the woman gives birth and is relieved of her pain, a bear comes out of its cave and helps her. The bear licks the newborn's arms and hands, gathers some bush and covers the baby so that it will be warm and then calls for help. At that moment the merchant and the caravan are transformed into stone. (253-254)

Armenian bear stories often come up in hunting stories, narrated by men, in which the bear appears as intelligent, unpredictable, and very human.[3] The bear is also presented as sexual. In these anecdotes the bear appears as the ideal embodiment of sensuality, sexual desire, and sexuality.[4] There are numerous stories of women running away with the bear, where the bear can be seen as the embodiment of women's desire. Each of these stories makes a different "statement" about the bear. The meanings given to the bear by Armenians can be compared to those given to the hyenas among the Beng of the Ivory Coast as analyzed by Alma Gottlieb (1989). One can only make sense of the bear and the multiplicity of the contexts in which it appears in Armenian narratives through the notion of polyphony and a world of Bakhtinian heteroglossia. Armenian meanings given to the bear are reminders that we live in a world containing a multiplicity of viewpoints (Bakhtin 1981).

Among the Armenians the bear is perceived as both good and bad, presented as a "mirror" of the human self, and often portrayed in ambiguous terms. In his studies of the oral tradition of the villages of Artzakh, Nagorny, and Karabakh, the prominent Armenian ethnographer Erouand Lalayan (1988) came across a number of different stories involving bears. In the Vananda Khatchen region, the tradition claims:

> [A] bear has been buried in the churchyard of Ptksaberg. The bear is believed to have brought in from the nearby mountains the huge rocks of which the church has been built. The church was almost completed, except for one last huge stone. After a long search the bear finds the missing block and in the

process gets injured. To this day, the villagers claim to see the blood stains on the stone walls of the church. The bear passes away after helping the master mason put in place the last stone. The master then buries the body near the church. Pilgrims light candles and conduct ritual sacrifices on the stone tomb of the bear. In the same region, the bear was believed to have been a miller. When it had stolen too much, God had become angry and had transformed it into a bear. To prove their point, the villagers say that when a bear is killed, it brings its paws together in the form of a cross. (172-173)

Attributing human traits to the bear is common among Armenians. For instance, Avedik Isahakian, a well-known figure in Armenian literature, suggests that bears do not like those who are not "straight forward" and who have "roundabout ways" in his parable entitled, "The Bear and the Snake" (see Arartian 1987: 47-48). Another example can be found in the parable, "The Lion and the Little Bear" by Armenian satirical writer Nichan Beshigtashlian, in which bears are portrayed as having very bright, critical minds (see Araratian 1987: 57-58).

Women and Bear Stories

There are a variety of folktales transmitted orally from one generation to the next among Armenians that are related to bears and young women. The first Armenian story I heard about a woman running away with a bear was when I was an adolescent. The story was told to me by a woman in her 80s. She claimed it was a true story, involving a relationship between a bear and a young woman. Many years later, when reading Canadian author Marian Engel's novel, *Bear* (1976), I was struck by the similarity of this story to the protagonist in Engel's novel who also falls in love with a bear. The woman who told me this story stressed that this had transpired in her own life time to a woman she had grown up with in her native Armenian village:

There was no running water, at the time. One had to get water from a spring. Usually, getting water from a spring or source was the responsibility of women and young women used to go in groups to get water from the spring. The process of bringing water in clay containers from the major water source of the region was a fun ritual. The women used to be relaxed and would sing popular songs. A bear who used to drink water from the same spring, and liked to hear the young women sing, had apparently fallen in love with one of the young women. Then one day the bear, it is believed, abducted the young woman.[5] Her family and friends searched for her in vain. Most people forgot about the incident and everyone went about their everyday routine as usual. Years passed by. The woman's brother continued the search. After several years the brother found his sister. To his surprise, the woman had given birth to little furry children with the bear. She seemed to be happy with the bear. The brother, it is said, became furious at the sight of these in-between beasts and killed them all, and took his sister by force back to culture. In the village, the woman, the story goes, refused to return to "culture." She had lost her speech—she never spoke again and lamented the death of her offspring through wild sounds.

The woman who told me this story emphasized that the woman may not have actually been "abducted" by the bear, but rather chose to run away with it. This story is similar to a number of number of Armenian folktales about women running away with bears, where the notion of desire[6] is about the yearning to be "free," as well as about women's desire to know and unravel their selves and their identities.

Different versions of this story express or dramatize a relationship between "nature" and "culture," deconstructing this very dualism that is inherent in Cartesian logic. The following is an alternative version of the woman and bear story, passed down through generations of western Armenian women:

A beautiful young woman goes to gather wood for cooking. After preparing the bundle of wood, the young woman, while trying to carry it on her back crashes under an unusual weight. When she turns her head to see what this extra weight is, she catches glimpse of a bear holding her back. The bear carries the girl to the mountain, to its den. The two fall in love and the woman bears three furry babies. After a few years, her brother finds her. He kills the furry babies and forcefully returns his sister to the village. The young woman refuses to speak and laments the loss of her children.

Although not all stories involving women and bears focus on the theme of abduction, it is a predominant theme. But there are many that take a different approach. The following is another recorded "true" story, told by Zeynal, a well-known Kurdish leader who collaborated with Armenians at the turn of the twentieth century:

There used to be a very beautiful young woman in our mountains. The young woman was engaged to an equally beautiful (handsome) man. The couple was taking a walk on the mountains and reached the Havlora Mount. They stopped in front of a cave. Just as they were about to kiss, the rock under the young man dislodged under his feet, causing him to fall and die. The young woman started to cry in grief and wanted to throw herself after him. At that moment, a bear came out of the cave, embraced the young woman, and started speaking to her in Zaza—a Kurdish dialect. The bear empathized with the young woman and expressed its condolences. The young woman did not speak Zaza, only Armenian. Nevertheless, she understood what the bear was trying to communicate. The woman asked the bear to retrieve her fiancé's body from under the hill. The bear understood her and retrieved the young man's body. The bear nurtured and fed the young woman for forty days. By the time the forty days were over, the body had decayed. The bear and the young woman then buried the body. The young woman and the bear fell in love and understood each other's language. They became husband and wife and had several offspring who became the patrilineal ancestors of Zaza Kurds. The grandchildren of the oldest son were the Khremnk Kurds and Zeynal was their elder. The younger son's grandchildren were the Demlik Kurds. The latter were more numerous, but were subject to Zeynal's people. This is the reason that the Khoremnktzik have not been allowed to hunt bears.

Killing bears is also taboo among the Khanty in western Siberia, as well as among other northern peoples particularly where the bear "is a representative of a people's godly ancestor" (Pentikainen 1995: 175). The taboo on bear hunting reminds one of the prevalence of this theme of animal-ancestral relations in the context of discussions of totemic[7] classifications.

Armenian bear stories, similar to First Nations stories of women and bears—such as those recorded by Catherine McClellan (1970)—may be interpreted in a variety of ways. McClellan suggests these folktales strengthen the separation between Nature and Culture and serve as teachings about gender relations. However, Georgina Loucks (1985) argues these stories can be seen as questioning the status quo, rather than affirming patriarchal relationships. As Kaarina Kailo (1993) has also shown,

Espousing, becoming intimate or identified with either a She or He-bear (literally, or symbolically) is a major taboo, for this threatens the phallic economy of high/low, human/animal, human/natural, civilized/primitive, natural/supernatural, female/female—perhaps the most hair-raising of all—woman/animal. (116)

It is precisely because of this transgression of nature and culture that Marie-Françoise Guédon (1994), writing about women and bears in her self-reflections on fieldwork among the Dene, stresses: "Women are not supposed to tell bear stories, or even pronounce the name of 'that which walks upright,' 'the big one,' because of the story of the girl who married the bear, and of the story of a she-bear marrying a man" (45).

I read Armenian stories of women and bears—or what remains of them—as metaphors for the loss of true gender complementarity—an application of the Nature/Culture dialectic to Armenian culture. These stories are not just scripts for gender identities, as Peggy Reeves Sanday (1981) has suggested, but are ways of resisting and transgressing the categories of gender, culture, and nature.

Bear symbolism involving women and bears cuts across many cultures. As Lou, the fictive character in Marian Engel's novel *Bear* (1976) states:

Ursus Arctos, ours, orso … inhabits the mountainous districts of the Alps, Pyrenees and Arctic circle. Also Siberia, the Kamchtkan Peninsula and North America. The Laplanders venerate it and call it the Dog of God. The

Norwegians say, "The Bear has the strength of ten men and the sense of twelve." They never call it by its true name lest it ravage their crops. Rather they refer to it as "Moedda-aigja, semen cum mastruca," the old man with the fur cloak. (53)

There are many legends and myths surrounding the bear, all of which transgress the Nature vs. Culture binary. In these stories, the boundaries between human and animal collapse and one transcends the limits of being a gendered being. As discussed earlier, among the Armenians, the bear appears to be "humanized." This, as Paul Shepard and Barry Sanders (1992) state, is related to the physical appearance of the bear and its humanlike upright posture (xi). The bear must learn to become a bear (Swanson 1997: 21), just like humans learn to become Armenian, American, Lebanese, Canadian, or Japanese.

However, among Armenians there is no evidence of the kinds of cults associated with bears that can be found in the neighbouring ancient Greek society, where vases discovered in temples suggest the existence of a ritual involving young girls who "act as bears" prior to marriage:

> During their initiation the young girls dressed in characteristic yellow robes … and mimicked the behaviour of she-bears. Shedding these robes symbolized abandonment of the "bear life" in order to enter a new stage of life, the phase of puberty, to be followed by marriage. (Zaidman 1992: 343).

The bear cult in early Greece has been seen as the socialization and "taming" of prepubescent girls into "nubile" young women (Zaidman 1992: 344). The stories are thus not just about the passage from nature to culture: they defy any dichotomous conceptualization of nature and culture. This is in direct contrast to western thought and the Judeo-Christian tradition, as has been pointed out by Carol P. MacCormack (1980), that sees humans as different from animals and culture as distinct and contrasted with nature. As MacCormack states: "The female-male contrast can be understood as a further metaphoric transformation of an allegedly universal nature-culture contrast" (1).

It is also believed that human beings, as a species, and through our capacity for culture, have made the transition from nature to culture:

> From our capacity to make discriminations, such as between "us" as a kin category and "other," and our ability to know rules of incest avoidance and marriage exogamy, we are capable of the Rousseauesque social contract in which we give up a state of nature, which means incest and the social isolation of small kin groups, for reciprocating kin ties and social contracts with others. (MacCormack 1980: 1)

For MacCormack (1980), basic human needs are natural and yet with social rules and regulations to control them, the fulfillment of these needs becomes central to culture. Nature itself becomes a cultural category—a concept—and 'nature' and 'culture' become cultural constructs in contrast to each other (1). In western thought, therefore, Nature and Culture have become contrasting dichotomies. Furthermore, western paradigms dictate that men are associated with culture and women with nature. However, this is by no means universal. The Armenians of Anjar, in the Bekaa valley of Lebanon, for example, believe the opposite is true. Men are wild, they need to be tamed by women, and marriage is the taming process (Aprahamian 1990, 1989).

Bear Stories as the Desire to Transcend Patriarchy

Among the Armenians patriarchy has become a common-sense reality and expresses itself in the dominance of heterosexuality. In fact, Armenian "nationalist discourses pathologize homosexuality and normalize heterosexuality" (Kassabian and Kazandjian 1998: 33). The Armenian bear stories can be read as scripts that provide a forum or space to literally run away from patriarchal constraints on desire. The young women running away with bears can be also interpreted as a coming-of-age story. Among Armenians in Armenia, as Andrei Bitov has observed (1992: 69-73), children are given complete freedom until puberty. At the onset of puberty, however, children are made "invisible" and treated through strict discipline. The contrast is dramatic and sudden. The young women feel like their "desire is stolen from them ... in order to impose a history or morality in the form of a specific social role or identity" (Gooldchild 1996: 171).

> Through narrating the bear stories women re-claim womanhood as becoming a woman "involves entering the plane of desire completely, like Alice in *Alice in Wonderland* through the looking-glass." In this context, "Becoming ... proceeds by way of a becoming animal. Unlike humans, animals do not participate in the strata of significance and subjectification ... and expressing territories" (Gooldchild cited in Deleuze 1990: 236).

My research on women and bear stories in the Armenian context led me to an examination of Armenian folktales. The folktales and legends that Armenians have included in their canonized versions and published collections do not include any stories about women and bears. The tendency has been to include in the canon stories that put emphasis on androcentric social justice. The best known and most studied legend in the epic of Sasma Tserer-Sanasar Baghtasar, David of Sassoun, Mher (see Der Melkonian-Minassian 1964, 1972), focuses on the theme of justice from a male perspective. Another story that is significant to Armenian identity formation and re-invention is the legend of the crying cliff by A. Leylani (see DerKaloustian 1929: 47-51).

This (crying cliff) rock formation located near the Armenian village of Keboussieh in Mount Moussa used to be a shrine. The belief was that inside the crying cliff resided Conscience, who had come into our world in the form of a beautiful maid, named Tekghin. She had come from a legendary world like a goddess holding a green olive branch and carrying on her shoulder a pot full of the essence of happiness. The path that she had crossed in her journey had been covered with a variety of flowers. However, the cities and villages refused to give this beautiful woman permission to enter. Hit and stoned by the guards of cities, palaces, and villages, Tekghin took refuge in Mount Moussa. In the forest she met her sister Varvara. Together they sung a song that tamed the wild beasts and drove the mermaids, *tsovanushner*, into Mount Moussa where they danced around the two sisters. The rulers and city guards heard of the singing and sent their troops to Mount Moussa. Varvara was killed by the soldiers. The mermaids were transformed into blind *egheramairer* (women who sing at funerals) and the mountain itself was transformed into a dark thick forest. Tekghin had run away and taken refuge in the cliff. Since that time, the cliff with its red tears[9] continues to "cry over the lost Conscience in this world." One day, the people believed, when rulers, kings, and princes no longer exist, Tekghin (Conscience) and justice would again appear in the world (Aprahamian 1990, 1989).

My quest to make sense of the exclusion of the stories about women and bears from the collected canon of Armenian legends and folktales led me to engage in a historical study of gender relations among Armenians and in Armenian mythology. Doing so meant facing a history that for Armenian people has been marked with tragedy and devastation, culminating in the 1915 genocide—a genocide which remains unrecognized and unpunished. In this, self-conceptualization issues of gender and class are undermined, as Micaela Di Leonardo (1984) points out, "The vision of ethnic community or for that matter, 'Nation'… ignores class, regional, demographic—but especially gender-differences within ethnic populations/or a Nation" (229). In addition, the geographic location of Armenia has made it a place where, as Sanday (1981: 231) has pointed out, "The seeds of sexual equality and male dominance existed from the beginning of written history" (231).

As I discuss elsewhere (Aprahamian 1998), gender relations among early Armenians were known to have been complementary (23). Although descent was patrilineal, the head of the household was the eldest woman. The role of the male in impregnation was undermined. Water was considered to be the source of impregnation. This early belief is still present among Armenians. Every year during the second or third weekend in July, Armenians celebrate "Vartivar" (the festival of Water/Roses/and Love) dedicated to the pre-Christian deities, Asdghig and Vahakn. During the celebration young boys throw water on girls and women.[10] During the pre-Christian period great emphasis was put on the link between water and fertility (Tsovinyan 1984: 67).

The pre-Christian belief system involved a series of gods and goddesses headed by Aramazd. The mother of all was Anahit—"*e park azgis mero ev ketsutsich*," the pride of the Nation and the source of its continuity; "*mayr amenayn zgastutiants*," Mother of all prudence; "*shunch ev kendanutiun ashkharhin hayots*," breath and life of the Armenian world; "*barerar amenayn mardkants,*" benevolent for all humanity (Agatangeghos cited in Zaidman 1992: 7a). Among other goddesses there were Asdghig—the deity of love, beauty and wife of Vahakn and Nane—the goddess of wisdom/knowledge and inventiveness as well as of home economics. The name, today, is applied to the grandmother or the eldest daughter-in-law (mother-in-law) of a household. The Armenian woman was "*tan chrag,*" the light of a home: "Armenians believe that woman is the keeper and maintainer of life and therefore she should live longer.... It is cold and gloomy in a house without a woman" (Tsovinyan 1984: 68).

With the introduction of Christianity as a state religion in Armenia in 304 AD, the cults associated with Anahit continued. The early churches were named after women martyrs: Gayane, Hripsime, Marine. Women continued to be significant as public leaders. There are numerous accounts of the importance of women in politics and public life—in particular of aristocratic women. The queen was as important as the king in the monarchy. The emphasis on family values and kin ties reinforced Armenian patriarchal values. The Armenian woman was the head of the household. She was responsible for the planning of the activities related to the maintenance of the household. As such she was also responsible for the division of labour. However, she reached this position only at a relatively old age and through it, she became a source for transmitting patriarchal values. At the same time, against this backdrop of patriarchal values, the bear stories of women running away from culture and male dominance continued to be transmitted orally from one generation to the next.

With the end of Armenian kingdom in 1045 AD, we see the beginning of sub-jugation of Armenian women. During the short-lived Cilician monarchy (ninth century until the fourteenth century), there was a trend toward Europeanization, marked with emphasis on morality and religious piety. However, for Armenian men and women, the "real" transformation in gender relations and identities took place during the Ottoman domination that lasted over six hundred years. During this period, Armenian values became more and more repressive toward young women.

The second half of the nineteenth century and beginning of the twentieth century is marked by attempts of Armenian women to organize for change (Aprahamian 1998).[11] Until the genocide of 1915, Armenian women at-tempted not only to liberate themselves but were also engaged in the liberation struggle of their oppressed nation, conscious that "the liberation of women necessitates the liberation of all human beings" (Rowbotham 1972: 11). In spite of the efforts of many Armenian women to liberate themselves, how-ever, they continued to be challenged by a history of women's oppression in which "Armenian mothers-in-law held power over their daughters-in-law at the behest of a patriarchy that excluded women from positions of authority in community institutions," as well as contemporary version of sexual politics that silenced women in marriage, in relationships, and in community orga-nizations (Avakian 1998: 66).

The story of the Armenian women's liberation movement is seen by many as the "re-capturing" of the pre-Christian and pre-foreign occupation gender relations and identities among Armenians—a state where women were not only confined to the domestic sphere. These discussions, however, do not deal with the continuity of the oral transmission of women and bear stories nor with the exclusion of these stories from the canon of Armenian folktales and legends. The discourse was thus influenced by European values and interpreted as deconstructing categories of gender, culture, nature.

I encountered in my journeys among contemporary Armenian women a continuous re-examination of their history and the history of the European and North American women's liberation movement. It is amazing that in spite of different historical experiences women and bear stories have continued to be narrated and women continue to pass them on even today.

Armenian women are known to have played a significant role throughout history, especially as warriors in the struggles for survival that have marked Armenian history (Darbinian 1993: 6). However, during the post-stateless period from the eleventh century until the present, Armenian women were not allowed to carry arms. Often, women had to disguise themselves as young men to be warriors. When discovered, they were subject to ridicule. The presence of women among the *fidayi* liberation movement during 1896-1907 was considered a bad omen (Darbinian 1993: 6). During Sovietization "women /were supposed to be freed/ from all forms of slavery and humiliation" (Bilshai 1957: 22).[12] However, none of that hope materialized[13] and Armenian women were faced with double standards much like their counterparts in the Soviet Union.

As noted by Ester Reiter and Meg Luxton (1991), Soviet views assumed women and men have quite different natures. This implied a "celebration of femininity" and a glorification of motherhood. During the Sovietization period in Armenia, women entered the labour force as doctors, nurses, engineers, skilled labourers, agriculturalists, etc., and yet continued to be responsible for domestic labour. They became party members, workers, and slaves in their own homes. Men were not expected to provide housework. Childcare remained the responsibility of women. In addition, women were and are expected to please men and obey them, including their fathers and brothers as well as husbands. "Despite a situation where women make up 51 percent of the work force, they continue to be defined in terms of their responsibilities outside of paid work. Thus proposals for restructuring don't seem to take into consideration the impact on women's employment" (Reiter and Luxton 1991: 68). Armenian women themselves maintain and perpetuate these values still today. Not surprisingly, a review of Armenian literature also indicates many assumptions about gender differences as biologically determined and "preclude an analysis of gender hierarchy and male privilege" (Reiter and Luxton 1991: 55).

Women are also perceived in two extreme dichotomies: either as mothers or as prostitutes. As Varsik Mekerditchian (cited in Aprahamian 1998) writes, women are reduced to sex objects in Armenia. An Armenian women's magazine,

Nareg/Narek (the name of an Armenian saint associated with healing), offers the following to contemporary Armenian women:

> Do not argue with your lover. In his presence do not engage in any conversation with others…. Admire him; Be caring; Repeat to him that you love him; Never attempt to discipline him; Sometimes cry in his presence, tears would soften his heart; Whenever he wishes to kiss you, be ready even if you are not feeling well; Be polite and flexible….[14]

It is in this context, then, that stories of women and bears are still being narrated, shared, and re-narrated among Armenian women.

During my recent visits to Armenia, I often received contradictory messages from the women I encountered. Women with post-secondary education still wish to please men. When a man enters a home, he is surrounded with caring women who give him all their attention. Young women do not wish to give birth to female infants, and pray to be "blessed" with male children. At the same time, however, women recognize the need for women's grassroots organizations to improve their lives by providing resources to support the inclusion of women in diverse work-related, professional, and political sectors. Armenian women also continue to give priority to the liberation struggle of the Armenian people. There is a strong belief in a moral imperative to alleviate the pain that has befallen the nation and to be collectively strong in order to heal. Although women are still invisible in the current public arena, it should be noted that Armenian women have always been at the forefront during times of crisis—from the 1988 earthquake to the uprisings in the early stages of the Nagorno-Karabakh movement (Aprahamian 1998). Despite having been at the forefront of this movement, however, Armenian women today remain relegated to the background.

The Armenian women I met during my visit in the summers of 1992 and 1993 felt the need to make themselves more "visible" and were looking for ways to organize and break away from feelings of guilt toward the "moral imperative" put upon them by virtue of the tragedies that have befallen on their "nation" throughout history. As Selma James (1972) states: "Women are finding more and more that there is no way out but a complete change. But one thing is clear. Things can't go on the way they are. Every woman knows that" (79).

During my September 2006 visit to Armenia, much had changed. There were more women's organizations that were present at public meetings including at the Armenia-Diaspora official conference. Nevertheless, in the political sphere women are still not well represented, making up only nine percent of the elected representatives in the Parliament of the Republic of Armenia.

There is much that remains to be explored in Armenian women and bear stories. The details of the Greco-Roman practices, including the initiation rites, need to be studied further. The lack of evidence for Armenian bear cults must also be examined in light of the following: 1) the pre-Christian archaeological material—the inscriptions, writings, and oral history—was systematically destroyed by the clergy and state officials during the early phase of the adoption of Christianity as a state religion (304 AD); and 2) as Chaké DerMelkonian-Minassian shared with me in an informal interview (1999), nineteenth-century Armenain scholars interested in folklore were selective in their collection of the oral histories of the Armenian populations. One of the pioneers in this field was a priest, Karekin Servantzianz. He took great pains to justify that what he was doing would not contradict the Christian and "civilized" vision of Armenians about themselves. Stories about women marrying bears would have been seen as too much of a challenge to the Judeo-Christian patriarchal vision to be included in any collection of folktales or legends.

Other aspects that need to be studied further are the use of symbols in the stories including Armenian notions of water and fertility; the colour red/ blood as a symbol of life along with the colour green; as well as the fertility of the bear, the snake, the moon, and women, each of which is characterized by cycles of death and renewal.

I have suggested in this paper that the Armenian women and bear stories can be interpreted as spaces for resistance in the context of the nation's culture. The fact that they continue to be told, despites efforts to suppress them in the canon, indicates contemporary Armenian women's desire to self-actualize, to move beyond the constraints placed on them by Armenian patriarchal culture, tradition, and family values. The women and bear stories are not only a form of resistance to patriarchal ideologies but also spaces for dialogical thinking outside fixed categories in a genderized, racialized, dichotomized world. Armenian women are protecting these stories, are continuing to pass them down to younger generations, validating and affirming their desire to be free of patriarchal constraints. The She-bear, the Bear/woman goddess, is re-claiming her space and place in time and history, and in today's Armenia.

[1]One can ask: could these stories be seen as a counter-hegemonic discourse against "authority," patriarchy, "canonized" narratives?

[2]The translation from Armenian of this story and others in this paper are mine.

[3]There are many hunting stories. In one such story narrated by Armenians of Mount Moussa in the Beka'a valley of Lebanon, the story is as follows: one day in the homeland of the people when a group of men were in the woods hunting small birds, they noticed a large bear nearby. They hid themselves, as they had no weapons that could help them protect themselves against the bear. They saw through their hiding place how the bear took two large fallen logs and made a bridge (or a crossing) over a deep narrow low-stretch of land between two hills. The men noticed that the bear crossed the other side and returned to the first side again. Afterwards, the bear disappeared. The men got out of their hide-out and removed the bear's bridge to see what would the bear do. To their horror they saw the bear come running holding two young boars. When the bear reached the place where it had put the logs and made the bridge, it looked in great fear. Soon

a group of boars attacked the bear and killed it on the spot. The men watched incapable of doing anything.

[4]In Armenia many tell stories about bears and sexuality. In one version, a French tourist and an Armenian married man have an affair. The next time the tourist comes to look for the Armenian man, he tells her that he is not available, but his brother is. The French tourist asks about the sexuality of the brother. The Armenian man's response is: "Well, my brother, had a relation-ship with this bear once. The bear has been so satisfied that we are getting honey since then."

[5]The abduction theme is recurrent in the stories. I had trouble with the theme. It reminds one of rape and yet when one takes into account that the women prefer the abduction over patriarchy one wonders how to interpret these stories.

[6]In any case, "Desire is collective" (Gooldchild 1996: 196).

[7]The term "totem" derives from a native North American term "*ototeman*," which means "he is my relative."

[9]One has to explore this further. Red tears could very well be menstrual blood.

[10]Throwing water is also common in other cultures. Among the Finns and Sami (Saami) red water symbolizes fertility.

[11]Many women's organizations emerged during the second half of the nineteenth century among the Armenians living under Russian, Turkish, or Iranian domination. The early organizations were calling for equal education for men and women and aimed to liberate women from the repressive domestic sphere. Among these early organizations were: *Azganever Hayuhiatz Miyutiun* (Armenian Nationalist Women's Union); *Miyatzial enkerutiun* (United Society); *Dprotzaser Tiknantz Enkerutiun* (Educa-phile Women's Society). The members of these organizations were of up-per of upper-middle classes. These organizations considered the liberation of the Armenian woman as a pre-requisite for the liberation of the Armenian people as a whole. Other organizations were closely linked to the political organizations that aimed to liberate the region from repressive political regimes. One such attempt was the *Narodnaya Volia* (People's Will) movement.

[12]Lenin's position, as stated in his speech on September 23, 1919, delivered at the fourth Moscow city conference of non-party working women was that, "Owing to her work in the house, the woman is still in a difficult position. To effect her complete emancipation and make her the equal of the man it is necessary for housework to be socialised and for women to participate in com-mon productive labour. Then women will occupy the same position as men" (Lenin 1965: 69).

[13]As Tatyana Mamonova (1984) points out, however, "The Soviet woman is edu-cated in an atmosphere of falsehood. Beginning in childhood she is told that she is emancipated and that she is fully equal with men. Yet she is not taught about her highest function: to give birth to the next generation..... Ideally, a woman is expected to have children, be an outstanding worker, take responsibility for the home, and, despite everything, still be beautiful" (xx).

[14]See Kouyoumdjian (1993) for a critique.

References

Aprahamian, Sima. 1998. "Armenian Women Organizing: Resistance and Change." *Hai Sird* 153 (November): 22-27.

Aprahamian, Sima. 1990. "A Multitude of Overlapping Identities: A Lebanese Armenian Community in the Bekaa Valley of Lebanon." *Armenian Review* 43 (1) (Spring): 67-83.

Aprahamian, Sima. 1989. *The Inhabitants of Haouch Moussa: From Stratified Society Through Classlessness to the Re-Appearance of Classes.* Unpublished doctoral dissertation, McGill University, Montreal.

Araratian, K. 1987. *Hatentir arakner (An Anthology of Rarables).* Antelias, Lebanon: Armenian Catholicosate.

Avakian, Arlene Voski. 1998. "Validated and Erased: A Feminist View 'Back to Ararat'." *Armenian Forum* 1: 61-68.

Bakhtin, Mikhail M. 1981. *The Dialogic Imagination: Four Essays by M. M. Bakhtin.* Ed. Michael Holquist. Trans. Caryl Emerson and Michael Holquist. Austin: University of Texas Press.

Bilshai, Vera. 1957. *The Status of Women in the Soviet Union.* Moscow: Foreign Languages Publishing House.

Bitov, Andrei. 1992. *A Captive of the Caucasus.* Trans. by Susan Brownsberger. New York: Farrar, Strauss, Giroux.

Darbinian, Vladimir. 1993 "Kin azatamartikiner (Women Liberation Warriors)." *Aspar* 1 (1): 6.

Deleuze, Gilles. 1996. *The Logic of Sense.* London: Athlone.

Der Melkonian-Minassian, Chaké. 1972. *L'épopée populaire Arménienne David de Sassoun: étude critique.* Montréal: Les Presses de l'Université du Québec.

Der Melkonian-Minassian, Chaké. 1964. *Contes et légendes arméniens.* Beirut: Editions Kirk.

Der Kaloustian, M. 1929. Siro sgih (Chalice of Love). Beirut: Hraztan Publications.

Di Leonardo, Micaela. 1984. *The Varieties of Ethnic Experience: Kinship, Class, and Gender among California Italian Americans.* Ithaca: Cornell University Press.

Engel, Marian. 1976. *Bear.* Toronto: McClelland and Stewart.

Freud, Sigmund. 1950. *Totem and Taboo.* London: Routledge and Kegan Paul.

Gooldchild, Philip. 1996. *Deleuze and Guattari: An Introduction to the Politics of Desire.* London: Sage.

Gottlieb, Alma. 1989. "Hyenas and Heteroglossia: Myth and Ritual Among the Beng of Cote d'Ivoire." *American Ethnologist* 16 (3): 487-501.

Guédon, Marie-Françoise. 1994. "Dene Ways and the Ethnographer's Culture." *Being Changed by Cross-Cultural Encounters.* Eds. David E. Young and Jean-Guy Goulet. Toronto: Broadview Press. 39-70.

Hagopian, G. A. 1974. *Nerkin Basenin azgagroutyoune ev banahiousoutyoune (The Ethnography and Oral Tradition of the Inner Basin Region).* Erevan: Hayastan Publications.

Irimoto, Takashi. 1996. "Ainu Worldview and Bear Hunting Strategies." *Shamanism and Northern Ecology. Papers presented at the Regional Conference on Circumpolar and Northern Religion, Helsinki, May 1990.* Ed. Juha Pentikäinen Berlin: Walter de Gruyter Publisher. 293-304.

James, Selma. 1972. "A Woman's Place." *The Power of Women and the Subversion of Community.* Eds. Mariarosa Dalla Costa and Selma James. Bristol, England: Falling Wall Press., 57-79.

Kailo, Kaarina. 1993. "Furry Tales of the North—A Feminist Interpretation." *Simone de Beauvoir Institute Bulletin*: 104-126.

Kassabian, Anahid and David Kazandjian. 1998. "You Have to Want to be Armenian Here: Nationalisms, Sexualities, and the Problem of Armenian Diasporic Identity." *Armenian Forum* 1 (1): 19-36.

Kouyoumdjian, Rita. 1993. "Narek te pornekagroutyoun? (Narek or Pornography?)." *Horizon* 14 (46) (April): 7-18.

Lalayan, Erouand. 1988. *Collected Works. Volume 2.* Erevan, Armenia: Academy of Sciences, Institute of Archaeology and Ethnography.

Lenin, Vladimir I. 1965. *On the Emancipation of Women.* Moscow: Progress Publishers.

Lisitzian, Stephan. 1981. *Lernayin Karabaghi hayere (The Armenians of Mountainous Karabakh).* Erevan: Armenian Archaeology and Ethnography Institute.

Loucks, Georgina. 1985. "The Girls and the Bear Facts: A Cross-Cultural Comparison." *The Canadian Journal of Native Studies* 5 (2): 218-239.

MacCormack, Carol. 1980. "Nature, Culture and Gender: A Critique." *Nature, Culture and Gender.* Eds. Carol MacCormack and Marilyn Strathern. Cambridge: Cambridge University Press. 1-24.

Mamonova, Tatyana. 1984. "Introduction: The feminist movement in the Soviet Union." *Women and Russia.* Ed. Tatyana Mamonova. Boston: Beacon Press. xiii-xxiii.

McClellan, Catherine. 1970. *The Girl Who Married the Bear.* Publications in Ethnology, no. 2. Ottawa: National Museum of Civilization.

Pentikäinen, Juha. 1996. "Khanty Shamanism Today: Reindeer Sacrifice and its Mythological Background." *Shamanism and Northern Ecology.* Ed. Juha Pentikäinen. Berlin: Mouton de Gruyter. 153-182.

Reiter, Ester and Meg Luxton. 1991. "Overemancipation? Liberation? Soviet Women in the Gorbachev Period." *Studies in Political Economy* 34 (Spring): 53-73.

Rockwell, David. 1991. *Giving Voice to Bear: North American Indian Myths, Rituals, and Images of the Bear.* Colorado: Roberts Rinehart Publishers.

Rowbotham, Sheila. 1972. *Women, Resistance and Revolution.* London: Allen Lane, The Penguin Press.

Sanday, Peggy Reeves. 1981. *Female Power and Male Dominance: On the Origins of Sexual Inequality.* Cambridge: Cambridge University Press.

Shepard, Paul and Barry Sanders. 1992. *The Sacred Paw: The Bear in Nature,*

Myth, and Literature. New York: Viking.

Swanson, Diane. 1997. *Welcome to the World of Bears*. Vancouver: Whitecap Books.

Tapan, Noyan. 1998. Groong Armenian Network. August 21. Online: <http://groong.usc.edu>.

Tsovinyan, Tsovinar. 1984. "I'm from Armenia." *Women in Russia*. Ed. Tatyana Mamonova. Boston: Beacon Press. 67-72.

Zaidman, Louise Bruit. 1992. "Pandora's Daughters and Rituals in Grecian Cities." *A History of Women in the West I: From Ancient Goddesses to Christian Saints*. Ed. Pauline Schmitt Pantel. Cambridge, MA: Harvard University Press. 338-376.

Eden Bare Poem

In Eden Bear and woman
sleep in each other's arms
Under a Maple tree in bloom
They share a common bond of love

In the garden of Eden
A Maple tree, a bear
and a woman, bare
As they unmask, rediscover a bond of blood,
They unveil and expose their essence.
Devoid of pretense, unafraid
They are linked by blood
Having to face their Creator

In Eden, Maple trees, Bear and woman
share the secret of the life of blood
Out of Eden; Their hearts are heavy
Their eyes cry! Their souls mourn!

Out of Eden! In the cold world
Blood is spilt. Blood of death.
Blood gushes and splatters!
As a bullet hits a child, a woman, a bear.

As one generation after another
wastes blood.
In the name of righteousness
They wear they say the mask of truth.
Invoke the Creator by name.
Secretly worship the destroyer.

Their words are from the lips

Under their mask ugliness lives
their secret is revealed.

They are not thankful for life
They lust over Creation.
They need to conquer
To rule over the world.
They act as though
They have dominion over life
Dominion over death.
These monsters would be godlike.
Yet in their world God is dead.
Because they are killing nature
in the name of the Creator.

In Eden bear and woman
Sleep in each other's arms
Under a Maple tree in full bloom
They share a common bond of blood.

Out of Eden, Tree, Bear, and Woman
Eden is in their soul.
Because they remember
the sacredness of blood.

For woman blood is sacred
Out of her blood comes life.
In the veins of bear also
flows life.
And Bear is a fierce protector of life.
Oh! But what about the tree
it has no blood.
What about the tree
The tree has no blood only sap.

The sap is sacred
In the Maple tree
and promises new life.
As spring warmth comes back
and flows, then is heated
Sap changes into a syrup
that points to sweetness of life

A woman in the throws of passion

and as the blood rushes in her veins.
Her body releases a sweet smelling sap.
That is as sacred as life.
Woman and tree share a bond of life
Live by the laws of Creation in Eden
In Eden, in their oasis, God and Goddess
are alive.

Day and night act as life and death
So Bear, woman and tree
Each day as they wake to life
and are in awe
They offer thanks
Because they remember they are not eternal.

They dream, they visualize
They feel, they hope that one day soon
Eden will be at hand.
At midnight on a summer's day
Listen to the trees whilst they pray
Look at bear offer thanks
See woman whisper
Feel the wind carry her words.

In Eden bear and woman
sleep in each others' arms
Under a maple tree in full bloom

Dedicated to Kaarina Kailo, my inspiration.
March 28th, 1999.

JÜRGEN W. KREMER

*Bear*ing Obligations

1

Raven scouts. Among the Germanic-Nordic peoples Raven flies as emissary by the names of Huginn and Muninn—Intent or Consciousness or Mind, and Memory. The Twin Ravens of the shaman. The shaman transforming into Ravens. The Ravens transforming into shamans. Twinship indicates a special relationship between the realm of humans, animals, and spirits. It also indicates the internal, integrated dual aspects of the shaman (as mind and memory, female and male, human and animal).[1] Raven assists those who desire and know how to *see*, prophecy, shamanize, sing, make offerings, heal, sit in council in a *seeing* way. Raven is known to be a smart bird, a bird with a long memory. Raven may put a healing leaf on you if you are in need: in *Völsunga saga*[2] Raven brings a leaf to Sigmund who puts it on Sinfjotli's wound, healing it instantly. Raven is also known to have a solar connection. As we travel from the Germanic-Nordic lands of my birth and ancestries farther east raven also appears as Big Raven, world creator and high or primary spirit. Other traditions have different relationships with raven and tell different stories. There are many stories about raven as trickster, for example.[3]

Raven is one of the ways in which we can stay embedded in participatory consciousness: as a scout raven represents the other side, so to speak, the side of what we are embedded into, all the nature relations we are woven into, and Huginn and Muninn speak to us from that other side, truly: that side of *ourselves*. And this *ourselves* is not the egoic, heroic, inflated, or idealizing expansion of egoic consciousness into our nature relations (as control of nature), but the obverse: the remembrance of our consciousness together with all our relations, our relations expanding into our awareness, our participation in their existence becoming conscious. Raven is my way of participating in reality and of telling the stories of my increasing participation as I reconnect and recover my Germanic and Nordic roots and their interconnections with other peoples. This work is done from my current place of settlement on Turtle Island.

So, *Bear*ing Obligations is the story of Raven caring for and carrying a bear story and the obligations that arise from knowing this story.[4] As Raven scouts he brings back a story of bear, a story shared freely and generously with Raven.

My story begins with summarizing considerations of the epistemological framework I am using. It then describes a raven journey to the Arctic North of Europe, where I am told a bear story. The considerations of Ravenmemory receiving and holding this particular story lead to the exploration of some specific aspects of the bear in Eurasia, particularly the bear's thumb, bear twins, and the bear oath. The older layers of the relationship between bear and raven lead into a discussion of the presence of the bear in Old Norse mythology. A personal dream is part of the final reflections of the meaning of the bear, particularly the she-bear, for today. Reflections on gender identity are woven throughout the story as part of the remembrance process.

2

I know of many ways to tell a story. There are so many. At one end of the spectrum we have stories that don't appear to be stories at all, the stories each of the euro-centric sciences tell, for example. Then we have the scientific story of evolution, which is much more of a conventional narrative than is apparent in most other scientific knowledge. At the opposite end of the spectrum we have stories that are sorted in the possibly interesting, exciting, entertaining, or educational, but definitely also dubious category of fairytale, folktale, myth, and the like.[5]

We can read stories that clearly appeal to our linearity and our cognitive minds in the purest rationalistic forms we can imagine. And we can also read stories that confuse the logic of linearity and reach deeply into less linear apprehensive capabilities. The observation that we live in a storied universe has the double valence of being all too obvious (thus trivial) and being profound. Its valuation depends on, or is correlated to, whether we relate to the narrative universes we live in primarily as a world of rights or primarily as a world of obligations: if we live in a narrative universe of civil rights (as they have emerged as part of modernity), then the narrative aspect of reality is not particularly meaningful. However, if we live in a world where law and ethics express themselves more as obligations than as rights, then consciousness of the narrative nature of reality is how such obligations are carried through time, community, land, and ceremony (cf. Peat 1994). Stories tell of obligations. It is obligatory to tell stories. *Bear*ing Obligations is a story that can be located in the process of the participatory mind.[6]

The European Enlightenment Philosophy put the final touches on the development of a non-participatory, dissociative mind process, the enthronement of linear causality, and the imperial grasping of the appearances of reality in a globalizing quantitative reduction (presumably resulting in the control of what is conceived of as objective reality itself). Subsequently, systems theory and various postmodern movements have undermined the sense of reality control that the eurocentered grand narrative attempted to create (cf. longer discussion in Kremer 1986, 1991, 1997). Sandra Harding's (1997) pertinent summary of the situation—"since the perception of scientific claims as universal, objective, and rational is itself locally constructed, not an internal, transcultural feature of any truly scientific process, any appeal to such notions should carry no more authority than the claims can command on other grounds!" (45)—leads us to the remembrance of the local knowledge systems eurosciences were attempting to destroy as their "predatory conceptual frameworks" (Harding 1997: 64) were developing as integral part of the conquest and the appropriation of native cultures.

As the various postmodern challenges result in the beginning breakdown of eurocentered confidence and hubris, a twofold dawning recognition emerges: the realization that indigenous peoples continue to exist contemporaneously without ever succumbing entirely to the colonial and globalizing forces arising from the grand narrative (appearing as crude and brutish economic powers as well as its more subtle educational and purportedly civilizing forces); and secondly, that locality, historical moment, cultural roots may matter more than Enlightenment Philosophy allowed us to acknowledge. In short: all peoples have indigenous roots that may matter more at this historical juncture than even the various postmodern strands are able to see or willing to admit. The critical opposition of postmodernity to the construction of the idealized grand narrative is left behind, before, and beside by the process of the indigenous mind in its two-fold nature: the continued contemporary presence of its participatory process and the recovered presence of participatory consciousness, whether by people with contemporary or recent indigenous roots or with historically more remote indigenous ancestries (such as members of most cultures located in what is now called Europe, and her eurocentered colonial relatives elsewhere on Mother Earth).

This third process—that has always been there—sees itself neither as a member of the eurocentered Enlightenment traditions, nor in postmodern or other opposition to the discursive practices of modernity.[7] Outside of the baits constructed by this particular opposing pair (good subjects of modernity vs. bad subjects deconstructing modernity) non-subjects take care of the obligations they see for themselves. While the third process or indigenous discourse can argue quite powerfully against both positions, it needs to be noted that argument is not its natural mode of conduct. Teaching and learning occurs via modeling, observation, storytelling, and presence (aware living) rather than via direct instruction, persuasion, or argument. The stories of obligations this third process bears can be told, and the fulfillment of the prerequisite personal and collective ceremonial and non-ceremonial endeavours can be shown and shared. While such endeavours are also deep knowing activities, they are far removed from the pursuit of knowledge for knowledge's sake. This process is associated with what Genevieve Vaughan (1997, 2004) describes as gift economy or the criteria Heide Goettner-Abendroth (2004) provides for her understanding of matriarchal societies.

The following table attempts to give a summary of the terms used in this article (they are defined as part of and through the context of my narrative). It is a collection of catchwords given here as indicators for the various processes I am referring to:

Table 1

Eurocentered discourses		Indigenous discourses	
dissociative consciousness		participatory or integrative consciousness	
opposing pair		integrative pair	
first and second process		third process	

Modern Consciousness	Critiques of Modern Consciosness	Recovering Indigenous Consciousness	Indigenous Consciousness
"good subject" of modernity	"bad subject" of modernity	developing non-subject	non-subject of modernity
unconscious of participation in the phenomena	breakdown of un-conscious participation	regaining conscious participation in the phenomena	conscious participation (integrative states of consciousness)
singular Truth	multiple truths	re-contextual-izing truths and Truth locally and historically	locally and narratively contextualized truths and Truth
his-story	her-stories story revealed as his-stories	recovering female aspects of stories; remembering multiformous gender identities	multiply engendered stories: Freyja-Freyr, Nerthus-Njörðr, twins, metamor-phoses, spirit marriages
belief in objective reality	assertion of narrative realities	recovering ancestral narrative realities and anchoring them in present ecology and historical moment	communally and locally anchored narrative realities

Modernity		Postmodernity	Indigenous
emphasis on rationality (rationalism) and science (scientism)	recovery of reasonableness	reasonableness	reasonableness
imperial, masterful, bounded self	non-imperial self, unbounding	re-connecting self	connected self
individualism	individualism	intentional communities	natural communities
belief in progress	progress (albeit questioned in appearance)	linearity struggling for balance	belief in balancing, rather than progressing
emphasis on monocausal, linear explanations	variegated linearity, multicausal, systemic explanations	cyclical linearity	cyclical linearity as explanatory mode
dissociation from nature, community, integrative states of consciousness	suffering from dissociation	recovering participation in the phenomena	participation and integrative states of consciousness
exchange economy	globalization, exchange economy	gift economy	gift economy
colonialism, globalization, missionization	post-colonialism	decolonization	beside, outside and inside of colonization; sovereign imagination of self and community

For a person like myself, the recovery of indigenous mind is the epistemological framework for any inquiries like this one into bear or the spirit of bear.[8] Its fundamental assumption is that the dissociative and pathological, continuous split from aware participation in the phenomena (that is, the unconsciousness of our participation, and consequently the imperialistic and controlling grasping of what is made into facts as they appear at an illusory distance) stands in the

149

way of the resolution of our ecological crises, the discontinuance of colonialism, equitable relationships with indigenous peoples, balanced gender relationships, etc. One of the foundational prerequisites for the renewed participation in the phenomena as we attempt to know and as we live is the remembrance of our indigenous roots, and therefore the recovery of a consciousness process, which can be called indigenous. Thus the process of knowing is not seen as separate from nurturing something or somebody or from being nurtured by knowledge.[9] Healing the split from participation means the inclusion of the history of dissociation as part of any knowing activity (which is in good part the history of the European enlightenment and modernity).[10] Obviously, all peoples have indigenous roots. Contemporary Native people are quick to point this out, and they feel that it is highly significant that so many people who regard themselves as modern, have little regard for or interest in the oftentimes complicated layers of their ancestries. It is not just a matter of integrity in relation to Native peoples that obliges us to step out of dissociative epistemologies, but it is even more the obligation to knowing and nurturing without denial that forces us to seek the reconstruction of participatory knowing.

Stories told in this mode are not primarily evidential, they are much more injunctive: guidelines for narrative and ceremonial participation in a culturally specific world at a specific time and place. Bearing obligations. Carrying out obligations. Celebrating them. Dancing them. Feasting. Justificatory or evidential cognitive moves (causal explanations, proofs) in the abstract are not primary. Justification and evidence consist in the more or less successful pursuit of a nurturing conversation that consists of the balancing of human beings within and without, between each other, balancing them with place, with story, with history, with ancestry, with animals, with plants, with the time cycles.

Healing—in the indigenous sense of the Indo-European root word *kailo*, whole and holy—is just one particular aspect of this indigenous conversation with all beings (spirits).[11] Healing, making sacred, wholing is necessary when things are particularly out of balance, when there is individual sickness or collective imbalance, wounding, or illness. But carrying out obligations on an ongoing, day-to-day basis by aware participation in the nurturing conversation is also always healing, staying in wholeness, staying in relation, staying in participation—it is maintaining sacredness where everything is sacred, and where the split into secularity is imbalance, illness, and pathological dissociation.[12] In indigenous understandings healing and the enacted knowledge of creation and origin are not separate; in a most profound sense healing means to put oneself at the place of creation and to track one's steps from there. This is the work of remembrance of the she-bear, the bear ceremonial, and the twin ravens.

Thus the goal of the indigenous consciousness process is not knowledge or the justification of abstract theories. Even modeling is not its goal, though each instance of the presence of indigenous mind is also a model. The goal is balanced living, becoming present and being present in a particular place and at a particular time to the obligations that arise from one's being there (no matter how we may construe our getting there in the first place). Knowing and being in this way is a participatory activity (participatory with everything that surrounds us) that properly should be written as one word: beingknowing. "[Elders] learn the earth's secret language by quietly observing. It is a secret language called knowledge that releases the spirit from stone and heals by tone of voice and by changing sickness into elements that flow instead of blocking life" (LaPena 1998: 18). The participatory aspect refers to the processual fact that individuality or personality does not find its boundary in the thickly encapsulated egoic consciousness or self of eurocentered construction, but individual consciousness extends through permeable and fluid boundaries of self into the consciousness realm of other beings, whether human, animal, plant, rock, or star (and vice versa!). The goal of the nurturing conversation is the fulfillment of obligations, because happiness and balance, health and fulfillment are the likely results of such endeavours and presence.

The distinctions between the various postmodern consciousness processes and the recovery of indigenous mind process are important, especially since they are emerging historically during the same time period and share certain similarities (see also Table 1). Wisława Szymborska's (1995) poem, "Conversation With a Stone," illustrates the major distinction between the indigenous mind process and the dawning of ancient memories during the postmodern critique of modernity quite precisely:

"You shall not enter," says the stone.
"You lack the sense of taking part.
No other sense can make up for your missing sense of taking part.
Even sight heightened to become all-seeing
will do you no good without a sense of taking part.
You shall not enter, you have only a sense of what that sense should be,
only its seed, imagination." (32)

The various postmodern critiques contain the seed of participation: imagination. Indigenous consciousness, however, is the actuality of the sense of taking part. It is the practice of the nurturing conversation and ceremonial balancing in beingknowing.

This particular story of *bear*ing obligations is told in the framework of participation, however constrained by the given format of the printed page. Stories told in this way have to be anchored in the personal and cultural weave of the storyteller.

There are—at least—two catches to telling a story in this way: the first is our eurocentered obsession with linear monocausality, and the second our obsession with abstraction.

Our predominant monocausal thinking habits (even when our dreaming, our somatic experiences, our reading of mythology put us in touch with other modes) lead us to think of remembering raven or bear as a simple intent reaching from us as agents into the remembered realms of raven and bear stories and ceremonies, reaching into older realms of histories, places, or ecologies. While we can ultimately only write and authorize from the perspective of human consciousness and individuality (even when there are moments where we may feel as nothing but the scribe in a much larger script), it is easy to overlook a crucial facet of participatory consciousness: as embedded awareness it is part of a multicausal weave making the remembrance of raven and bear, put simplistically, a two way street. It would be more accurate to speak of such a process of remembrance as a woven or networked multicausal process with many intentional origins, meeting points, causes, and effects. To write in such a fashion in the English language is near impossible, since its noun and action-oriented structure is most suitable for the expression of monocausal linearity and objectification (Alford 1980; Bohm 1980: 32ff.). Indigenous languages are generally, and naturally, closer to the expression of this participatory mode (see Hinton 1994 or Whorf 1956 for examples). Other than that what truly matters is the lived practice of the quotidian of participatory consciousness.

The eurocentered obsession with abstraction is a little easier to address. We value the summarizing abstract concept that pulls everything together, that strips what we see of what is considered non-essential. This is one of the things that makes it often difficult to learn indigenous languages; they are steeped in the specificity of observation and knowledgeable ongoing participation in the lives of all our relations (the rich Sámi vocabulary for snow, reindeer, and various features in the landscape may serve as an example here). The bear or the cave bear or the bear ceremonial are abstractions that leave out the specific adaptations, the specific nurturing conversations of bear, cave bear, and bear ceremonialists in a particular ecology and at a particular time. While such abstractions can be useful and reasonable for certain purposes, they can also lead us to disregard what is its ceremonial beingknowing practice: the celebration and enactment of an ecologically, historically, and communally specific understanding of balance. It is not that abstractions per se are inevitably bad, however, their reification and hypostazation increases normative dissociation.

We desperately need images that remind us of balanced ways of being (such as the she-bear). With it comes the obligation to take care of the power, gift, and memory contained in it. We need to unfurl the rich and diverse knowledge contained in such abstract seed images to its full extent. If we don't come to understand our own historical obligation to the bear as who we are individually and culturally, as people living in particular places (Standoff, San Francisco, Utsjoki, Archangelsk, Ottawa…) and carrying particular cultures and ancestries, we continue to act and think in the mindset of modern or postmodern consciousness. Then we are wasting the power not just of an image, but we are violating what it means to participate in the awareness of bear ancestry—in short, bear abuse. Without this part the full power of the image cannot come to bear. Indigenous consciousness and recovered indigenous consciousness means that we don't just know where we stand in relation to the bear, but that we are willing to heal the splits we have suffered so that we can be with, know, and celebrate with the bear again. Bearing obligations. Then the bear is not a symbol, but the bear spirit is invited to become part of our presence.[13] As long as we talk about the archetype of the bear only we remain within the psychological realms of modernity and postmodernity.

And then there is this: I can only tell my story of raven learning about bearing obligation in the fragmentary, tumbly way it is coming to me; images juxtaposed with bits of stories; abstract and concrete intermingling; storytelling and reflection, commentary interwoven. The Ravenstory of bear exhibits the scars of colonizing history. For me bearing obligations means sitting with all this jumbled material. Sitting with it as a man. One part of a raven pair. In 2008. It means while talking about the bear I need to tell it as raven and the particularity of my autobiographical context. There are many ways to tell a story. This telling happens outside of what good subjects and bad subjects deem necessary when talking about bears.

3

Scouting Raven, remembering Raven, Muninn, travels northward. Toward northern Europe, the Arctic. His mission is an old trade, an old exchange of knowledge. He had remembered a calling from childhood, a calling that was connected with illness. Before he had found ways to answer this call he had migrated to Turtle Island to seek healing for the wounds he carried in his body from Hitler's abuses of the old stories in his place of birth in Northern Germany, along the Elbe River, where the Myrgings had lived two thousand or so years ago; and where way before that reindeer hunters had populated the banks of the gigantic river close to the southernmost reaches of the ice sheet 10,000 or so years ago. He had given away, fasted, and remembered Muninn inside of himself. He was now following the guidance Ravenmemory provided. Such travel is different from tourist travel. It is travel with story, dream, ceremony, travel with relations. It is movement not in isolation, but movement in interconnection. Presence to interconnection (for details of this story see Kremer 1997a).

This particular ravenstory begins on Turtle Island. The dominant, eurocentered story of the origin of Native American peoples tells us about their travel across the Bering Strait some 20,000 or 30,000 or 40,000 years ago (and this date seems to get pushed back further and further, see Stannard 1992).[14] This is contrary to the stories of many Indian tribes that tell of their presence in a particular place since earliest memory. The most significant issue here is not whether, who, when, and how many people actually came across the Bering Strait at various times, but whether this particular aspect of evolutionary thinking is used in a racist fashion to justify (implicitly or expicitly) the European colonization of Turtle Island, the genocide of Native American tribes (and, yes, all the other issues are significant issues subsequently). The full story of human migrations will only be told again once the stories of all the Native American tribes can be heard as true stories (no longer to be dismissed as self-delusional folklore). The eurocentered way of telling the story of evolution is shaped into neat linearity and monocausality ("out of Africa").[15] However, this particular telling, at least in its eurocentered version, dismissively excludes much material that is deviant. We have the Hupa Indian story of having been in their particular place on the Klamath River of Northern California for always. We have the Hopi story of migration way eastward (the lost white brother, *pahana*, who carries a part of the prophecy tablet) (Waters 1963). We also have Hopi stories about their emergence in South America (Blumrich 1979). We have Navajo stories of travel westward across the Bering Strait. We have sculptures in Mesoamerica and South America that indicate contact with people from the Middle East, Africa, China, and Europe. The list of deviant facts is too long to give in full detail (cf. Kremer 1998 for further details). We have the Olmec sculptures in what is now Veracruz on the coast of the Gulf of Mexico that clearly show an African connection. In the Huasteca region, especially among the Totonac, pole dancers to this day perform what appears as an acrobatic feat but is in its essence the celebration of an ancient calendar as the ceremonialists slowly revolve and descend around the center pole. The Azteco-Mayan calendar does much more than our 365-day calendar. It also pays attention to much larger cycles or the turning of the ages. During the time of preparations for my trip north I also had the opportunity to watch this ceremony.

And on the other side of the ocean, not far from the farthest reaches of the Mexican Gulf Stream, I found a petroglyph depicting just this very ceremony. As I was doing my ceremonial work on my northerly travels it became apparent that this was my stepping stone on my return from Turtle Island to the north of Europe as I was deepening the remembrance of my roots. I had read the description of where to find this particular petroglyph. I had seen the image reproduced in some guidebook, but had not found it among the major rock carving sites of Bohuslän, Southern Sweden. I inquire at the museum in Tanum. Nobody really seems to know. After a while I manage to obtain some vague directions to the site. It is raining hard as I walk for a mile or so in rubber boots and rain gear across harvested fields and through small stands of trees. No sign of the petroglyph in question. I return to the museum and ask for more specific directions. People dig into the archives to get me more details. I notice how this deviant fact has been the hardest to find of all the rock carvings I have been looking for here. It becomes clear that I had been in the right area, in fact, that I must have been very close. I return and manage to find this extraordinary rock carving.

The image of the tree from which the *voladores* are descending is the central part of a rock-carving panel that is 9 x 6 meters in size. It is very low on the ground as the field descends into a small riparian valley. As I am recovering my own interconnectedness it is my obligation to honour the interconnections that have been there before. While my mode of travel between continents on this occasion has been by plane and car, this movement as an aspect of my participation in the nurturing conversation obligates me to make an offering at this juncture as a way of getting from here to there in ancestral, participatory consciousness. I *blót* and chant.[16] I see ancestors responding to my *talk*, a talk of *count*ing the ages in the old way and *recount*ing old interconnections.[17] What is at work is a raven chant, Ravenmemory Muninn struggling for awareness of the account in front of him.

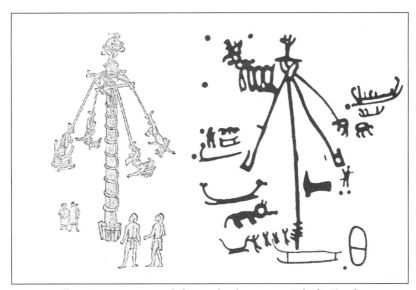

Illustration 1: Mexican voladores and rock carving in Bohuslän/Sweden

I went from Germany to Turtle Island to heal my personal wounds of disconnection from my shamanic and indigenous roots; now I have to travel in full awareness of where the healing process has brought me.

4

I have arrived in the North, one of the places where the Nordic or Germanic people had cultural exchange with the Sámi people. As linguistics show, these exchanges go back at least to post Proto-Uralic times when old Indo-Iranian idioms were adopted in the Sámi language, after 4,000 BCE (Sammallahti 1990, 1998). The woman across from me is a Sámi *noaidi*, somebody who practices seeing with the drum as the Sámi people and their ancestors have done for hundreds and thousands of years (as indicated by rock carvings). This practice is also known for the Nordic people as well as pervasively for all the indigenous neighbours east of the Sámi people (Bjarnadóttir and Kremer 1999). The *noaidi* tells her version and seeing of a story of *Father Bear and the Daughter of the Forest Spirit* (Kallio 1995).

This is a story from the Sámi and Samoyed tribes about the ancestor bear that has been preserved especially among the Samoyed tribes.

The bear is big and strong. The bear is very clever. Powerful bear, the old tradition tells, is Máddu (the root, the origin) or Máttar (ancestor) of the northern tribes. The Sámi call the bear Áddjá (grandfather) or Áhkku (grandmother), and the Samoyed tribes—the Enets, Nenets, and Nganasan—call him, for example, Ihčče (which is the same as Sami Áhčči, father). The bear has many names and has always been shown the greatest respect. One other name for the bear is Luoðuid Eadni, the mother of the wild. The Green Daughter of the Forest Spirit is called Pynegusse in the Samoyed language, and *Ruonánieida* or *Ránanieida* in *Sámegiella (meaning Green Daughter or Girl)*.

Long ago the brown Father Bear *(Ihčče)* and the beautiful Green Daughter of the Forest Spirit *(Pynegusse)* got married. When the frosty winter came they went to sleep the heavy winter sleep through the long, thick winter darkness in Father Bear's warm lair.

When the mild spring came and the bright light shone again, then the first human beings were born. They were quite small and naked. The Father Bear and the Green Daughter of the Forest Spirit took care of the small human beings and nurtured them well. And after that more human beings were born and they all lived peacefully and happily in the green, protective lap of the Forest Spirit for a long, long time.

But then, suddenly, strangers came to the land of the Father Bear and the Forest Spirit, and the strangers had sharp weapons and drank blood. They went to Ihčče—the Father Bear—and demanded bread. But Ihčče gave them stones instead of bread. Then the strangers went back to their father, who was Kristus and who had taught them to drink blood, and said: "See, Ihčče gives us stones instead of bread!"

So Kristus sent more people with more weapons back to the land of the Father Bear and the Forest Spirit. And the soldiers of Kristus went to war against Father Bear, the Daughter of the Forest Spirit and their children, and they scattered them. The strangers killed and destroyed. It was a terrible time for the children of Ihčče and Pynegusse.

Ihčče, the Father Bear, was forced to escape, and he went very far, to the other side of the Big Sea. And there the Bear Ancestor went to sleep in the secure lair of the Mountain of Dreams; and there he dreams good dreams for everybody. Pynegusse, the Green Daughter of the Forest Spirit, is patiently waiting for him—she knows that Ihčče, the Bear Ancestor, will awaken and return home when the time has ripened.

Then they will gather all their scattered children and bring them back home into the deep lap of the Forest Spirit.

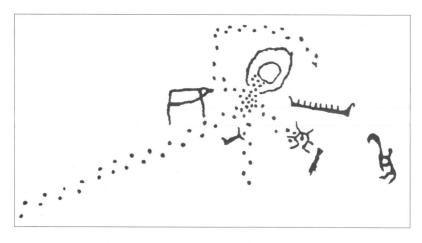

Illustration 2: Rock carving from Álaheadju, Sápmi,
possibly illustrating a narrative of bear origin

I have carried this story with me over the years. Most important in my mind is the question of what it will take to bring the bear back so that all the children can gather again in the participatory process with bear and forest spirit.

The affront and outrage in this story is, of course, that the people of the dominant societies (the Christian missionaries) are given stones instead of bread. The invaders and persecutors of the bear people take this as an insult rather than as what it is also, as the Szymborska poem reminds us: the possibility to reconnect with earliest Earth memories, rock knowledge. Instead of unwrapping this gift they are offended by this confrontation with their own indigenous roots. They act out their dissociation in colonial violence (rather than following the models presented by the figure of Jesus, they enact his patriarchal institutionalization; cf. Ani 1994). The advance of normative dissociation has been illustrated quite pertinently by Samuel Beckett (an important author for some of the deconstructivist literary discussions) through the protagonist of one of his major novels, *Molloy* (1951): he sucks on sixteen pebbles in a carefully designed mathematical scheme—he is so enwrapped in the existential dilemmas of modern being that neither anger about his social condition nor memory of connected knowing are among the responses to his rock intake—he is so far removed from participatory consciousness that all he can be preoccupied with is his abstract scheme rather than the sensory and mnemotic power of the pebbles.

The story the Sámi *noaidi* has told me is of ancient origin. It carries an old seed. It emerges from an old web of knowing and being. But this particular version is not an old story. It is as recent as the beginning of the colonization of the Sámi and Samoyed people and their relatives (cf. Solbakk 1994; Kuoljok 1993). Missionization in Sápmi became stronger during the 1500s. The Samoyed colonization by the Russians was pretty much synchronous. Trading and taxing (single, double, and triple taxation) began in Sápmi around the 1300s. The bear story reflects upon the arrival of the eurocentered mind and consciousness process (at that point primarily in its Christian form). It is a story of the retreat of the indigenous mind.

The nucleus of this story is, of course, ancient: the marriage between the wild woman of the forest and the bear, the wedding with the ancestral spirit, the shamanic spirit connections, the origin of the first humans, etc. (Metamorphoses and mixed marriages are an internationally widespread theme in indigenous stories.) These themes are part of the world of balance and the nurturing conversation. And, in its modern version, the disruption of the ancient way of striving for balance. It leads back to the times of what we have to call the *sacred* hunt—but the word sacred only needs to be added after the split between sacred and profane—a split that did not exist at the times of the sacred hunt, because hunting was done within the context of story, obligation, and ceremony—fundamentally, there was no profane way to go hunting. There was only the hunt and the right and obligatory way to conduct the hunt.[18]

On my northerly journey of remembrance there is no casual listening. I have been given a gift that needs caring. Sharing it, passing it on is one way to do so.

Since I have listened to this story I am bearing an obligation. Just as making an offering at the petroglyph or spirit rock in Tanum is obligatory on my journey of recovery.

In the participatory mind there is no such thing as accidental information. Ravenmemory Muninn scouting is as much intentional as it is being intended, being woven. Hearing a story like the one shared above is a teaching, is guidance; now the story needs to be nurtured, I need to feed the story inside of me. I cannot merely archive the story. It is now part of the relational web in which I am moving. It is becoming part of my remembrance, part of my instruction.

Raven scout Muninn returns from his mission in the Arctic Circle, from among the Sámi people, to his place of settlement, Turtle Island.

5

I grew up with raven. Or more accurately, the absence of raven. A burning absence. It took much preparation, fasting, singing, conversing with my relations, speaking of intentions (praying), to realize what would have been obvious had I been raised in a tribal context: raven was part of my *fylgja*, my company, my follower, my protective spirit (similar in meaning to the Sámi *gázzi* or *kaddz*) (De Vries 1977; Bäckman 1975; Kallio 1997). As I am exploring the older stories of my ancestors and the cultures they were related to or in exchange with, I am finding that raven has been an important presence since long ago.

Most well known from recent mythology and history is probably the connection with Óðinn, on whose shoulders Huginn and Muninn are said to have been sitting according to the Old Norse stories. They were his scouts. He would send them out to survey the battlefields in particular. In the Old Norse and Germanic traditions (also in the Celtic traditions) we find echoes of the connections between ravens and shamans. These echoes are reverberating even through the patriarchal and warrior consciousness of Viking times. In the Elder Edda, we read the following words by Óðinn (here speaking in the form of Grimner, meaning hooded or disguised):

Huginn ok Muninn
fliúga hverian dag
iörmungrund yfir;
óomk ek of Huginn,
at hann aptr ne komit,
ó siámk meirr um Muninn.
(Neckel, 1927: 59)

Hugin and Munin fly each day
Over the battlefield Earth.
I am anxious for Hugin that he returns not
But I fear more for Munin.
(Titchenell 1985: 168)

I have often wondered about the meaning of the last line quoted. Why fear more for Muninn than Huginn? The interpretation I have come to has to do with the increasing danger of losing an understanding of where we come from and what it means to live in that way. Cultural amnesia. This would be the loss of original instructions (Horn 1996; Mails and Evehema 1995),[19] and their celebration, enactment, and embodiment. Maybe the words even reflect Óðinn's self-awareness that he himself is a significant step in the increasing loss of participation and connection to ancient teachings; naturally the fear for loss of memory or losing Muninn would be greater then (alternatively it could signify his fear of loss of control in case he does not have a precise map of even the oldest layers and practices).

Part of my work with Native American Elders and medicine people was purifying my perceptions of spirits by reconstructing their older, balancing, and nurturing function in my understanding. Once I could see beyond the warlike overlay Óðinn had been given during the last one thousand years plus, it became easier to be with raven. It became clear that Óðinn is, of course, an inflated, late appearance of the ancient village shaman, who had now shapeshifted to serve the Indo-European needs for masculinized power and control, seeds that more and more transformed into the eurocentered visions of reality. This is very apparent when we look at Snorri's descriptions of Óðinn in *Heimskringla*:

> [Óðinn] had the skill which gives great power and which he practiced himself. It is called [seiðr], by means of it he could know the fate of men and predict events that had not yet come to pass; and by it he could also inflict death or misfortunes or sickness, also deprive people of their wits or strength, and give them to others. But this sorcery is attended by such wickedness that manly men considered it shameful to practice it, and so it was taught to priestesses. Óðinn knew about all hidden treasures, and he knew such magic spells as would open for him the earth and mountains and rocks and burial mounds. (Sturluson 1987: 11)

This quotation gives us both a sense of the ancient shamanic roots of the Óðinn figure as well as the Christian overlay of the times when Snorri (a Christian himself) wrote this down (the association of the old practices with the devil, evil, and the feminine). It shows the common ambivalence toward shamanism as regards the possibility of harmful interventions by powerful practitioners. And, finally, it alludes to the "unmanly" things that are rumoured to be part of the practice of *seiðr*. To what extent this practice relates to actual sexual practices remains unclear in the literature, but what is clear is that *seiðr* fits less and less the increasingly rigid, dichotomized, and masculinized social understanding of gender roles. Visionary seeing was considered women's business, and something a warrior should not indulge in.

The information from one of the holders of traditional knowledge in Tuva/Siberia was helpful in this process of purification and raven remembrance. He faxed me the following: "*Kuskun.* The raven is the shaman's faithful and favourite informant. The magical quality of ravens is always present. Wooden figures are often carved of the black raven. Because of the bird's vigilance, keenness, and wisdom, shamans wear, as a rule, two raven spirits on their shoulders" (Kenin-Lopsan 1997: 35). An image uncanny in its likeness to the Old Norse depiction of Óðinn.

We find the relationship between the shaman and raven further illuminated in a Yakut story (Findeisen 1970: 159-161) entitled *Der älteste Sohn des "Schwarzraben" vermählt sich mit einem irdischen Mädchen, das daraufhin zwei Rabenkinder gebiert, die später zu Schamanenpriestern werden* (The oldest son of "Black Raven" marries an earthly girl who gives birth to two raven children who later become shaman priests). The firstborn son of Chara-Suorun, who lives in the upper world, gives the woman detailed instructions as to where to give birth to their two children:

> There grows a three-part tree, a larch. Go there and give birth! Two black raven nestlings will enter the world. Barely born, and after emitting raven screams, they will fly away and sit on the lower thick branches of the same larch tree. Then circumambulate the tree three times, hitting it with your undergarments, whereupon the ravens will fall headfirst onto the skin you have spread out.… After only three days they will cry like children, and both will change into boys. The name of the elder is Dshanai-Bytschykyj, and the name of the younger is Öksökülech-Örgön. Once the latter turns forty years of age, he will become a shaman, but the first will become one in his forty-first year. (my translation)

This story allows us to enter the culturally contextualized history of the double raven, in this case as a twin pair of shamans. In this story we find three themes that are relevant for the discussion of gender issues in the context of the recovery of indigenous mind epistemologies: 1) Metamorphosis (fluid boundaries between the human and natural worlds, one particular example or form of participation in the phenomena); 2) intercourse between humans and animals; 3) twins. (These gender-related themes can also be found in the interactions between humans and bears, and will be discussed below. Ravens, like bears, do not allow easy gender identification.)

Twins have carried a special significance among the peoples of the Eurasian north since ancient times. The special powers accorded to them always have the double valence of being potentially dangerous (especially if not treated properly) or beneficial (thus in some cultures dichotomously seen either as harmful or beneficial). According to Mircéa Eliade (1964), the twins in Indo-European mythologies are benefactors, healing mortals, protecting them from harm, rescuing seamen and so on (cited in Cheavalier and Gheerbrant 1994: 1048). Lidija Ashihmina (1992), talking about Sibirian early history reports that the "specific ritual role of twins in primitive [sic!] family groups is noted by many investigators (A. M. Solotarev, V. V. Ivanov). The majority of peoples thought the unnatural twins' birth to be malformation, and twins themselves and their parents were considered to be dangerous and frightful. The idea that fertility depended on twins favoured the reconsideration of twin rituals in the style of twin and their parents' sacralization. In many cases twins and their parents were associated with animals—it is known that animals are characterized by great fecundity" (27). Of course, among the oldest identifiable layer of Old Norse mythology, the stories and incidents around the Vanir, we find a similar sacredness or specialness in the then acceptable sibling marriage.

In our current sexist times it is difficult to imagine what balanced gender relationships can all look like. It is clear from my reading of the Old Norse records that even amidst the late evidence we find clear traces of an understanding of gender quite different from our own. Régis Boyer (1991) has remarked that the Old Nordic cultures show "a distinct tast for androgynes, among the first of which we must place Fjörgyn(n) (male or female depending on whether we give him/her one or two *ns*[20]), not to mention the couple Freyr-Freyja. This tendency must be an extremely profound one, since it has never disappeared from the Nordic view of the world" (230). It is worthy of note that this Vanir stratum of mythology reaches into pre-patriarchal times when female spirits, especially Freyja (usually called goddess or the great goddess of the north), were highly significant.

Within my own cultural heritage we actually find one poem that seems to give us one of the seeing or scouting reports the twin ravens were known for. This Eddic poem is entitled "Forspjallsljóð" or "Hrafnagaldr Óðins"—the Prophecy or the Magic Song of Óðinn's Ravens.[21] When I first worked my way through the poem, however, it struck me that the origins of this poem must be very old, something which I have found confirmed since.[22] This poem can be considered the report of Huginn's and/or Muninn's *seeing*. It is a prophecy about the renewal of the Earth Spirit (*Jórunn* reborn as *Iðunn*), a *ragnarök*, a fateful moment for those who reign (*ragna* from *regin*, *rök* meaning fate, lines of events). According to a number of indigenous stories, calendars, and astronomical observations we are approaching just such a fateful time as the equinox precesses (cf. Kremer 1998; Bjarnadóttir and Kremer 1999; Colorado 1988 for more detailed discussions). *Ragnarök* is the cyclical renewal that we can relate to the shift in vernal star constellations because of the wobble of the earth axis, and the different meaning each age has (Simek 1995: 330-332; see Kyselka and Lanterman 1976, for a basic explanation of this phenomenon; also De Santillana and von Dechend 1969 and Waters 1975). *Völuspá* gives a vivid description of this time, here in the words of a seeress, a *völva*:

Sól tér sortna, sígr fold í mar,
hverfa af himni heiðar stiörnor;
geisar eimi við aldrnara,
leikr hár hiti við himin siálfan.
Sér hon upp koma öðro sinni
iörð ór ægi, iðiagræna:

falla forsar, flygr örn yfir,
sá er á fialli fiska veiðir.
(Neckel, 1927: 14)

The sun turns black, the earth sinks below the sea,
no bright star now shines from the heavens;
flames leap the length of the World Tree
fire strikes against the very sky.
She sees the earth rising again
out of the waters, green once more;
an eagle flies over rushing waterfalls,
hunting for fish from the craggy heights.
(Terry 1990: 7)

The seeing of the ravens is very similar in content and structure to the *völva's* report that I have quoted first to highlight the feminine side of this endeavour:

Dofna þá dápir,	Then wanes the power.
detta hendr,	Hands grow numb.
svífr of svimi	A swoon assails
sverfl áss hvíta;	the white sword-Áse;
rennir örvit	Unconsciousness reigns
rygiar glyggvi,	on the midnight breath;
sefa sveiflom	Thought fails
sókn giörvallri. (14)	in tired beings. (23)
Riso raknar,	Up rose the gods.
rann álfraudull,	Forth shone the sun.
nordr at niflheim	Northward to Niflheim
nióla sótti;	night drew away;
upp nam ár Giöll	Heimdal once more sprang
Úlfrúnar nidr,	up upon Bäfrast,
hornþytvalldr	Mighty clarion-blower
Himinbiarga. (26)	on the mountains of heaven. (26)
(Hrafnagaldr Ódhins)	(Titchenell 1985: 267-8)

Raven's seeing into the changes of the ages is relevant here if we are to contextualize the remembrance of the she-bear in an indigenous understanding of the cycles of time and changes in the meaning of life for humans. The embattled and shuddering world tree is analogous to the axis around which the *voladores* enact, remember, and celebrate their calendar. This may be why the image of the rock carving where I made my offering was of such obvious significance to the Old Norse. The content of raven's report in the prophecy of *Hrafnagaldr* indicates that its roots are likely to be found in the oldest layers of known Norse mythology, thus reaching into times when the female and male presumably were balanced in a different way. Many prophecies among Native peoples talk about the necessity for human beings to change their ways during the current change of the ages in order for Earth to regain balance and in order to survive (among the multitude of examples see Mails and Evehema 1995). The strengthening and return of the bear, with particular emphasis on the she-bear and other marginalized gender aspects of this presence, can be seen as a timely duty for human beings following the instructions provided by the current *ragnarök*.

Illustration 3: Bear from the Chauvet cave (possibly about 30,000 years old)

The scope of what the raven reports in the prophecy of this magic song[23] can be seen as being equal to the role of raven in the easternmost Eurasian traditions. We find the Chukchi calling Big Raven at times "the outer garment of the Creator" (Czaplicka 1914: 257); they also represent spiritual beings called *viyolet* (assistants) as raven or half a raven and offer to them a share of the sacrifices. The Koryak see Big-Raven as sent by the Supreme Being to order human affairs, "to carry out certain reforms in the already organized universe, and [he] was therefore, so to speak, a reorganizer and first man. He is also a supernatural being and a powerful shaman; and his name is mentioned in almost every incantation in shamanistic performances" (Czaplicka 1914: 263).

Across the sea from the Chukchi we find stories like the following among the Indian tribes of the Northwest Coast of Turtle Island: "When Raven spirit and Black Raven are working this land, they put coves in it where you can come in when it's blowing—a place where you can come ashore.... Just after the earth's crust was formed, Raven made the tree. Why did he make this tree? He made it to shelter us" (Colorado 1988: 50-51). The tree also plays a significant part in the understanding of rootedness, origins, and indigenous sciences in these regions.

From very early on we find raven as part of the landscape of the Eurasian complex. As a twin pair they have carried a particular medicine of *seeing*, a medicine connected to the feminine. This is the place from which I was listening to the bear story, it is the raven context of carrying the story. And bear has been part of this Eurasian complex also.

6

The association between bear and human beings is very old, like the connection with raven. We have evidence of early Neanderthal hominids killing cave bears 49,000 years ago (Erd, Hungary) (Campbell 1983). Ceremonial bear burials found at Drachenloch, Switzerland and elsewhere indicate the bear's early ceremonial significance (Campbell 1983). While we find conflicting interpretations of the evidence, it is nonetheless reasonable at this time to assume that the bear has had a special significance reaching into Neanderthal times.[24] The position it takes in the later cave drawings associate the bear rather easily and obviously with ancient understandings of renewal, reincarnation, honouring of ancestors, and shamanic practices related primarily to people living by hunting and gathering. At least since Irving Hallowell's 1926 publication we are aware of the circumpolar significance of the bear who is clearly an essential protagonist in the indigenous lifeways of the Eurasian complex.

Juha Pentikäinen (1989), when discussing the Kalevala, is among the scholars who have addressed the connections among the peoples of Eurasia. Besides the bear, the elk, or reindeer, and the raven, most obviously, the Tree of Life or "the 'Tree of the World' is one of the most essential elements in northern Eurasian shamanistic rituals" (165) (some scholars suggest bear and elk/reindeer in particular as the older cultural layers) (Ashihmina 1992). In the discussion of the range of sources pertinent to the current discussion, Pentikäinen concludes that "it is more likely that Scandinavian saga literature, the Edda as well as the witches' songs, and ancient Finnish poetry are partial manifestations of folklore and mythology which is common, in part, to northern Eurasia" (173). He then makes a statement that is helpful in delineating the larger context of the "indigenous roots" I am talking about in this article:

The existence of the same phenomenon in ancient Scandinavian epic, in Finnish and Saami tradition, and also among the Altaic and Uralic peoples indicates its great age. The wide distribution of shamanism in the arctic area indicates that it is certainly one of the deepest layers of northern Eurasian culture and may have been practiced by these peoples even before they journeyed to their present dwelling places thousands of years ago. If this is true, the connection would date back four or five thousand years, to a time when ancient contacts reigned between the Uralic and Indoeuropean or Aryan peoples. It is possible, although unlikely, that this does, in fact, indicate a genetic, linguistic, and cultural relatedness extending beyond mere contacts. (Pentikäinen 1989: 192)

The bear is clearly a significant aspect of the landscape of the Eurasian complex. This allows us to discuss the various manifestations of bear together while keeping the difference in ecology and historical time in mind. The general associations of the bear are well summarized in the literature, albeit often in an overgeneralizing and romanticizing manner to the detriment of specific ecological, cultural, and gender critical understandings. Paul Shepard and Barry Sanders (1985) assume some association between humans and bears since about 700,000 years BCE, with the earliest evidence of possible bear ceremonials dating to 40,000 BCE or thereabouts, and engraved objects and parietal art in the Franco-Cantabrian area beginning about 30,000 BCE or so. They assume a bear mother myth and a slain bear ceremony beginning about 40,000 BCE or so. Marija Gimbutas (1974) has provided evidence of the significance of the bear as part of the Old European "civilizations of the goddess," with sculptures dated to the sixth millennium BCE.

From all we have as evidence it seems reasonable to conclude that the bear is an animal that had great significance at the times of earliest reconstructable history, and that this significance was connected in some fashion with an understanding of Earth as mother and provider, with the she-bear as an expression of, and celebration of, this understanding; as such it is also connecting with a human way of beingknowing commonly labelled with the words "hunter, gatherer, and forager." The subsequent shift toward an increasing masculinization of beingknowing and dissociation from the environment is an indicator of the increasing human imbalances and disruptions of the conversation with bear (together with an emphasis on the strength of the bear, and less and less on the performance of bear ceremonials as the bear also synchronously physically begins to disappear in various parts of the Earth). Where we have been able to reconstruct an early understanding of the bear it seems clear that it is associated with a participatory lifeway based in an understanding of the cycle of nurturance, with the ancestral she-bear as a provider as well as a significant connection to shamanic practices. The generalizations just made are dangerous in the sense that they disregard much of the local specificity (crucial for today's ecological healing and balancing), and that they include some bold inferences from what we know from contemporary indigenous people who are practicing (or who have until recently practiced) bear ceremonials. With these caveats in mind we can appreciate these generalizations, and move on to more culturally specific beingknowings of the bear.

For the Western Siberian tribes Ismail Gemuev (1989) observes that humans are transformed into bears after death. Here "the bear was [sic] connected both with the world of the living people and that of the dead, which made the nature of this image dual. Hence the man [sic] had to take special measures so that the bear should recognize him [sic!] as 'one of his [sic] own kind' and should not do him [sic] any harm" (181). Every bear embodies the soul of an ancestor (180).

Éva Schmidt's (1989) discussion of the bear among the northern Ob-Ugrians is an example clearly indicating the rich weave of living and knowing the bear can be a part of. She summarizes her analysis as follows:

> The concepts of the component systems can briefly be summarized under the name "bear," signed "upper (sky)," "lower (earth)," "intermediate (forest-, human-)," "spiritual," etc. The bear vertically connecting all three worlds is a blending of two mediators—namely, 1) of the mediator between the upper and

the intermediate worlds; and 2) the mediator between the intermediate and the lower worlds. In what follows, we shall concentrate on the latter. (190)

Given current gender imbalances and prevalent sexism it seems important to focus on those reasonable generalizations that see the bear associated with Earth, underworld, etc. rather than with Sky (an aspect to which this article does not attend, tempting as the stars are). For the northern Ob-Ugrians Schmidt (1989) points out "that bears with a 'lower,' 'earth' sign have a maternal dominance, while those with an 'upper,' 'sky' sign have a paternal dominance" (196).

In discussing the aspects of the bear that seem particularly relevant in today's recovery process, Schmidt (1989) contends that "the concept of descent from an underworld parent … accounts for the bear's links with everything that pertains to the other half—the dead, the ancestors, spirits, hidden fecundity and rebirth, otherworldly possessions and knowledge, heroes and healers descending to the underworld—in brief, the totemic world-picture" (197). While these excerpts can hardly do Schmidt's work justice, they are a clear reflection of the process of the participatory, indigenous mind. Part of this rich lifeway is an understanding of bear as mother, father, guardian, shaman, ancestor, helper, keeper of the bear oath, hero, etc. Such multiform understanding is an illustration of the multicausal process of the Native mind. While Schmidt struggles to nail (so to speak) the complexities, missing pieces, apparent contradictions into a cohesive whole, participation contextualizes these pieces with precision in the practice of the bear ceremonial.

I want to focus now on three aspects of the bear particularly relevant for my raven explorations: the toe and thumb of the bear, the connection to twins, and the bear oath. Gemuev (1989) has surveyed archaeological artifacts from "Western Sibiria and the Preuralie" where we find images of the bear or bear paws with four toes on one of the front paws. He comments that among the Selkups

in [the] case of a "great shaman" the process of the dead man's [sic] transformation into a bear was accompanied by cutting off the man's [sic] thumb, as according to the early belief that the thumb was a receptacle of soul and strength. (183)

He summarizes his findings as follows (English of the original uncorrected):

The image of four-toed bears (or four-toed bear paws among shaman fetishes) seem to embody the personality of the "great" shaman that has become helping spirit of the shaman possessing these attributes (i.e. the image of the helping spirit merges with that of the shaman ancestor). The fact that the bone of a cut-off shaman thumb was a transmitter of shaman power and strength corresponds (perhaps already in the pre-shamanic period) to the concept of the thumb as of a receptacle of soul and strength. If the dating given by Černecov to the archaeological finds with "four-toed" bear images is right, we must conclude that religious beliefs connected with the bear in the described (or close to it) form were characteristic of the West Siberian population not later than in the second half of the first millennium B.C. Later this tradition penetrated into the culture of subsequent ethnoses (including the Selkups) and came in a relict form to our days. Similarity of details connected with bear cult in the religious concepts of different peoples from Western Siberia to the Far East enables one to think of a certain religious and ideological unity of this vast region's population in the second half of the first millennium B.C. and the beginning of the first millennium A.D. (Gemuev 1989: 183-4)

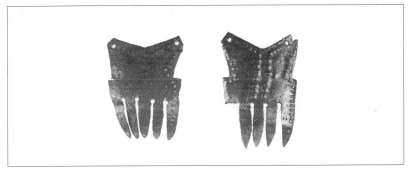

Illustration 4: Bear paws, Evenk shaman sacred objects

The significance of the thumb finds an echo in the medieval literature of both Scandinavia and Ireland, as Hilda Ellis Davidson (1989) points out. Here we find "the motif of the placing of the thumb in the mouth as a means of acquiring wisdom," a "ritual gesture" connected with shamanic seeing (66ff). For example, in *Völsunga saga*, Sigurd touches the roasting heart of the slain dragon, then puts his thumb in his mouth, and immediately understands the speech of birds and receives messages from them.[25] The Irish hero Finn mac Cumaill was asked by his companions to put his thumb under his tooth of knowledge "to find out what kind of trouble they were in, what could save them, and whether this was the end of their lives. 'I will,' said Finn, 'for a man should do his best when he is in dire straits.' He then put his thumb under the tooth of knowledge so that the truth was revealed to him about the trap that had been prepared for them and how they could be rescued from it" (Davidson 1989: 71). The use of the thumb to gain wisdom and poetic inspiration is also found in a tale concerning young Taliesin. "It seems that the thumb was thought to be particularly sensitive to the supernatural" (73). Jakob Grimm (1966) has recorded that "the thumb was sacred, and even worshipped as thumbkin and Pollux = pollex" [pollex is Latin for thumb]. He also noted that in the Netherlands the space between the thumb and the forefinger when stretched out … was called … *Woedenspanne*" (160). This measure brings us back to Óðinn (Wotan) as shaman, making the distance between forefinger and thumb the shaman's measure. The thumbkin, according to Grimm—*Däumling, petit poucet, peukalo*, etc.—was considered part of the elves (Old Norse álvr), and food offerings were made to him (448-451).[26] Björn Jonsson's (n.d.) interpretation of Eddic texts as star lore brings the thumb via Pollux (and Castor), the contemporary constellation Gemini, safely back to the origins of creation: he equates them with Vili and Ve, the sons of Burr, the giant of creation,[27] and the entire constellation Gemini is interpreted as Ymir who is sacrificed for the sake of world creation (with the constellation Taurus looming nearby as the cow of creation Auðumbla). While this may look like leger-de-main, it should not come as a total surprise: the work of seeing and healing starts at the source of creation and is connected with the ongoing process of creation—this is the fount of energy for such endeavors—and if the ritual gesture of the thumb

Illustration 5: Siegfried's thumb (Rasmus rock, Jäder, Södermanland, Sweden)

in the mouth facilitates the entrance into this level of participatory beingknowing—so much the better. What we remember in the story of the thumbkin, its elfin presence in fairytales, and what we see present in recent times as the honouring of the sacred bear and shaman thumb may connect us into an old, maternal matrix of bear knowing.

Ravens seem to make their appearance within the Eurasian complex frequently in twinned form. However, we also find a relationship between the bear and twins that is significant for our discussions:

Five generations ago, the great-great-grandmother of the Nivkh Khugan gave birth to the latter's grandfather. She then gave birth to twins who died. One night, on her way to the place reserved to women, she again gave birth to twins. The children were hairy and fur appeared on her face and hands. When people went out and gave light with birchbark (torches) to where she was lying, the twins suddenly died and she went crazy and began to sing. She sang how she followed her bear cubs through the thick forest, through a clearing and then to the mountain. She reached a stone house. She went in and said she was to live there from now on. She gave the death rattle and died. (Delaby 1984: 214)

The Nivkh (Gilyak) see a strong connection between twins and "men of the mountain" or bears (alternatively to "men of the sea"). One of the children is said to be the Nivkh child, the other one the bear child. The twins are part of the balancing cycle with bear: "The twins' death means their going back home, to the mountain, among the bears. Afterwards, the bears offer as a compensation bear cubs that the hunters catch in the forest. When the bear cubs have grown in captivity, the Nivkh will send them back to those of the mountain during a bear festival together with offerings of food" (Delaby 1984: 217). The bear twins appear here as significant go-betweens bridging the world of humans and the ancestral world of the bear.

The significance of the bear is within the Eurasian complex is also apparent when we observe how the network of obligations culminates in the bear oath. We can consider it the supreme expression of a universe of balance or appropriateness. "Through the institution of the bear oath, bears form, as it were, a controlling super society, sent down from the divine sphere, over human society" (Schmidt 1989: 199). Lauri Honko, Senni Timonen, Michael Branch and Keith Bosley (1994) explain the oath as follows: "Sworn on the name of the bear, it was the oldest, most powerful and most binding oath that a Khanty or Mansi could take: 'May the bear eat me if my oath is false!' An oath sworn during the festival was witnessed by the bear itself; at other times the bear was represented by an old skull, pelt or tooth" (126). Another description is as follows: "The suspect physically insults an object symbolizing the bear (a part of the bear's body), saying, '[may] the bear tear me apart in requittal if the charge is true'" (Schmidt 1989: 199).

An oath is a particular moment and highlight of consciousness in which the subjective intentions of the speakers are uniting with the ancestral, totemic, and ecological context from which they are born. While tremendous awareness of this lifeworld must always be there for the sake of survival, the bear oath presents a tie that surpasses the quotidian by connecting subjective intention with origin of being. We can imagine that the bear sculpture in the cave of Montespan from Magdalenian times[28] or the bear skull placed on top of an altarlike boulder in the Chauvet cave (with the paintings dated to the early palaeolithicum of about 30,000 BCE) (Chauvet, Deschamps and Hillaire 1995) might have served similar purposes. What has remained as the contemporary bear oath may have been at those times an oath of obligation to the medicines and powers invoked during initiatory and other ceremonial endeavours. While this is mere speculation, we know about the importance of the bear oath in contemporary times.

What we can glean from the available evidence is that the bear can rightfully be considered a central actor in the Eurasian indigenous understanding of balance. The bear ceremonials continue to be a contemporary expression of this view[29] that can be traced much further back in history to its possible mother, woman, and earth-based roots in early known human history. Balance is an energetic model of mutual obligations. Balancing is a way of beingknowing quite different from what we call a mythic or primitive or ethical universe. "Each time the hunter or fisherman [sic] sets out, his [sic] knowledge of these phenomena

169

has to be assessed anew in the light of prevailing conditions. As he [sic] lays his plans, he [sic] must judge which spirit forces will be in ascendancy that day, and decide accordingly on a strategy which balances the practical needs of the chase with the spiritual imperative to remain in harmony with supranormal master and guardians of the environment" (Honko et al. 1994: 118). These kinds of mappings and observations (cf. also Brody 1981), the multitude of clues and forces available to hunters and others, amount to what can rightfully be called an indigenous science, in which astronomical (seasonal cycle, etc.), meteorological, ecological, historical, etc., observations and memories converge to create a matrix of knowledge that is affirmed and celebrated in the bear ceremonial, for example. All this finds its expression in a particular mythology, oral history, ceremonial cycle, ethic, etc., but the basis for it all is not moral or mythic or fantastic or unconscious: they are expressions of a scientific knowledge of what is required to be in balance at a particular place (ecology) and time (seasonal and larger astronomical cycles) in the context of the history of the community making such observations.

Felicitas Goodman (1990) is among the people who have looked toward hunter-gatherers (and horticulturalists in her case) as a model for balance in general and ancient trance practices in particular (for critical reviews and research see: Kremer and Krippner 1994; Woodside, Kumar and Pekala 1997; Cardeña 1997). The bear ceremonials are, of course, primarily associated with hunter-gatherer societies. Goodman (1988) has expressed the view that hunter-gatherers "live a life of total balance, because *they do not aspire to controlling their habitat, they are a part of it*" (18; italics in original).[30] She sees hunter-gatherers as occupying "the full expanse of the ritual canvas" (34) identified by her as "the gripping drama of birth" (32).[31] Goodman states that hunter-gatherers "use the trance not only for curing, which is done in all types of societies, but especially to undertake a spirit journey" (42); she ascribes to them an "*ethic of appropriateness toward the habitat*" (58; italics in original). She further explains that "wrongdoings among hunters … are corrected or avenged not on the basis of an absolute good-evil dichotomy, but by considerations of appropriateness" (86).

The generalizations Goodman (1988) makes need to be read with caution, especially since the variety of hunter-gatherer societies is vast. Thus we find cultures—somewhat correlated with complexity—that are egalitarian, while others are hierarchical (generalizing statements regarding the status of women are difficult); in some of them warfare is rare, in others it is rather common; some practice slavery while it is absent in others; while some encourage competition, others do not tolerate it; etc. (Kelly 1995). While "no social scientist today would say that members of industrial society are more evolved than modern foragers" (Kelly 1995: 337), it seems to be more challenging to prevent stereotyping and idealizing when looking for models of balance among present and past hunter-gatherers. This may be especially true when we reconstruct the ancient past in attempts to find guiding and healing images. If we succumb to our need to abstract, then the result of such efforts might be a stereotypical and idealizing image of *the* "original" hunter-gatherer society performing *the* bear ceremonial. However, we have to assume "that modern diversity stems from original diversity in the foraging adaptations of behaviorally modern humans" (337). Robert Kelly (1995) further points out that hunter-gatherers "can be used to support any image of human society, generous or greedy, violent or peaceful, monogamous or polygamous, attentive or aloof to children, and so on" (338).

Such diversity among hunter-gatherers is not necessarily in contradiction to Goodman's (1988) generalizations or to my own statements regarding balance and the participatory process (they are made at a more abstract level than the categories just mentioned), but it should serve as a reminder that while it is almost inevitable in my current writing that I use abstractions, such as "balance," it is at the same time mandatory to ground such concepts in the specific indigenous science of our ancestries. It is only then that we can do them full justice, bring them to life, and get the seed they contain to sprout. After all, most of us no longer live in hunter-gatherer societies, so, in order to derive any meaning from inquiries like this one, we need to remember what *our* bear is; we need to follow the story of the loss of connections with the bear (or their thinning), and as we grieve these changes (many of them undoubtedly made by our ancestors with the best of intentions for the sake of survival) we can conceivably renew a pursuit of balance that is eminently relevant for the current times. It is so much easier for us to project onto hunter-gatherers idealizing images of balance, than it is for us to develop images of balance that address the varied histories of domination, colonization, missionization, racism, sexism, genocide, and the like. It is so much easier to split or go single focus (various forms of dissociation), than to plunge into the despair as we canvas the full picture of violence that has accompanied what is so often called the "civilizing" process or the line of "progress" (mirrored in the increasing loss of the bear ceremonial). Idealizing Native peoples or societies of early human history is indeed the retro-romanticism of which Ken Wilber (1995) accuses neo-shamanism and other aspects of the New Age. While reconstructions of ancestral bear ceremonials are a necessary part of the remembrance process, these are hardly the sole or final purpose. They need to become an ingredient in the meaning of bear balance for us—at least most of us—city dwellers today. Such an image may even be harder and more difficult to develop as part of an ongoing participatory indigenous mind process rather than as dissociated, mental reconstruction of earlier bear ceremonials.

The narrative universe of balance is an energetic model of mutual obligations. While this is frequently expressed or seen within a particular ethic or moral system of right and wrong (cf. the language of some of the Hopi prophecies, for example) (Mails and Evehema 1995), it can also be understood as a way of living that is analogous to the physics a tightrope walker has to contend with: losing one's balance is not a moral issue, it is a mistake in judging or executing particular energetic constellations (body, wind, pole); failure is not morally wrong, however, it can be deadly. The obligations to the bear and the bears' obligations to human beings in a particular place and at a particular time are just that: humans and bears are tied together in a dance of balance, and failure to fulfill one's obligation is like a misstep on the tightrope. (Much of the moral language we find in some of the reports is probably the result of Christianization and its concepts used by native people in order to make the bear ceremonial and bear stories intelligible to their colonizers.) The connections between bear and humans are like the threads woven by norms: a web or network of obligations.

7

The importance of the structure above vs. below is a common feature within the Eurasian complex. It is reflected in the moiety system of the Khanty (Ostyak) and Mansi (Vogul), for example. Here the *mós* phratry is connected with the sky people, consumers of raw meat, with the goose as the totem and a connection to the solar World Surveyor Man among the Mansi; the *por* phratry is connected with the underground people, consumers of cooked meat, with the bear as totem and a connection to the Sacred Town Elder among the Mansi (Honko et al. 1994: 71; Schmidt 1989: 216).

> Some scholars draw attention to matriarchal and totemistic features in Khanty and Mansi bear cults. Both peoples have long identified themselves as members of one of two moieties, por and mós. The por moiety's claim to descent from a bear may explain why the members of this group uphold the rules of the bear cult more carefully than members of the mós moiety. Among the latter, customs associated with bear cults appear to have been adopted later; moreover only certain features of the cult were adopted, in particular those concerned with the entertainment aspect of the festival. In this connection, it is interesting to note that among the stories told during the festival is one of how a bear gave birth to the first por woman, who became the primordial mother of the tribe. (Honko et al. 1994: 126)

Schmidt (1989) ventures after her detailed analysis of bear material that

> …several tempting ideas for reconstruction might arise—for instance, that, in the old days, cult leaders of the por moiety, with the help of the bear, mediated toward the underworld, while those of the mos moiety, through the forces symbolized in the present-day World Surveyor Man, did the same toward the upper world; that, in the tradition of the bear-killing mythical heroes, the representatives of the moieties kill bears with signs opposite to their own—the sons of the Town Lord killing an "upper" bear, the World Surveyor Man a "lower" one etc. (228)

We find a reflection of this upper-lower structure also as part of the bear ceremonial among the Tungusian peoples. The literature on the bear ceremonials is replete with references to the hunters blaming somebody else, like the Russians, for the killing of the bear. However, as Hans-Joachim Paproth (1976) points out, the role of the raven is often significant in this regard, especially among the north Tungusian peoples. Often hunters exclaim *kuk!* in imitation of the raven as they are conducting the ceremonial bear hunt. The raven is, of course, known to be a companion to the hunter, even pointing out to the observant human where wild animals can be found. During the ceremony, when the bear head on display is asked who was the killer children speak up as witnesses for the raven's deeds.[32] Raven makes appearances during the ceremonial on several occasions, and two ravens (men wearing raven masks) may even attack the bear physically. Paproth interprets all this not just in terms of the natural behaviour of ravens, but also in terms of the relatedness of humans through the bear and raven spirits. He discusses the connection of the Tungus tribes with the Chukchi and Koryak tribes in whose mythology the raven plays a significant role, as mentioned previously. Members of the in-law-kin (*Schwägersippe*) play a significant role during the bear ceremonial.

Einerseits war der Bär gleichsam ein Verschwägerter des Menschen, andererseits verkleideten sich die Teilnehmer des Rituals als Fremde, im gegebenen Falle als Raben, um den Bären zu betrügen. Mit Menschen, die eine fremde Sprache redeten, die den Rabenkult hatten, konnten die Tungusen in eheliche Verbindungen treten. Folglich konnten auch diese Leute ihre Verschwägerten sein. (On the one hand the bear was quasi brother-in-law of humans, on the other the participants of the rituals dressed as strangers, in this case as ravens, in order to deceive the bear. The Tungus could enter into into marital relationships with people speaking a foreign language, people of the raven cult. Consequently, these people could also be their brothers-in-law. (120-1; my translation)

The structural analogy between the sky and earth-related moieties among the Khanty and Mansi, and bear (northern Tungus tribes) and raven connected peoples (Chukchi and Koryak) is apparent. The raven thus is a significant player in the relational web of the bear cremonial, marital relationships, and intertribal exchange. In certain parts of Siberia we find the raven in relationship with the bear and part of the ceremonial, albeit as the in-law that gets blamed for the bear's death. The scouting flight of the raven is a part of the web of the interrelated hunting communities and their bear ancestors. During the Old Norse times of Óðinn we find the shamanic raven seeing primarily connected with warrior activities, and the bear has remained primarily as the bearskin worn by berserkir—an indication of the dissociation that has occurred since the disappearance of the bear ceremonial in these regions.

A review of the literature yields some ancient relationships between raven and bear. According to Cervantes' *Don Quixote*, King Arthur, *arctus*, the bear, "converted into a *raven*: que anda hasta ahora convertido en *cuervo*, y le esperan en su reyno por momentos" (Grimm 1966). Alexander Marshack (1991) reproduces an bear image engraved onto the head of a raven from much earlier, palaeolithic times; interestingly the bear is shown with a dart in its throat and is bleeding from mouth and nose.[33] This could be seen as the speculative possibility of a relationship between bear and raven such as we find among the northern Tungus.

Records indicate that raven (like eagle and falcon) has been especially significant since the earliest beginnings of shamanism, reaching as far back as the neolithic and the palaeolithic times (*The New Encyclopedia Britannica* 1988). These are the times when bear was particularly significant. Some of the bird images in cave paintings may well be ravens, although identification is frequently difficult. However, the palaeolithic image of raven engraved in schist from Gönnersdorf on the Rhine (Germany) is very clear as raven or crow (a distinction that did not and does not always matter to Native people) (Gowlett 1993: 130).

As I travel with the bear story from the far north I realize these aspects where raven is relationally obligated to bear.

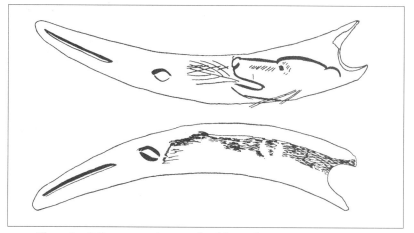

Illustration 6: Bear engraved on ravenhead (bâton from Massat, Ariege, France)

8

The strong presence of the bear—to this day—among the Siberian and Fennoscandian indigenous populations led me to wonder about the presence of the bear in the Germanic-Nordic cultural complex, especially its oldest identifiable layers. It appears that knowledge of the bear, bear stories, and bear ceremonials is correlated to the physical presence of the bear vs. its disappearance over vast stretches of Europe (even in northern Fennoscandia we now only have 500 brown bears as a result of intense hunting during the nineteenth and early twentieth century) (Bernes 1996). The best known presence of the bear in the Germanic stories (from Tacitus on) may be in the form of the *berserkir*, the ones donning bear skins for the sake of spiritual and physical battle power, and in order to gain entry into the warrior's paradise *Valhöll*.[34] The nature of the reports indicate that this seems to be a late appearance of the bear spirit that now has taken on this purely masculinized, warring appearance in accordance with the dominance of Óðinn, who they are associated with. (But even this connection with the bear still carries practices of altered states, etc., with it.) We also find the bear mentioned in various sagas as spirit and as common first name. The importance of the bear becomes clear when we remember such appellations as *ásbjörn*, sacred bear. Through the berserkers the bear has frequently become associated with Óðinn, however, Þórr carries the bear as one of his kennings (Sturluson 1987: 156).[35]

Remembering the bear in my own ancestral traditions means working my way backward through the various splits and dissociations that have emphasized one particular aspect of the bear only: its strength and ability to fight if necessary. True enough, there is an image of warriorship in here that could present an antidote to current military approaches: the sacred warrior in an individual fight vs. the soldier pushing computer buttons for mass destruction (with the distinctions between virtual wars in video games and actual wars conducted from computer screens gradually disappearing). Addressing this masculinization means retracing our steps from misappropriations in Hitler's genocidal activities, the mass killing of witches during the European Middle Ages, the aberrations of Viking raids and abuses of women, to the various war-oriented Kurgan invasions intermixing with and/or suppressing the populations already present in what is now called Europe.[36]

However, bears usually leave tracks, even when their disappearance is considerably earlier than in the Sámi story. In the case of Old Norse written documents it leads to a very early part in the creation story: At the beginning of Völuspá (stanza 2) the völva reports about the giants born at the beginning of time, the nine worlds, the giantesses, and the tree of fate. Then she talks of the giant Ymir (stanza 3), and the creation of Earth:

áðr Burs synir	until the sons of Burr
biöðum um yppðu,	raised the lands,
þeir er Miðgarð	they who made
mæran skópu.	the great Miðgarðr. (Pálsson, 1996: 47, 61)

Hermann Pálsson glosses burr as "a son," and relates it to the same root as the verb *bera*, to bear. Burr is thus etymologically connected to the reconstructed Indo-European root complex *bher-* with its four major semantic fields "to carry (bear children), to bore (cut, pierce), brown (bright), and to cook (bake)."[37] I would contend that this is the place where the older understandings of the bear are hibernating in the Norse creation story (together with other hermaphroditic, androgynous or bisexual beings as well as a gynocentric view of things). The bear may very well be part of an older cosmological understanding that we also find reflected in the cow *auðumla* (*auðr*—riches, *humala*—without horns): the urcow (born from salty ice)—an image obviously connected with Earth Mother (and analogous to the presumably earlier indigenous uses of the image of moose or reindeer) (Ashihmina 1992).

Auðumla fed the ancient frost-giant Ymir, who subsequently gets sacrificed by Burr's sons[38] in order to create Earth. Such creation of Earth is common among Indo-European cultures (cf. Lincoln 1986), but can also be found in Sámi mythology as rendered by Fjellner (Schwaar 1996: 37).[39] As the following quote indicates, the theme of hermaphroditism or androgyny weaves itself through Norse mythology:

> Sigurðr represents the hero of the Mother Goddess. In fact, Freyja/Óðr, Frigg/ Óðinn, Skaði/Njördr, Skaði/Óðinn and even Skaði/Loki can be understood as the sexually fluctuant expression of the whole creative power of the Great Goddess, just as the primordial androgyn is a figuration of the whole of the world. In this light, Sigurðr's constant collusion with and passive dependence upon women or telluric elements—bound as such to the Goddess—would lead to the thought that the hero was originally a female… Sigurðr is not a hero according to patriarchal criteria, even if the development of the story provided him with more "virile" virtues like strength or sexual ability. It seems clear that Sigurðr receives his ultimate identiy from the women who create, mark, define and end his life. (Gouchet 1997: 289).

These couples and sibling couples are increasingly, as they approach Viking times, described in masculinized terms. In Fjörgyn and Fjörgynn, Nerthus and Njörðr, Freyja and Freyr we may find the clearest link to the primordial times of Ymir, as well as the ancestral bears Burr and Buri, thus connection with creation out of the primordial oneness.

All the activities within a shamanic universe require spiritual work with the source of creation.[40] Such balancing of the strong male identification with the feminine during *seiðr* can only have been highly suspect at the time when the stories of Óðinn were told. No wonder Loki accuses Óðinn of homosexuality (in Lokasenna).[41] No wonder *seiðr* was slandered with the suspicion of improper sexual rites. While the possibility of sexual ceremonial proceedings during seiðr certainly exists (maybe as some form of Nordic Tantric practice) but is difficult to ascertain from the sources, we can be sure that the Old Norse author writing about seiðr must have been highly suspicious of spiritual work that required anything resembling androgynous presence (especially when involving men). Of course, what the *völvas*, the seeresses, were doing was connecting with the origins of creation, particularly human creation (we can think here of the imagery of the tree of life with three women at her root spreading the fertilizing clay of *auður*); the sacred or magical chanting called *varðlokkur* was instrumental in this (as in earlier times presumably the drum).[42] The sexual heart of *seiðr* may very well have been the primordial androgyn we find described in shamanic traditions:

> In certain cultures, there exist shamans and shamanesses who claim gender transformation, and manifest a symbolic sex change. On much rarer occasions—for example, in Malay—they may actually undergo an anatomical change. As a result of their psycho-physiological predispositions (bisexuality) or androgynous physical characteristics (hermaphroditism), these shamans

appear to combine in their persons the feminine (earth) and the masculine (heaven) principles. In other words, they represent the complementarity of bipolar unity, the union of opposites. (Ripinsky-Naxon 1997: 49)[43]

The sacrifice of the original androgyn was something the Old Norse people needed to see as a thing of the past, a necessary act for subsequent differentiation, evolution, and the rise of patriarchy. For those practicing *seiðr* the requirement of androgyny may have remained as the source of their seeing and healing—instead of a thing of the past it is the everpresent origin.

The presence of the bear in the pre-Indoeuropean layers in the North can be noticed and appreciated, for example, in the mesolithic amber bear from Resen Mose mentioned earlier. Marshack (1991) concludes after a detailed analysis:

> It was not an object made once for "hunting magic" nor an object of decoration, since it had no hole but had to be held in the hand. Its story or use was, then, repetitive or periodic, and mythologically its meaning was continuous.... In one way or another, each pattern was an act of participation in the story of the bear. We can conjecture, but not know, their meanings. If the multiple angles represent sky, cloud, or water, and the structured hatches represent spirit nets or even notation, and unstructured groups represent markings made while saying a rite, we would have symbolic art and markings comparable in scope—if not precise meaning—to those found in the Paleolithic. (355)

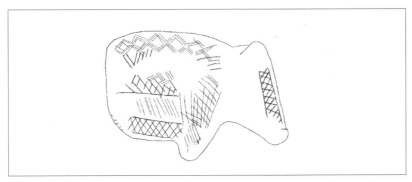

Illustration 7: Amber bear (from Resen Mose, Jutland, Denmark)

The old Nordic-Germanic peoples managed to make the power of the bear part of their violent purposes. Today the healing of bear can only mean the remembrance and celebration of the she part of the bear—*before* the bear can be honoured in the complexity Schmidt (1989) describes the she-bear needs care. This can be identified as a requirement for the recovery of indigenous mind among those who have lost their lived awareness of the bear ancestor, and who are in the process of restitution.

9

A few years ago I dreamed of bear. In the dream it is winter. I am out camping in the wilderness. In the distance I see an emaciated bear cross the railroad tracks near where my tent is. The bear comes toward me and transforms into a young bear as it gets closer. The fur now shows the markings of a young boar: it has bright, luminescent stripes running the length of its body. The bear then collapses close by and dies.

Bears normally are not up during wintertime walking about in the snow. Something important, some terrible hunger (physical or other), must have brought the bear out of hibernation. Hibernation is often seen as the time of renewal and deep, sustained dreaming. The bear has obviously suffered either prior to or during hibernation as is apparent by its malnutrition. But maybe she was so thin because of feeding its young ones in the den, as bears do. (Maybe a twin birth had overly stressed the bear's body.) As bear approaches me she goes through a transformative renewal, becomes young again, but then does not have sufficient energy to live. Young bears do not have stripes like boar piglets; these stripes looked quite radiant and striking, almost as if the bear had put on body paint for this renewal. In my mother tongue German, boar piglets are called *Frischlinge*, fresh ones; it is both the one newly born, but also the one to be given away as sacrifice (Mitzka 1960: 219). The bear is trying to come back, make itself new. For this it has put on special markings. As it is trying to come back it stresses an ancient side: it gives birth out of itself (as the primal giant Ymir gives birth to the world through its sacrifice), and the association with the boar piglet brings it into the realm of the ancient Vanir spirits Freyja and Freyr (a magical boar with golden bristles is said to be one of their important animals). The young bear collapses right in my view, since the proper nurturance has not been provided. The bear sacrifices itself in front of and for me in this dream, just like the bear gets sacrificed during the bear ceremony. I had this dream not quite one year before I was told the bear story. In the context of the bear story I was told in Sápmi and my work with raven, it is easier now to garner more meaning from the dream.

In the Sámi/Samoyed story the bear escapes "to the other side of the Big Sea," he goes "very far." When I look at a map of the circumpolar regions the place that seems obvious as the bear's destination across the Arctic Sea is Turtle Island (there really isn't anything else, excepting Greenland, a place for polar bears and not forest bears). In this reading of the story Turtle Island, both with its Aboriginal peoples as well as its settlers, seems implicated in some form in the awakening of the bear and the "return home when the time has ripened." And the story continues: "Then [Pynegusse and Ihčče] will gather all their scattered children and bring them back home into the deep lap of the Forest Spirit."

The Sámi/Samoyed story relates the disappearance of the bear to the arrival of Christian colonization of Sápmi and the neighboring Samoyed lands. This process had begun in the 1300s, and gathered strength in the 1500s. In 1521 Native Americans made a decision at Tenochtitlán in Mexico "not to talk, not to share … knowledge" (Colorado 1996: 7). Oneida Native Pamela Colorado (1996) comments further:

> People knew then, through our scientific practices, that we were entering a time they called the Dark Sun, which would go on for 468 years. During this time, consciousness would go through darkness…. They said that after the 468 years there would be a new sun, which started in approximately 1987. This is in the Aztec calendar…. What is prophesied at the end of the Dark Sun is that the condor (i.e., the land of the South Americas) and the eagle (the land of the North Americas) will be re-united, and the knowledge of the earth—and you must understand that when we say "the earth" we don't just mean the physical earth, we refer to something which you might call "energy"—the knowledge of the earth will come out again and the knowledge that we have will become whole. *The ancient knowledge will rise again, only this time the key to it is integration, and we have to do it with "all the directions."* (7 and, 8; emphasis added)

If we look at the historical meaning of the bear story from this perspective, then we can glean some further possible meaning. The ancient knowledge of balance as celebrated in the bear ceremonial and related stories joined the hibernation of indigenous wisdom on Turtle Island as part of the cycle of darkness described in the Aztec, Mayan, and other calendrical observations. The return of the bear means the recovery and integration of traditional, indigenous knowledge. The indigenous knowledge of all the directions of the sky are needed in this process. This does not just mean the Native American peoples on Turtle Island, and the

*Illustration 8: Bear changing into young bear with boar piglet markings
(author's arrangement and drawing of rock carvings from Álaheadju, Sapmi)*

Sámi and Samoyed people of the Arctic Circle, but also the European settlers on Turtle Island as well as in the Arctic North. Making knowledge whole can be read as the gathering of the scattered children and bringing them into the deep lap of the Forest Spirit, making beingknowing whole through the remembrance of balance, the opening of the indigenous knowledge preserved in ancient petroglyphs, buildings, sacred sites, etc. The rock carving in South Sweden where I made my offering holds the count and account for this change.

Working within this epistemological process of participatory knowing or the recovery of indigenous mind is always interesting and full of surprises. As I am writing this I remember that the first step on my journey to Sápmi was a place that is connected with the Hopi migration stories (an exploration beyond the scope of this article), and that the second preparatory step was in Mexico.[44] As part of that trip I made an offering on a mountaintop altar outside of Mexico City, where an Aztec Indian—much to my surprise—sang the Sámi song *Gula! Gula!* (Listen! Listen! by Mari Boine); he did not know about my travel plans to Sápmi. I also went to the center of Tenochtitlan, the Templo Mayor, in the middle of contemporary Mexico City. It was in this place—at that time an island in a lake—that the decision to hide their knowledge was made two years after the beginning of the Spanish conquest in 1519.

> Nobody said that it was the Dark Sun because of the coming of the Europeans. The Europeans had come thousands of years earlier … but then the relationship was different. Who tells the sun how to move? Not the Spanish! We don't like what's happened, we surely didn't want it. On the other hand, that's life itself; that's the cycles of life. Perhaps the best way to say it is that we really value accommodation as a universal principle—accommodation to life is more important than judging what needed to happen. Now what is important is that we are entering a new sun (Colorado 1996: 10).

As part of this trip to Mexico City I also watched the *voladores*, and learned about the Azteco-Mayan calendar that records these cycles. The petroglyph at which I made an offering in Southern Sweden is an image linked to this understanding of the ages. In this context the meaning of the new sun is the reconnection and remembering of indigenous knowledge from all the directions. The ravenseeing in *Hrafnagaldr* describes the terrible time of the change, the in-between, the renewal. Working with the bear through raven eyes has allowed me in retrospect to acknowledge what had happened at that time and what has been constellated.

The bear story has continued since. The *noaidi* who told me the story visited California, where she was visited by bear during her shamanic work of *noaiddášeapmi*. And then there is the place where I do much of my personal work related to the process I am describing in this article. The local Indians have disappeared from this area as part of the pervasive genocide in California (they were first herded to a neighbouring area, then across a mountain range into another region of California; many died of the diseases brought by European settlers, others were simply hunted down and shot). For me, as somebody working through the historical and personal impact of the German genocide of the Jewish people, it seems a fitting place to do this work. Bears are still present here. The black bears leave many traces of their presence, however, they are extremely shy, because once a year they are hunted for one week. I had the good fortune to see two of them tussling with each other not too long ago. The significance of the bear for the Native people of this area is apparent once we know that they used to bury their dead in bearskins (Goldschmidt 1978). Recent work with the land has led us to identify two bear stones in the landscape (one of them a female figure as well as a bear). Work at these sacred sites is the work with the grief about the disappearance of the Native people from this place, as well as the honouring of the renewal she-bear brings. This is the emergence of my own bear story.

10

If we assume that the ordeal of the postmodern critiques has left eurocentered thinking without the possibility of persuasive objectifying sciences as final arbiters of truth, then the alternative is to accept that no matter what (whether consciously acknowledged or acted out unconsciously) all inquiry is a form of participatory knowing, or: the reality we live in is a narrative universe (Kremer 1992a, 1992b). What we call truth or fact or reality is never a mere reflection or mirroring of the *Ding an sich*, but we always participate actively in the construction of what we call truth or reality. The examples of objectifying sciences, hermeneutic inquiry, and archaeomythological investigation are all ways of creating a story about the world as we perceive it (and thus construct) with the help of these methodologies. All this is not to say that there is no *Ding an sich*, or that anything goes (as Paul Feyerabend [1984] would provocatively have it), or that we can make it all up through some voluntaristic or decisionistic acts, or that there aren't any constraints on the narrative universes we can create, or the truth claims we can make, or that there isn't such a thing as sloppy research—in fact, it does something rather curious: it increases the responsibility of inquirers to understand their personal, historical, geographical, ecological, gendered, and cultural situatedness in order to avoid sloppiness. It is in this sense that the awareness of our participation in a narrative universe increases our burden in terms of integrity, self-reflectiveness, ethical and other value considerations.

These stories coming forward from older times have an interesting quality. There is no casual reading of them as there is no casual reading of this particular story. This means now that you, the reader, know something about raven, and even more about bear, the question is whether you pick up your obligation, whether you retreat into the modern mind or discover what your own obligations are. To your own tradition, your own roots, your place of settlement, the places of your ancestors. Really, there is nothing moral about this. It is about spiritual seeing, health, balance, seeing spirits. It is about staying in balance. However you conceive of your own task in that regard, this story is now a part of your weave.

The revival of shamanism presents, at least so it seems, a profound desire for integral knowing and being. The interest in goddess cultures, ecology, mythology, Asian spiritual practices, the bear, etc., are all expressions of this desire. The extent to which these trends will become real depends on the reality and completeness of the conversation they create. Such conversation needs to include the memory of the historical breaches which created the lacks which led to the modern desire for shamanic experiences, connection with the land, well-told stories, etc. There is no way to leap back to anything, but the possibility to be nurtured from what in Old Norse is called *Urðarbrunnur*, the source of memory, exists—and it contains many things ranging from feminism, to the fights against classism and racism, the history of colonialism, the ideals of the civil society—and on ... and on ... including the root memories of our cultures. We cannot allow ourselves to avert the gaze from anything. We also have to struggle with the shadow aspects of indigenous being. While the recovery of indigenous mind does not inevitably lead to political action, the third process of non-subjects nonetheless implies a profound critique of modern societies, as it implies an ecological critique, as it challenges a number of understandings of gender and gender roles—and on. This is critique by virtue of decolonization and presence of recovered indigenous practices non-subjects conduct within the dominant social formations. Through such practice it is a radical ideology critique of modernity and postmodernity from an indigenous perspective—with the possibility of a recovered indigenous conversation which facilitates the mutual witnessing of the twisted roads human beings have walked. Such recovery and witnessing is not so much a process of critique or opposition as it is the doing of what non-subjects must do in order to recreate balance. Maybe out of the tears about the grievous things our ancestors have suffered and committed, amidst all their achievements, then will arise laughter and appreciation as the joy of the local truth ceases to be a call for dominance. As the Mayan calendar approaches its end, as so many indigenous traditions are sharing their teachings again openly, as the *voladores* celebrate the change of the ages in Mexico as well as in Scandinavia, and as the tree of life once again shudders during yet another *Ragnarök*, we may find the strength not just to remember what the bear has to teach us about balance, but also to embody this ancient knowledge for the future.

The return of bear ceremonials for those who have discontinued them—and we have to keep in mind that there are individuals and peoples who have never discontinued them—could be a folkloristic, superficial, nostalgic, or romantic performance. But it could also mean everything the recovery of indigenous mind and roots implies: a ceremonial place for laughter, grief, honouring, horsing around, remembrance of obligations, apologies, and more. This is the richness, the *auður*, of the bear ceremonial.[45] This is healing. The inclusion of the dark and light prevents us from mere nostalgia and dissociated romanticism, and allows us to celebrate our obligations to bear. So that there be a nurturing conversation where we are. So that there may be greater balance. So that the relational web of bear and raven and human can be an ancient presence for our future well-being.

John Mohawk has stated that "I don't want people to adopt Indian rituals because

I want people to own *their own* rituals. I want them to come to ownership out of experiences that are real experiences to them, that mean something to them. Then I'll come and celebrate it with them" (17; emphasis added). This necessitates the painstaking work of remembrance, reconstruction, and recovery—with the history of forgetting as part of the reality of the experiences. The bear can serve as a measure for this work:

> In the spring, Bear marks his territory on the tree. Stretching as far as possible, Bear uses his claws to score the tree. Other bears passing by are challenged to meet his standard. If they cannot reach the mark, they leave the territory. For the Native scientist, the tree is not merely science but science interwoven inseparably with life. We meet the mark or die. Like the Bear passing through, no one watches us, the science relies on utmost integrity. (Colorado 1988: 51).

This is what is required of us in the process of decolonization—the re-invigoration of nurturing conversations—*criar y dejarse criar*—and the recovery of gift giving as a central communal process.

11

he raises his arms
he raises his voice
twin ravens fly
down to the depths of memory founts
up up toward star writ laws

down twin ravens fly
as he raises his drumstick
as he raises his chant
down to the roots
down to the riches
white clay of auður
the woman of memory
the woman of measure
the woman of becoming
down to the three
that gave life and destiny
to the trees on the beach
ash and alder
sacred trees
the first humans
three women usher twin ravens deeper
to beginnings

origins from bear
bear mother bear father
matrix of creation
cycle of regeneration

up twin ravens fly
as he raises his drumstick
as he raises his chant
twin ravens climb
the ancestor shuttle way
bilrost
milky way
star ladder
ravenmemory ravenmind
enter the eye of the eagle
shaman star
ancestral light and law
twin ravens enter the circle of elders
grandmothers grandfathers
hear our song
hear our drum
hear our need
elders wait for the offering
ravens sacrifice
memories
painful memories
of armor and berserkir and witchhunts
ravens purify
rapes and killings
elders point
into the depth of the forest
twin bears walking toward the village
elders offer
the thumb
of the great seeress
and point the way

twin ravens fly
as he raises his drumstick
as he raises his chant
into the middle of the forest
twin bears offer their lives
as Earth renews herself
twin bears twin ravens

revolve
around the life tree
nailed to the star of the north
revolve
counting great years
revolve
celebrating the dawning age
renewal
twin bears offer their lives
twin ravens wed twin bears
they touch the hearts
and the thumbs tear the final veils
of unknowing and unseeing
she
bears
marry twin ravens
one couple turns skyward
to hunt among the stars
one couple turns earthward
to hunt in ceremony

he raises her drumstick
she raises his chant
grandmothers! grandfathers!
I honor
bearmother
I purify
my imbalance
I swear
to bear
the memories
into this age
drumming ceases
chanting closes

Thanks go to Jacqueline Whitmore for her generous support for the graphics of this work.

[1]This notwithstanding the fact that the *grammatical* gender of Huginn and Muninn is masculine; Huginn is the definitive form of hugi, meaning: *the* thought, intent, etc.; Muninn is connected to the verb muna, to remember (De Vries 1977).
[2]See translation by Jesse L. Byock, *Saga of the Volsungs* [sic] (1990: 45).
[3]See Peter Goodchild, *Raven Tales* (1991) for an introductory overview of raven

mythologies.

[4]Luce Irigaray (1985) is among the feminist authors who have attempted to reconstitute the discourse of women by developing modes of expression not governed by phallocentrism. This story is an analogous attempt from the perspective of reconstituted indigenous consciousness: rather than being governed by the rules of the dominant discourses (either in affirmation or in opposition), it attempts to exemplify in its style what its content is. As such it is also a story of initiation and is best read in this way. In my opinion and analysis, the alternative of merely retelling mythic stories of raven or bear does not exist for those of us who have left their indigenous roots far behind and who are part of and complicit in the colonizing forces oppressing and destroying Native peoples; it would be the pretense of wholeness where the scars of history need to be healed before such storytelling can be envisioned with integrity. Awareness of these scars is part of the contemporary possibility and opportunity for wholeness.

[5]Dubious as far as validity issues around their content is concerned: "Historical validity (euhemerism)?" "Ancient memories?" "Psychological, maybe Jungian validity?" "The truth of myth?" "Astronomical validity of star lore?"

[6]By participatory mind process I mean the following: The interaction with the phenomena of reality occurs as a process of embedded consciousness that is experienced, lived, and known as part of nature with permeable boundaries between self and phenomena. It is a synthetic or integral type of consciousness process. Images are a significant part of this mind process (see Kremer 1994 for further discussions.)

[7]Yvonne Dion-Buffalo and John Mohawk (1994) outline three choices that colonized peoples have in response to cultural colonization:

They can become "good subjects" of the discourse, accepting the rules of law and morals without much question, they can be "bad subjects" arguing that they have been subjected to alien rules but always revolting within the precepts of those rules, or they can be "non-subjects," *acting and thinking around discourses far removed from and unintellegible to the West*.... In a world composed of fewer than a dozen distinct civilizations (including the metropolitan West) plus 3,000 to 5,000 distinct indigenous societies, the range of possible experiences is very great indeed. These are the autochthonous peoples whom such luminaries as Arnold Toynbee wrote entirely out of history. Much of what remains of the range of human potential for creating versions of reality exists in the framework of the arts, stories, oral traditions, music and other cultural manifestations of these peoples. Their lived and dreamed experiences are the world's richest sources of exploration of the human potential. Gaining access to these experiences will not be easy. Not only are the voices of these distinct "others" remote, the channels of communication are practically non-existent. Few individuals from tribal societies write novels or history texts (35; emphasis added).

Analogous choices apply to members of colonizing societies: They can be part of the majority discourse, they can oppose the majority discourse and be deviant, or they can become non-subjects (decolonize) by working to recover their own indigenous roots in order to participate in discourses far removed and intellegible to the West. As decolonizing non-subjects they may re-enable themselves to establish genuine channels of communication and knowledge exchange with indigenous communities.

[8]For longer discussions of this stance see my various publications in the reference list from 1997 to 2005, beginning with "Shamanic Inquiry as Recovery of Indigenous Mind."

[9]The nurturing conversation as foundational aspect of participatory or indigenous consciousness has been discussed extensively by PRATEC:

> The conversations held between persons and the other inhabitants of the world are not primarily engaged in for the purpose of "knowing reality." They are engaged in as part of the activity of *criar y dejarse criar*, of nurturing (raising) and letting oneself be nurtured (raised). The verb *criar* is used to speak of raising children, animals, plants, relationships, etc. It is the activity that fosters the growth and development of any potentiality or generativity. It is a fundamentally mutual or reciprocal activity: as one nurtures one is simultaneously nurtured. The action in the world does not leave the actor untransformed; acting in the world is being in relationship with that world, so the language of conversation is more appropriate than the language of knowledge. There is here no knower and known, no subject and object. Rather there are actors in relationships of mutuality. By acting one transforms not only the world but oneself as well. Therefore it is a fundamentally dynamic world, always moving, always changing, always in flux. There is, as it were, no simple act of knowing as we moderns understand the term for such knowledge-acquiring activity presupposes that there is something to be known, irrespective of who knows it.
>
> This is not to say that conversing with the world does not involve cognitive faculties, it of course does, but that the activity is not primarily and certainly not exclusively a cognitive one. *Criar* demands not only understanding but love, tenderness, patience. But it is to say that the point of conversation is not the attainment of knowledge through the interrogation of nature, it is rather to generate and regenerate the world and be generated and regenerated by it in the process (Apffel-Marglin 1994: 9).

This is also a definition of the process of balance, or what the Iroquoians call *skanagoah*, the "good mind," a place of stillness and peace (Colorado 1988). The Hopi call this *suyanisqatsi* (as opposed to *koyaanisqatsi*; Lomatuway'ma, Lomatuway'ma, Namingha and Malotki 1993). In Old Norse the equivalent term is *friður* (Grönbech 1954).

[10]We can broadly define three types of relationship to participation: 1) Unconsciousness of participation in the phenomena during modernity; the splitting from nature, feminine, spirit(s), etc.; ongoing, thus pathological, cultural or normative dissociation. 2) Awakening to the awareness of participation in the phenomena in postmodern, deconstructivist, and systems theories as well as in the recovery of indigenous mind process. 3) Continuing awareness, observation, and celebration of participation in the phenomena among people in their

indigenous mind.

[11]In an indigenous context healing is not a matter of manipulating isolated, monadic individuals for the sake of health, but understanding the individual's place in the cosmos as they relate and are related to the place where everything and everybody comes from, and intervening within that framework as is appropriate and necessary; physical healing is an aspect of this process. The following quote indicates that this is contained even in the early Indo-European traditions that gave rise to the imperialistic moves of Eurocentrism. Lincoln (1986, 118) concludes after his survey of Indoeuropean traditions: "It is not just a damaged body that one restores to wholeness and health, but the very universe itself.... The full extent of such knowledge is now revealed in all its grandeur: the healer must understand and be prepared to manipulate nothing less than the full structure of the cosmos." This is in obvious ways related to the etymology of "to heal," which is connected with the German *heilen*, and the Indoeuropean root *kailo*, referring to a state and process of wholeness (the word "whole" also being related to this root). But "to heal" is also connected to "holy" (as is German *heilen* to *heilig* or Icelandic *heill—heil—heilög*), which points to the older layers of understanding healing through remembering the history of language.

[12]This worldview does not preclude failure in the sense of what appears as serious imbalance to us today (violence in its various expressions)—only the idealization and romanticization of indigenous peoples, as the flip side of imperialistic destruction, allows for such imaginations. Of course, indigenous peoples have never lived in a perfect world, the ideal of balance is always and at best a temporary achievement—staying in balance is always a tremendous struggle individually and communally. For example, traditional Hopi stories describing situations where things are out of balance (*koyaanisqatsi*), are very educational in this regard; see the *Hopi Ruin Legends* (Lomatuway'ma et al. 1993). However, it should be noted that much, if not most, of what is written on the shadow aspects of indigenous living is seen through the highly prejudical eyes of the colonizers, especially Christian priests and missionaries, and that much of this information is erroneous or sensationalized (feeding simplistic evolutionary stories of primitve vs. civilized modern). (For a pertinent critical discussion see Hassler [1992a, 1992b] re Aztec human sacrifice; or Peter-Röcher [1996] re cannbialism.) The projection of European shadow material onto native peoples has led to their internalization of colonizing forces that get acted out through alcoholism, family violence, etc. This provides the native context for any discussion of present and past imbalance. Nonetheless, anybody engaging in indigenous discourse today needs to grapple with an indigenously contextualized understanding of human sacrifice, cannibalism, sexism, slavery, and the like, beginning with one's own ancestries.

[13]I have discussed the difference between the modern interpretation of, e.g., raven as symbol as part of the dissociative knowing process, and the indigenous understanding of it as spirit elsewhere (Kremer 1995). All this is not to say that psychological language and theories are not potentially very helpful in clarifying

and working with the process of recovery of indigenous mind. However, it is important to be mindful in which discourse it places us. For people socialized in an increasingly psychology-centered narrative universe the habitual tendency to psychologize spirit is strong.

[14]Stannard (1992) comments that there is no barrier to the possibility of human entry into the western hemisphere 60,000 or 70,000 years ago, although the current prudent estimate is 40,000 years ago.

[15]It should be noted that the mono-regional theories of human origins are at this point significantly more persuasive from the standpoint of genetics, for examples. Finch (1991: 49) discusses the difficulties with Wolpoff's theory of multiregional evolution; see also his detailed discussion of race and human origins *ibidem* that corrects racist biases in the way the evolutionary story is commonly told. At this point I am unable to reconcile the various stories tribes hold (particularly Native Americans and Australian Aborigines) with current genetic and linguistic data.

[16]The Old Norse word *blót* for offering or sacrifice is etymologically connected with the meanings of chanting, singing, or prophecying. The word "singing" is also connected to prophecying (Watkins 1969). The Old Norse seeing ceremony *seiður* has chanting as part of its root meanings (cf. Bjarnadóttir and Kremer 1998).

[17]Counting and recounting are part of the etymology of the word "to talk," *del-* (Watkins 1969).

[18]As Honko et al. (1994) describe aptly: "As [the hunter] goes about his [sic] work, animals, plants, trees and rocks all possess a character and individuality of their own. The reverence necessary in their presence and the way in which they must be addressed cannot be understood properly by anyone not brought up in that culture. Animals and the topographical features of the landscape communicate to the experienced hunter promises, warnings and threats.... In short, knowledge of the supranormal is an essential part of the hunter's or fisherman's [sic] mental map of his [sic] territory" (118).

[19]Original instructions can be understood in the following fashion: "Words about purpose, words rooted in our creation, words that allow the human being an identity beyond the illusion of civilization" (Horn 1996: 49).

[20]Fjörgyn, the mother of Þórr, means earth or land in Old Norse, Fjörgynn is the name of a god, "the male subsidiary form of Fjörgyn," maybe the name of an old thunder god (connected to the Lithuanian Perkunas); (De Vries 1977; Simek 1995).

[21]See Titchenell (1985) for a complete translation and some commentary; Old Norse corpora online have the original text available. This poem is usually not included in the canon of the Elder Edda, since its style suggests that it was written later (the manuscript is eighteenth century). (Additionally, its content is not easily accessible.)

[22]According to Stefán Karlsson, an expert in Old Norse manuscripts, and Jónas Kristjánsson, director of the Árni Magnússon Institute in Reykjavík (Bjarnadóttir 1998).

[23]*Galdr* is magic song in Old Norse (*galan*—to sing, especially in relation to birds:

cf. nightin*gale*, a bird seen as particularly capable of magical song in the north of Europe); the old seeing ceremony *seiðr* was also done with chanting, with *varðlokkur*, meaning also magic songs.

[24]On the one hand we find Rowley-Conwy's (1993: 70) critical discussion of the Drachenloch find resulting in the "verdict: a chance arrangement magnified by wishful thinking" (70), on the other hand we have Campbell's (1983) extensive interpretations of "the master bear" (54-56) (which contains one qualificatory clause only). Even though not all the evidence for very early ceremonial connections between humans and bears may be holding up, I believe that there is currently enough substantive material to support such notion. An intervening variable here is, no doubt, the presuppositions of those needing to have early humans be as "primitive" as possible for their evolutionary scheme, vs. those who have ideologies leading to the enhancement of the capacities of early humans. Ideology as an intervening variable in the reading of evidence is a crucial factor. Two things need to be kept in mind here: As Gowlett (1993) and others have pointed out, "through the past 30,000 to 40,000 years the brains of modern *homo sapiens* were similar to our own. Physical and cultural evidence points to lower levels of mental ability and craft skill in the earlier periods. Nevertheless, we may have to concede that the foundations of many basic human skills were laid 1 or even two million years ago, rather than at the origins of our own species" (345). Additionally, many of the dates of early human history seem to get pushed back further and further implying the presence of intelligence and skills previously not suspected at that those points in time.

[25]*Fingr* can mean thumb or finger in Old Norse. Old illustrations clearly show the dragon slayer sucking his thumb (see Davidson 1989: 68).

[26]It is beyond the scope of this article to explore the apparent connections with the psychology of infant thumb sucking, and the necessary distinctions between regressive (pre) and transpersonal (trans, as ritual gesture) thumbsucking in detail. While Wilber (1983) has introduced the dichotomous notion of the "pre-trans fallacy," Washburn (1998) suggests a more dialectical view: "a refusal to yield to what *was* pre is at the same time a closing of oneself to what *could* be trans. In this case, one *does* need to retrace old ground, and refusing to do so has the consequence of forfeiting the possibility of attaining higher ground" (80). This quote seems pertinent to the ritual gesture of thumb sucking for the sake of shamanic seeing and poetic inspiration. Beckett's protagonist might have been better off to suck his thumb in a ritual gesture in order to connect not just with the personal maternal matrix, but also the spiritual ground of being.

[27]More about this below.

[28]See Bahn and Vertut (1997) for views not commonly shown in photos; they make the bear nature of the sculpture more obvious than most photos.

[29]See the photos from 1985 and 1988 in Honko et al. 1994; the video of the same bear ceremonial available for viewing at the Arktikum in Rovaniemi, Finland; and Milovsky (1993).

[30]For the sake of completeness, let me give a fuller picture of Goodman's view

(without critical commentary on my part). Regarding other social formations she comments: "[*Horticulturalists*] *began aggressively asserting control over the habitat*" (19) (about twelve to ten thousand years ago). "While the dominant cultural idea of the hunter-gatherers is balance, that of the horticulturalists is metamorphosis" (20). Regarding agriculturalists she comments that they have "the illusion of power, of being able to exert control over the habitat" in common (25). "Instead of being plagued by guilt feelings toward the earth, agriculturalists are beset by paranoia toward "bad" plants—weeds—and toward equally "bad" animals that intrude on their fields, all of which are to be exterminated in order to protect the harvest" (27). Her view of nomadic pastoralists is that what they "have in common is that although they do not actively modify their natural environment, they are not part of it either.... With the habitat also possessing a sacred aspect, the animals thereby assume the role of the mediator, the bridge or messenger between the habitat and its alienated children" (28-29). Lastly, "urbanites are divorced from the habitat.... [They] have no guilt feelings toward the habitat. The motivation of many environmentalists instead is more that of an antiquarian who wants to preserve rare books" (29). (See, for example, also Honko et al. 1994: 70ff.)

[31]She (1988) bases this summary primarily on a review of South American Indian ceremonials (32).

[32]It should be noted that in other traditions other birds also get blamed. For example, the Sámi seem to blame the cuckoo.

[33]Marshack (1991) interprets the bird from Massat (near Les Trois Frères) as waterbird (it is not apparent which one it would be), however, it could just easily be seen as a raven (which strikes me as the more likely image in this context, especially when compared to other raven images in native cultures).

[34]See Metzner (1994) for a useful discussion.

[35]Interestingly, he is also the one who cross dresses (in order to recapture his stolen hammer he dresses as Freyja and is offered to the thieving giant as bride in exchange for the hammer).

[36]One aspect of the Indo-Europeanization of the earlier populations may have been the increasing physical and ceremonial disappearance of the bear. From my review of Nordic petroglyphs it appears that the bear is no longer in the picture with the arrival of Indo-European peoples, farming, and the Bronze Age. The bear head from Bodum (Ångermanland, Sweden) is 5,000 years old (Erikson and Löfman 1985) and the amber bear from Resen Mose (Jutland, Denmark) is dated to the mesolithic (Marshak 1991: 351ff.). (Erikson and Löfman [1985] interpret the latter sculpture as wild boar.)

[37]See also the overview provided in Shepard and Sanders (1985: xi-xix). They divide the meanings of the Indo-European root into the categories navigation, transportation, and transformation.

[38]These are Buri´s or Búri´s grandsons; conceivably also related to the root complex *bher-*, alternatively connected with *búa* (De Vries 1977: 65).

[39]Schwaar's (1996) translation *Jubmel schafft Land für das Sonnenvolk* is based on

Daga Nyberg's prose versions of Fjellner's "homeric" renditions. Because of the loss of the original Fjellner manuscript it is difficult to determine the extent of his own enriching additions. We find an echo of this cosmogony in the Finno-Ugric myth of the world egg, where the pieces of the egg change into earth, sky, moon, and stars (see Honko et al. 1994: 69); the other common Finno-Ugric cosmogonic myth is that of the earth diver.

[40]This statement warrants much explication (manuscript in progress), however, this much should be said here: For the purposes of the current discussion we can understand this connection with creative energies in Bennett's sense (1964), or, for example, in the neuroscientific sense of ecstatic hyperarousal or mystical rapture, and samadhi or nirvanic hypoarousal (e.g., Fischer 1986). Navajo medicine man Hanson Ashley (1993) has described the necessity to return to the center of creation and to retrace one's step from there, if healing is to occur.

[41]*Loki* says:

En þik síða kóðo kóðu	But you once practised seið
Sámseyjo í,	on Samsey,
ok draptu á vétt sem völur;	and you beat on the drum as witches do,
vitka líki	in the likeness of a wizard
fórtu verþjóð yfir,	you journeyed among mankind,
ok hugða ek that args aðal.	and I thought the hallmark of a pervert.
(Neckel 1927: 98)	(Larrington 1996: 89)

[42]See Bjarnadóttir and Kremer (1998) for more detailed discussion.

[43]See, for example, Plato (1961) in the *Symposium* (189eff.): "For though the term 'hermaphrodite' is only used nowadays as a term of contempt, there really was a man-woman in those days, a being which was half male and half female." Also in the Christian tradition: "In a letter of EUGNOSTOS THE BLESSED, whose two manuscripts were discovered in Egypt not that long ago, we read that the Father gave birth, entirely off himself, to an androgynous human being. This person, joining with his Sophia (spiritual wisdom), in turn, gave birth to an androgynous offspring (Illumination), who owing to its masculine name is a Saviour, and on account of its feminine name is Sophia, also known as Faith (Pistis). The last two became the parents to six other pairs of spiritual androgyns. Clearly, we can see here allusions to the spiritual Androgyny of Christ, who consisted of '*the power and Sophia of God*' (I Cor. 1:24). Word (power) and Wisdom (Sophia), the masculine and the feminine aspects, were merged within a unified essence, personifying Christ as a true intermediary between heaven and earth" (Ripinsky-Naxon 1997: 56).

[44]I would like to acknowledge Pamela Colorado's vision and the students from the Traditional Knowledge Program who traveled with us.

[45]*Auður* is an Old Norse word that is related, among other things, to the fertilizing activities of the three norns under the tree of life, and carries a distinct woman-centered connotation in this context.

Illustration Credits

1: Left image: author's edited computer image based on catalogue Lebendige Vorzeit (Archäologisches Institut der Universität Uppsala), p. 19; right image: author's edited computer image based on author photo of rubbing).
2: Author's edited computer image based on Sveen (1996), p. 47.
3: Author's line computer line drawing based on Chauvet et al. (1995), p. 23.
4: Author's edited computer image based on Gemuev (1989), p. 184.
5: Author's edited computer image based on Davidson (1989), p. 68.
6: Author's edited computer image based on Marshack (1991), p. 238.
7: Author's edited computer image based on Marshack (1991), p. 354.
8: Author's edited computer image based on Sveen (1996), p. 49.

References

Alford, Danny K. H. 1980. "Demise of the Whorf Hypothesis." *Phoenix: New Directions in the Study of Man* 4 (1,2).

Ani, Marimba. 1994. *Yurugu.* Trenton, NJ: Africa World Press.

Apffel-Marglin, Frédérique. 1994. "Development or Decolonization in the Andes." *Daybreak* 4 (3): 6-10.

Ashihmina, Lidija I. 1992. "Reconstruction of Imaginations of the Tree-of-the-World in the Population of the North Suburals in the Bronze and Early Iron Ages." *Suomen Varhaishistoria Fornion Kongressi* 14-16 June 1991. *Studia Historia Septentrionalia* 21: 23-33.

Ashley, Hanson. 1993. Personal communication.

Bäckman, Louise. 1975. *Sájva.* Stockholm, Sweden: Alqvist and Wiksell.

Bahn, Paul G. and Jean Vertut. 1997. *Journey Through the Ice Age.* Berkeley, CA: University of California Press.

Beckett, Samuel. 1951. *Molloy.* London: John Calder.

Bennett, John G. 1964. *Energies.* Charlestown, WV: Claymont.

Bernes, Claes. 1996. *The Nordic Arctic Environment.* Copenhagen: The Nordic Council of Ministers.

Bjarnadottir, Valgerður H. 1998. Personal communication.

Bjarnadóttir, Valgerður H. and Jürgen W. Kremer. 1999. "The Cosmology of Healing in Vanir Norse Mythology." *Yearbook of Cross-Cultural Medicine and Psychotherapy.* Eds. Holger Kalweit and Stanley Krippner. Berlin: Verlag für Wissenschaft und Bildung.

Blumrich, J. F. 1979. *Kasskara und die sieben Welten.* Düsseldorf, Germany: Econ.

Bohm, David. 1980. *Wholeness and the Implicate Order.* London: Routledge and Kegan Paul.

Boyer, Régis. 1991. "Elements of the Sacred Among the Germanic and Norse Peoples." *American, African, and Old European Mythologies.* Compiled by Yves Bonnefoy. Chicago: University of Chicago Press. 226-234.

Brody, Hugh. 1981. *Maps and Dreams*. Toronto: Douglas and McIntyre.

Byock, Jesse L. 1990. *The Saga of the Volsungs*. Berkeley, CA: University of California.

Campbell, Joseph. 1983. *The Way of the Animal Powers*. San Francisco: Harper and Row.

Cardeña, Etzel. 1997. "To the Editor." *Anthropology of Consciousness* 8 (4): 163-167.

Chauvet, Jean-Marie, Éliette Brunel Deschamps, and Christian Hillaire. 1995. *Grotte Chauvet*. Sigmaringen, Germany: Thorbecke.

Cheavalier, Jean and Alain Gheerbrant. 1994. *Dictionary of Symbols*. New York: Penguin.

Colorado, Pamela. 1996. "Indigenous Science." *ReVision*, 18 (3): 6-10.

Colorado, Pamela. 1988. "Bridging Native and Western Science." *Convergence* 21 (2,3): 49-67,

Czaplicka, Marie Antoinette. 1914. *Aboriginal Siberia*. Oxford: Clarendon.

Davidson, Hilda Ellis. 1989. "The Seer's Thumb." *The Seer*. Edinburgh: John Donald. 66-78.

De Santillana, Giorgio and Hertha von Dechend. 1969. *Hamlet's Mill*. Boston: David R. Godine.

De Vries, J. 1977. *Altnordisches etymologisches Wörterbuch*. Leiden, Netherlands: Brill.

Delaby, L. 1984. "Shamans and Mothers of Twins." *Shamanism in Eurasia*, Ed. Mihály Hoppál. 214-230.

Dion-Buffalo, Yvonne and John Mohawk. 1994. "Throughts from an Autochtonous Center." *Cultural Survival* (Winter): 33-35.

Eliades, Mircéa. 1964. *Shamanism: Archaic Techniques of Ecstasy*. Princeton, NJ: Princeton University Press.

Erikson, Bo G. and Carl O. Löfman. 1987. *Scandinavian Saga*. Stockholm, Sweden: Natur och Kultur.

Feyerabend, Paul. 1984. *Wissenschaft als Kunst*. Frankfurt/Main, Germany: Suhrkamp.

Finch, Charles S. 1991. *Echoes of the Old Darkland*. Decatur, GA: Khenti.

Findeisen, Hans. 1970. *Dokumente urtümlicher Weltanschauung der Völker Nordeurasiens*. Oosterhout, Netherlands: Anthropological Publications.

Fischer, Roland. 1986. "Toward a Neuroscience of Self-Experience and States of Self-Awareness and Interpreting Interpretations." *Handbook of States of Consciousness*. Ed. Benjamin B. Wolman and Montague Ullman. New York: Van Nostrand Reinhold. 3-30.

Gemuev, Ismail N. 1989. "Bear Cult in Western Siberia." *Uralic Mythology and Folklore*. Eds. Mihály Hoppál and Juha Pentikäinen. Budapest and Helsinki: Ethnologica Uralica 1. 179-185.

Gimbutas, Marija. 1974. *The Goddesses and Gods of Old Europe*. Berkeley, CA: University of California Press.

Goldschmidt, Walter. 1978. "Nomlaki." *Handbook of North American Indians:*

California. (Vol. 8). Ed. Robert F. Heizer. Washington, DC: Smithsonian. 341-349.

Goodchild, Peter. 1991. *Raven Tales.* Chicago: Chicago Review Press.

Goodman, Felicitas D. 1990. *Where the Spirits Ride the Wind.* Bloomington, IN: Indiana University Press.

Goodman, Felicitas D. 1988. *Ecstasy, Ritual, and Alternate Reality.* Bloomington, IN: Indiana University Press.

Goettner-Abendroth, Heide. 2004. "Matriarchal Society: Definition and Theory." *The Gift/Il Dono. Athanor* 15 (8). Ed. G. Vaughan. Rome, Italy: Meltemi editore. 69-80.

Gouchet, Olivier. 1997. "Sigurðr and the Women." *From the Realm of the Ancestors.* Ed. Joan Marler. Manchester, CT: Knowledge, Ideas and Trends. 278-292.

Gowlett, John. 1993. *Ascent to Civilization.* New York: McGraw-Hill.

Grimm, Jakob. 1966. *Teutonic Mythology* (4 vols.). New York: Dover. Originally published in 1883-1889.

Grönbech, Wilhelm. 1954. *Vor Folkeæt i Oldtiden.* German: *Kultur und Religion der Germanen.* Darmstadt, Germany: Wissenschaftliche Buchgesellschaft. Originally published 1909-1912.

Hallowell, Irving B. 1926. "Bear Ceremonialism in the Northern Hemisphere." *American Anthropologist* 28.

Harding, Sandra. 1997. "Is Modern Science an Ethnoscience? Rethinking Epistemological Assumptions." *Postcolonial African Philosophy.* Ed. Emmanuel Chukwudi Eze. Oxford, UK: Blackwell. 45-70.

Hassler, Peter. 1992a. "The Lies of the Conquistadors." *World Press Review* (December): 28-29.

Hassler, Peter. 1992b. *Menschenopfer bei den Azteken?* New York: Lang.

Hinton, Leanne. 1994. *Flutes of Fire.* Berkeley, CA: Heyday.

Honko, Lauri, Senni Timonen, Michael Branch and Keith Bosley. 1994. *The Great Bear.* New York: Oxford University Press.

Horn, Gabriel. 1996. *Contemplations of a Primal Mind.* Novato, CA: New World.

Irigaray, Luce. 1985. *Speculum of the Other Woman.* Ithaca, NY: Cornell University Press.

Jonsson, Bjorn. n.d. *Star Myths of the Vikings.* Swan River, Manitoba: Jonsson.

Kallio, Biret Máret. 1995. Personal communication.

Kallio, Biret Máret. 1997. "Noaidi: The One Who Sees." *ReVision* 19: 37-41.

Kelly, Robert L. 1995. *The Foraging Spectrum.* Washington, DC: Smithsonian.

Kenin-Lopsan, Mongash Boraxooevich. 1997. "Tuvinian Shamans and the Cult of Birds." *ReVision* 19: 33-36.

Kremer, Jürgen Werner. 2005. "Tricksters of the Trans/Personal: Mythic Explorations of Constructions of Self." *ReVision* 27 (3): 34-43.

Kremer, Jürgen Werner. 2004a. "Ethnoautobiography as Practice of Radical Presence: Storying the Self in Participatory Visions." *ReVision* 26 (2): 5-13.

Kremer, Jürgen Werner. 2004b. "Mythic Storytelling: Re-envisioning Stories from the North." *ReVision* 27 (1) (Summer): 19-30.

Kremer, Jürgen Werner. 2004c. "Remembering Ancestral Conversations." Afterword. Betty Bastien. *Blackfoot Ways of Knowing: The Worldview of the Siksikaitsitapi.* Calgary: University of Calgary Press. 184-193.

Kremer, Jürgen Werner. 2003. "Healing the Impact of Colonization, Genocide, and Racism on Indigenous Populations." *The Psychological Impact of War Trauma on Civilians: An International Perspective.* Eds. S. Krippner and T. M. McIntyre (with B. Bastien, R. Kuokkanen and P. Vickers). New York: Praeger. 25-37.

Kremer, Jürgen Werner. 2002a. "Radical Presence." *ReVision* 24 (3): 11-20.

Kremer, Jürgen Werner. 2002b. "Shamanic Initiations and Their Loss: Decolonization as Initiation and Healing." *Ethnopsychologische Mitteilungen* 9 (1,2): 109-148.

Kremer, Jürgen Werner. 2000a. "The Cosmology of Healing in vanir Norse Mythology." *Yearbook of Cross-Cultural Medicine and Psychotherapy 1997.* Eds. H. Kalweit and S. Krippner. Mainz, Germany: Verlag fur Wissenschaft und Bildung. (With Valgerður H. Bjarnadóttir.) 127-176.

Kremer, Jürgen Werner. 2000b. "Millennial Twins: An Essay into Time and Place." *ReVision* 22 (3): 29-42.

Kremer, Jürgen Werner. 1999. "Reconstructing Indigenous Consciousness: Preliminary Considerations." *Ethnopsychologische Mitteilungen* 8 (1): 32-56.

Kremer, Jürgen Werner. 1998. "The Shadow of Evolutionary Thinking." *Ken Wilber in Dialogue.* Eds. Donald Rothberg and Sean Kelly. Wheaton, IL: Quest, 1998. 237-258.

Kremer, Jürgen Werner. 1997a. "Recovering Indigenous Mind. "*ReVision* 19 (4): 32-46.

Kremer, Jürgen Werner. 1997b. "Shamanic Inquiry as Recovery of Indigenous Mind: Toward an Egalitarian Exchange of Knowledge." *Was ist ein Schamane/ What is a Shaman?* Eds. Amélie Schenk and Christian Rätsch. Special issue of *Journal for Ethnomedicine – Curare* 13: 127-142.

Kremer, Jürgen Werner. 1997c. "Transforming Learning Transforming." *ReVision* 20 (1): 7-14.

Kremer, Jürgen Werner. 1996. "The Possibility Of Recovering Indigenous European Perspectives On Native Healing Practices." *Ethnopsychologische Mitteilungen* 5 (2): 149-164.

Kremer, Jürgen Werner. 1995. "Perspectives on Indigenous Healing." *Noetic Sciences Review* (Spring): 13-18.

Kremer, Jürgen Werner. 1994. "Practices for the Postmodern Shaman?" *Proceedings of the 10th International Conference on the Study of Shamanism and Alternate Modes of Healing.* Ed. Ruth-Inge Heinze. Berkeley, CA: Independent Scholars of Asia.

Kremer, Jürgen Werner. 1993. "The Past and Future Process of Mythology." *Proceedings of the Ninth International Conference on the Study of Shamanism and Alternate Modes of Healing.* Ed. R.-I. Heinz. Berkeley: Independent Scholars of Asia.

Kremer, Jürgen Werner. 1992a. "The Dark Night of the Scholar." *ReVision* 14 (4) (Spring): 169-178.

Kremer, Jürgen Werner. 1992b. "Whither Dark Night of the Scholar?" *ReVision* 15 (1) (Summer): 4-12.

Kremer, Jürgen Werner. 1991. "Contemporary Shamanism and the Evolution of Consciousness: Reflections on Owen Barfield's *Saving Appearances*." *Open Eye* 8 (3): 4-5, 9.

Kremer, Jürgen Werner. 1986. "The Human Science Approach as Discourse." *Saybrook Review* 6: 65-105.

Kremer, Jürgen Werner and Stanley Krippner. 1994. "Trance Postures." Re-Vision 16 (4) (Spring): 173-182.

Kuoljok, Kerstin Eidlitz. 1993. *Nordsamojediska folk*. Uppsala: Ursus.

Kyselka, Will and Ray Lanterman. 1976. *North Star to Southern Cross*. Honolulu: University of Hawaii Press.

LaPena, Frank. 1998. "In Vision We Can Balance the World." *News from Native California* 12 (2): 18-19.

Larrington, C. *The Poetic Edda*. Oxford: Oxford University Press..

Lincoln, Bruce. *Myth, Cosmos, and Society*. Boston: Harvard, 1986.

Lomatuway'ma, Michael, Lorena Lomatuway'ma, Sidney Namingha and Ekkehart Malotki. 1993. *Kiqötutuwutsi: Hopi Ruin legends*. Flagstaff, AZ: Northern Arizona University.

Mails, Thomas E. and Dan Evehema. 1995. *Hotevilla*. New York: Marlowe.

Marshak, Alexander. 1991. *The Roots of Civilization*. Mount Kisco, NY: Moyer Bell.

Metzner, Ralph. 1994. *The Well of Remembrance*. Boston: Shambhala.

Milovsky, Alexander. 1993. "Hail to Thee, Papa Bear." *Natural History* 12: 34-41.

Mitzka, Walther. 1960. *Etymologisches Wörterbuch der deutschen Sprache*. Berlin: Walter de Gruyter.

Mohawk, John. "Indigenous Creation-Centered Spirituality" (interview with Charlene Spretnak). *Creation* 16-18 (September/October).

Neckel, Gustav. 1927. *Edda*. 2 vols. Heidelberg: Carl Winters Universitätsbuchhandlung.

New Encyclopedia Britannica, The. 1988. Vol. 26. Ed. by Philip Goetz. London: Encyclopædia Britannica. 64-67.

Pálsson, Hermann. 1996. *Völuspá*. Edinburgh: Lockharton Press.

Paproth, Hans-Joachim. 1976. *Studien über das Bärenzeremoniell*. Uppsala, Sweden: Religionshistoriska Institutionen.

Peat, F. David. 1994. *Lighting the Seventh Fire*. New York: Birch Lane.

Pentikäinen, Juha Y. 1989. *Kalevala mythology* Trans. R. Poom. Bloomington: Indiana University Press.

Peter-Röcher, Heidi. 1996. "Köpfe gekocht." *Der Spiegel* 8: 214-215.

Plato. 1961. *The Collected Dialogues*. Eds. Edith Hamilton and Huntington Cairns. Princeton, NJ: Bollingen.

Ripinsky-Naxon, Michael. 1997. *Sexuality, Shamanism, and Transformation.* Berlin, Germany: Verlag für Wissenschaft und Bildung.

Rowley-Conwy, Peter. 1993. "Was There a Neanderthal Religion?" *The First Humans.* Ed. Göran Burenhult. San Francisco: Harper. 70-73

Sammallahti, Pekka. 1998. *The Saami Languages.* Karašjohka, Sápmi: Davvi Girji.

Sammallahti, Pekka. 1990. "The Sámi Language: Past and Present." *Arctic Languages: An Awakening.* Ed. Dirmid R. F. Collis. Paris: UNESCO.

Schmidt, Éva. 1989. "Bear Cult and Mythology of the Northern Ob.Ugrians." *Uralic Mythology and Folklore.* Ed. Mihály Hoppál and Juha Pentikäinen. Budapest and Helsinki: Ethnologica Uralica 1. 187-232.

Schwaar, H. U. 1996. *Sápmi.* Frauenfeld, CH: Waldgut.

Shepard, Paul and Barry Sanders. 1985. *The Sacred Paw: The Bear in Nature, Myth and Literature.* New York: Viking Penguin.

Simek, Rudolf. 1995. *Lexikon der germanischen Mythologie.* Stuttgart, Germany: Alfred Kröner Verlag.

Solbakk, Aage. 1994. *Sámi Historjá 1.* Kárášjohka, Sápmi: Davvi Girji.

Stannard, David E. 1992. *American Holocaust.* Oxford: Oxford University Press.

Sturluson, Snorri. 1987. *Edda.* Trans. Anthony Faulkes. London: Everyman.

Sveen Arvid. 1996. *Rock Carvings.* Finnmark, Norway: Trykkforum.

Szymborska, Wisława. 1995. *View With a Grain of Sand.* New York: Harcourt Brace,

Terry, Patricia. 1990. *Poems of the Elder Edda.* Philadelphia: Univeristy of Pennsylvania Press.

Titchenell, Elsa-Brita. 1985. *The Masks of Odin.* Pasadena, California: The Theosophical University Press.

Vaughan, Genevieve. 1997. *For-Giving.* Austin, Texas: Plain View Press.

Vaughan, Genevieve, ed. 2004. *The Gift/Il Dono. Athanor* 15 (8). Rome, Italy: Meltemi editore.

Washburn, Michael. 1998. "The Pre/Trans Fallacy Reconsidered." *Ken Wilber in Dialogue.* Ed. Donald Rothberg and Sean Kelly. Wheaton, IL: Quest. 62-83.

Waters, Frank. 1975. *Mexico Mystique.* Athens: Ohio University Press.

Waters, Frank. *Book of the Hopi.* New York: Penguin, 1963.

Watkins, Calvert. 1969. "Indo-European and the Indo-Europeans." *The American Heritage Dictionary of the English Language.* Ed. William Morris. NY: American Heritage. 1496-1550.

Whorf, Benjamin Lee. 1956. *Language, Thought and Reality.* Cambridge, MA: MIT.

Wilber, Ken. 1983. *Eye to Eye.* New York: Anchor.

Wilber, Ken. 1995. *Sex, Ecology, Spirituality.* Boston, MA: Shambhala.

Woodside, Lisa N., V. K. Kumar and Ronald J. Pekala. 1997. "Monotonous Percussion Drumming and Trance Postures: A Controlled Evaluation of Phenomenological Effects." *Anthropology of Consciousness* 8 (2,3): 69-87.

CHRISTOPHER G. TROTT

The Gender of the Bear

Bear Symbolism and the Third Sex Among the Inuit

In the winter of 1922-1923 anthropologist Therkel Mathiassen was forced to stay on Southampton Island due to adverse ice conditions. During this period he was able to observe and record in some detail a series of shamanistic seances performed in the community. While Mathiassen never published his accounts of the performances, the leader of the expedition, Knud Rasmussen (1929, 1930), included excerpts from his diary in the published monographs of the expedition. Neither Rasmussen nor Mathiassen provide adequate contextual background for these sessions, primarily because the Inuit blamed many of their problems on Mathiassen and his activities in excavating archaeological sites on the island. One of the most striking series of seances focuses around the attempt to cure a woman called Nanoraq from various persistent ailments. During the sessions Nanoraq confessed to a number of transgressions and through these was to be cured of her problems. Despite these efforts Nanoraq persisted in her complaints, but the shamanistic activities ceased, probably because, as Jarich Oosten (1984) has suggested, the real focus of the activities was on the annual "New Year's" ceremonies[1] and not particularly on Nanoraq's problems (378).

The shaman performances highlighted the cause of Nanoraq's illness in terms of ritual transgressions. Mathiassen notes, however, that the shaman himself attributed her problems to the fact that Nanoraq had beaten her little daughter so much that her arm had turned bad (Rasmussen 1930: 111). Already there are two explanations in place for this illness. Oddly enough, Nanoraq's own explanation seems to have been ignored by the investigators. "Nanoraq says that since the bear was shot she had been afraid more and more each day that passed, and at last she fell ill. The skin, head and legs of a bear must not be taken home at once, but must first be cached; the result of this is that half of the bear's skin has now been eaten by dogs" (Rasmussen 1930: 108). Oosten (1984) is the only investigator to have picked up on this point, explaining that "Nanoraq's name means 'polar bear skin,'" and it is clear that she felt related to the polar bear. This is not surprising when we consider the great importance of the namesake relationship in Inuit society and in particular the important symbolism of the bear" (387).

Oosten fails to elaborate any further, but I believe that this small anecdote takes us to the heart of a number of critical issues dealing with the relationship between women and bears among the Inuit and, in a more general sense, the puzzling problems of the nature/culture relationship as articulated through the categories of gender. Oosten points in the right direction when he invokes the namesake relationship, but it would be rare that the meaning of a name, in and of itself, would have much influence on the problem at hand. Much more critical is from whom and in what context Nanoraq received her name: if she had received her name from a shaman who sought to sustain her life by giving her the name of one of his familiar spirits, then Oosten's hypothesis could be sustained (Saladin d'Anglure and Hansen 1997). There is no evidence to support this line of reasoning, however.

The incident described by Mathiassen and analyzed by Oosten points to the intersection of two metaphorical frameworks within Inuit cosmology: bear symbolism and gender categories. The literature on Inuit symbolism is extensive in both of these areas, but only Saladin d'Anglure (1986) has attempted to show the links between the two. In this chapter, I will examine the existing discussions within each of these areas and then develop an alternative hypothesis about the relationship between these two metaphorical fields that will further bring into question our understanding of Inuit cultural categories. Through her work with the Yup'ik Eskimos of Alaska, Fienup-Riordan (1984) has argued that the cycling of animals through life and death constitutes the key metaphor in Inuit thought, while Saladin d'Anglure (1986) has argued that sex and gender constitutes the central metaphorical axis for Inuit. By looking at the relationship between bears and gender it is now possible to resolve this dichotomy.

The Metaphor of the Bear

There is no doubt that the polar bear (*nanuq*) takes on a symbolic significance among Inuit far beyond its importance in their diet. In one of the earliest, and only, theoretical considerations of Inuit society, Marcel Mauss (Mauss and Beauchat 1979) pointed to the fundamental division between land and sea in Inuit cosmology, clearly reflected in the taboos which separated the preparation of caribou skins and meat (land) from either seal or walrus meat and skins (sea). The polar bear has the peculiar property of being a land animal that lives and hunts primarily in the sea. In the fall and spring, bears hunt seals on the land fast ice by attacking them through their breathing holes, while in the summer bears move onto the ice flows to continue seal hunting in the open water. Rarely will bears remain on land in the summer and they are not known to hunt caribou, primarily because bears cannot move as swiftly on the land as they can in the sea. To follow Mary Douglas's (1966) line of argument, bears are thus categorically ambivalent and thus logically potentially sources of "pollution."

Nelson Graburn (1976) has noted that the *nalunaikutanga* or distinctive features of the polar bear are the incisors, the claws as well as the tongue. For Graburn this speaks to the bear's "striking power" most represented in the fact that the bear is often portrayed in sculpture battling its only serious opponent, the walrus

(7). The distinctive features of the polar bear noted by the Inuit should warn the reader of an ethnocentric bias created by classifying polar bears with other types of bears where, in western terms, the distinctive feature is the bear's whiteness. Within the universe of the Eastern Arctic Inuit there are no other bears, although they are aware of "land bears," and thus the classificatory paradigm is significantly different.

Most important is the fact that bears exhibit a direct parallel with human activity. Here we begin to note the dichotomization of the bear in terms of the sexual division of labour. Bears, like men, are primarily hunters and more particularly seal hunters. Like humans, bears hunt seals on the ice through breathing hole techniques. Indeed Vladimir Randa (1986b) has argued that Inuit learned breathing hole hunting techniques through their observations of bear behaviour. In an early analysis of bear symbolism, Bernard Saladin d'Anglure (1980) argued that bears were the archetypal symbol of male power. For Saladin d'Anglure this appeared in three forms:

1) Bears are the greatest opponent for male hunters and as such are the most prized prey for men. Exceptional value was placed by men on hunting bears, and in some senses one could not be a "real man" (*angutimarik*) without having captured a bear.
2) As hunters themselves bears constituted the primary model for male hunting activities. Bears thus represented male hunting prowess at its best.
3) Bears appeared frequently as shaman helpers and since it was thought that most shamans were men, they were thus primarily men's helpers.

These conclusions accorded well with the available data and the thinking of the time, despite the obvious androcentrism of their formulation (84-85).

But this formulation overlooks another very important part of the bear's annual cycle. Like humans, bears built dens in the winter out of the snow that are similar in shape and size to igloos. The dens are primarily the spaces of female bears who give birth to their young while in the dens and then reappear in March to begin hunting on the ice. In the same way, igloos are primarily women's spaces and are occupied by the Inuit in the darkest part of the winter. The literature is clear that igloos are women's spaces and are metaphorically parallel to the uterus and the vagina (Saladin d'Anglure 1977a). The life cycle and hunting activities of bears directly parallels that of humans thus providing a critical juncture between the natural world and the human world that allow humans to think about their own cultural constructions. This is well known and can be seen in the taboos surrounding the killing of a bear that indicate that the bear corpse receives the same death rites that humans do. A female skin must be hung in the igloo for three days with the appropriate women's instruments (*ulu, qulliq*) laid alongside, while a male skin is hung in the igloo for four days with men's knives (*savik*) and hunting implements laid alongside.

There is thus plenty of evidence for articulating metaphorical parallels between human activity and bears, which the Inuit are keen to exploit. But we already have begun to indicate that the parallels not only apply to men's lives, but to women's as well. In cosmological terms, bears inhabit the sleeping platform of the "Man in the Moon" (Aningat) who controls caribou (land animals) and represents both male sexual virility and hunting prowess. Aningat is also one of the primary sources of shamanic insight and it is the bears that occupy his sleeping platform that become shaman familiars. Bears are thus centrally located in the primordial male symbol among the Inuit. At the same time bears also protect the sleeping platform of the "Mother of Sea Beasts" (Sedna[2]) where she keeps sea mammals when withholding them from humans, usually due to infractions of the taboos surrounding menstruation. One must also note that when Sedna's father comes to join her at the bottom of the sea, he wraps himself in a polar bear skin and lays down on the sea shore (the fluctuating boundary between land and sea). The combined ambivalence of the sea shore and the bear skin transport her father into the "spirit" world at the bottom of the sea. What is key to note here is that in the primary opposition established in Inuit cosmology, the bear is separately situated on both sides of the boundary.

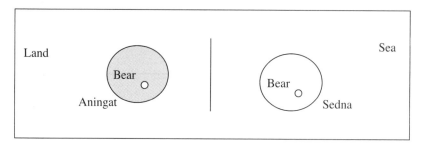

Figure 1: Bears within Inuit cosmological structures

In the third spiritual realm, that of Narsuk, the bear also appears as an important operator. Parallel to the changes in size from giant, to human, to dwarf that take place in the story, the bear appears alternatively as a bear, a fox, and as a lemming depending on visual perspective and relative size. In the sequence of creation stories outlined by Saladin d'Anglure (1991) bear, fox and lemming are among the original animals prior to the creation of caribou and sea mammals. The fox is also a categorically ambivalent creature as it occupies the sea shore and scavenges on the carcasses left by polar bears.[3] The lemming has the odd property of being a land animal that periodically during its population cycle throws itself into the sea. The Inuit are clearly exploiting the parallelism in the classificatory ambiguities of these three animals, transforming the parallelism into a distinction based on size.

In two publications, Randa (1986a, 1986b) has intensively examined polar bears from both a zoological and cosmological point of view. Randa's zoological evidence provides a scientific basis for the symbolic expressions of the Inuit. Randa is concerned primarily with the classification of bears within Inuit thought and concludes that bears operate as the mediator between the land/sea, hunter/hunted, and animal/human dichotomies in Inuit thought. He concludes, "*Pour revenir à l'ours polaire, s'il a si fortement frappé l'imaginaire des Inuit, c'est en raison de sa tendance naturelle à chevaucher la frontière des catégories contrastives construites socialement*" (Randa 1986b: 168).

Models of Gender

In "sociological" terms, Jean Briggs (1974) examines the evidence for patriarchy and explores the arguments surrounding the equality and inequality of the sexes among the Inuit in her discussion of "Eskimo Women: Makers of Men." She finds substantial evidence to support both positions, but none that is conclusive. Briggs concludes that male-female relations among the Inuit are fundamentally ambivalent. She attributes this to the flexibility of Inuit social forms that makes Inuit society so adaptable to the variable ecological conditions in the arctic. While it seems to me that this flexibility is what needs to be explained rather than constituting an explanation, I think her focus on ambivalence is important. At this level the symbolic ambivalence of the bear thus constitutes an excellent metaphor for male-female relations. To see this one needs to look more closely at how male-female relations are constructed in Inuit society.

An important aspect of Briggs' (1974) discussion is the cases she notes where women perform what are usually understood as men's activities, and where men perform women's activities. Since Naomi Giffen's (1930) paper, researchers have been aware of the strict division of labour among Inuit. But Briggs' argument points to the fact that the division of labour may be qualified by other circumstances. In the cases cited by Briggs in a family that has had a series of girls, one of them will be chosen by the father to learn male hunting skills and thus brought up as a boy. Thus while there may be a strict division of labour, the people who perform that labour are not so strictly defined. For Briggs this again speaks to a fundamental flexibility in Inuit society that also forms the core of the gender system as well. People may move between the gender role categories, where circumstances dictate.

Saladin d'Anglure (1977b) took up the challenge set forth in Brigg's article and argued that violence against women, and consequently patriarchy, was endemic in Inuit thought and practice. As evidence he cited the myth where the original two humans were males and, desiring to reproduce, one of the men became pregnant. When the child was ready to be born the other male recited some magic words that caused the penis to split and turn into a vulva whereupon the child was born. In addition, Saladin d'Anglure points to the Arnapaktuq myth where a battered wife dies and her name soul moves through a series of animals until finally as a seal she is captured by her own brother and enters into her brother's wife to be born as his son. For Saladin d'Anglure this evidence establishes a fundamental patriarchy among the Inuit.

Yvonne Guérin (1982) challenged this argument by questioning the textual evidence of the myth of first humans, and asking if the text said *inuk* (human) rather than *anguti* (male) would this not suggest an androgynous origin for humans thus qualifying the strict patriarchy of the text? Saladin d'Anglure (1986) has replied by pointing out that the original Inuktitut text does indeed say *anguti* (male) and thus the argument holds (49). Guérin also challenges the interpretation of the Arnapaktuq myth by pointing to the variations of the myth across the arctic, only some of which begin with a battered wife while many others begin with women, children, or men. Furthermore she questions the arguments based on the prevalence of female infanticide (especially among the Netsilik Inuit) as indicating a fundamental preference for boys as opposed to girls. She examines the material surrounding the spirits of children who either die through abortion, are miscarried, or are killed shortly after birth. In Greenland these spirits are especially dangerous to hunters and can bring bad weather. Shamans must struggle to capture and kill these spirits. On the other hand in Alaska, if a hunter can capture the spirit of the dead child and use the dried corpse as a hunting charm, then these spirits can be very beneficial to the hunters. Guérin thus provides evidence that the rigid patriarchy proposed by Saladin d'Anglure might be qualified, and might at least be ambivalent in the terms suggested by Briggs (1974).

Saladin d'Anglure (1986) has re-evaluated the evidence by asking what the contexts for such ambivalence might be, and in so doing has shifted the argument to different grounds. The basis for such gender role ambivalence may not be based on pragmatic circumstances but on fundamental properties of the Inuit understanding of gender. This is well illustrated in the cover picture of the 1982 edition of *Equinox* magazine which shows a woman hunter from Iglulik.

Saladin d'Anglure's (1986) point of departure has been the naming system whereby children, through the inheritance of names, take on the social gender of the namesake despite their evident biological attributes. Each person is made up of four elements: the blood from the mother's blood, the bones from the father's sperm, the flesh from the game animals, and the name soul from a recently deceased person. When a person dies, the name soul rises up out of the body and searches out a pregnant women, into whom they enter and form a new human being. The fetus then has a certain amount of volition as to what sex it may choose to be when born. Although the data is difficult to assess it appears that fetuses are generally thought of as male, but that as the child leaves the uterus (understood metaphorically as an igloo) it can choose either male (knife or harpoon) or female (ulu or stone lamp) implements and thus determine its sex. During the birth process a child may change its sex and the penis is absorbed internally to become a girl (*sipiniq*). While it is logically possible for a female fetus' clitoris to grow into a penis, this seems to happen so infrequently that none of my informants could recall a case. Saladin d'Anglure concludes that approximately two percent of the population are *sipiniq*. At birth the child is socialized according to the gender of the person who last held the name and not according the their biological sexual characteristics. This socialization is indicated through the clothes the child wears (there are distinctive male and female outfits), the length and style of hair, and the tasks the child is trained to perform. Thus approximately 15 percent of biological girls are acculturated as boys and similarly for biological boys. This is further complicated by the fact that a child may receive multiple names (usually four or five in the Iglulik/North Baffin district, but this may go as high as eleven names) from ancestors of different genders and thus have multiple genders according to which name is in use. Furthermore, more than one child may share the same name, thus creating a system of *avvariit* or "halves."[4] Saladin d'Anglure (1986) has pointed to the fact that a combination of circumstances is usually required before a complete gender transference takes place: multiple names of the opposite gender and circumstances such as those outlined by Briggs (1974). In other cases partial transformations may occur: the child will be dressed as a boy one day, a girl the next; the child may be split so that half of their hair is long and the other short and their clothes are designed with a male and female side. At puberty,[5] the child's gender roles were realigned to their biological sex.[6] Thus when I had mistakenly treated an eleven-year-old girl as a girl and was informed by her playmate that she was in fact a boy, she was able to respond quite clearly that she had not been a boy for two years. For girls socialized as boys, their first menstruation was usually marked by them visiting each house where the occupants declared what a great hunter the child was and how s/he had captured such large game as walrus or whales. After this the child's clothes were changed and she was taught to sew. For boys the transformation of gender occurred when they captured and distributed their first game.

This cursory summary of the evidence suggests that Inuit understandings of gender are constructed in a markedly different way from those in the West. Firstly, it suggests that people can and do change their gender over the course of their lives. Secondly it suggests that a single person may in fact have multiple genders (given that they have a number of names). Thirdly, it suggests that gender may be situationally defined. One of the consequences of gender derived from names is that the children are in fact the ancestors returned to the living. As an example, I will point to a situation where I was hunting one spring with a middle-aged man. This man was a well-established hunter in the community, had raised and provided for a family, and as far as I was concerned was clearly male. A group of much younger men came to our camp one evening and immediately began making ribald sexual jokes with this man, asking to touch his genitals. I soon discovered that these younger men had the name of the older man's namesake's husband, and thus they were treating him (jokingly) as their wife. Situationally he had become a woman.

Further evidence for ambivalent gender relations can be found in Inuit cosmology. In the myth of human origins and the Arnakpaktuq myths, already presented, we see further evidence of changing genders. In addition, a careful analysis of shamanism has shown firstly that not only is the proportion of shamans to the general population much higher than anticipated, but that there were also many more female shamans than had been predicted (Saladin d'Anglure 1988). Saladin d'Anglure and Hansen (1997) have further shown that shamanism is linked to the naming complex and that those who become shamans are more likely to have been transgendered. Much more important has been the analysis of ritual activity where significant transvestite transformations take place culminating in the exchange of spouses. Shamanism also provides a further field for gender transformation among the Inuit.

Clearly Inuit gender relations are constructed in terms outside the western frame of reference, and this difference has led to some debate as to how to conceptualize these relations. Briggs (1974) continues to use a two-gender model that leaves male and female gender categories correlated with gender roles, but argues for an institutional flexibility allowing people to move back and forth between various gender roles. Saladin d'Anglure (1986) has argued that the variety of gender expressions in Inuit society call for an additional gender category, "le troisieme sexe." These overlapping and variable gender relations have led him to conclude that these man-woman/woman-man figures at birth, in childhood, and throughout shamanism constitute a separate sociological category, the "third sex" which is neither male nor female, and both male and female at the same time.

As adults, Inuit men and women fulfill the gender roles assigned to their sex, although within specified contexts those who have had differential upbringings will also perform the roles of the opposite sex. It is mainly within the context of kinship references that the ambiguities will remain, although I have argued that the significance of this lies in the fact that it creates a structurally ordered set of ongoing relations between people and land rather than creating an intermediary gender (Trott 1995).

Linking Bears and Gender

In 1982, I presented an ethnographic puzzle in the form of a small carving with a bear's head placed centrally within a stylized representation of a vulva. My informants had told me that the carving was "all about women," and given Saladin d'Anglure's male-oriented interpretation of bears I sought to elaborate in what sense bears could also "stand for" women. At that time I pointed out that while men stood in a relation of opposition to bears, women stood in an homologous relation to bears. While men stood in danger of being hunted and killed by bears through the instability of the predator-prey relation, women stood in danger of transforming into bears through the relationship between their reproductive cycle and the life cycle of the bear (Trott 1982).

In his important paper where he applies of the concept of the "third sex" to the Inuit, Saladin d'Anglure (1986) has proposed that an *axis mundi* emerges along the connections between the changeable sex of the fetus (*sipiniq*), the sexual variability among children and the transformations that take place at puberty, and the sexual ambiguity of shamans. Within the Levi-Straussian structuralist framework that forms the basis of Saladin d'Anglure's theory this is a logical conclusion. The primary opposition between male and female is mediated and transcended by a third category that "resolves" the opposition given in nature. The mediation of the "third sex" within the gender system appears coded in animal terms as the bear. In the same way that the bear mediates the opposition between land and sea animals, the "third sex" mediates gender relations, and thus the two appear as homologies of one another. From this perspective, bears are then the most appropriate animal to be used as shaman familiars. Graphically one can represent this position as follows:

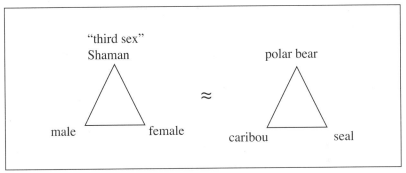

Figure 2: Homological Relations between gender and animals

The bear is therefore also the "third sex," both male and female, and neither male nor female.

This is a substantial argument that we need to take very seriously. Nevertheless, it overlooks the rather important point that men and women each stand in a fundamentally different relationship to bears. One of the striking elements is that when one discusses bears with Inuit men and women one encounters very different responses. Women inevitably say that bears are *iqsinaqtuq*, "frightening," and give a shudder to express the fear. One would not be surprised to find such a response as indeed bears are very frightening and can be dangerous, but what was surprising was the similarity of the responses from different women that suggested a standardized cultural response for women. On the other hand, men almost inevitably became animated and excited when discussing bears and would enter into stories of various risky adventures in capturing bears (usually other hunters adventures as it is inappropriate to talk about one's own prowess). On a number of occasions inquiries into bears evoked stories of one man who had jumped on the back of a bear and garrotted it with his harpoon line. In addition, the men would talk about the polar bears ability to hunt seals, killing them with a single blow of the paw, and then eating only the blubber and leaving the remainder of the carcass. At least on the emotional level there were very different responses.

Mythologically, Randa (1986a) has shown that bears are very prominent and figure primarily in contexts where social conflicts cannot be resolved. In these cases, one of the partners will transform into a bear and seek vengeance on the other partner or on the other members of the social group. What must be noted is that it is always women who transform into bears while men will marry bears who fluctuate on the border between bears and women. One of the well known stories concerns a man who had three daughters and when the eldest reached the age to be married he shut her up in an igloo alone. The girl gradually transformed into a bear and broke out of the hut. The father with his wife and two younger daughters gave chase but the bear turned on them and ate the father. The mother and two sisters protected themselves by laying out skin stretchers in a circle and sitting within. The bear sniffed at the ring of skin stretchers and then wandered off. It is thus the women's ability to construct a (circular) boundary out of distinctively women's tools that protects the family. The story explores both the reality that women can transform into bears while at the same time maintaining that it is the women who must construct and maintain the boundary between humans and bears. There is a clear association here between a women's reproductive cycle, eligibility for marriage, and the creation and manipulation of boundaries that permeates all the stories about bears and women.

Randa (1986a) notes further that bears are also frequently adopted by women to replace children that have been lost. Not only does this appear in the corpus of myths, but stories from my informants in Arctic Bay also indicated that bear cubs were often adopted in practice. This would suggest that women can also stand in a "mothering," nurturing relationship to bears as well.

Bears do not therefore collapse the categories of maleness and femaleness but maintain the distinctiveness of the relationship between the two. There is no logic of synthesis or mediation here, but rather the attempt to hold in place the terms of the opposition while seeing them as related. The same argument can be applied to the categories of gender. I am not convinced therefore that a third sex exists among the Inuit and the symbolism of the bear parallels such a conclusion. Indeed, I would argue that given the ambiguities of gender in Inuit society, the gender of each person only becomes evident as men and women construct and demonstrate their gender through the practical activities they undertake. Thus in the social division of labour, one does not hunt because one is a man, rather one's hunting ability demonstrates that one is indeed a man. The significance of marking a boy's first catch is thus that the boy has demonstrated his maleness and is thus in the position to give away his first game. For a parallel with girls, first menstruation is clearly marked by isolation (as seen in the myth of the girl transforming into a bear above) and by tattooing. As the myth shows, though, first menstruation is the process of transformation, possibly into a woman, possibly into a bear. Tattooing tries to hold the girl onto the human side of the boundary through the parallels between the girl and the woman in the sun (Saladin d'Anglure 1991) and the use of soot to mark boundaries.[7] Only when a girl produces her first child does she become "fixed" as woman, and, parallel to the boy renouncing his first game, the girl must renounce her first child to the community through adoption.[8] Ritually, symbolically, and metaphorically each child, whatever their gender as a child, is made into either a man or a woman. Because of the strict division of labour among Inuit, I would agree with Briggs (1974) that there are only two genders. What remains in question is how those two genders are internally constituted and how they then relate to one another. I would propose that a quite different symbolic logic is at work that allows the analyst to account for the "flexibility" Briggs has seen within the Inuit data.

Not all authors agree that gender does form the essential line of symbolic differentiation among the Inuit. Ann Fienup-Riordan (1984), on the basis of her data from the Yup'ik Eskimo of Alaska, has argued that the human/animal distinction, the maintenance of boundaries between these two through injunctions (taboos), and the ritual passage between these two realms appear as the basic symbolic modality. Fienup-Riordan's and Saladin d'Anglure's positions can be articulated through understanding that the production of animal products and the reproduction of human and animal life form the nexus of Inuit and Yup'ik ritual. Inuit discourse can be seen to run along two axes, male-female and animal-human at the same time (Oosten 1989).

Towards an Inuit Epistemology

A different "logic of the concrete" needs to be articulated for this ethnographic situation. Rather than a logic of opposition and mediation, or of thesis-antithesis-synthesis (to put it in its philosophical frame), we need to see a logic of embeddedness and complementarity. What I mean by this is that in any pair of oppositions the distinction between the two terms will be maintained, but each term will always invoke the other by the fact that a piece of one term is already embedded in the other term. The classical *ying-yan* model of the Chinese is the most evident example of such a position:

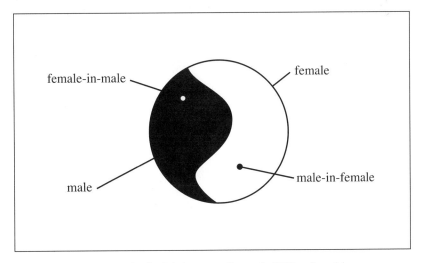

Figure 3: Gender Relations according to the "Chinese" model

In this model binary aspects of reality (male/female, animal/human) oppose and complement each other to form a unified whole (represented by the circle). Within each aspect lies a portion of its own opposite, thus overcoming the apparent mutual exclusion of the two terms. This model seems to work well for the understanding of gender among the Inuit where male and female, especially in practice, complement each other while at the same time each man and each woman contains within them an aspect of the opposite (given through their names) that becomes situationally and momentarily evident. There are two problems with this model: 1) it requires one to assume that ultimately everything comes together into a united whole; 2) it cannot account for homological symbol of the bear; and 3) it does not allow for movement between the categories.

The philosophical drive toward unity is probably a western intellectual imperative, and has recently been brought into question not only by post-modern thought but also by David Turner's (1985) reflections on Australian Aboriginal thought. Earlier work on Inuit social organization has suggested that the Inuit maintain a balance between what Turner has called an incorporative and federative logic of organization, that never allows one to collapse into the other. The "federative" links created by the history of names over an area divides the domestic groups as both the husband and wife maintain the ties given to them by the name. At the same time residential associations at the level of the household and the local hunting group create "incorporative" relations that set local task groups in competition for resources (Trott 2000). In the origin myth discussed above, it must be noted that *two* men emerge from the earth, and from their activities further distinctions are created in the universe. Further Graburn (1972) has noted, "There is an inherent symmetry in carvings of most single-creature figures and there is very often bilateral symmetry (*idluriik* = two equals as a pair) or complementary symmetry (*aipariik* = two complements as a natural pair) in the multi-figure sculptures, the type of symmetry being appropriate for the creatures modelled" (168). Interestingly, *idluriik* is also the term for "cross-cousins" and "song partners" while *aipariik* is frequently used for husband/wife couples. This linguistic and artistic model suggests that Inuit recognize at least two modes of relating pairs.

It is not possible, then to reach back to a single monadic existence in Inuit thought? If one postulates an unmediated dualism (at least) in Inuit thought the question then becomes how to create relationships between the terms.

In terms of gender, every male in some sense contains an aspect of the female and every female contains an aspect of the male. This is most evident in those children who have been socialized cross-gender and as adults perform the tasks assigned to both sexes. In a further dimension, Saladin d'Anglure and Hansen (1997) have noted that male shamans always have at least one female helping spirit which he equates with the sex-linked naming system. For him, this cross-gender linking provides the shaman with the ability to move back and forth between the various realms, male and female, living and dead. But one could equally well argue that the opposition is not so much transcended as maintained and that each

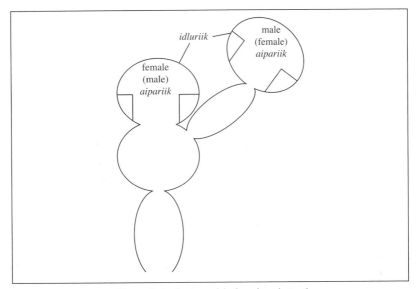

Figure 4: An Inuit model of gender relations[9]

person has some ability to enter into both realms.

The bear is not so much a cosmological mediator (in terms of transcending and combining the land/sea dichotomy), as a cosmological operator. The bear (and the shaman) provides the logical term that makes up the linking "passage" or path between the two terms. The bear is not then an internally unified figure, but an internally divided figure: there are two bears, male and female, who within each of them contain the seeds of its own opposite. It is precisely this property of an animal containing within it two figures that makes the bear such a powerful object of thought.

This argument links to Fienup-Riordan's (1984) analysis that Inuit symbolic thought consists of the construction and maintenance of boundaries, with the ritual opening of a passage to move outside of those boundaries. I would argue that the reason for this in Inuit terms is because any enclosed boundary already contains within it a piece of its own opposite—this opening the way for a passage.

Conclusion

This allows us to return to the initial ethnographic problem: what was Nanoraq's illness? In the transcription of the seance, the shaman reviews the various offences committed by Nanoraq. Most of these have to do with eating certain foods or working materials that were forbidden while she was menstruating (in this case sealskins), while other offences include combing her hair shortly after the birth of a child, hiding a miscarriage, and having sexual intercourse while menstruating. In other words, nearly all of Nanoraq's offences relate to her reproductive cycle. At the same time one must take into consideration that the seance was part of a much longer series of events that leads Oosten (1984) to suspect that Mathiassen was observing the *tivajuut* ceremony that takes place at the shift from summer land hunting to winter sea ice hunting. During this sequence the entire universe is recreated through confronting the productive and reproductive activities of the entire group. At this point of cosmological crisis and renewal, Nanoraq stood in real danger of transforming into a bear herself because of the offence against the slain bear and because she embodied in her reproductive capacity the transformative power of the bear. The shamanistic seance effectively resolved this problem, despite the fact that it did nothing to cure her physical ailments and indeed may never have intended to do as much.

For too long anthropologists have worked with the nature/culture dichotomy established by Levi-Strauss. Inuit ethnography shows that there are clear boundaries between the animal and the human, the living and the dead, male and female, but that each of these terms contains the other within it while simultaneously providing a passage between the two. It is this conceptual framework that leads to the series of cycles and transformations between each of these realms that are acted out in human and animal bodies and through rituals.

I would like to thank Drs. Kaarina Kailo and Sima Abrahamian for inviting me to participate in the workshop on "Transgressing Boundaries" at the 1997 Canadian Anthropology Society Meetings and for their enthusiasm for this project. The ideas in this paper have been tested on numerous patient classes of undergraduate students at Concordia University and the University of Manitoba, as well as my graduate seminar in Native Studies at the University of Manitoba. I would like to thank all of the students for their input. I would also like to express my ongoing intellectual debt to David Turner of the University of Toronto for the support, encouragement, and continually fresh ideas over the years.

[1]These "New Year" ceremonies are the *tivajuut* ceremonies extensively analyzed by Bernard Saladin d'Anglure (1993) and also by Blaisel and Oosten (1998).
[2]Only Boas (1964) records the name of the "Mother of Sea Beasts" as Sedna. This figure goes under a wide variety of names among Inuit (see the table in Swinton [1980]) and is more commonly known as Uinigumasuituq, Nuliajuq, or Arnaaluk Takanaaluk. I have retained Sedna as this is the term that has seeped into popular usage.
[3]Hugh Brody in *The People's Land* (1975) notes, "Trapping and skinning foxes from shoreline camps thus constituted a violation of the land-sea opposition, and may well have defied taboo. If so, it is an outstanding example of how economic readjustment erodes deeply entrenched belief systems and transforms the social practice which was moulded by such beliefs" (129, fn. 4).
[4]In North Baffin terminology. In South Baffin such relationships are referred to as *atikuluk* and in Nunavik and the Belcher Islands as *sauniq*.
[5]The transformation took place at puberty in the pre-settlement period. Cur-

rently the children are changed when they go to school since this gender system confuses the non-Inuit teachers.

[6]Hélène Guay (1989) has recorded some remarkable stories of young women resisting this transformation when told by their mothers.

[7]See Fienup-Riordan (1984) for the importance of the use of soot to mark boundaries among the Yup'ik

[8]Saladin d'Anglure (1993) has shown these two renunciations as demonstrating the control of elders over youth. The interpretation here suggests that the process of renunciation is much more important in establishing the children as social beings. For a comprehensive theory of renunciation the means of creating social relations see Turner (1996).

[9]This figure is copied from Boas (1964: 138, fig. 106).

References

Blaisel, Xavier and Jarich Oosten. 1998. "La logique des échanges des fêtes d'hiver inuit." *Anthropologie et Sociétés* 21: 19-44.

Boas, Franz, 1964. *The Central Eskimo.* Lincoln: University of Nebraska Press.

Briggs, Jean. 1974. "Eskimo Women: Makers of Men." *Many Sisters: Women in Cross-Cultural Perspective.* Ed. Ed. Carolyn J. Matthiasson. New York: Free Press. 261-304.

Brody, Hugh. 1975. *The People's Land.* Harmondsworth: Penguin.

Douglas, Mary. 1966. *Purity and Danger: An Analysis of Concepts of Pollution and Taboo.* Harmondsworth: Penguin Publishers.

Fienup-Riordan, Ann. 1984. *Boundaries and Passages: Rule and Ritual in Yup'ik Eskimo Oral Tradition.* Norman: University of Oklahoma Press.

Giffen, Naomi M. 1930. *The Roles of Men and Women in Eskimo Culture.* Chicago: University of Chicago Press.

Graburn, Nelson H. H. 1976. "*Nalunaikutanga*: Signs and Symbols in Canadian Inuit Art and Culture." *Polarforschung* 46: 7.

Graburn, Nelson H. H. 1972. "A Preliminary Analysis of Symbolism in Eskimo Art and Culture." *Proceedings of the XL Congress of Americanists* 2: 168.

Guay, Hélène. 1989. "Socialisation et employs salaries: Une ethnographie des femmes Inuit d'Igloolik." *Culture* 9: 3-24.

Guérin, Yvonne. 1982. "La femme inuit dominée: creation mythique allochtone?" *Anthropologie et Sociétés* 6: 129-154.

Mauss, Marcel and Henri Beauchat. 1979. *Seasonal Variations of the Eskimo: A Study in Social Morphology.* London: Routledge and Kegan Paul.

Oosten, Jarich G. 1989. "Theoretical Problems in the Study of Inuit Shamanism." *Shamanism: Past and Present.* Eds. Mihaly Hoppal and O. J. von Sadovsky. Budapest: ISTOR Books.331-341.

Oosten, Jarich G. 1984. "The Diary of Therkel Mathiassen (1922-23)." *Shamanism in Eurasia.* Ed. Mihaly Hoppal. Gottingen: Edition Herodot. 377-390.

Randa, Vladimir. 1986a. "Au croisement des espaces et des destines: *Nanuq* «marginal exemplaire»: Un cas de mediation animale dans l'Arctique central canadien." *Études/Inuit/Studies* 10: 159-170.

Randa, Vladimir. 1986b. *L'Ours Polaire et les Inuit*. Paris: Société d'Études Linguistiques et Anthropologiques de France.

Rasmussen, Knud. 1930. "Intellectual Culture of the Carbou Eskimos. Iglulik and Caribou Texts." *Report of the Fifth Thule Expedition, 1921-24*. Copenhagen: Gyldendalske Boghandel, Nordisk Forlag.

Rasmussen, Knud. 1929. "Intellectual Culture of the Iglulik Eskimos." *Report of the Fifth Thule Expedition, 1921-24*. Copenhagen: Gyldendalske Boghandel, Nordisk Forlag.

Saladin d'Anglure, Bernard. 1993. "The Shaman's Share or Inuit Sexual Communism in the Canadian Central Arctic." *Anthropologica* 35: 59-103

Saladin d'Anglure, Bernard. 1991. "The Mythology of the Inuit of the Central Arctic." *Mythologies*. Yves Bonnefoy, ed. Chicago: University of Chicago Press. 25-32.

Saladin d'Anglure, Bernard. 1988. "Penser le «féminin» chamanique ou le «tiers-sexe» des chamanes inuit." *Recherches Amérindiennes au Québec* 18: 19-50.

Saladin d'Anglure, Bernard. 1986. "Du fœtus chamane: la construction d'un «troisième sexe» inuit." *Etudes/Inuit Studies* 10: 25-114.

Saladin d'Anglure, Bernard. 1980. "Nanuq Super-Mâle: L'ours blanc dans l'espace imaginaire et le temps social des Inuit de l'Arctique canadien." *Études Mongoles* 11: 63-94.

Saladin d'Anglure, Bernard. 1977a. "Iqallijuq ou les reminiscences d'une âme-nom inuit." *Études/Inuit/Studies* 1: 33-64.

Saladin d'Anglure, Bernard. 1977b. "Mythe de la femme et pouvoir de l'homme chez les Inuit de l'Arctique central (Canada)." *Anthropologie et Sociétés* 1: 79-98.

Saladin d'Anglure, Bernard and Klaus George Hansen. 1997. "Svend Frederiksen et le chamanism inuit ou la circulation des noms (*atiit*), des âmes (*tarniit*), des dons (*tunijjutit*) et des esprits (*tuurngait*)." *Études/Inuit/Studies* 21: 37-74.

Swinton, Nelda. 1980. *La Déesse Inuite de la Mer/The Inuit Sea Goddess*. Montreal: Montreal Museum of Fine Arts.

Trott, Christopher G. 2000. "Structure *into* Practice: A Theory of Inuit Music." *Indigenous Religious Music*. Eds. K. Ralls-MacLeod and G. Harvey. Aldershot: Ashgate Publishing. 183-197.

Trott, Christopher G. 1995. "The Cannibal Theme among the Inuit: a case study in inversions." *Igitur* 6-7: 17-37.

Trott, Christopher G. 1982. "The Semiotics of Inuit Sculpture: Art and *Sananguat*." *Recherches Sémiotique/Semiotic Inquiry* 2: 337-359.

Turner, David H. 1996. *Return to Eden: A Journey through the Aboriginal Promised Landscape of Amagalyuagba*. New York: Peter Lang.

Turner, David H. 1985. *Life Before Genesis: A Conclusion*. New York: Peter Lang.

SUSAN BRIGHT

Bear Watch

Polar bears in Churchill wait long summer days ravenous and white
until wind blows cold and sideways from the north, freezing the sea
so they can venture out to hunt. White giant bears with galaxy eyes
and wet black noses locate seals through ice and thirty feet of arctic
water, then feast when pups come up for air, scarlet food on ice.

If winter comes too late, Polar Bear fathers eat their children, which
is why we dream of them. In Manitoba, they stalk delicious goblins
in plastic costumes on Halloween. Sometimes one snatches a wee child
trudging from house to house in sub-zero wind that is too hot for Polar bears.
They roll to cool their bellies and would loosen the collars of their white

fur coats if they could do it. If, in this hot and furious hunger, Polar Bears
venture too close to town or reach for meat set out in traps at the dump,
they end up in bear jail which is three Quonset huts divided into stalls
with giant bears inside them. They'll get no food until the ice comes.

They wake from wild dreams of flying, from drug-induced stupor.
They fly through skies full of hammock nets hung from helicopters that
pick up polar bears and transport them away from humans who do not
wish to become food, though many wear bear caps.

Polar bears in Churchill don't seem to hate us though, come close
enough to inhale the fascinating scent of tourists in glass vehicles
whose tires are as tall as a bear standing up. Polar bears are curious,
come to look at humans who come to look at bears, to shoot film,

spend money, take pictures, sip scotch in heated cabins late at night –
two species nose to nose with little sense of the sacred names
either whispers in the night.

Bear Woman

The central image of a she-bear embodies both the physical prowess, and the supernatural powers of the bear. In the vignettes within the mandala, the bear is portrayed as the "sacred dreamer" when hibernating; as the protective mother when nurturing her cubs; and as the goddess Kali, collector of skulls, when she is attacking.

The bear-woman has the ability to enter the "dream-time" at will, as when she wears the bear-skin, in the centre of the mandala. The dragonflies decorating the perimeter of the mandala also reinforce the theme of the "dream-time," representing the ability to fly between worlds.

This painting celebrates the energy of the bear as expressed through women.

The Girl and Grizzly

This is another story of girl who married bear.

This girl and her sisters went to pick berries. She takes the lead. Her berry string broke. Those berries spilled.

"Help me pick them up."

"Pick them up yourself," they say. They go ahead. One by one they pass her. None help her.

As she work, nice young man came to her. "There's nice big bunch up here. Let's pick that one." She's single, so she went with him. They went little higher. Bog tree, log fallen over there. They went under it.

"Let's camp here," he said. Before they go to bed he hit her on the head. That's to fix her mind, so she'll never think of home. He's really grizzly bear. He look like person to her though. He tell her, "If you wake up in morning, don't look at me."

They camp. Next day, pick berries all day long. That evening they walk under log again. That's really a year every time they walk under log. When they camp, that's winter camp in den.

Seems just like a day to her.

When they camp he say to her. "You stay here. I gopher hunt." That's the second night. He tell her, "If you wake up before me, don't look at me."

Next day, same again. She never see what he do with berries. But she knows he's not saving. "Save for winter," she say.

"Just eat them. Don't worry about winter," he tell her.

Third day is the same. They walk under log, camp. He hunts gophers. Brings back lots of gophers. They eat. "Why don't you save for winter?"

"Don't worry. Winter will take care of itself," he say.

Fourth day is the same. They go under tree, camp. It's four years now since she left.

Next he says, "This place down here, my mother and father put up fish. Let's see what those people do. I'll go down, see if people are there." He leaves her there. He walks down to notify them. It's grizzly camp.

"I've got wife coming," he tells them.

They all turn to human for her; really they're grizzly. People there, they feed her, that mother and father.

They all tell her not to look at them if she wake up first in morning. Two, three times they help her. One morning she wake up, open her eyes. She sees big grizzly hand on her. She's scared. She looks around, sees all bears, all grizzly.

He woke up. "Why did you look at me? Didn't I tell you?" He turn into human for her. "Now you know." But her mind is still fixed from that slap.

Every day they fish there.

One day he say," See that smoke over there? Don't go into that camp."

She gets curious. She sneak over. She sees human being sit down and here it was her aunt on her father's side. She was lost a long time ago. No wonder grizzly didn't want her to see her because she's human.

She look up. "My niece, my niece. You here too? Long ago it happen to me too. Grizzly save me. Don't stay here. You go back home. I can't. I have two kids. I can't leave them. You have no kids. You might as well go home. In morning bring little balsam tree top. Bring jack pine tree top and spruce tree top. Bring buttercup tops too. Bring whetstone. Bring me little grease. And bring me bladder of *Tlo* fish—that little fish with big head, little thin body. Fill that bladder full of water. You bring all that next time you come.

It takes time to get those things. Next time she sneak over she give all that. That's third day since she see her aunt.

"Okay, I'm going to fix them. Tomorrow you're going to try. When you hear someone coming, take off. If they catch you, they'll kill you. You got to get home. When they come put this buttercup stem comb through your hair. Then throw back. Buttercup stems will grow up so thick behind you, you can't get through. Next take jack pine tree top comb. Put through hair, throw behind you. Then spruce tree top, the same. Then balsam tree top. It will make thick trees, slow them up. They can't travel. Then put grease on your mouth. You won't be hungry," her aunt tell her. "Then throw stomach of water and with it throw whetstone. That will make lake with bluff across it. Then you'll come to lake. Man will be there. He'll save you."

That girl took off. Halfway up mountain she hear people. They're close. She did all those things. Buttercup stem comb then jackpine tree top, then spruce top, then balsam. Then she put grease on mouth. After she threw bladder and whetstone she made big lake with bluff across. She run, run. She came out on lake. Saw that man in middle. "Help me, help me," she holler, "save me."

That man come to shore. "Grizzly chase me," she tells him. "Save me and I'll marry you."

"I've got wife," he told her.

"I'll be your slave then."

He took her, just a little way out.

"Go farther, farther."

"Nope," he doesn't.

Three grizzly bears came running up. The rest gave up, I guess. One was her husband.

That man hit boat with stick. Boat took off. Those bears swim in. When they're close he hit with stick again. That boat took off. Finally he gets tired of that. Finally he spit on his spear, then threw it in water. He hit all three bears. One by one they float up, dead. He took that spear, wash off. Put it in boat.

"You hungry?" he ask. In bow of boat is Tlingit style cedar box. "Good meat in there. Eat." She eat dry meat, grease. She never eat for so many days.

He's fishing for frog, that's for his wife. Then he went home. Just before he gets home, he tells her, "I've got wife already. When she's eating, don't look at her. She kill lots of women. I'll take a chance with you. Don't look when she eat. Don't get up out of bed if I'm out."

He tell his wife he save that girl. He made her camp across the fire.

Next morning he hunt. "Don't look at her," he say.

Quite a while stayed with them. He sleeps with her instead of his wife.

Finally one time she wonder, "Why not look at his wife?" He's out. She look through that gopher robe and watch that woman eat frogs.

"Ach!" That woman feels it. The frog get stuck. Right then both those girl's eyes come out. That wife's power does that. It dug both that girl's eyes out.

He comes back, sees those eyes of blood. He pretend not to notice.

His wife says, "You brought back nice wife. All she does is sleep." He knows that young girl is killed.

He brought back what he killed, frogs, for her. That's her food. He pretend to fix his spear.

"Hey, what if you hit me," that wife say.

Right then, he kill that frog lady. He burnt her up so she's never come back.

He looked for that young girl's eyes. He has power too. He put back those eyes so she get up again.

He brings good meat to her, seal. "Let's move camp. I don't want to stay where I kill frog woman. I'm human. That frog turn into woman and I had to marry her. I don't feel right for long time now. If we move camp, I'll lose that funny feeling.

She's gone four and a half years by then. Four years with grizzly and half year with this man. She think about her home

That man asks her, "Are you lonesome?"

"Kind of," she says.

"Well, I'll take you home." Then go in his boat. That boat can go anywhere. The land where her father and mother are.

"Go up and see your father and mother, and if you want, you can come back. I'll wait, but if you don't come back, I'll leave."

She goes to them. She tells them, "I want you people to welcome him." So they did, and they live happily ever after. Those people accept them. Five years later, she's back.

This story was originally published in My Stories Are My Wealth, Mrs. Angela Sidney, Mrs. Kitty Smith, Mrs. Rachel Dawson. *As told to Julie Cruikshank. Copyright © 1977 Council for Yukon Indians. Reprinted with permission by Ida Calmagen, Mrs. Angela Sidney's daughter.*

Helena Junttila, "Levitation," oil on canvas, 200 x 120 cm, 2002. Private Collection.

WACOQUAAKMIK

The Warrior Way and the Bear

A Personal Narrative

This article is a personal narrative of the author's development of his political philosophy as a warrior and a member of the Bear Clan. Based on one of the foundational stories of the Anishnaabe tradition, it combines family history, childhood reminiscence, and meetings with other Indigenous people around Canada and in Russia. It draws upon observations of how the bear lives its life, and how this has been incorporated into belief and cultural values by First Nations people, to posit a series of thoughts on the responsibility of the warrior within the Anishnaabe tradition, and within the context of contemporary struggles for Indigenous rights.

In the beginning of all things, before the beginning of time, the people lived in the sky. There in the sky they had no use for many of the things we need here on the earth today. The weather was always warm and beautiful and they had no need of clothing or of building shelters; all of the food they needed grew on plants and was easily picked; they spoke the same language as the animals and there was no warfare with them. Life in the skyworld was good.

There were, living in the sky, two small children, a boy and a girl, and they were walking through the forest one day when they saw a very large tree. Being curious, as children are, they went to investigate and they saw it had great long roots going into the ground. One child looked at the other and they decided they would dig down to see where the roots went to. They began to dig and the hole grew deeper. They kept on digging and the hole kept getting deeper. The roots still went down further and they dug and they dug. The hole got very deep. Peering deep down into the hole the children thought they saw some light. Becoming very excited the children leaned further over the edge and looked deep down into the hole where they thought they saw the light. As their bodies craned forward all of the sudden they lost their balance and they tumbled down into the hole. They fell and they fell for a very long time holding onto each other's hands. Finally with a loud thump they landed on the earth.

It was dark on the earth and cold and wet and the Skychildren were very frightened. Picking themselves up from the ground they set out to find out where they were. As they travelled they became much more frightened. They could hear strange animals in the bush roaring and whispering alternately, speaking in

221

languages they could not understand. Their bodies were experiencing cold for the first time in their lives and their bellies were becoming hungry. They did not see any of the plants they were familiar with and did not know what to eat. The boy picked up a stick from the ground and tried to chew it … ppphhhtt! It was bad-tasting and hurt his teeth. Comforting each other and crying the two finally took refuge under a great rock where they were out of the rain. In desperation they cried out to the Creator to have pity upon them for they were wet and cold and sad and hungry and they wanted to return to their home in the sky.

The Creator, looking down from his home, heard the cries of the Skychildren and saw how wretched and pitiable they were on the earth. So he sent Grand-mother Bear to take care of them and teach them the things they needed to know to live on the earth. Coming to the Skychildren, where they were hidden under the rock, Grandmother Bear called out to them in the language of the Skypeople. The children were so happy to hear somebody calling them in their own language they came running out to embrace her. Grandmother Bear took the Skychildren in her arms and held them close to her body in her fur until they had dried off and become warm. Seeing how hungry the children were she fed them with milk from her own teats while she sung them lullabies. Once the children were fed and rested Grandmother Bear told them to follow her and she took them to her home.

The Skychildren lived with Grandmother Bear for many years and in that time she taught them many things about how to live on the earth. She taught them which plants were good to eat, which were sweet, like the tiny strawberries, and which ones could be used to heal the body. She taught them how to hunt and how to defend themselves against danger. She taught them how to make cloth-ing for when the weather got cold and wet, and how to construct a shelter to be safe and warm when they were away from home. Grandmother Bear taught the Skychildren all that they needed to know about living well on the earth.

Still, the Skychildren missed their home in the sky and they often talked about it and wished they could go back to it. One day as they were walking in the forest their hearts grew so troubled with the memories of their home in the sky that they cried out to the Creator to have pity on them and to help them go back home. Looking down from the place that he lives the Creator's heart was touched by the cries of the Skychildren for they were so wretched and pitiable.

The children walking further into the forest came upon a very large and very tall pine tree. Looking up at the tree they could see that the top of the tree reached all the way to the sky. Extremely excited the children tried to climb the tree but the trunk was much too big for them to get their arms around and they could not get a hold with their moccasins as the trunk was too smooth. They tried many times to climb the tree but they could not and as the day grew darker and nightfall approached they became very discouraged and made their way back to Grandmother Bear's home. That night they were so sad they could not eat their supper. Grandmother Bear asked them what was wrong and they told her how they missed their home in the sky and how much they wanted to go back to it.

They told her about the tree they had found in the forest whose trunk reached to the sky and their unsuccessful attempts to climb it. As Grandmother Bear listened to the story her heart became sad for the Skychildren because they missed their home so much and sad for herself because she knew that if they went back to the sky she would miss them very much. Taking the Skychildren in her arms she told them that they must not be sad as bears were very good climbers and that she would help them return to their home in the sky.

Arising early next morning Grandmother Bear made herself and the Skychildren a hearty breakfast because she didn't know how long the trip to the sky might be. She began packing her backpack with the things she might need for the journey. First she packed in some loaves of fresh-baked bannock she had made earlier that day. Then she put in a container of lard and some sugar and tea. Then she thought she better put some extra moccasins in … and maybe an extra dress … maybe even a really nice dress—just in case she met some good-looking men bears. By this time the pack was getting pretty full and heavy. Looking at it Grandmother Bear thought: "Well I better pack my cookstove too. You never know what there'll be to cook on up there."

The pack grew bigger and bigger, a needle and thread, a thimble, some beads, her big iron frying pan … and bigger and bigger … don't forget the teapot … and bigger. Finally, after she had packed almost all of her house inside the pack Grandmother Bear was ready. With a tremendous grunt she hoisted the pack on her back and she and the children set off for the big tree in the woods.

Arriving at the tree Grandmother Bear instructed the children to wait on the ground and that she would climb the tree all the way to the sky and then throw down a rope she had brought in her pack and then pull them up. Balancing the giant pack on her back she dug her claws into the big pine tree and started to climb. She could see way up to the top of the tree where it reached the sky. She made it halfway up and looked down at the children who looked like tiny ants on the ground below. The pack seemed to be growing heavier the higher up the tree she climbed. She kept on climbing and was three-quarters of the way to the top and the trunk was getting much thinner … then the wind began to blow. Holding tightly to the trunk Grandmother Bear swayed back and forth with the tree … that pack sure was getting much heavier …. Gathering her strength she climbed further up the trunk towards the sky. The wind was blowing harder and the trunk was really swaying and the pack felt heavier than even before. Grandmother Bear gathered all of her strength and with a final gasp of energy moved towards the sky … then crack! The pine tree broke and Grandmother Bear, her heavy pack and all, fell back to the earth. And so they say that since that time the Skychildren have never been able to return to their home.

In the 1830s, the United States of America began the process of Indian removals from around the Great Lakes basin. Following the defeat of the Tecumseth at the Battle of Tippecanoe, the government of the United States of America began the process of Indian removals from around the Great Lakes basin. This was motivated partly by revenge for the Anishnaabe Nation siding with the British in the War of 1812, and partly strategically as the British continued to maintain fur-trading posts, and good relations, with many Indian people on the American side of the Medicine Line. Removing the Anishnaabek would not only deny the British influence south of the Lakes, but would prevent a pan-Indian military alliance such as the one organized by Tecumseth. It had the added advantage of opening up Indian lands rich in timber and mineral wealth located on the south shores of the Great Lakes and lands for settlement of an ever-increasing population. Whatever the motivations the American government embarked upon a systematic removal of the Shawnee, Delaware, Chippewa, Pottawatamie, Odawa, and other Indian people to barren lands located west of the Mississippi River. Many Indian people refused to go along with the forced removals, and those who had culturally-close relatives in Canada sought refuge north of the Medicine Line. This diaspora between the 1820s and 1850s saw over 30,000 Indian people travel north to take refuge in Canadian Indian communities ranging from Walpole Island near Sarnia to Garden River near Sault Ste. Marie.

At the time of the removals Indian communities that chose neither to flee nor to be removed to the west entered into war with the American government. One Chippewa family in Wisconsin was a part of one of these communities, and was *mukwa dodem*, or Bear Clan. Foreseeing the inevitable result of prolonged battle with a larger and better-equipped force of soldiers, known to Indian people as *Kisi Mokomon* (or Long Knives), they instructed their children that when the battle began they were to flee in a canoe that was hidden in some bushes and to follow the Islands around Lake Superior until they reached Canada. These children, having seen their parents murdered by the Long Knives, did as they were told and over many days of island hopping along the shore of Lake Superior finally reached Sault Ste. Marie. From there they went to the Indian settlement at Garden River, where they were adopted into the Crane Clan (*Cheechalk Dodem*). As they grew they stayed together and when they were older they moved further east to Thessalon and Mississagi at Blind River. These three boys were called Jackpine, Morningstar, and Bobiwash. These names are still common at Mississagi. In this way the Bear became Crane.

In the Anishnaabe tradition every clan within our great lodge has a set of responsibilities. People born, or adopted, into a particular clan are bound to the responsibilities of their clan. The first responsibility of the Bear Clan is justice as bears are responsible in council meetings to ensure that all voices are heard fairly and then to see that the common will is carried out. Secondly, they are responsible for healing, as bears hold the oldest medicine within their bundles—the knowledge of which herbs and plants can be used to treat which ailments. Hunters and trappers who have lived around bears many years assert that if a bear is sick, they will seek through the bush until they find the plant that they need and then they will eat it, and occasionally even prepare it in a specific way, to cure themselves. Beyond this herbal knowledge though, Indian people, like many Aboriginal people across the globe, believe that the bear has a great and ancient spiritual knowledge and is our closest relative as humans. Thirdly, as warriors, bears defend the perimeter of the community. Although adult bears are not great social creatures the mother bear keeps its cubs very close for one of the longest periods of any mammal. Young bears often den with their mothers until they are three years old. Any person who grew up or travels in bear country is familiar with the adage, "Do not get between a bear and her cubs." This fierce caring, ascribed as a maternal instinct, may be at the root of what relates to the Bear Clan people's particular sense of responsibility for the defence of the their communities.

The Crane Clan people on the other hand were related to the Bird people and as such they had a leadership role. The birds, and particularly Meghizo the Great Eagle, have been given the responsibility by the Creator to watch over Indian people and ensure that we are following the ceremonial ways which reflect that we still know who we are. The Crane People have a further responsibility to speak on behalf of the people. A crane has a very large beak and makes a loud and distinctive clacking noise with its beak that can be heard from very far away when you are in the bush. Thus Crane People have that responsibility among our people. My people being both Bear (by birth) and Crane (by adoption) have all of the above responsibilities. This role was understood by my ancestors, and as early as 1850, from this small family of refugees, my Great-Great-Great Grandfather, who signed his name, Wacoquaakmik (The Breath of the Land), to the Huron-Robinson Treaty, was accepted as a headman on the north shore.

In Wisconsin in the eighteenth and nineteenth centuries there was a legendary warrior society, closely associated with the bear people, that was called the Ogitchiidaa (Big Heart Warrior Society). Many members of this warrior society stayed to defend the villages and homes of the people while giving others the chance to flee and live. Membership in the Ogitchiidaa was not determined by age or sex but by bravery and a willingness to sacrifice oneself for the people. In times of battle the Ogitchiidaa would tie a rope around themselves and then tie the other end of the rope to a war lance stuck in the ground. There they would make their stand to hold off the enemy. The Ogitchiidaa could only leave their place on the battleground when the enemy was defeated or when they were dead. Our people have many great songs about the bravery and the exploits of the Ogitchiidaa. It is said that the hearts of the Ogitchiidaa were like the hearts of a bear.

When I was a child I would go out with the members of my family into the bush where we would pick wild blueberries. We would go for many days to pick berries for our food in the winter. They would be frozen or turned into jam and a few of them might find their way into a potent kind of blueberry wine. We also would make money as kids by selling baskets of berries door to door to the white people in town. From a very early age we encountered black bears when we were in the berry bushes. They were never cause for alarm. We were told to respect them and to not bother them and they would do the same to us. I learned that during that time of year when the sun was hot and food was plentiful that the bears grew lazy and content to feast on the sweetness nature offered them. In the restfulness of summer the bears would store up reserves of fat that would get them through the long winter's hibernation. We picked our berries side by side with the bears and I do not recall any instance of trouble with these bear people, and we learned as human people to respect them and not to provoke them in any fashion. In my memory of that warm and wild place of my childhood bear and child exist together in a great summer sweetness.

When I was in my early teens I went on a camping trip to Killarney Park in the La Cloche range, with a class from my high-school. The trip took place in the fall. We had much freedom on the trip once we had pitched our tents and taken care of some chores like gathering firewood and hauling buckets of water from the lake for cooking. I called to my then best friend Mark to take a walk in the bush with me. I was not carrying anything with me, although I wore a belt knife (standard camping gear) but Mark was carrying a small hatchet with him. As we travelled along the path further away from the campsite we spied some large broad tracks in the dust along the trail. I immediately identified them to Mark as the tracks of a young bear. He grew quite excited and insisted that we follow them. I was not so sure but didn't want to appear frightened so I agreed. We followed the bear tracks for another half-hour along the trail to where they disappeared behind a high ridge. As we climbed the ridge Mark grasped the hatchet tighter, convinced the bear might be just beyond the ridge. Neither of us really gave much thought to what use a small hatchet might be against a bear. As Mark came over the top of the ridge, with me following close behind, the bear came over from the other side. Letting out a terrible scream of fright Mark turned, knocked me over in his haste to run away and threw the hatchet down to the ground. The bear, a small yearling, gave an equally frightened woof, turned and ran away down the other side of the hill. I went tumbling down the hill and only at the bottom did I realize that blood was pouring from my left thumb where Mark had hit me with the hastily thrown hatchet. Wrapping a neckerchief around my thumb I headed back to the camp and found Mark about 100 yards down the trail, convinced that I had been attacked by the bear. To this day I have a scar on my left thumb to remind me of that incident. That scar is also one of the identifiers used on my Indian Status card, which proves to the government that I am an Indian.

In 1980 I was working for the summer at the South Tall Cree Reserve in Northern Alberta near Fort Vermilion. One hot and very dry day my friend Harvey Auger and I were out driving around the back roads in his pick up truck. We had been down to a spot on the river to pick some wild mint for use in tea and for medicine. Having picked a good bunch of mint we were headed back to his house when Harvey slowed the truck down and came to a stop. Pointing off to the side of the road he showed me a small bear standing on his hind legs beside a tree. We watched the bear for a few minutes and I asked Harvey if he was going to shoot the bear. Harvey said no and indicating the rifle behind the seat said I could. I said I was not interested in killing it either and we watched for a while longer and then continued on our way. I asked Harvey why he didn't want to shoot the bear. Harvey told me that the last time he had killed a bear was many years ago. It was a young bear, like the one we had just seen. He shot the bear but hadn't killed it outright and the wounded bear came crawling towards him on its belly. It had its paws over its eyes and was crying like a little baby that was hurt. The sight of this broke his heart and from that day he never killed another bear. He looked at me at the end of this story and said:

"You know when a bear is skinned he looks just like us—just like a person."

In 1987 I travelled to Northern Saskatchewan to pursue research related to my dissertation. I was planning to travel the Churchill River from Pinehouse to LaLoche and back south to Green Lake by canoe, stopping in the summer fishing camps to collect oral testimony from Chipeweyan and Cree people living along the river. My paddler Karl and I began the trip in Pinehouse and had to wait a few days for all of our arrangements to be made before we could set out on this eight-week trip. One afternoon I followed a bush path out of town. I was a mile or so out in the bush when I heard somebody walking—it sounded like a man. I looked around but could see nobody. I kept walking and could still hear another set of footprints faintly echoing my own. I looked around again but didn't see anyone. I kept walking but decided I would head back towards the lakeshore through the bush and follow the shoreline to town. I made a figure eight so I crossed over my own trail a couple of times and I saw in the bush a parallel set of bear tracks following mine. The bear had followed me and watched me the entire time, but other than the faint sound of his footsteps I heard nothing and was not bothered. He followed me all the way to the lake and then part of the way back to town before losing interest. Friends who live in the Arctic had told me before that when a bear walks s/he sounds like a person but until that day in the bush outside of Pinehouse I had not realized how true this was.

In 1995 I was invited by the Khanty-Mansi people of the Ob River region of Central Siberia to travel to and speak at their first self-government conference. After much serious negotiating with my travel agent, who had to be convinced that such a place existed, I set off on this journey. I flew to Frankfurt and from there to Tallinn, Estonia. In Tallinn I met with a colleague from the University of Toronto, Dr. Harri Mürk, who had facilitated the trip. After a week in Tallinn we set out in a bus to St. Petersburg and from there hitched a ride on an Aeroflot flight with a group of Estonian construction workers to Surgut. In Surgut we boarded a river boat and travelled with a folklore festival for three days up the Ob River to Khanty-Maansisk. This journey to the other side of the world was an important turning point in my life. I wore my ribbon shirt, a traditional Anishnaabe ceremonial garment, to official functions to honour the people I was meeting and their lands. This shirt, made for me by a friend, is decorated with several representations of bears and the elbows have bear claw designs worked into them. As I learned about the Khanty, the Komi, and the Mansi people I realized how central the bear was to their existence and their identity. In a very direct way I was brought close and into the heart of these people.

As the boat travelled towards Khanty-Maansisk there were occasional moments when we were able to slip away from the constant police surveillance on the boats.

227

One of the stopping places was a Potemkin Village of sorts, where a number of Khanty Elders tended a fire and were present to meet visitors. As I got off the boat and approached the Elders who were sitting on logs and reindeer mats in front of a Bear shrine, I knew that it was required that I honour this bear spirit in some fashion. I went back to the boat and I found my *semaa* (tobacco). The *semaa* was given to Indian people by the Creator as a comfort and to aid in our prayers. When the tobacco is burnt in a ceremonial way the smoke rises and pierces the sky bringing our prayers to the Creator. I brought the *semaa* to the Elders and had my patient interpreter Piret, an Estonian journalist, explain to the Khanty Elders what the tobacco was for and ask permission to put it in the fire and pray. The Elders agreed and watched with great interest as I prayed before the Bear shrine and offered my tobacco. At the end I sat with them and shared some water and we talked. One of the most elderly men there looked at me and taking my hand in his said: "You are one of us."

I asked my interpreter if he could explain what he meant by that as I was obviously not a Khanty. The old man further explained. "In your heart you are one of us. You are one of the Bear People."

Later on that night, I sat on the deck in the bow with one of the Khanty Grandmothers travelling with the boat. It was around four a.m. but still very bright out and the river was very quiet except for sounds of an accordion disco, which was being carried on one of the other boats some distance away, and the never-ending vodka party in the stern. This older lady had adopted me, called me her grandson, and insisted on singing lullabies to me in Khanty and making small gifts for me. As we sat and talked with my interpreter of how the Khanty had lived before the Russians, this Grandmother turned an anguished face to me and with tears running from her eyes asked me: "How will the little people survive?"

I sat there holding her hand with tears streaming from my own eyes and I had no answers for her. The only truthful answer was that I did not know if the Khanty would survive the disease, loss of culture, environmental degradation, and other pressures which they were subjected to and which had already wreaked such an immense toll on their people. At that moment my political philosophy matured and developed far beyond where it was. I had always believed as an Indian in Canada that all of my actions and decisions were political—that is, they all had political consequences. My life was bounded by a sense of responsibility related to the negotiation of presence and power within the rubric of Indian-Clan-People-Community vs-White-Family-State-Canada. The realization that came to me on the Ob River that night was that the struggle could not be carried out in terms of the negotiation of space within the state because the state itself considered my continued existence as an Indian person to be subversive. This changed the rules of the game forever. When a people seeks, either consciously or not, the extinction of another group of people the only rational position is war. In taking a position of war against a much stronger enemy the only rationale maxim then is "by any means necessary." The defence of the people is a clan responsibility for all people who are *mukwa dodem* (Bear Clan), and indeed for all Aboriginal people, and the people take their lesson from the mother bear who defends her young cubs not out of malice or vengeance, but out of love. This is among the first and hardest of lessons that Bear Warriors have—that what is done is done for the love of the people. This is the way the old warrior society of the Ogitchiidaa conducted itself—sacrificially and with such love for their people that they would give of their lives.

In the village of Khanty-Mansisk I met with the sister of a leading Khanty activist from the region. He had been killed two weeks before this by the Russian police who beat him to death in his jail cell where he had been locked up on a fabricated charge. Speaking quietly with each other under the ever-watchful eyes of the not-so-secret police following me, she appealed for help in getting the Khanty story out to the world. As oil and gas production has increased in Khanty and Komi territories human rights violations have also increased as the people are forced off of their reindeer pastures so that oil and gas wells can be installed. The night following my address to the Khanty Self-Government Conference I received a message that the Elders were inviting me to a Bear Wake ceremony to be held that night. When a bear is killed its body is waked for seven nights and all people in the village are expected to come and make offerings to the spirit of the bear. I arrived at the site of the ceremony and took my seat near the Elders (Shamans) who were conducting the ceremony. A few hours into the ceremony two police cars pulled up and disrupted the proceedings. Loud yelling in Russian quickly turned to violence as they kicked and destroyed the Bear shrine. After beating the two shamans conducting the ceremony they took them away in their cars. Pulling their guns they indicated that I and the others who were there needed to leave and I went back to the boat. At the time I left Khanty-Maansisk one of the Elders was still unaccounted for. It was clear from this message of intimidation that Indigenous people of Russia were subject to the same brutal and equally oppressive treatment as other Indigenous peoples around the globe. It was also clear that the state feared their spirituality and was intent on suppressing the great and powerful symbols of power among them much as the Canadian government did with Indian people in Canada in the 1890s with the so-called Potlatch Laws.

As a warrior who has been involved in many different actions and in many different and dangerous situations across Canada over the years I have often had the opportunity to talk to young people who are attracted to the romanticism of the struggle. These discussions are often very difficult. The media has to a large extent glamourized and demonized the image of the warrior in conflicts across Canada from Oka to Gustafson Lake to Ipperwash. The image of the warrior with bandanna over face toting an AK-47 is far removed from those warriors who understand their roles and carry them out within the context of traditional clan responsibilities. As I have thought about this I have had to contextualize it within the knowledge that I am bound by as a member of the Bear Clan. I have come to the conclusion that there are several lessons for the warrior to be drawn from the ways bears live. These are listed below with no particular priority attached to them.

Nurture

As already discussed bears care for their young for as long as three years, a longer time than most mammals. Indian people often use the expression "for the seventh generation," meaning that the things we do must be done with forethought for the impact they will have unto the seventh generation to come after us. The business of being a warrior needs to be focused outside of self. It is done first and foremost for the children and those things that are done must be done with regard for that.

Love

This has already been discussed earlier. The business of being a warrior is about love and protection. I think that because most wars have been the preserve of men that, aside from shallow patriotism and jingoism, the element of personal love as a motivation has been discarded among warriors. Yet, love for one's own people is perhaps the only justification for violence and needs to inform how we treat other people even while at war with them. A well-known Elder who had fought in the Pacific theatre, in Indo-China, told me that it was in the midst of that conflict that he gained consciousness. He said that one day as they were razing a village in the jungle he was struck by the thought that the people they were killing, the village they were destroying, was one of brown people just like himself. This realization helped him to realize who the enemy really was and directed his life's work to peace and building bridges of understanding between all people.

Defence by Any Means Necessary

When a bear defends its young or its territory it will use any weapon at its disposal. A bear will rarely attack an aggressor without warning—the threat is a part of the battle and if it is successful, then that is the best kind of battle as the young are protected and nobody is really hurt. However once the battle is engaged the bear will use its claws, teeth, weight, voice, and anything else it can to win. The conclusions from this are obvious to the warrior, but they also suggest a whole range of options prior to engaging in violence. Once engaged in violence, however, every effort and strategy must be employed to ensure success.

Healing

Within the Anishnaabe tradition the bear holds ancient and powerful medicine. All warriors must also take responsibility for healing those who are traumatized by war, declared or undeclared. Ninety percent of the wars being waged around the globe, or that have been waged since 1945, have been undeclared wars between Indigenous nations and states, or between Indigenous nations themselves. The vast majority of these have been territorial disputes. In many places (i.e., Borneo, Ireland) generations of children have been raised their entire lives within a war zone. Other fourth world nations and states have recently entered into peace processes (i.e., Guatemala) with similar statistics and their people are in desperate need of healing from war trauma. While some characterize this as post-traumatic stress syndrome, this definition may be too limited as it does not adequately deal with the effects of cultural destruction and spiritual alienation within Indigenous/state conflicts. To deal with these the people will have to reach back to ancient traditions and specific cultural knowledge—they will need to go back to the bear wisdom and power that is at the heart of human societies. While this is not exclusively a warrior responsibility, warriors need to learn how to participate in that process in a way which honours their role in the struggle while it moves their nation forward from conflict.

Omnivorousness

A bear is an omnivore, it eats what it can and is curious to go and try anything new, sometimes to its own detriment. When I lived in Northern Alberta there was a bear who visited our cabin every few nights. We soon learned not only to keep garbage out of its reach bur also not to leave cans of motor oil on the back step. The bear would pick up the cans in its teeth, punch a hole in it, and drink the oil. The bear seemed to enjoy this immensely but it had some obviously disastrous effects on its stomach. I think what this speaks to for those who follow the way of the bear is the need to be curious and not to discount any knowledge as unimportant or uninteresting. The more that is known about the world, the more natural curiosity that is exercised and encouraged, the better the thinking will be. We need to be omnivorous in the pursuit of those things that feed our mind and our souls. In this we must also be careful not to shy away from the bitter or hard things but to accept these as necessary for our continuing and lifelong education.

Hibernation

One of the things that black bears practice is hibernation. I think that what this speaks to is the need for rest periods and the need to conserve resources for those rest periods. Nobody can sustain a struggle for twenty-four hours a day forever. There needs to be judicious thought given to resting. In order to make this a reality resources must be conserved, much as the bear puts on fat during the late summer and fall, for that period. What do bears do when they hibernate? They dream. I believe this is an essential part of how a warrior receives direction and strength. In our dreaming (visioning) we enter another world where we commune and take spiritual direction. This relates also to fasting, for bears take no water or food during their hibernation. Similarly when Indian people fast they take neither food nor water and it is during those fasting periods that we gain our power as well as answers to the difficult questions we face.

Universality

As I have travelled in many places around the world I have learned that many peoples have the same foundational cultural relationship with bears as Indian people do. This speaks to me of the universality of the human family and the need to have an internationalist perspective in the struggle. The struggle of the Khanty and the Komi is my struggle because we were related at the beginning of time.

Sweetness

All people need sweetness in their lives. Bears actively seek out sweetness in their diet. They eat blueberries, they raid honey trees and beehives, and in the spring you will see these great creatures with their long tongues, curling back their lips and delicately picking the tiny sweet wild strawberries. I think that for people this translates as the need for sweetness in our lives. We need to feed our souls by contact with other people, by conversation, by dance and joy. We cannot live austere Calvinist lives and maintain a human dimension to our role in the struggle. While we recognize the need for discipline we deny self-imposed austerity, except for the purposes of conservation of resources, as above. The heart that is not joyful and is not sweetened by life is the one that moves from love to hate as a motivation for the struggle.

The Easy Life

Bears are notorious creatures for being seduced by garbage dumps and people. They get used to the good life provided by people's garbage and soon become "garbage bears." I think there are many examples of people involved in the struggle who have spent so much time dining at the table of their oppressor that they have been seduced into forgetting who they are. This is a caution to both those who are seduced by this and those who are intent on the seduction—in the end, bears who become garbage bears are killed because their expectations are still framed only within their own frames of reference. Revolutionaries who are co-opted usually suffer the same fate.

In the preceding essay I have not attempted to provide a definitive or exhaustive argument for warrior consciousness arising out of bear knowledge. What I have done is to present some personal narratives for how I have, as an Anishnaabe warrior and somebody who is *Mukwa Dodem,* come to have some ideas about my role in that particular struggle. There is much more to be said and much more to be learnt. In the morning when I put my sage and my tobacco in my smudge shell and I pray I give thanks to the four directions. When I turn to the north I give particular greetings and honour to that Great Bear Spirit who lives in that place and I ask for one more day so I might learn from that Grandfather the path that will help the Skychildren live well here upon this earth. *Chi Meegwetch.*

KARI SALLAMAA

Chant of the Bear

The time has come
for the bear to sigh his song
his fur, his nails hushed
From his blood, shed by spears
he imbibes the rhythm
from the maiden's womb
imbibes the warmth
as the humble bride dances

The scent is crisp
when the maiden leads the bear
toward his death
the history of his kin

With gold chains
the bear rises back to his father's heaven
The woman remains
now aged, just recently bride
no one who loves the bear
can hold him back for long

The woman prepared a salty tongue
to hear the bear sing for thousand years
Generations, gold chains
bind him to us

If you are the offspring of the bear's woman
if you still have faith in the word
the maiden's womb
perhaps you can then discern
the spell written on a grand piano

Translated into English by Mirka Pohjanrinne

Maureen Enns, "Transitions," mixed media: canvas, painting, oil and acrylic, 5' x 6', 1993

Bear

Becoming Bear

A few meters from Bear Creek in northeastern Iowa there is a vagina-shaped cave. Its narrow entrance is tall enough to enter without stooping, but one can touch the sides with ones hands. Roof and floor remain flat, but the walls taper towards the end. The cave is long enough to lie down and remain protected from the weather. Each of the sandstone walls has been inscribed over and over again with the same symbol for the vulva. This symbol—two facing vertical ellipses with a vertical line between them—in some Anishnaabe traditions means both the human vagina and Earth. (Vulva images, some similar and some with a different design, are found in the earliest human decorated caves, going back tens of thousands of years, as well as around the world.) Nearby, archeologists have found the remains of an Oneota village. This area abounds with the famous low mounds created in the shape of theriomorphic deities; the terrestrial deity so depicted nearby is Bear.

Another cave by Bear Creek is similar save that it has images besides the many representations of the vulva, including a bison by the entrance and a tortoise at the rear; both images (Bison in her female aspect) also represent Earth in Native traditions. At the rear wall of the shelter there are three inscribed bear paws. If one sits at the natural shelf on the rear wall, one can place each of one's hands in two of the bear paws.

Given Anishnaabe practices that continued well into the twentieth century in nearby southeastern Minnesota, the function of these caves is clear (there are other caves or rock shelters in the area that have been defaced or the images weathered away). Girls becoming women at the onset of menarche went—and traditional women still go—into isolation for their first major four to eight day seclusion-fast to have a vision in order to establish a personal relationship with a spirit(s). These relationships are understood to be essential to continue to live and to make positive contributions to one's community. Males undergo similar fasts around the same time in their lives, but for males, there is no specific physiological marker for adolescence as menarche is for females.

During menstruation women are considered especially sacred; their spiritual power is then so potent it can overwhelm those of males. Hence, traditional women seclude themselves, as they have no wish to weaken their men folk. At the onset of the first menstruation, women are more than ever spiritually powerful, but this power being new is uncontrolled—potentially dangerous to those around them and themselves. Thus, women at menarche seclude themselves for the sake of their community and to learn to use their new spiritual power. During this fast, the elder women of the community will come to instruct them.

Outside of the patriarchal monotheistic traditions (normative Judaism, Christianity, and Islam), where only one sex is considered sacred, menarche everywhere is the most sacred period in a woman's life and often her community as well. It is a time not only of physical transition from childhood to adulthood but also of spiritual maturation. In some of the Anishnaabe traditions, menarche is called "Becoming Bear."

Why Bear? All around the northern hemisphere, bears are or were considered the most sacred of the terrestrial beings. Of the few circumpolar rituals, the bear sacrifice was the most potent. These rituals, being circumpolar would go back tens of thousands of years and are among the earliest of human religious activities. The other rituals are pyroscapulamancy—prognosticating through the reading of cracks in the dried scapula of herbivores caused by the application of a heated rod or coal—and heat rituals known by various names, including "sauna" and, de-sacralizing, "sweat-lodge" ("Spirit Lodge" in the Anishnaabe tradition).

Bear sacrifices still take place in Siberia and among the Ainu in far northern Japan. In this sacrifice a young bear is raised by the community—in some, suckled at the breast of a human woman. When the bear approaches adulthood, it is ritually sacrificed. The body is decorated and treated with complex rituals of respect. Evidence of rituals directed towards Bear can be found in European caves going back nearly 20,000 years. Traditional Native Americans even now, when a bear is killed for food and hides, but especially for its fat, which is used for nutrition and for healing, treat it with greater respect and more complex rituals than any other hunted animal. But in northern North America, the bear sacrifice seems to have been replaced by a dog sacrifice.

What both bears and dogs have in common with regard to sacrifice is their closeness to humans. Dogs, of course, become part of our families, and to sacrifice a dog is like sacrificing a member of our family. Bears structurally are similar to humans. If you have ever seen a bear skeleton, you will have noticed that it is very human-like in appearance. I would suggest that both the bear and the dog sacrifices are in effect human sacrifices using a substitute that, in different ways, is very close to humans.

But this does not explain why Bear is a major deity, for dogs are not deities in the circumpolar cultures. As with another major theriomorphic divine analogy of Earth, Bison, the sex of the Bear is important. In their male aspects, both the bison bull, and particularly the now extinct Plains grizzly bear exhibit ferocity, and as a spirit, give warrior power. Portraits of nineteenth-century great warriors of the Plains show them wearing grizzly claw necklaces. On the other hand, Bison as female—for example, White Buffalo Woman of the Lakota—signifies the nourishing power of earth. Especially on the Plains, the bison was the main provider of hides for teepee coverings, meat for food, bones for tools, and sinews for sewing.

In the woodlands of north-central and northeastern North America, necessities for existence were provided by several beings: deer, moose, wapiti, and the woodland bison. Bear provided large thick furs and a large amount of fat, fat being essential to the diet—the herbivores mentioned having little fat on their bodies. But far more important in spiritual understanding is the life of bears. Female bears den up in the earth during the winter and emerge from the earth in the spring with new life, their cubs. So human females at menarche enter small caves or small fasting wigwams (or a separate room in an apartment in modern urban dwellings) and crawl out after four to eight days now capable of bringing forth new life.

During the menarche fast, the young women bonded with Earth. Either in the fasting hut or the floor of the cave, they sat on the earthen floor; their sacred menstrual blood flowed onto and merged with the Earth. If they were near a stream or creek, they could hear the flow of the Earth's blood, as their own blood flowed from their vaginas. When near rock walls, if soft, they inscribed the symbol of vulva/Earth on it; if the rock was hard, they painted the symbol with their menstrual blood. These young women have become not only one with Earth, but, emerging from the earth or crawling out from the small opening of the lodge, one with Bear; hence, the term for menarche, "Becoming Bear."

Bear Healing

But bears represent more than the bringing forth of life, important as that is. Bears are similar to humans in a number of regards. For one, bears are highly intelligent. I have myself observed a bear coming across a situation changed from the previous day in a complex way. The bear sat down on its haunches in front of it. And then, with no hesitation, the bear got up and acted in a way that decisively solved the problem with no trial and error. Clearly the bear had sat down to ponder a solution and then confidently acted on it.

Bears, like us, are omnivorous. This is highly important to humans. For as we migrated into new areas, we could observe what the bears ate and know that it was a suitable food for us as well. Our sharing the same taste for a complex variety of foods is readily apparent for those who have picked berries in the same patch with bears—to be avoided, of course, if there is a mother bear with playful cubs, as we might end up between the mother and her cubs and thus be in danger of her motherly protective instinct.

Bears also come down with the same illnesses that we do. Again by observing the herbs and other medicines they eat to heal themselves, we can learn of the medicinal plants in new areas. Thus, Bear is the pre-eminent spirit for healing.

Those who have a special relationship with Her and have Bear power are frequently healers, unless it is a vision regarding the ferocious aspect of Bear, and He gives them warrior power. Bear is often depicted on early Sacred Pipes with effigies, particularly in the Northeast, connoting their use for healing rituals.

While many of those who have a special relationship with Bear have been given knowledge of the healing herbs and roots, others heal with the life energy of Bear. In the Anishnaabe Midéwiwin understanding, Bear carries onto this world life for the people, symbolized in the Midéwiwin birch bark scrolls by a sign for Bear carrying a pack filled with life-force on its back. (Bear as warrior also guards the four portals of the Midéwiwin lodge.) The ability of Bear to provide life-force and to heal is so great that there are stories of Bear—Bear Herself directly, not through a human intermediary—visiting a recently dead human and bringing the corpse back to life.

This life energy is the life-force of Earth, which literally "bears" us in two ways: when we walk on the ground She bears us up on Her surface, and She is our ultimate Mother: She bears or births us. And as the ultimate Mother, She nurtures us. It is She who provides the plants and animals on whom we depend for sustenance to continue to live. Bear is Earth in Her living terrestrial form.

People rarely if ever have direct visions of Earth, but they do of Bear. Hence, to have a special relationship with Bear, for Her to assist one with Her power, may also give one access to Her power, Her life-force, for healing.

For those cultures whose societies are divided into clans linked to theriomorphic deities, those of the Bear clan may have a degree of warrior power or healing power, but unless they also have a vision of Bear creating a special, personal relationship, that power is attenuated. Thus, healers may be of the Bear clan, but more important, they have been given by Bear either special knowledge of healing herbs or the ability to pass on Her life energy to assist the weak and ill.

Encountering Bear

Bears exist, as all living beings—which includes bodies of water, particular rocks, thunder, and so forth—in varying combinations of two modes: what we perceive from ordinary consciousness and from (light to heavy) trance consciousness. Hence, whenever we encounter Her, she may be "bear" as animal or "Bear" as spirit. Since we cannot know in advance the nature of the encounter, it is best to always treat bear/Bear as Bear. This means, out of respect, not to address Her as "bear" but as "Grandmother" when greeting Her.

Grandmother and Grandfather are the terms by which spirits are traditionally addressed, as they are honourific relational terms. From a Native perspective, all beings are related, and each of us exists in concentric circles of relationships. From smallest to largest, these are the circles of family, clan, other-than-human beings, and the Four Directions plus Zenith and Nadir (the entire cosmos). Elders are given the most respect, and all spirit beings are elders.

Hence, when we encounter Bear in the woods or in our visions, we speak respectfully to her and address her by an honourific, usually "Grandmother" or as some do, "Spirit" (*manido*). She may walk on by or She may stop to talk to us. Or, if we need her fat and meat to survive and have asked her to come to us and offer herself, after respectfully addressing Her, we kill Her.

After killing Her, we thank Her for the gift, the self-sacrifice, of Her life. We treat Her body with the greatest respect, skinning and butchering Her with the proper rituals, and decorate parts of Her body as a sign of our gratitude. We then ask Her to come back again when we need Her, because we kill Her in the flesh but not in the spirit. If treated with the proper respect and gratitude, She will return when we again need Her.

The Western literature in this regard is often misleading. Western culture is hierarchical and monotheistic. Thus Westerners tend to assume that if Bear is understood to be a spirit, it must be a single ruling spirit. So in many books, you will find that theriomorphic spirits are discussed as a "Master" of the species, such as a Bear, and only that single being is divine.

In cultures that have transformed their economy from gathering-hunting to herding-gathering, since humans control the herds, it is assumed that there is a single spirit in charge of the species, and it is that spirit to whom humans offer sacrifice in gratitude for the gift of the animals. But in such cases, the single spirit is female not male, for nurturing through the providing of food is invariably understood as a female role, continuing the nurturing of breast-feeding. Thus, among the Saami and Siberians who herd reindeer, sacrifice is offered to the Mistress of the Reindeer, not a Master of the Reindeer.

But gathering-hunting traditions, save for the dog, who may have domesticated us, have no domestic animals. Animals that provide food are utterly natural. So there is no notion of their being subject to anything, let alone an overarching spirit. More important, these cultures are egalitarian, and leadership is a matter of a community voluntarily accepting leadership for specific tasks, but anyone can opt out. Thus, the concept of a master of anything could not exist. Hence, our respect is due to each and every bear on encountering Her as the spirit, Bear, not to any Master of the Bear, as Western literature tends to indicate.

Demonizing Bear

The two major theriomorphic female deities are Bear, with Her associations with Earth and life, and Owl, the powerful hunter and spiritual presence of the night associated with Moon. (Anishnaabe women may hold Moon Ceremonies during the full moon.) It is these two major deities that under the influence of Christian missionaries have been demonized. Owl was made into a harbinger of death, and Bear became the symbol of evil sorcery.

Very early, Christianity not only demonized the female Earth of the gender complimentary Sky-Earth pair of cosmic deities, turning Earth into Hell, the abode of Satan, but demonized all human women, save the eternally virginal Mary, with the doctrine of Original Sin. In China, we have documents from the seventeenth century noting that Christian missionaries vehemently objected to the Earth part of the Imperial sacrifice to Sky-Earth. So the demonizing of female spirits by Christians theologians and missionaries was early, continuous, and worldwide.

In cultures with an understanding of people having power derived from a personal relationship with spirits, it is understood that this power can be used to help or harm others—harming an enemy is considered to be helping one's community. Whether used for good or evil, the choice is made by the human, for the spirits are morally neutral in offering their assistance to those with whom they have chosen to relate. In these communally-oriented traditions, acting solely for personal benefit is considered the epitome of evil. In traditional times, those considered to be using spiritual power in this way were liable to be killed as being an extreme danger to their community. Hence, it was far from being common.

But as these cultures increasingly came under Christian influence and missionary control, all of the beneficent spirits were considered Devils and having a relationship with them evil. It came to be understood that all those who had power from these relationships were doing it for selfish, perverse reasons and were wicked. Grotesquely twisting the beneficent healing power of Bear to be an evil deity, such persons in some Anishnaabe traditions were called Bearwalkers. Bearwalkers became a label for evil sorcerers, and Bearwalking the term connoting working in conjunction with spirits.

It was understood that Bearwalkers physically turned into large bears, or sometimes into giant dogs, and traveled about at night to carry out their evil deeds. If such a bear or dog were shot, on dying they turned back into their human form. In other words, they had become were-creatures. But this understanding actually demonstrates that many in the culture no longer understood the meaning of having power through a relationship with a spirit.

In actuality, with a relationship such as with Bear, one can merge in various ways with the spirit, but it is a spiritual not a physical merging. Again, one can travel with the assistance of a spirit, but it is a spiritual journeying not a physical one.

I have a friend who is a traditional healer and who is a "flyer." With the assistance of spirits she can travel to those she is helping and she enjoys the flight experience, looking around as she travels. But that does not mean she has to put on warm clothes or carry oxygen for high altitude flights. Her body stays put; it is one of her "souls" that is flying. (All cultures, save for the monotheistic ones, understand humans to have two or more souls; one can go off traveling while the other maintains life in the body.) I have traveled by merging with Bear, but as bears do not fly, it is a matter of being here and then there, with no sense of travel in between. Again, it is one of my "souls" that travels; my body goes nowhere. Hence, the relatively late Anishnaabe concept of Bearwalking not only is almost certainly due to Christian influence, but it is actually impossible, since it assumes an actual physical transformation of the Bearwalker. Such transformation is a European fantasy not a Native understanding or practice. Moreover, necromancy is often associated with Bearwalking, and that is also a European concept.

The influence of Christianity on Anishnaabe traditionalists has been waning since the 1970s. From that time, there has been an increasing revitalization of Native religious modalities. In Canada, Christian control of reserves ended in the 1970s, and the last of the notorious Christian controlled boarding schools closed in the 1980s. The true understanding of Bear has returned, and She is again understood to be the most powerful of the healing spirits.

Most of the topics touched on in this article have been dealt with in greater detail and with references in the following books by the author: Offering Smoke: The Sacred Pipe and Native American Religion *(University of Idaho Press 1988);* The Spirits are Drunk: Comparative Approaches to Chinese Religion *(State University of New York [SUNY] Press 1995);* Through the Earth Darkly: Female Spirituality in Comparative Perspective *(Continuum 1997);* The Mystic Experience: A Descriptive and Comparative Analysis *(SUNY Press 2004);* The Deities are Many: A Polytheistic Theology *(SUNY Press, 2005); and* Native North American Religious Traditions: Dancing for Life *(Praeger 2007).*

Her Gift

I first encountered Bear in late adolescence when I was motivated, for some un-remembered reason, to hike alone along the crest of the Smokies in the southern Appalachian Mountains. Camping one night at a lean-to near a road, I stopped some older local men from throwing stones at Her. The next year I went back, and She walked the same trail with me and slept near me for several days, my strength and endurance increasing enormously. Since then, I often encounter Her, especially when I lived on an island in central Ontario for many years from when the ice melted until it formed again. There, I saw Her every day, and she left muddy paw prints on the log wall of my cabin.

Our encounters culminated over a quarter century ago. On the fourth night while fasting in northern Ontario, She crawled into the tiny fast lodge, filling the remainder of the space my body did not take up. She taught me a healing ritual and gave me a healing song. That song was not just for me but for the Anishnaabe community where I was fasting. Now, as I am reaching the end of my life, I give this song to the community composed of the readers of this anthology.

I can but pass on the words, for that is what She gave me; the tune I use came later. I sing it in the Anishnaabe language, but the song was given to me from Her mind to my own, not from Her vocal cords to my ears, so the language is irrelevant. Whatever language is most meaningful to you is suitable. Each line should be sung twice within the verse, and the verse four times:

On my claws you shall walk,
By my spirit you shall live.

—Mazhakwat Makwa (Colour-of-Sky Bear, a.k.a. Jordan Paper)

KAARINA KAILO

From the Unbearable Bond to the Gift Imaginary

Arch-aic Bear Ceremonials Revisited

The Bear festival, ceremonial, and stories related to them have intrigued research-ers from ethnographers, archeologists, linguists, folklorists, and anthropologists to historians of literature for hundreds of years. The stories that concern me in this book, the narratives dramatizing the relationships between women and Bears,[1] are not only recurrent themes in Arctic, Greek, and Roman mythologies, but their traces and fragments are found across the world, including mountain-ous regions of Armenia. Although the stories are as much part of the heritage of westernized countries as of First Nations or Indigenous peoples, it is mostly the latter that have retained them in active and respectful memory through oral tradition and performance (see Loucks 1985; McClellan 1975, 1970).[2] As an academic topic, the narratives—addressing women's relations with the mysteri-ous, religious, erotic, spiritual entity, and totem forebear—provide multifaceted case studies and a rich narrative matrix for revisiting the dominant research on Bear ceremonials. The narratives also represent a woman-friendly, yet gender-balanced core of a socio-cosmic imaginary that can help question, displace, and even replace the dominant master imaginary of western culture.

The cross-cultural body of narratives about wo(men) and Bears has gener-ated interpretations mostly through the eurocentric male "gaze"/perspective. The eurocentric male perspective situates the women and Bear narratives in the context of the Bear ceremonial that some see as evidence of the practice of the very first religion (Frazer 1890; Sarmela 1991: 209). Research going so far back in history is bound to be to speculative, educated guesswork even when based on the selected evidence. However, numerous multidisciplinary findings allow us, in this anthology, to posit that the stories hark back to a life-oriented, pre-patriarchal era in Old Europe and North America.

Researchers' biases (on which I will elaborate) are present and manifest in nu-merous ways when it comes to the study of Bear ceremonials, and the worldview of which they carry traces. These biases can range from a focus on the killing and hunting of the bear (male activities), to the taken-for-granted sexual politics of so-called "primitive" cultures, which I prefer to call "cultures of life." These studies often include an emphasis on the male gender of the Bear, the totemistic forefather, and the role of the participants at the Bear feast. In general, these dominant studies fail to connect the women and Bear narratives to the all-male hunting dramas as part of a broader historical configuration—the shifts from goddess, or matriarchal cultures to patriarchies focused on monotheism and an exclusionary, hierarchical worldview that privileges, or rather only acknowledges, male godheads.

Mary Condren's (2002) research on the gradual overwriting of goddess-centered cultures, evidenced by changes to the festivals celebrating the ancient Pagan Goddess Brigit in the Irish-Celtic context, provides one worthwhile theoretical framework for my comparative research. In her analysis of the historical trajectories of Brigit as a metaphor of women's wisdom and power in early Europe, Condren focuses on Brigit's links with the cycles of life and death, foregrounding a social ethics based on feminine creativity rather than the male reproductive consciousness (see also O'Brien 1983). In this article, I also speculate on the ways in which the womb-and-tomb celebrating ethos of the ancient Bear religion or worldview was eventually replaced by a more exclusively tomb-oriented and life-denigrating ethos. While the former corresponds with the values ascribed to "gift economies," the latter prioritizes exchange (Vaughan 1997), male reproductive consciousness (O'Brien 1983), heroism, resurrection, guilt, expiation, and hierarchical relations between humans, men, women, and nature. My research on the topic of women and Bears in the North (Kailo 2005a, 2003, 1996, 1993) has led me to detect in these narratives traces of gender-equal "cultures of life," which are also referred to as matricentric, matriarchal, egalitarian cultures, or manifestations of the give-back economies of gift-based societies.[3] I also draw on ecofeminist theories that I find in harmony with the values of the gift economy (i.e., Plumwood 1993).

My article, then, seeks to contribute to feminist spirituality and cultural studies by foregrounding the evidence of Bear-honouring cultures of life as the most distant background of the "masculated" (Vaughan 1997) Bear ceremonial. I will also evoke the shifts in discourses and worldviews that have taken place in several cultural and temporal frameworks between the matricentric eras and the increasingly more patriarchal exchange economies. My aim is to lift, or at least to pull aside, the academic veil on the repressed, suppressed, or forbidden contact between women and Bears within the context of world renewal festivals. I bring forth the elements that support the thesis of a gift-circulating, life-oriented worldview prior to the male-exclusive and death-oriented Bear rituals. Although there is a wealth of research on artefacts and other symbols of feminine creativity and matriarchy, they have not to date been linked this closely with the Bear religion, particularly from a feminist perspective. I will show that comparative research materials on the women and Bear narratives suggest that men and women had gender-segregated but gender-equal life-enhancement and rebirth-oriented rituals beyond assumptions of cultures dominated by only one gender—the very gender being also contingent and constructed across history. Indeed, pre-patriarchal times should not be approached as the mirror image of hierarchical, androcentric, and exclusionary patriarchies. Although fertility and survival-oriented rituals have evidently placed mothers, bears, and other symbols of reproduction or cyclical time measurement in the center of their social imaginaries, it seems that the male phallus has likewise commanded positive ritual attention. My approach toward the women and Bear narratives consists in listening to and looking at the evidence through a non-binary approach, which I term "the gift gaze,"[4] and which recognizes fluid dualities rather than categorical and hierarchical dichotomies.

Traces of the women and Bear narratives are evident in a life-celebrating socio-cosmic matrix which honours especially the icons of regeneration, foremost of which are mothers, birds, bears, bees, caves, and snakes. Such a focus should not be reduced to a "cultural ecofeminist agenda," assumed to be by definition rooted in biological essentialism and reverse sexism. Doing so would reify the eurocentric dualistic imaginary. In contrast, I seek to foreground a wholly other imaginary beyond the patriarchal western imagination, while recognizing the difficulty of positing anything foolproof about imaginaries that existed so far back in time. Since models of womanhood, mothering, and the feminine have been defined via the male gaze in a sentimental and dualistic way, we need to redefine the very context in which gender is assumed to be immutable, giving up the taken-for-granted patriarchal sex/gender system as universal (Moore 1988). The philosophy of the gift is an attempt to think of difference itself differently, while recognizing that it is also not mere speculation (Kuokkanen 2007). Contrary to stereotypes circulated often for ideological reasons (i.e., Binford 1979; Hodder 2004),[5] ecofeminists, or researchers of matriarchies or women-centred religions, are not a homogenous group of "essentialists" glorifying women or mothers while demonizing men. It is worth considering how the imaginary body itself is coded with constructed notions of "feminine" or "masculine" forms of creativity, and exposing how such an arbitrary coding has led to the suppression and appropriation of the "feminine" forms of the sacred——and the concomitant privileging of male elite power structures. For Moira Gatens (1991) "there is a contingent, though not arbitrary, relation between the male body and masculinity and the female body and femininity. To claim this is neither biologism or essentialism but rather to acknowledge the extremely complex and ubiquitous network of signification and its historical, psychological, and cultural manifestations" (149). It is to the imaginary body that we must look to find the key or the code to enable the decipherment of the social and personal significance of male and female biologies as lived in culture, as part of a particular worldview, and the set of discursive practices underlying this worldview.

Critical debates about whether or not gender-equal, life-oriented societies have preceded patriarchies in the very forms through which scholars have sought to confirm their thesis, do not lessen the relevance of such research. Redressing the balance of research engaged through male or male-identified eyes can only leave us with a skewed sense of the past. On the other hand, since women have been the objects of centuries of misogynistic male philosophy that has demonized us from Aristotle (1908-1931) and Schopenhauer (cited in Nagl-Docekal 2000) to Freud (1953-74, 1933), providing women with more positive representations of their socially-constructed gender cannot be reduced to an alleged hatred of men, or "reverse essentialism." It is a symptom, rather, of the dualistic mindset and exchange economy where luck or success is seen to be limited: hence, to foreground positive representations of female creativity is seen as wresting something from men. Men (although by no means a homogenous group) have had centuries to circulate philosophies, histories, myths, and other discourses in their own image. To label women's interest in their self-defined, even strategically essentialist, cultural traditions as biologism is to perpetuate rather than decenter masculated power structures.

By what methods and approaches can we best get beyond the biases and naturalized assumptions of the dominant research, which perpetuates the values/assumptions of the exchange economy and the master imaginary (concepts I will elaborate on in the next section)? How might one recognize such evidence? Why must women and Bears be kept from close encounters and from crossing each other's paths (typical examples of the patriarchal stage of the Bear festival)? Although my research is focused on Finno-Ugric, particularly Finnish Carelian and Sami (Lapp) Bear narratives, I will draw on cross-cultural materials[6] that highlight my research interests and provide points of comparison from Northern Europe and Indigenous North America. Similar elements of a gift-circulating worldview have travelled across the continents even before the modern age of globalization. If the Greco-Roman gods and goddesses have numerous counterparts in the most distant parts of the ancient world, it is no doubt because of large-scale exchange and circulation of cultural ideas. Just as there are affinities between Arctic and Northern male gods and their middle eastern counterparts, one can detect similarities of values, ways of living, and of practising rituals among what I term "cultures of life," following Mary Condren (2002), among others. As my method, I contrast cultural materials on life-renewal rituals even from the ancient and modern Kabyle culture of Algeria, where one can still find strong evidence of a life-honouring woman-centred worldview, thereby reminding us that if matricentric, based on a maternal social imaginary, continue to exist today, there is no rational reason to *a priori* posit patriarchy as universal. I will begin by elaborating on the theoretical concepts which in my view are best suited to bringing out new perspectives on women and Bears, as well as on the Bear ceremonial.

Theoretical Concepts and Perspectives

The search for relevant parallels to help make sense of the women and Bear narratives has carried me backwards in history to the classical mythological tradition on the one hand, and to an exploration of the Arctic, Indigenous, and Nordic/ Northern narratives on the other. A focus on the oldest layers of human history, as well as the entire range of cultural goods common to old Europeans, Celts, and "invading" Indo-Europeans, brings to the fore the appearance of goddesses of regeneration and transformation linked with Bear. They range from Cybele, Artemis, Diana, Hera, and Hestia to Juno among the best known ones. However, by extending their range to include the goddess myths of lesser diffusion from Louhi, Helga, and Dea Artio to Ursula and beyond (Kailo 1996), we can deepen the cross-cultural evidence of a gift-circulating, Bear honouring imaginary. At the same time, Mary O'Brien's (1983) theory of male reproductive consciousness, Genevieve Vaughan's notions of the gift and exchange economies (2007, 2006, 2004a, 2004b, 1997), and Heide Goettner-Abendroth's (2000, 1995, 1991, 1988) classic studies on matriarchies provide useful theoretical approaches for teasing new lines of inquiry out of the male-centered Bear festival. The aim of evaluating the primary materials that I have been gathering over a decade compels me to adopt an inter- and multidisciplinary approach—a kaleidoscopic and multiethnic gaze—to make up for the lack of available data and reliable research on the topic. The aggregation of this part archaic, part modern material helps to bring forward and reclaim new interpretations of the rich symbolism associated with the women and Bear narratives and the festivals and worldview to which I link them.

Notions of the "evil" eye or the "powerful gaze" are a recurrent topic in cross-cultural studies of *arch*-aic societies (the very term "archaic" can be linked to the Greek word for Bear, *arctos*; thus my spelling of *arch*-aic). It is not surprising then that one of the dominant and highly symbolic power-related aspects of the women and Bear narratives has to do with the taboos placed on women not to look at/gaze upon the bear that has taken them in the narrative, and on the killed Bear that is being celebrated in the Bear ceremonial. I suggest that the women and Bear narratives and historical evidence of the Bear ceremonial reflect the desire to sever and conceal the women's and the Bears' mutual gaze and bond, the red thread running through many of the cross-cultural wo(men) and bear narratives. This aspect of the narrative and the ceremonials has not received much, if any, critical attention. Scholars are content to note, mostly in passing, that this prohibition attests to beliefs of women's "polluting" (related to menarche) influence, or the danger that the Bear represents to women. I will elaborate on this taboo relation-ship by pointing to the power relations that are in the center of contemporary research on gendered politics and discourses, from media studies to art history. My aim is to remove the wool that has been pulled over our eyes, not in order to revert the evil (colonizing) gaze but to help radically change academic paradigms towards recognizing and accepting the im(possible) gift (Kuokkanen 2007) of Indigenous epistemes. A thorough examination of the theoretical perspectives is necessary as we need new methods to be able to revisit history and open new spaces for gynocentric revisions—the re-creation of history as herstory.

The Unbearable Gaze and Epistemic Power

How can we change patriarchal relations of looking? If patriarchy informs our political regimes, our economic systems, our culture, our language, our unconscious, then it is not surprising that a male perspective is dominant in representation. How can we shift this perspective and inscribe a female gaze into the heart of our cultural life? (Gamman and Marshmen 1989: 1)

The theory of the gaze, at its origins a psychoanalytical concept (Mulvey 1989), is appropriate in many ways for addressing the gendered agenda behind women's "forbidden gaze," which occurs and reoccurs in the wo(men) and bear narratives as well as in the context of the Bear festivals. It epitomizes the gradual veiling over and suppression of the history of matricentric cultures of life. I begin with the "unbearable" gaze which condenses two historically contingent and gendered views on human/human as well as human/animal relations. As a paradoxical concept, the "unbearable gaze," contains a reference to both the male gaze,[7] a dominant concept in academic research, and the particular case of the "unbearable" bond between women and bears. However, it also represents what is unbearable and overbearing for the woman/bear on the one hand, and for patriarchy on the other.

The consequences and symptoms of the sexual politics that have led to the overwriting, suppression, and censoring of life-honouring societies are evident in the co-optation of the Bear Goddess, Kallisto (Geminder 1984; Reischl 2004; Wall 1988), and her cross-cultural variants. The wo(men) and bear narratives range from stories of a Bear/woman marriage to tales of seduction, even rape. They attest to patriarchal sexual-textual interventions whereby stories told from women's perspective give way to tools of moral guidance with efforts made to consolidate male supremacy through mythic and narrative rape (Pratt 1994: 353). The Kallisto history/myth/narrative/story effectively illustrates the power mechanisms, whitewashing, and other strategies of mind colonization that have led to women's loss of mythic and political power and gynocentric knowledge. The "unbearable" gaze, present in the wo(men) and Bear narratives, captures the dominating stance both of those who pushed women into the margins of the social imaginary, and of malestream scholars who unwittingly perpetuate this exclusion by taking it for granted. The key concepts relevant for my research, then, are on the one hand, the related concepts of "the male gaze" and "master imaginary,"[8] and on the other, "the gift gaze" and "gift imaginary," which are part of my interdisciplinary ecocritical approach.

Before I elaborate on the gift imaginary, which refers to the ideal of a circular rather than strictly hierarchical model of human/human and human/animal relations, I reflect on ecofeminism/ecocriticism and the stereotypes with which it has been belittled and demonized. Ecocritical perspectives in literary studies (Glotfelty and Fromm 1996) have been gaining ground along with French feminists' efforts to empower women through a new strategically essentialist gynocentric language of their "own" (i.e., Cixous 1980; Cixous and Clément 1986; Irigaray 1985). Both epistemic orientations help uncover woman-empowering dimensions in traditional research as such approaches bring two neglected/suppressed dimensions ("nature" and women/gender, among other things) to the center. Australian ecofeminist Val Plumwood argued in *Feminism and the Mastery of Nature* (1993) that "the dualism of Reason and Nature—a dominant cultural narrative of human and rational hyper-separation from, opposition to, and mastery over a passive and enslaved nature underlies the irrationality we see in the modern ecological crisis" (3). Like Carol MacCormack and Marilyn Strathern (1980) among others, she recognizes that nature is itself a contingent cultural construct. As Plumwood noted at a conference in Madrid in 2000,[9] ecological feminism involves nothing less than turning around the direction of western culture, which continues to inscribe this disastrous opposition on more and more of the globe: "To shake the conceptual foundations of these systems of domination we must unmask more fully the identity of the master hidden behind the neutral guise of the human and of the ideals of rationality" (1993: 68). Because both ecofeminist and matriarchy-related research is often assumed *a priori* to be essentializing, I stress, like Plumwood (2003) that a critical ecological gaze needs to break the false dichotomy of nature and culture in the forms they have taken also within feminism, which she calls "Feminism of Uncritical Reversal" and the "Feminism of Uncritical Equality." Plumwood claims that the first position accepts and embraces the identification of woman with Nature and the underside of reason, leaving the dualistic construction of Reason and Nature largely unquestioned, reversing their value and power, so that women's "closeness to nature" becomes the truly valued human characteristic in place of male-associated distancing from it" (1-2). The first position is also assumed to embrace merely the nature-side of the dualism. The second position, for its part, ranges from liberal to postmodern feminism, although it is dangerous to reduce any position to a black-and-white category. Socialist ecofeminists like Janet Biehl (1990) exemplify, however, the "nature-phobic" side of the equation, moving women from the "lower" nature side of the dualism and idealizing rationality and culture, uncritical of the idea that the overall dualism is itself the problem (Kailo 2003). Plumwood (2003) argues that "the Feminism of Uncritical Equality takes the critical edge off feminism as a larger cultural critique and also destroys its capacity to create common ground with other social forces. It also works poorly for most women, since those who will find equality in what are essentially male terms will always, given women's socialisation, be only an elite few" (1-2). Like Plumwood (2003), I also extend the concept of equality to include other than the human species and advocate as she does:

> an ethical order with its own values and standards of sharing, generosity, and radical equality between species, and with its own stringent obligations to recognise the other as equally positioned, as potentially food and always more than food. The anthropocentric denials of western culture have set the stage for this conflict of perceptions, but less anthropocentric alternatives such as the framework of reciprocity are still alien to the thinking of western culture and in conflict with the modes of life and rationality it has developed.... [T]he task now is to develop alternative frameworks and models like the reciprocity model which can address these conflicts as a practical ethic for contemporary life and a source of critical, ethical and ecological remaking of our food relationships. (35)

What ecofeminism in its cross- and interdisciplinary variety adds to epistemic diversity and a politics of affinity rather than sameness (Kailo 2006a, 2004a, 1998) has to do with its explicit concern with environmental issues and ecologically sustainable attitudes. Ecofeminists consider the objectifying and utilitarian stance of "masculated" capitalistic patriarchy (Vaughan 1997) in its various manifestations to be the root of the oppression of women and nature and a major source of multidimensional violence affecting all.[10] Developing more ethno- and gender-sensitive approaches can provide us with a more accurate view/sense of cultures rooted in imaginaries and epistemic styles of reasoning (Meyer and Ramirez 1996: 90) that challenge the tenets of white mythology and the many naturalized epistemic conventions.[11] Marija Gimbutas (1989, 1982), noted for her pioneering work on the goddess symbols and culture at Çatal Huyük, has been challenged by many scholars who point out that male virility, embodied in a bull god with horns, was also an object of worship (see Ruether 1992). The gender equality of Minoan society has also been questioned on the grounds that patriarchies had already developed to some extent in that era (Leahy 1998). The women and Bear narratives allow us to speculate, however, that a very different social imaginary can be linked to the Bear ceremonial's oldest layers than what scholars so far have been able or willing to admit. Feminist modes of "reversal" allow us to do justice to cultures of life, thus honouring, not objectifying the category labelled by western scholars as "nature." Either/or questions or claims fail to do justice to an imaginary that may well have defied such dualisms. The centrality of a maternal symbolic order does not mean total marginalization, even less a devaluation of male symbols or status.

The Master and Gift Imaginary

The concept of the "imaginary" is best known in its use by Jacques Lacan (1997 [1966]), the well-known French psychoanalytic theorist.[12] For my purposes, it refers to the imaginary relationship of individuals to their real conditions of existence and is that complex of symbols, images, or representations of reality which mask the historically contingent ecological, material, and spiritual dimensions of life (cf. Althusser 1984). The term also refers, in my usage, to the dominant representational and discursive orders of thought that guide thought, perception, and values during particular historical periods. Instead of referring to a symbolic order in the Lacanian tradition, I refer to a social order as the institutional core of regulations, laws, dominant practices, and rituals, which I see as having among other dimensions clearly gendered and power-related aspects.

With the concept of the master imaginary (Kailo 2006a), having some affinities with Plumwood's (1993) master identity, I refer to the historically and geographically dominant western paradigm and worldview to do with human values, identity, nature, reason, spirituality, and consciousness, which set elite men in the center as an unrecognized, but prioritized norm. It represents the concealed psycho-social and fantasy-related framework in which the male gaze is embedded and which is also reflected in academic mainstream research. In the spirit of O'Brien's (1983) sociological notion, "the male reproductive consciousness,"[13] I seek to capture with the concept of the master imaginary how modern eurocentric "human" desire, masking its current heteromasculated norm, is intimately linked with power and gendered projections of patriarchal supremacy. The master imaginary covers and refers to the artificial and arbitrary dichotomies that have allowed mostly white heterosexual elite men (as well as assimilated Indigenous and non-Indigenous men and women assimilated and integrated through mind colonization to the modernity of master narratives and the constantly evolving mechanistic ways and values of "modernization") to dominate nature, women, and people of colour, as well as men defying the heterosexist/heteronormative and often homosocial gender contracts.[14] The devaluation of the realms not associated with "reason"—mother, the Goddess, the feminine, and nature—linked with the woman-positive imaginary of reproduction—are my particular concerns here. Among the central elements of the master imaginary, as it has developed in the course of patriarchal history, are assumptions and projections of non-egalitarian difference (i.e., men vs. women, humans vs. animals, matter vs. spirit, reason vs. emotion). They are the ideological tools through which the ruling classes have sought to control, subjugate, and label the "other."[15] The master imaginary also has at its core an ordering of reality related to sex/gender and species systems and other intersectional variables of difference, and represents a combined backgrounding of the gifts provided by women, the "subaltern" (Spivak qtd. in Winant 1990) and nature. The master model or identity has been embraced by both individuals and social institutions, and for Plumwood (1993), it "has been arrived at by exclusion and devaluation of women, women's life-patterns and feminine characteristics, as well as by exclusion of those others and areas of life which have been construed as nature" (29). Emotional detachment and the fallacy of "objectivity" making possible the objectification of nature (formerly understood as organic), enabling humans to turn it into something soulless and mechanical, are likewise elements of the master imaginary (cf. Merchant 1989). Traces of the gift imaginary and the attendant social order honouring Bear, Bear goddesses, bees, snakes, caves, and other paradigms of regeneration and/or hibernation are present in different degrees in two main matrices that I extrapolate from the narratives of wo(men) and Bears: those attesting to the ritual worship of (giving worth to) life renewal and those showing evidence of a shift toward the iconography and symbolism of death, hierarchy, violence, and the ultimate denigration of the sanctity of women, the maternal symbolism and logic, and the earth (cf. Merchant 1989; Ruether 1992).

It needs to be pointed out that the master and gift imaginaries are contrasted heuristically, to allow us to distinguish between gendered and ethnocultural epistemes, as tools for thinking of difference differently. The concepts are not mirror images of each other, but rather, allow for marginalized gift economies to be re-interpreted in a different voice. The gift imaginary represents an ancient-modern non-binary logic but also contains within it elements of exchange and negative power. It is not useful to idealize cultures of life, which no doubt have their shadow side; the etymology of the word for gift in most Romance languages derives from the Latin *dosis,* a "dose" as, for instance, of poison. In German, *gift* has come to mean only poison. Jacques Derrida (1981) looks upon the gift as a *pharmakon*—a Greek word that also means both "remedy" and "poison" (63-171). In developing the concept of the gift imaginary I thus recognize the way in which any ideology or worldview carries the seeds of its undoing, its negative and positive impact. But gift logic remains a non-binary one in its basic premises, and in its impact (stressing interconnectedness rather than hierarchy as a mode of organizing human and human/animal relations). We need academic epistemologies and approaches that recognize other than Eurocentric systems of knowledge and ways of knowing, ones that challenge the hegemony and hierarchy of epistemes which serve hegemonic interests (cf. Kuokkanen 2007: 56-58). The heuristically dualistic set of discourses, which recognizes the overlapping/dialectical nature of gift and exhange perspectives, does not serve to consolidate hierarchical dichotomies that form the core of the master imaginary. Rather, through the gift gaze, I analyze elements in archival and other texts so that we can see better what has been *a priori* excluded. The male reproductive consciousness—based on appropriating and denigrating the female forms of biological and symbolic creativity—has, in contrast with this model, served the goals of hierarchical and exclusive modes of social organization. The master imaginary, and the worldview I associate it with, is based on a practice of power as "power-over," which manifests in an asymmetrical distribution of cultural, mythic, material, epistemic, and immaterial resources between elites, men, and women.[16] At worst, it manifests itself as intolerance and as reductively anthropocentric ways of perceiving and evaluating life and other life forms, as well as other members of the extended community of living beings. The master imaginary as "psychic reality" is also related to the exchange economy, the rise of private property and ultimately, capitalism, which grounds its politics in the exchange and accumulation of goods, and where women and animals are often the prime currency of trade. However, the desire to control the "other" (women, Indigenous peoples, animals) also has sexual and socio-political dimensions.

In contrast, the gift imaginary refers to a collective psychic reality grounded in a non-hierarchical relational attitude, better reflecting the ways in which identities, knowledge, and relationships with the natural environments are constituted, as revealed above all by Indigenous theorists and feminists (i.e., Armstrong 2007; *Adivasi Justice is to Live in the Forest* 2007; Kuokkanen 2007). One of the founding premises of the relational gift-based model of the world is that of responsibility and interdependence/intersubjectivity across the flexibly conceived human and animal domains echoing Plumwood's ecological ethics (2003). The ethics—to use modern terms—are to "look after" or care for the land; only through interspecies mutuality and respect can one ensure abundance and survival. Emphasizing the turn-taking of gift circulation ensures a stable, survival-oriented social order. The cultures of life to which scholars often refer as matriarchies with their matrix of icons of regeneration provide important examples of gift-circulating societies in their vast variety. Before I elaborate on the narratives of wo(men) and Bears, I describe key notions of Genevieve Vaughan's theories (2007, 2004a, 2004b, 1997) in which she combines semiotics, linguistics, Marxist theory, and feminist criticism of economic models. Vaughan's theories add yet an important dimension for understanding how the focus on property and accumulation by the evolving patriarchy, hegemonic masculinity, and master imaginary, developed an economy based on exchange rather than the gift imaginary (a care-based holistic economics and worldview).

The Gift and Exchange Economies

Since Marcel Mauss's (1969 [1923/24]) influential *The Gift: Forms and Functions of Exchange in Archaic Societies*, the gift and gift exchange have been frequent topics of inquiry within the field of anthropology.[17] In contrast to other theorists of the gift, Vaughan addresses the gift in a gender-sensitive way in her book, *For-Giving: A Feminist Criticism of Exchange* (1997), and in "walking her talk," i.e., practising the gift in her own life.[18] Vaughan's formulations of the tension between the gift and the exchange economy as gendered categories provide the theoretical lens through which the oversights and selective biases of malestream research can be exposed and situated.

Vaughan (1997) posits two gender-related although not essentialist worldviews or logics, one based on gift giving/circulation and another one based on the philosophy of patriarchal exchange economies. Vaughan relates these worldviews to two basic economic paradigms which co-exist and of which the gift paradigm likely has been more dominant in the past. They are logically contradictory, but also complementary. However, reflecting the asymmetrical power relations that in many societies subjugate women and their "gift labour" (i.e., unpaid work), the latter tends to be invisible and undervalued while the one associated a patriarchal order is highly valued and recognized. Vaughan has come to recognize and state explicitly that many Indigenous cultures also express the worldview of gift circulation, or of "giving back" (see Armstrong 2007; Kailo 2004b; Kuok-kanen 2004b). In pre-patriarchal/non-patriarchal societies the gift economy likely formed and still forms the dominant ethos whereas today the exchange economy is predominant and thoroughly naturalized. Vaughan explains that Gifts require the turning of attention from the giver toward the receiver. Gift giving is other-oriented, satisfying the needs of, and ascribing value to another while exchange, which requires an equivalent value in return, is ego-oriented and directed toward the satisfaction of the exchanger's own needs. As Vaughan (1997) points out: "Even our greeting 'How are you?' is a way of asking 'What are your needs?'" (31). However, needs-fulfillment easily degenerates into forced emotional labour and care in a situation of strict gender roles and capitalistic arrangements. Exchange creates separation and seeming independence on the basis of a deeper dependence, and manifests itself today as dependency on the market economy. Gift and give-back rituals create a multifaceted community whereas exchange tends to lead to a collection of isolated individuals (Vaughan 2006: 94). For Vaughan (2006), the patriarchal exchange economy, and the mindset it reflects, has in the course of history incorporated the gift paradigm, rendering the worldview or logic of women (for all their ethnocultural differences) invisible through incorporation and renaming.[19] It may be necessary to stress that this form of economic-cultural philosophy is historically contingent and variable. Gift economies have likely always included trade. Likewise, advocates of the exchange economy may well have also practiced the gift. The point, then, is the preponderance of the exchange paradigm that has buried the gift perspective under its normative weight, giving rise to the need to (re)valorize the gift and redress the imbalance by making the gift more visible, also as something to be taken into account as part of the methodological toolkit.

Vaughan (1997) notes that the kind of recognition that takes place with the exchange gaze fits with the exchange paradigm and looks at nature and humans as manipulable, mechanical, without Gifts or need for gratitude and bonding. It echoes what Carolyn Merchant (1989) has written about the shifts from an organic to a mechanical view of life. It is Vaughan's specific and unique contribution to feminist theory and practice to point out that gift giving has not been recognized as a social paradigm and logic, but has been marginalized as a merely private way of looking at the world. It is not seen as political (in the sense of the personal being political), and as part of a widely spread social imaginary. Likewise, the gift imaginary, if seen as relating only to women, will likely be dismissed as belonging to women's private sphere (although it was the norm for all members of gift-circulating societies). The exchange gaze has replaced the gift gaze as the norm, concealing the operations of the gift economy as a naturalized women's labour and mode of economic distribution. The ecofeminist stance that I advocate recognizes collective eco-social needs (rather than the accumulation of capital) and the effort to ascribe value to all living beings. Without such values, as a scholar one may not find evidence for the gift, the selection and combination of facts and scientific materials being always also an effect of personal bias. It would be simplistic and reductive to claim that men and women across time and space have been characterized by these two logics, but the key issue is what impact different social imaginaries have on gendered and other values (cf. Leahy 1998). The attempt to trace how the Bear Goddess/Forebear/Guardian has been replaced by the Christian Eve, Brigit, and Virgin Mary among other figures, and historical shifts, would reveal that two main types of relatedness may have intersected and been the identificatory pattern of both women and men at different historical junctures (cf. Condren 2002).

For Sami scholar Rauna Kuokkanen (2007), the gift continues to pose a threat to prevailing modes of thinking and interaction that she argues characterizes contemporary transnational capitalism in the same way that countless other gift practices posed earlier a threat to "civilization" and the emerging nation-state of Canada. This threat was considered so serious that it was outlawed by the early colonial authorities and later erased by various, sometimes very ambiguous and insidious forms of cultural imperialism (Kuokkanen 2007: 46-46). One reason to also prohibit the gift today is that the current academy is deeply rooted in the ideology of exchange (Kuokkanen 2007), which I argue has led to nothing less than a predatory corpocracy. Indigenous gift philosophies do not limit the gift to mere exchange, counter-gift, and debt, contrary to what many analysts of the gift, like Derrida (1981), claim. Kuokkanen (2007) states "...it is important to notice that we are not talking about 'archaic' societies or gift practices in the past, but *epistemes* that continue to influence the way in which many people think and behave today" (56-57). One cannot be sensitive to traces of a matricentric, matriarchal worldview if scholars are not trained to even recognize the possibility of other possible worldviews. How can they, therefore, approach difference differently?

I will thus summarize the key aspects of peaceful societies or "matriarchies" first as approached by Mary Condren (2002), and then, in a more elaborate form, as defined by Heide Goettner-Abendroth (2000, 1995, 1991, 1988), a German scholar and pioneer of matriarchal studies. She has studied past and present matriarchies for over 30 years and has developed ways of methodologically testing and proving the existence of such alternative, woman-empowering social systems.[20] These fori for circulation of knowledge about gift- or life-oriented cultures have yielded important proof to challenge persistent claims that real alternatives to patriarchy and the naturalization of humans' basic aggressive, ego-oriented nature never existed.

Matriarchal Societies

Mary Condren (2002) has demonstrated how the shift from matricentric to patriarchal societies gradually came to be concealed in the historical Irish context she has researched:

> In early Irish society, women's power rested on social networking and ties to their children.... It could even be argued that the emphasis on material wealth became the crucial leverage point for wresting power from women. If material wealth was not the basis for female power, wealth was not unimportant. (63-64)

Condren provides an insightful interpretation of the reasons why the cultures of life in which the worship of the Goddess was centered came to be transformed.

It is important to be familiar with some of Goettner-Abendroth's (2007) research results, core insights, and clarifications to do with matriarchal research, above all the assumptions often circulated in the academe that have served to discredit such inquiries. Among other things, she stresses, with the authority of her extensive research in this field, that matriarchies simply do not refer to a reverse patriarchy—a reversal of gendered power relations—with women and mothers as oppressors of men. She posits that one can translate "matriarchy" more accurately as "mothers from the beginning," while "patriarchy" translates correctly as "domination by the fathers." She bases her findings on historical studies exposing the increasing characteristics of domination of non-matricentric societies to which Condren's (2002) and many other scholars' research attests.[21] Goettner-Abendroth (2007) points out that originally, in terms of etymology, the Greek word *arché* came to have a double meaning. It now means both "beginning" as well as "domination" (100) (see also Sanday[22] 1998). I suggest that Arkas, the Greek Bear-Son of Zeus and Artemis, the Bear Goddess, can also be related to the word *arché*, perhaps even to the people of Arkas, Bear ancestors of the Arcadians.

It is challenging, as well as stimulating, to foreground the evidence, in light of which this etymology and its links with Bear festivals, as well as with the Irish/ Celtic festival of Brigit, may well point toward a one-time imaginary privileging of both mothers and Bears as its key symbols of reproduction and life renewal. Could "archaic" and "*arché*" thus be interpreted as "Bears and Mother Goddesses at the beginning?" Could Bears and Mother Goddesses be the primal matrix of socio-cosmic relations that were followed by the overwriting and reversal of these beginnings and the values/symbols with which they were associated, eventually co-opted and appropriated by Church leaders for a different purpose and with semantic reversals of their more originary meanings? Goettner-Abendroth's point about a gendered difference in political organization and values is corroborated by the gendered yet gender-blind elements of Oedipal myths examined in Sigmund Freud's *Totem and Taboo* (1950). The story of Oedipus is clearly a violence-oriented myth of domination by men and fathers that contrasts with the woman/Bear origin story and matricentric festivals like that of the Irish Bridget (Ó Catháin 1995). Even in historically recent versions of the Bear festivals, the primal bond between women and Bears is the metaform of an imaginary where women give birth to and/or nurture/marry the Bear. It is a narrative honouring the cycles of life and death with particular esteem attached to the symbols of life energies and renewal.

In cultures of life there appears to have been great respect for the women's ability to give birth and produce new life, together with other beings and phenomena associated with the cycles of birth/rebirth. Since life was sacred, so were mothers, bears, bees, snakes, and other paradigms evoking cyclical time measurement or renewal. With respect to bears specifically, "… through its hibernating habits, the bear acted as a time indicator with respect to the seasons, its biocosmic rhythms subtly responding to changes in light and darkness. The hibernation of the bear acted as a stable, reliable sign of the limits of the seasons and became a dominant symbol of the entire transition from summer to winter and back again" (Bäckman 1983: 38). Other recurring elements in the paradigm of periodic death and renewal are the menstruation huts/bear's dens and caves, which contain in their symbolism a non-dualistic coming together of tomb/womb, life/death.[23] However, the valorization of mothers did not necessarily entail demonization or subjugation of non-mothers (just as the notion of "interconnectedness" in ecofeminist and Indigenous studies in no way evokes reverse discrimination). In contrast, in Freud's *Totem and Taboo* (1950) we can see an "origin story," the myth of Oedipus, that epitomizes the (unconscious?) reversal of the values of the gift imaginary and naturalizes through psychoanalysis the imaginary of death, murder, patricide, and violence against women. The mother does not feature in this story. The sons want to kill their father in order to gain access to the tribe's women. *Totem and Taboo* is allegedly about patricide and original sin as the root cause of human guilt and the need for rituals of atonement. From the point of view of women and cultures of life, however, it merely describes and dramatizes the matricide that is one dimension of patriarchal culture, and the fall into patriarchal time and space. As Condren (2002) notes, the fall into patriarchy has had devastating consequences for the "banished children of Eve" (43). Gift-identified wo(men) have no reason to embrace Freud's misogynistic primal myth; the totemistic marriage between the primal ancestor and Bear with its theme of human/animal interdependency and social responsibilities would be much closer to the heart of women's (and men's) identity themes beyond any claims of biological determinism. Why would women consciously embrace a myth that sets them up as objects of male trade in women? And would all men wish to identify with a master narrative that dehumanizes them and their mother relationship?

Goettner-Abendroth (2005) exhorts researchers not to shy away from the provocative connotation of the term "matriarchy," both because research in this field is so under-focused and important and because only continued efforts to venture into this tabooed area of research will bring about a different mindset (even enabling such research). She presents three heuristic criteria for matriarchal societies, which I add need to be studied historically and contextually whenever possible. The first criterion is economic. She circumscribes matriarchies as societies which practice subsistence agriculture and where land and house are property of the entire clan and not "private" property. Women have the power of disposition over the source of nourishment and there is a constant adjustment of the level of wealth by the circulation of the vital goods in the form of gifts at festivals. Matriarchies are thus societies of reciprocity embracing Vaughan's (2006, 1997) position that reciprocity may well have manifested itself as a turn-taking way of responding to collective needs. Among the social criteria Goettner-Abendroth (2004) lists matriarchal clans, which are held together by matrilinearity and/or matrilocality. The societies are rooted in social fatherhood meaning that they are often non-hierarchical and horizontal societies of kinship. As for the political criteria, the principle of consensus in the clan-house, on the level of the village, and on the regional level is a defining feature; the absence of classes and structures of domination characterize these egalitarian societies of consensus (Goettner-Abendroth 2005: 5-6). Goettner-Abendroth (2007) points to analogies between matriarchal research and the gift paradigm, providing an overview of some of the rules and regulations within matriarchal economies in different geographical and historical contexts. She confirms Vaughan's (2007, 1997) theory of the mothering logic, concurring that the matricentric worldview is *not* rooted in a romantic, idealized idea of motherliness as has often been portrayed in patriarchy, and which has led to the devaluation/trivialization and essentialization of mothering, seen as merely sentimental (cf. Melchiori 2007: 322) and private. In matriarchies, however, even men aspire to be like mothers (Sanday 1981), a metaform for a valued mode of relatedness and social logic among all humans, whatever the sex/gender system. Limits of space prevent me from doing justice to the breadth and depth of

Goettner-Abendroth's studies or to refer to the specific historic/cultural contexts on which she bases her analysis.[24] The point here is to question the assumption of the universality of patriarchy across time and space; an aggressive humanity based on crude self-interest that has also been challenged by scholars on the basis of strong evidence pointing to the contrary (Miedzien 1991). The above serves to contextualize my research and helps us retrace our steps back towards life-oriented cultures as a kind of "Bear-*archy*"—Bear at the beginning. I begin by outlining the broader context of studies on Bear ceremonials, and focus then on Finnish/Karelian (and some other Finno-Ugric) Bear narratives. I cite them as examples of the values and worldview of the gift imaginary in which the stories and their interpretations are most likely embedded.

Where Merchant (1989) dates the shifts in worldview to platonic ideology, and later, to sixteenth century mechanical notions of nature, Condren (2002) argues that the overthrow of the "Serpent," (the symbol of evil in the Christian "Adam and Eve" origin story), and an integral element of ancient Goddess cultures, was fundamental and crucial to the foundation of patriarchal culture. According to Merchant, the shift from matricentric to patriarchal cultures happened because imperial states needed "portable" gods as guarantors of their authority:

> If Israel was to grow as a nation-state, with all the entailed political and military trappings, Goddess religions would have to be overthrown. Allegiance would have to be to one god, Yahweh, and the central symbolism of the new religion would be based on Promise and History rather than on the Life and Cyclical Regeneration represented by the Serpent. (11)

In the geographic area that later came to be known as Finland, the emerging Christian patriarchy also preferred a monotheistic god over the polytheistic gods and goddesses or spirits of nature. The replacement of the serpent and related earth religions by a single male god was a development that affected most of Europe.

Bear Ceremonialism in the Northern Hemisphere—and Beyond

For David Rockwell (1991), "The affinities between the different practitioners of the bear rituals are remarkable because they link, in basic ways, peoples as diverse as the hunting gathering Cree Indians of James Bay and the reindeer herders of Lapland, the Athenians of classical Greece and eighteenth-century Great Lakes Ojibwa, Lakota visionaries and Danish warriors, European peasant farmers and Delaware Indian farmer-hunters" (93) (see also Campbell 1959; Edsman 1956; Frazer 1890; Hallowell 1926; Hultkrantz 1965; Paproth 1976).

While the theme of Bear as a multidimensional literary and mythic topic has been treated quite extensively in general studies on the mythological, literary, and socio-cosmic bearlore (i.e., Shepard and Sanders 1985), the relationship between wo(men) and Bears as a topic in its own right has been restricted to mostly North American literary studies.[26] The few existing woman-centred studies, although focused on historical perspectives on women and Bears, contain relatively few if any references to the Finno-Ugric/Circumpolar bearlore and even less, to an explicit (eco)feminist or ecocritical analytical framework.[27] Helga Reischl's (2004) dissertation is one of rare scholarly treatises centering on "The Woman Who Married A Bear," instead of reproducing the focus on men and the Bear ceremonial.

On a more general level, anthropologist Irving Hallowell (1926) pioneered one of the most comprehensive cross-cultural studies on Bear cults and rituals in his classic monograph, *Bear Ceremonialism in the Northern Hemisphere*. This study provided an influential frame for comparative studies on bear hunting rituals and also refers to Finnish Bear ceremonial customs. Hallowell's (1926) intention was to "survey bear ceremonialism in its widest aspects among the peoples of both North America and Eurasia" (23). He compared the bear hunting techniques of people throughout northern Europe, Asia, and North America and found striking parallels between the bear hunt of certain North American Indians and bear hunts in Scandinavia, Siberia, and Japan: "Throughout [these regions] hunters and others involved in the rites believed that the bear represented 'a supernatural being or power,' which governed either the supply of game animals or the supply of bears alone" (26). Hallowell also identified common elements of the hunting ritual:

First, the hunt took place in early spring while the bear was still sleeping in its den. Second, no one could refer to the bear except by metaphorical expressions or kinship or deferential terms such as "The One Going Around in the Woods," "Grandfather," or "Great One." Third, hunters called the bear from its den ("Grandfather, Come out! I am sorry I must kill you!") and killed it at close quarters with an archaic weapon—a club, an axe, or spear, or a knife. Fourth, the hunters made conciliatory speeches to the bear's spirit after its death. Fifth, the carcass became the focus of elaborate ceremonial attention in which it was dressed up in borrowed finery and offered food, tobacco, or decorated objects. Sixth, there was a communal, often eat-all feast of bear meat governed by numerous prescriptions and taboos and *emphasizing sexual differences*. Finally, the people respectfully disposed of the bones, especially the skull, by placing them in a tree. (qtd. in Rockwell 1991: 41-43, my emphasis)

Hallowell's description suggests that the Bear ceremonial was a religious event comparable to patriarchal, Christian religious rites addressed to a male-identified godhead and carried out in the context of a gender-specific social contract ("emphasizing sexual differences"). He concluded that the tradition may have originated in Eurasia during the Paleolithic age and migrated into the New World by way of hunters pursuing caribou herds across the Bering land-bridge. His interpretation is grounded in the historical-geographical method which focuses on the structural affinities of Bear cults across different Northern regions. The above summary described by Hallowell reveals that he does not consider shared elements other than those focused on the male hunting activity to be of relevance.

Although traces of Bear ceremonials have been recorded as late as the nineteenth century (Pentikäinen 2007: 82), as regards their most distant layers, there is reason today to challenge Hallowell's argument. If the tradition goes back to the Paleolithic times, which Marija Gimbutas (1989) and others have identified as the era of the Goddess, or of relatively gender equalitarian societies, Hallowell is misguided in restricting the Bear festival and ceremonial to the male-exclusive hunting framework. Although it is impossible to determine the historical origins of this material with accuracy, the worldview labelled by European scholars as "shamanistic" and "animistic" provides the most likely archaic context for Bear cults and the life-celebrating worldview of gift giving. Scholars from Marcel Mauss (1969) and Matti Sarmela (1991) to Hallowell (1926) and Rockwell (1991) do evoke gift economies and refer to the role of women but no reference is made to possibilities of *matricentric* gift economies and their remnants. Of course, gift economies do not necessarily equal matricentric societies: rather, we need to posit a continuum of gift-circulating cultures on which we might detect different stages and variations on gender equality or modes of interdependency contrasting with the myth of male autonomy where dependence on nature and women is denied and this form of relatedness naturalized.

David Rockwell (1991), in his extensive study of Bear cults, gives recognition to women's mediating and preparatory role: "A woman began the World Renewal Ceremony, when she dreamed the location of a bear in its den and directed the hunters where to find it" (169). Merely initiating a hunt leading to violent sacrifice may be, however, a far cry from the Bear woman's previous status as a central icon with bears, bees, and snakes also forming the semiotic web of life renewal and its complex socio-cosmic contours.[28] Next, I focus on the specificity of the Finnish-Carelian Bear festival, for it foregrounds most clearly my thesis regarding the way in which the matricentric gift imaginary is interlaced with the exchange economy/the master imaginary with its male-exclusionary feasts.

The Finno-Ugric Bear Ceremonial

The first description of a Finnish Bear ceremonial is attributed to Bishop Isak Rothovius at Åbo Akademi where he gave his much-quoted lecture on July 15th, 1640. Rothovius described "primitive" Finns growling and imitating the Bear at the Bear feast. The oldest and maybe the only full description of the hunting drama (*karhunpeijaiset*) is, according to Martti Haavio (1968), contained in the so-called *Viitasaari* manuscript which was evidently written by a clergyman from the parish of Viitasaari at the end seventeenth or the beginning of the eighteenth century. The manuscript contains a description of the bear hunter, preparations for killing the bear, the bear's "feast" or "wedding," and the way the bear's skull was finally carried to the forest and hung in a tree, the "bear-skull pine." The author also recorded the poems presented at various stages of the hunting drama. There are numerous bear skull poems and songs which were sung at the Bear feast, and which are a special feature of the Finnish ceremonial (Honko, Timonen, Branch and Bosley 1993). In describing the Bear ritual, Matti Sarmela (1983) refers to

"*Couvon päälliset tai Häät*" ("Kouko's feasts or Wedding"), with Kouko as the name of an honoured forefather: "Kouko's wedding seems to refer to the 'wedding' or 'funeral' of the primordial father of the kin or the forest, a feast during which the dead one's meat was eaten" (177-178).

As regards the central importance of Bear as god[dess] figure, Juha Pentikäinen (2007) finds evidence in recent investigations suggesting that bear images occur in ancient Finnish rock faces; they appear to be comparable to those found in Flatruet in Sweden, Alta in Norway, and on Lake Onega in Russia (147).[29] These and other rock paintings, artefacts, and cave findings provide some of evidence for the Bear religion (if indeed it is a religion since "religion" refers to organized, institutionalized forms of worship) or worldview. Recent research on the Bear ceremonial has dated its existence as far back as 33,000 years in Chauvet in southern France (Geneste cited in Pentikäinen 2007). The Roman historian, Tacitus (1942) described in 98 BC the people living North of Germania. He refers to them as *Fenni*, generally assumed to refer to the Sami people. His treatise contains speculation about *helluseios et oxinas* (likely the two clans of ancient Finno-Ugric peoples) which supports the thesis proposed by Kuusi (1963) that the first inhabitants or primal clans in the North during the Stone Age worshipped either the bear or the elk. Pentikäinen (2007) refers to "the archeological, verbal, place-name and ethnographic pieces of evidence, showing that clans devoted to both animals wandered in these regions in antiquity, even if the whole people may not have been worshippers of the elk or the bear" (14-15). Many scholars have pointed out evidence of the above-mentioned totemic worship in Finland as the historical background of the Bear ceremonial (Honko et al. 1993: 71; Kuusi 1963; Kuusi and Honko 1963; Haavio 1968, 1967). One of the most prolific researchers of the Bear ceremonial, Matti Sarmela has written about Bear feasts and related topics in numerous studies (1994, 1993, 1991, 1984a, 1984b, 1983). His cultural-ecological gaze highlights many aspects of the Bear drama that echo or reveal more explicitly the worldview or *episteme* contained within it: the gift or give-back imaginary and social order. As I will show, this aspect of the festival seems to suggest that the marriage of woman and Bear is a representation of the return of fertility, as is the case with the Sami maiden of Spring, Ravni who awoke the Bear and thus prompted the return of life (cf. Hammarstedt 1929; Kremer in this anthology). In *The Great Bear*, Lauri Honko (1993b) elaborates on Finno-Ugric festivities as expressions of what Marcel Mauss (1969) had referred to as the (primitive) gift economy:

The act of hospitality central to festivals and feasts had two functions. On the one hand, it emphasized one's own social position and the status of guests in relation to it. On the other hand, acceptance of hospitality also assumed reciprocity and the guest inevitably had in mind his own forthcoming duties as host, while the host did not forget that it would soon be his turn to act as guest. In this social exchange, not only bonds between individuals but, above all, between groups were defined and strengthened. The host demonstrated his perception both of his own standing and that of his guest by his behaviour and the scale of his hospitality. Sometimes a host might deliberately use the occasion to enhance his own prestige and humble his guest either by exaggerated largesse or by deliberately offering less hospitality than custom required. (259)

Although such practices may well have characterized the Finnish, Carelian, and Sami Bear ceremonial, there is evidence to suggest these practices were the norm. It is important to remember that Mauss's (1969) theories are reflections of his own twentieth-century values and assumptions. Honko (1993b) supports rather uncritically the taken-for-granted stance of Maussian scholars, according to which even gift circulation can be reduced to competitive, ego-oriented motives. It is necessary to make a sharper distinction between cultures that reify competition even in the framework of hospitality and those where gift circulation speaks to their more humane, care- and balance-oriented worldview. The interpretation of gift giving as concealing essentially competitive ego-oriented motives has been found insulting by many Indigenous scholars revisiting euro-centric research, and has also been challenged by academics in the Feminists for a Gift Economy network, which includes many Indigenous scholars who oppose these naturalized assumptions (see, for example, Armstrong 2007, Kuokkanen 2004a; 2007). Informed by the paradigms of modernity, many theories of the gift have, according to Kuokkanen (2007), failed to grasp the deeper meanings of giving gifts to the earth:

> Instead of viewing the giving of the gifts to gods and nature as a reflection of Indigenous worldviews founded on an active recognition of kinship relations that extend beyond the human realm, Mauss explains it as a "theory of sacrifice"; by his interpretation, people must enter into exchange contracts with the spirits of the dead as well as with the gods, who are the real owners of the world's wealth. For Mauss, "the idea of purchase from gods and spirits is universally understood." According to Mauss, the Toraya ... of the Celebes, Indonesia, are a classic example of people who believe that "one has to buy from the gods and that the gods know how to repay the price." The Toraya, however, see this relationship quite differently. According to them, Deata ("Creator") provides them with everything, and their gifts to Deata constitute thanks for the abundance they enjoy. Thus, for example, after the harvest, the Toraya hold a ceremony to express gratitude for the season. These practises are not considered purchases from the gods; rather they are expressions of thanks and of respect for the natural world. (28)

Kuokkanen further argues that classic theories "all downplay the uniqueness of the archaic gift, on the pretext that in order to understand it we must see it as an expression of constraints or motivations that are universal in themselves: economic interest, the prohibition of incest, the obligation to exchange, substitution of peace for war through social contract, the necessary subordination of the imaginary to the symbolic, or the sacrifice of a scapegoat in order to re-establish order among all members of society" (2007: 29). In our network meetings and academic knowledge-sharing discussions/seminars, the Feminists for a Gift Economy network has come to the conclusion that life-oriented economies involve the logic of the gift which does not imply "earning" the gift or "owing" something to the giver, and where the formation of the relationship through gift giving is not considered in negative terms. To quote Kuokkanen: "[it is not] a burdensome obligation, or a loss of one's individuality and independence" (2007: 29). Instead, it is a condition of balanced existence and ultimately, part of one's socio-cosmic identity which is not reducible to mere individualism: "The gift cannot be ignored or rendered to something else. In such a system and social order, if the gift is not recognized and received, it ceases to be a gift and the relationships formed through the gift are weakened and ultimately lost" (Kuokkanen 2007: 30). Adding important nuances to Derrida's (1981) argument that the gift is annulled when it is recognized, Kuokkanen maintains that in Indigenous philosophies, it is the very recognition of the gift that makes it possible. Echoing the views of Vaughan and of other Indigenous scholars (i.e., Quick-to-see-Smith 1993: 69), Kuokkanen argues that "we need to perceive Indigenous *epistemes* in another framework, within the logic of the gift of Indigenous philosophies (2007: 56-59). However, as Vaughan (1997) and Kuokkanen (2007) also note with their respective nuances, when the gift is taken outside the framework of abundance and care circulation, it does become impossible also for women and Indigenous peoples. This happens within the capitalist market economy where the creation of artificial scarcity is necessary to create needs and markets, and to thus ensure the accumulation of profits and capital by the elite.

The bias present in the masculated Bear research is evident in the very notion of sacrifice to which Hallowell (1926) also refers (above) and which also has a gendered dimension: sacrificing the Bear so humans might live (catch food). Elinor Gadon (qtd. in Owen 1998: 17) suggests that sacrifice involving violence and bloodshed has not been the ritual norm across time and space. It is known that women menstruating into the ground in the menstruation hut (prototype of the Bear's den and the Ojibway sweatlodge, or "spirit lodge" [see fn 21 in my introduction]) was a way of giving back and ensuring the turn-taking reciprocity between humans and the Earth on whose products they depended). Although women's biology is the source of the menstrual celebrations, it is not her "destiny" but the core of a social ethics and imaginary that need not be seen in opposition to male-focused feasts. Nor are gendered rituals coded in the sentimental and oppositional terms that characterize the master imaginary, where an imaginary social body is created through negative projections onto women's biology. In matricentric or life-oriented societies, feasts are important occasions for give-back rituals where social bonds are consolidated through the communal sharing of food and related festivals. When evaluating cultures of life and death, it needs to be stressed that there is no easy way to prioritize menstrual blood rituals over hunting rituals focused on death and resurrection, as ways of giving back to animal spirits or the Earth. It is possible that the gift was practiced prior to or beyond the need to kill animals, as in the Irish/Celtic festivals on which I elaborate later. The hunting rituals may have existed side by side with more life-oriented ones. They appear, however, to have evolved into the dominant communal feast whereby festivals/rituals reflecting the female life cycle were marginalized, then demonized. Nevertheless, there are significant nuances within situated Bear ceremonial practices even if they do involve the necessity of killing for survival needs. They may thus well be in alignment with the renewal of the life-oriented imaginary that I epitomize in the gift imaginary.

Val Plumwood (2003) does not address the Bear hunt in her extensive work on animal rights and vegan ethics. Still, I find her comments on the demonization of "holy hunts" as practiced by Indigenous people illuminating for understanding the differences between the gift and exchange perspectives. Having extensive knowledge of Australian Aboriginal cultures, she interprets the "relational hunt" of Indigenous peoples "as a hunting context which is usually only vaguely and ambiguously specified but one form of which may be taken to involve elements of respect or sacredness and to be strongly based on need"(17-18). She opposes the views of "ontological vegans" Carol Adams (1994: 104) and Marti Kheel (1995) for whom, in her view, "sacred hunting ceremonies are nothing more than the usual nasty business of corpse consumption and where talk of respect is no more than a bit of romantic waffle, a fancy piece of sleight of hand used to cover over the revolting, demonic facts of murder as usual..." (18). She notes that the concept of the "relational hunt" is sometimes misapplied or invoked in bad faith by those who cannot meet the stringent conditions such a reciprocity framework imposes. However, she suggests the two ecofeminists are ethnocentric in their implicit assumption that the concept of the "relational hunt" is invariably misused. I see such views as reflections of the cultural projections rooted in an internalized master imaginary. The "relational hunt" is dismissed by Kheel and Adams "on the grounds that 'it makes no difference to the animal' whether it is killed by a relational hunter who sees food as a sacrament that respects the animal as more than meat, or by a conventional one who sees the animal as meat and does not question the identification of food practices with domination" (Adams qtd. in Plumwood 2003: 17). Plumwood looks upon such an approach as reductionist and ethnocentric: "This is like saying that it makes no difference to you whether you are eaten by a hungry grizzly bear or killed in a Nazi concentration camp, and that where in both cases the result is your death the moral status of the latter must be the same as that of the former" (18). Indeed, through the exchange gaze, an animal's entire life can be instrumentalised and distorted in the most painful ways in the service of an unreflective and ungrateful human desire for meat, and, as Plumwood expresses it, "the 'more' than food that it is, is denied" (18). From the gift perspective, one can make use of an animal responsibly and seriously to fulfil an important need in a way that recognizes the "more" that it is and respects both its individuality and its normal species life, in a reciprocal chain of mutual use which must ultimately include both hunter and hunted (cf. Plumwood 2003: 18-19).[30]

Adams and Kheel do, in fact, reflect the kind of cultural bias that I see epitomized in the master imaginary, for they dismiss the entire concept of sacred meals with its contingent, yet clearly non-eurocentric understanding. They dismiss the "relational hunt" complex (which they see as including the reciprocity, sacred feasts, or gift/exchange frameworks) and provide an example of an "ecologically disembodied theory." This, then, reminds us that even ecofeminists in their variety have to a different degree internalized the epistemic, ethnocentric gaze that denies other cultures their paradigms of difference. If we dismiss the notion of sacred feasts as displaced aggression or as simple hypocrisy, in the vein of Mauss (1969) and Bourdieu (1997), we end up naturalizing the logic of exchange and hierarchy. Plumwood (2003) argues

> that in the present context of ecological destruction, it would be wise for us to adopt philosophical strategies and methodologies that maximise our sensitivity to other members of our ecological communities and openness to them as ethically considerable beings, rather than ones that minimise ethical recognition or that adopt a dualistic stance of ethical closure that insists on sharp moral boundaries and denies the continuity of planetary life. (19)

I also stress that the gift economies no doubt involved hunting or gathering-hunting and later agricultural practices, which need not have reflected senseless killing of wildlife. Hunting, too, has a different social meaning reflecting a different ethos when approached through the master or gift imaginary.

Bear Goddesses and the Matrix of Regeneration: Matricentric Traces Within the Bear Narrative?

> Gracious forest mistress,
> Golden forest master,
> order paws to turn,
> set claws on the loose!
> —Salmi, 1884, SKVR VII.5 3369
> (trans. C. Tolley, cited in Pentikäinen 2007: 87)

> "Bruin was not born upon the straw
> nor on the chaff of a kiln.
> Bruin was born yonder,
> the valuable pelt grew up
> at the Moon's, at the Sun's,
> on the shoulders of the Great Bear,
> on the back of the Big Dipper.
> Ukko, golden king,

old man of the heavens,
threw a tuft of wool onto the waters,
dropped s bit of down onto the billows;
that the wind kept rocking,
the turbulent air kept moving,
the spirit of the water swayed,
a wave drove long ashore
to the shore of the honeyed wilderness,
to the tip of honeyed headland.
Darling, mistress of the forest,
keen-eyed wife of Tapio's domain,
ran into the sea up to her knees,
into the billows up to her belt buckle,
seized the tuft of wool from the waters,
the soft bits of wool from the billows.
She swung it in its swaddling clothes,
rocked it on her lap;
from there she took her bird,
brought her treasure
to a silver box, to a golden swinging cradle.
She lifted the diaper strings,
the children's fine swaddling clothes
up to the bushiest branch,
the broadest leafy branch.
She swung her dear one,
rocked her darling
in the golden cradle,
in the silver strappings
under a fir with a luxuriant crown,
with a luxuriant crown, with golden foliage.
There she brought forth the bear,
brought up the fine-coated one,
in the roots of a scrub pine,
by a heavy pine
on the edge of a honeyed copse,
in the hearth of the hazy-blue wilderness.
    —*Old Kalevala* 378-432 (cited in Pentikäinen 2007: 138-139)

What evidence is there then of a possible matricentric stage in the Bear ceremonial prior to or parallel to the sacrificial rituals involving exclusionary gender politics, or alternatively, gender-segregated or transgender rituals? Historians of religion were among the first to consider the story of "The Girl Who Married the Bear" in the context of Bear ceremonialism. Carl-Martin Edsman (1965, 1960, 1956) has followed in the footsteps of Andrew Lang (1899) and Jane E. Harrison (1955) as one of the very first to point out a link between the different types of Bear myths and rituals in the context of analyzing Finnish Bear narratives. Carl-Martin Edsman (1956: 53) argues that the marriage rites of the Finnish Bear festival may be regarded as a fresh, dramatic representation of the mythical Bear marriage and adds that knowledge of these rites may have given rise to some Swedish marriage customs and linguistic expressions among country people, characterizing courtship and betrothal as Bear-capture (53). More importantly, however, the focus on marriage rather than hunting and killing may well attest to the traces of a more life-oriented culture with the paradigms of regeneration in the center of the social imaginary. The union of woman and Bear likely epitomized the sociocosmic imaginary of the union of all life forms, as several scholars to whom I will refer suggest. In such light, the Bear ceremonial could be seen as the androcentric equivalent of a more gynocentric women's festival (one that may not have been gender exclusive). Séamus Ó Catháin (1995) has made much of Edsman's thesis, in which he finds support for his interpretation of the woman-centred Festival of Brigit.[31] He believes himself cautiously justified in vouchsafing that the Irish/Celtic festival and traditions surrounding it are related to some of the basic elements and reflexes of an ancient bear cult and culture which, like the bear itself, found a lifeline to survival on the European periphery:

On the edge, in parts such as Lapland and Finland where bears still roam, the evidence for this is clear and explicit, though, admittedly, relatively late in terms of its documentation. At the other end of the scale, we have Ireland and Scotland, environmentally bear-less, but both boasting a culture with a long literary history, which preserves, as we have seen, a number of intriguing names for the bear. Here, I believe we can glimpse tantalizing reflexes of this same bear culture expressed through folklore and mythology as well as etymology. (Ó Catháin 1995: 35)

Many more elements in Ó Catháin's study (1995) help establish the assumption that links between woman-positive festivals preceded the masculated Bear ceremonial, as well as the links between the two, but I limit myself to the main cross-cultural elements recurring across Ireland and more broadly, the North. Etymological studies linking Bear, birth, the mounds in which life and death were both ritualized (the sacred womb-tomb and the related symbols of caves, bear lairs, and women's menstruation huts) command special attention. Ó Catháin alludes to a striking feature of the lexis of the Irish language, namely a profusion of names for the bear of which there are no less than eight: *art, math, mathgamain, milchobur, béithir, rustóg, úrsóg* and bear:

Old Irish *art*—Welsh *arth*, cognate with Greek *arctos*, Latin *ursús*—has a healthy Indo-European pedigree (yielded by the root **(H)rtko*—according to Hamp). Among the zoomorphic divinities of the Celts we may also note the presence of a Mercurius Artaios and especially a dea Artio whose names connect them with the bear. Preserved in this wise, we thus find in Celtic culture a vestige of earliest Indo-European civilization. As far as the word for "bear" is concerned, it is worth noting that this is not something which holds true for a whole range of other northern and western European language. In the Germanic and Balto-Slavonic languages, words based on the Indo-European root which gives us Irish *art* have been lost, falling victim to what philologists call "linguistic avoidance." In these languages a variety of new descriptions have been substituted for the original word. These include i.e., *björn*, "the brown one" in Scandinavia and *lokys* "the (honey) thief" among the Balto-Slavs. (27)

Shepard and Sanders (1985) add the following nuances to Bear's etymological meanings:

The Teutonic stem word *ber* is the forerunner of *bar*, the German for "bear," and such terms as "barrow," "burgh," "barn," "barley," "beer," "berth," "bereave," "berate," "berseuse," (or lullaby), "berg," "burgher," "bier," "bairn"; such proper names as the cities of Bern, Berlin and Bergen.... Among tribal Scandinavians and Eastern Siberians a human borne to his grave on a bier (sometimes a door taken from its hinges) was, in effect, brought to the grave on or in a bear, wrapped with bearskin, carried out of the tent or house through a special doorway, just as the hunted, slain bear was brought in by an entrance having no other purpose ... the Old English *burlic*, also from *beran*, means "exalted," and we know that the bear is widely associated with a holy mountain in myth and revered as a constellation in the night sky. The German word for "mountain"—*berg*—and the Latin root for "fortress" come from *bherg*, as do a passel of words of the bear in cyclical motion: "going away," as in its funeral rites; and, in other linguistic elements, engaged in "carrying in" or "bringing" a message of divine grace. The bear has for thousands of years been the master of souls, bodies and minds in transition. The syllable from which comes "bear" also produces "basket" and "amphora.".... (xiv-xv)

As the above etymologies suggest, Bear itself as a word captures numerous associations to do with the life-death cycle and the links with "basket" (Pandora's box?) likewise calls for deeper elaboration. According to *The Columbia Electronic Encyclopedia* (2001-2007) among other sources, "...(păndôŕə), in Greek mythology [is the] first woman on earth. Zeus ordered Hephaestus to create her as vengeance upon man and his benefactor, Prometheus...." Some scholars contend that Pandora's "box" may itself have been a mistranslation, and her "box" may have been a large jar or vase, forged from the earth (Kailo 2007). In fact, there is evidence that suggests Pandora herself was the jar. In Ancient Greece ... the jar was said to have been in a jar form because of the similarities between a jar and a woman's uterus. I have elaborated on this (Kailo 2007) to show how Pandora's meaning as the original mythic "All-Giver" (Greek, *dôŕə*) has itself been reversed into the opposite—the source of sinful curiosity and of all manner of scourges, i.e., the syndrome of woman-blaming.

The links between the Bear Goddess, the First Woman (Matri-*archy* meaning "mothers from the beginning"), and the Earth (womb/tomb) further lead us to the word "iron." Shepard and Sanders (1985) note that "...*Ber* is also cognate with *fer* and *ver*. From *fer* comes *ferrum*, the Latin for "iron," as well as "feral," along with "ferry," "fertile," and "ferocious" (xiv). In this regard, it is worth noting that Helga (or Helka) is another Finnish goddess of healing and rebirth, and still today, a spring festival, Ritvala Helka Fest, is celebrated annually in Sääsmäki, Finland, although the celebration bears a strong imprint of Christian values (Kailo 2008). Helka is in various ways associated with iron and feminine creativity. The soil in the area where her festival is celebrated is known for its high iron content, and Helka has been called upon to heal any harm caused by iron. She features in folktales as the mother of daughters referred to as Luonnotar (creatrix), which Martti Haavio (1967: 55) sees as representations of the feminine divine. Defying dominant western gender roles, Luonnotars' breasts in a nineteenth-century painting by Jouko Alanen are neither the objects of the male eroticizing gaze, nor the mere representation of nursing mothers, but are instead represented as producing iron (rather than breast milk) , true to many folk poetry descriptions (Lönnrot 1847, 9:1 266; 9:1 47-66). The historically recent associations of women with nature and with nurture, and men with culture, are thus here challenged in an image that situates the goddesses in the sky-world as creators of "culture" and technology without female biology being discarded. In many folk poems another important figure, the "evil witch of the north," Louhi and her variants are also linked with the bear as her mother. She has, however, often been deprived of a positive maternal role and has been demonized as either a devilish progenitor of illnesses or as Bear's enemy. For example, she appears as "Loviitar," an old wife and ancient hag who threw bits of wool into water (Hakulinen 1891: 3942) finally creating the bear. As Matti Sarmela notes (1991), in medieval peasant communities and their birth incantations, the bear has been handed over to the guardianship of saints. Now the bear is born from wool that Tuonetar, Pirjota (Saint Bridget), Virgin Mary, or some other saint has cast in the water. This epitomizes how the origin story of Bear has been transformed from pre-Christian times and a likely matricentric context to the Christian version idealizing Virgin Mary as having miraculous gifts of sewing. The bear she gives rise to is as harmless as the bear mother-figure. It is worth noting that in some variants of the folk poems about the origins of Bear, it is Ukko, the supreme pagan male god that casts the wool into the water, not the mother goddess. It is an example of the replacement of Goddesses or *haltias* of creation and life-giving with male godheads (Klemettinen 2002).

One needs to further analyze and explore the links between the underground world of *Hel* as a domain that condenses in its meaning death, return of vegetation like barley, and the rebirth of human and animal life. Ritvala's Helka was likely part of a feminine cult of the earth with the life producing and light aspects of the Goddess *Maaemo* (Mother Earth), and her specialized aspects linked to birth-giving, above all Helka-wife and the Golden woman (in Finnish *Helka-vaimo, Kultainen nainen, Kave, einesten emä*). The very name of the festival, Helka, refers to a goddess that the compiler of Finnish mythology, Christfrid Ganander (1997) in *Mythologia Fennica,* one of the earliest collected and published mythologies of the Finns, defined as the mother of Luonnotars, daughters of nature. The Luonnotars were responsible for maintaining the wholeness of nature. According to Ganander: "Helka, no doubt refers to Helga or Olga, alias sacred Helen: 'The Finns describe her as the good, *priski*, chosen wife, i.e. she is considered to be a most exemplary chosen woman and wise old woman who can together with Mary stop bleeding from wounds or *iron*-related damage'" [my emphasis](1997: 520). Helka, like Brigit (also referred to as the "exalted one" echoing the above etymologies of Bear) is clearly related to the other cross-cultural aspects of the Old European Goddess as metaphor of women's wisdom, of midwifery and healing: "in Savo a Helka figure mixed up with Virgin Mary has been called upon to come and help during delivery, echoing the role of the Golden Woman" (Heikkilä 2004: 402). The proper name Helka also harks back to the Scandinavian etymological matrix where *Hel*, helka, and healing form an ideational chain of associations with **kailo* as its most distant root (cf. Kremer in this anthology). The Swedish activist, artist and writer Monica Sjöö (1992) elaborates on the meaning of the German word *Hel* in *Return of the Dark/Light Mother or New Age Armageddon?* and allows us to infer that Helga and Helka are part of a word complex that may have been widely spread across old Europe:

> To the Scandinavians and Germanic peoples, Frau Holle, or Hel, was the fairy queen or Goddess of the otherworld and one entered her realm through the Neolithic mounds and long barrows, or the sacred mountains such as the Brocken in the Harz mountains in Germany, or Glastonbury Tor in Somerset in Britain. To the Christians, her uterine fiery shrine or cauldron/well became hell. The Celts believed that the winds were the spirits of the invisible dead who control the weather. In Welsh, words for the forces of nature are feminine, as are the words for oak and dragon. There is a great unbroken continuity between this world and the next; some of us are in a physical form and others in luminous bodies—worlds that co-exist and interface. The ancestors exist in all the elements: in fire from cremations, in air from the smoke of the fires, in earth from burials and in water from drownings at sea. We form a single community. (33)

As for the development that the above associations have undergone, it is revealing to follow the meanings ascribed to Bear in more recent times. Shepard and Sanders (1985) point out the links between *"arctos"* and "chief," with its scores of related words such as "archaic," "archbishop," and "archaeology," all referring to "overarching" primary sources and powers (xiv). From an overarching concept evoking human-cosmic interdependency, *arché* has become a marker of hierarchy, domination, authority, and power.

The very etymology of "Bear" thus points to its roots in civilizations of the Goddess and of bear-worshipping peoples. The Finnish words for Bear such as *karhu*, *kontio, otso*, have also been analyzed for their etymological roots or outlined in detail (Pentikäinen 2007; Schmidt 1989). Whether or not they directly relate to the above Indo-European linguistic traces of the life-death matrix, it is also worth remembering that myths and other cultural items have wandered nomadically across all of Old Europe, and it is artificial to designate any pure "ethnic" areas, state boundaries being themselves of course a recent historical development. The concepts removing Bear and woman from the sacred matrix of regenerativity have, however, followed similar lines of development as even the Finnish words *arkki-piispa* (arch-bishop) as loan words reveal. The develoment of the word "bear" thus epitomizes in many languages the shifts from birthing towards hierarchies—the Arch-bishops of the master imaginary and exchange economy where women, bears, and the sexual eros get reversed into polluting agents of "evil."

To elaborate on the matricentric roots of Finnish folk poetry and other evidence of by-gone eras with regard to the goddesses echoing the pagan Brigit, one of the most central goddess figures or matri-*archs* is, as we have seen, Louhi—whose very attributes and descriptions echo Goettner-Abendroth's references to matriarchy as "Mothers at the beginning." Feral, fertile, and ferocious, she is linked with Bear as her progenitor, nurse-maid and—in the patriarchal epic, Kalevala—as the Bear enemy. In a typical patriarchal reversal of her pagan role, she is currently described as a greedy old "Hag" who sends bears to wreak havoc on the heroic men of Kalevala (Kailo 2005a, 2006b). Other goddess or *haltia* figures likewise refer to primal mythic mothers. The language of the many Finnish skull poems sung at the Bear feast is recognized as being particularly old. Haavio (1967: 21-22) has recognized that some of the songs are a dialogue between *emuu*, "the female guardian spirit or original bear" and the hunters. This and the many references to rituals of rebirth point in the direction of a worldview in which bears, bear goddesses, and an imaginary of reproduction reigned over the master imaginary of hunting, killing, and expiating guilt. Although hunting under gift economies was a form of relational, "sacred" hunt (cf. Plumwood 2003), it gradually came to be attached to a more ego-oriented and violent symbolic order. There is also much evidence of the centrality of rebirth rather than the concept of "resurrection," which represents a shift towards the Christian concept with its gradual focus on the after-life rather than life on the Earth. According to Haavio (1967), the Bear ceremonial is based on the notion that successful hunting is dependent on the bear's guardian spirit, *Hongatar*, "Pine Mistress," who has the power to allow the hunter to catch a bear. A female guardian thus presides over the ancient Finns' economico-religious ritual in addition to being named in many poems and folklore materials as the Bear's primal mother and spouse. An attempt is made by the hunters to influence their fate with the skull verse by treating Bear with honour, according to the pact between humans and animals. Contrary to Hallowell's (1926) list of the Bear ceremonial's primal features, also present in the Finnish-Carelian Bear texts, is the role of powerful female spirit guardians as well as the emphasis on rebirth, which Goettner-Abendroth (2007) lists as a central feature of matriarchies. Sarmela (1994) reiterates the view shared by other Bear scholars that the Bear ceremonial expresses hunting peoples' common beliefs regarding reincarnation: the bones of large game animals returned back to the forest are reincarnated again and again and humans do not draw the anger of the bear's kin onto themselves if they honour the guardian and provide it with a gift. In many other ways, as well, the gift imaginary seems to have consisted in the recognition of the mutual needs of humans and other beings in a balancing act of interdependency and sustainability: the gifts given to providers of game and other food were meant to express gratitude and to endow them with worth, not mere "economic" value. Behind the ritual lies the notion that humans must not disrupt the natural order that consists of recurrent cycles of death and life. However, the returning of the skull and bones to nature as part of the resurrection rite seems to belong to a the patriarchal layer of the Bear rite. The notion of rebirth needs to be distinguished from that of resurrection and the returning of the bounty to the sky forebear (more recently, father). The belief in rebirth was also integral to matriarchies or to life-oriented gender equal cultures: a belief they express in many rites, myths, and spiritual customs (Goettner-Abendroth 2005). Rebirth is not an abstract concept of the transmigration of souls, as it later appears in Hinduism and Buddhism, but concrete: all members of a clan know that after death they will be born again to one of the women of their own clan, in their own clan-house, in their home village. Every person who dies returns as a small child to the same clan. Women in matriarchal societies were and still are greatly respected because they are able to grant rebirth.[32] A nineteenth-century pioneer of Finno-Ugric studies, John Abercromby (1898) summed up many of the non-dualistic core elements of Finno-Ugric "animism" or what is better termed as "life-centred cultures" (with particular reference to ancient "West Finns"):

Ancient spirituality is best considered a design in harmony, a striving for rapport between humans, nature, the elements, the sky, and the land beyond the sky, and of course, the earth and all its creatures. All the powers were initially seen as both good and bad, depending on their intrinsic nature, the way they are approached, their mood, and the conditions of the moment, as well as the context of their operation. For instance, the Bear Goddess Mielikki, guardian of bears and goddess of forest, is thus termed when propitious (literally, one that likes to please and fulfil desires); when unfavourable to prayers and sacrifices, however, her name, too changes to Kuurikki (the deaf one). (89f)

In Christianity, the triple goddess, referring to the major periods in a woman's life (virgin, mother, crone), as well as of the moon cycles, has been replaced by a dualistic representation of good and evil (i.e., whore/madonna). The Goddess Mielikki, that Abercromby (1898) speaks of, is not the *opposite* of Kuurikki; instead both are aspects of one being. Mielikki can also be seen as the Finnish

Goddess of Give-Back in that she presides over the needs for game, and fulfills hunters' need for survival. If respected, that is. If the circulation of the giving and sharing of nature's bounty is kept in motion, this Guardian is pleased and pleasing (the word *mielikki* has connotations with the Finnish verb *miellyttää*, to please, oblige):

> Keen wife of Tapiola,
> generous mistress of the forest,
> if I set off for the forest,
> let the forest at once be favourable.
> Be favourable to our men,
> reward our dogs.
> (trans. C. Tolley, cited in Pentikäinen 2007: 69)

To return to Ó Catháin (1995), he does not limit himself to describing a male-exclusive Bear ceremonial's Irish-Celtic traces, but links it with the Festival of St. Brigit—clearly a women's rebirth and regeneration/fertility festival. Ó Catháin notes that "the bear may have been identified by humans as a kind of biocosmic clock and even its behaviour taken as some kind of indicator of the nature of the individual life-span. Similarly, traces of the pattern set by its annual programme of sexual revivification may be seen in a number of the highly charged sexual images associated with the celebration of the Feast of St. Brigit some of which have already been adverted to above (38). Ó Catháin links Brigit's name to other socio-cosmic signifiers of regeneration and notes that its basic element means "to grow, to increase," signifying both physical growth as well as increase in size and stature (cf. Heiskanen's article in this volume on the meaning of Bear raising the life energies of nature). Likewise, Ó Catháin links St. Brigit's descent with her ursine and lupine connections and relates her to *Goa*, her counterpart in the Nordic world, who was remembered in the Gaelic folk tradition of Ireland and Scotland down to our own time (40-43). Ó Catháin also links Brigit, bear, and honey (45), adding to my list of signifiers of rebirth and other fertility symbols:

> the dog (from which [bear] is descended), the primordial cow, the bee ... the humble winkle and barnacle and the enigmatic oyster-catcher, the storied crane and other long-beaked birds also turn up. Plant life also features, with reference to angelica, rushes (straw), flax, various kinds of trees (especially alder, birch, oak, pine and willow) and mushrooms most prominent, while acorns, honey, milk and milk products and foods (principally butter), the crafts of spinning and weaving and the practice of transhumance are strongly represented too. Delicately reposing within a sophisticated web of sexual and fertility symbolism, these and a variety of other elements and images cry back in one way or another to the basic issue of procreation and productiveness.
> (Ó Catháin 1995: xi)

Ó Catháin (1995) has provided an in-depth comparison of those woman-centered ritual dimensions that in the context of Brigit's festival have received little, if any attention. His study supports the view that alongside male Bear festivals, there were women-only birth rituals. They involved giving gifts to the pregnant mother, and the festivals consisting of lewd sexual songs and dancing, which bring to mind the Hanti-Mansi Bear drama known for its erotic games in fairly recent history (Honko 1993c: 127-9). Ó Catháin's research adds credibility to my thesis of the coexistance of women's own special rituals, as well as the likelihood of the woman-bear-bee-snake-cave-moon connection pointing to matricentric societies. The Irish context involves a study of Brigit's pagan ancestors and the traces of rituals of life-enhancement in contemporary times. Ó Catháin (1995) attempts to widen the base for the further investigation and consideration of the "true" nature of Brigit and her festival while noting how the traces of the pagan goddess came to be suppressed: "The Irish country people ... became its recorders. They promoted the tradition ... assimilating it seamlessly into the deep Christian faith of Ireland, without allowing it to become totally submerged" (17). This led to a compromise of traditions between two saints, Brid in Kildare and another Brid continued until, already in decline, the traditions of Brigit, the old goddess and the Holy Woman, were swept to oblivion by the new culture of the twentieth century" (17).

Ó Catháin (1995) describes in great detail the intergenerational gatherings where women celebrate and enhance the cycles of birth, death, and renewal, in alignment with the agricultural calendar. In effect, the cult of St. Brigit, powered by many of the traditions associated with pagan Brigit, may have been the vehicle for transmitting ancient elements of the culture of the prehistoric era down to our own time (ix-x). As for the gift giving, it attests to the possibility that the Bear ceremonial may not have been restricted to the kind of give-back rituals to the Bear ancestor that had economic motivations and reflected the tenets of the exchange economy/master imaginary. More research is needed to determine whether the gift was a matricentric practice without a link to killing (the hunt), whether it was the female equivalent of the Bear religion, or whether men and women of matricentric cultures of life engaged in the kind of gift circulation where killing for food was necessary, but involved an ethics of mutuality and respect.

The Finnish Helka Festival at Ritvala, to which I referred earlier, gives reason to posit that there was a Finnish Give Back Festival similar to or having affinities with the Irish Festival of Brigit with its elements of helping nature raise its life force, in Irish *néart,* in Finnish *väki* (Kailo 2008). As for the female figure Pirjotar, echoing Brigit, more research needs to be conducted to relate her to the life/death matrix.

In the Finnish context, it seems that women rather than men were associated with the channels crossing the different layers of the universe. Were women the primary early shamans or was this important socio-cosmic role available to both men and women (or those bisexuals/two-spirited people who could identify with both)? Bear was not only seen as the mediator between different layers of the cosmos, but as the shaman-forebear who was kin to humans and mediator between human and animal realms. Bears enacted the drama of rebirth every spring, after having survived the entire winter in their dens by sucking their (honey) paws. This echoes the etymologies of Bear to which I have referred above. As Satu Apo (1999) has argued, this role unites women and bears:

> According to mythical and magic thought, all channels that link the main levels of the world, the middle, lower and upper realms, were places of "power," endowed with *väki,* a power of dangerous proportions. A woman's body belongs to the same paradigm as the various representatives of the world tree (sacrificial trees, the first where bear skulls were hung), cliffs rising out of the water or reaching heavenward, caves leading into the ground, crevices and cracks and fire places—particularly those situated in buildings—from which smoke rises to heaven. (11)

There are parallels with other European beliefs in this regard. For Condren (2002), an important set of symbols in ancient myths common throughout the ancient world included the Tree of Life and the Tree of the Knowledge of Good and Evil, which were the residences of the gods or goddesses. The elements in the description by Apo (1999) invite a deeper interpretation. As many sauna studies also reveal (i.e., Kailo 2005a, 2003), women, fire, birth-giving, ovens, hearths, and Bear are interconnected. Just as fire is considered a healing, purifying, transforming agent, as well as the agent allowing transformation from the raw to the cooked, similar attributes have been attached to water. The references to caves, trees, special cliffs, and crevices evoke ancient parallels between the cult of the dead and the celebration of life, and the symbolic sites where the fires of life and death are lit and extinguished in analogy with a woman's biological cycles. Makilam (1999) helps us revisit women-only rituals, where we can gather data best through cross-cultural comparative studies while recognizing the pitfalls of assuming unmediated and simplistic affinities:

> In Kabylia, the glorification of woman in her creative nature is present everywhere in the primary triangular motifs. The vital source of the feminine delta is conveyed by a triangle whose tip points towards the earth and its fertile V opens towards the sky. It is also drawn to represent a lamp, as well as the earthenware jug that, like the wooden ladle, collects water from the sky. It is therefore clear that the women consider themselves as human receptacles from which flow the earth's water and the sky's fire. (50-51)

Makilam (1999) finds the primary life principle represented in the fertile delta of the female body, often depicted as a diamond and a triangular schematization (48) (see also Irma Heiskanen's article in this anthology). Makilam also describes the affinities between bee hives and the art of reproducing the cycles of death and life:

Often represented, and sometimes drawn with red parallel lines, this diamond is called the bees' nest.... These drawings which are called in Kabyle by the names of the eye or the beehive all represent the female sex. For the Kabyle woman, as for all peoples who live in permanent contact with Nature, from this nest comes the sweetness of life, like the bees' honey. Bees have considerable importance in the minds and the traditional spiritual conception of the Kabyle, for they carry within them the sacred power of fertilizing the flowers of their natural environment. (49)

In Finnish folk poetry, Hongatar and Mielikki are the main Finnish bear goddesses but one must also mention Osmotar, mythic brewer of beer. The folk poems describe Osmotar in connection with ale making and associate her with yeast and the ingredients of fostering growth that are part of an alchemical creative labor. In Finnish Carelian folk poetry, the attribute "meady" is also a recurrent reference to the qualities of forests, the bear (including the bear's penis), women, and the sauna. It is the erotic juice of life that flows through all of nature and echoes also the life-renewing menstrual blood of women. The role of beehives is thus also present in cross-cultural woman-positive imaginaries.

The web of associations that I have singled out throughout my analysis of the women and Bear narratives and cultures of life is evident in matriarchies like the Kabyle society described by Makilam (1997). They may be far removed, geographically, from ancient Finland but similar values and conceptions of life and beliefs may well have characterized large areas of "Europe" and been transmitted and shared across many ancient borders from Middle East and Africa to the North and beyond. The same transmission of practices, has, after all, been found to characterize the Bear ceremonial as well.

From Traces of Matricentric Eras Towards the Master Imaginary

In the Finnish *Loitsu-runot* or *the Magic Poems of the Finns*, we learn that "the bear was born close to the moon, beside the sun, upon the shoulders of Otava (the Great Bear). From there he [sic] was let down to earth ... to a verdant thicket's edge. A forest maiden rocked him in a golden cradle, under a pine tree. The Virgin Mary acted as god-mother, and carried him to the christening" (Abercromby 1898: §193a). The primal creator of Bear, Louhi, has at some point in history been replaced by the Christian Mary, no longer the bear's mother but a "mere" godmother. The shift in the very meaning of the word godmother attests to the devaluation of the role of the Mother Goddess and is echoed in the Irish/Celtic materials as well. The hunting drama as transmitted to us through folk materials has also been looked upon as a reflection of human beings' efforts to resolve the mystery of life and death (cf. Sarmela 1991) and/or to undo the polarities of male/female, human/animal. It is important, particularly in view of this anthology's focus on nature, culture, and gender, to remember that the Finns, like many other peoples, looked upon Bear as half-animal, half-human, making the Bear ceremonial much more than a mere ritual of economic interests. The

Finnish Bear ritual indicates a stage during which the *hieros gamos*—the union of all entities in nature, cosmos, and society that might be considered separate—are united. The gift imaginary thus also contains in its overdetermination the existential dimension of a return to the time before separation, for which there are numerous terms with their specific connotations. I refer to it as Arctic Mysteria, leaving it up to the reader to project the deep meaning of such notions which are basically beyond the grasp of language. However, it is necessary to point out that such a cosmic, supernatural, psychoanalytical, or spiritual concept is itself a reflection of one's ethnicity and gender, among other variables. Spirituality among matricentric and Indigenous peoples is in many ways quite different from that of patriarchal spirituality, as seen for example, in Christianity with its emphasis on the beyond, on "heaven" rather than on earth.

Whereas matricentric communities looked upon death as a natural part of the cyclical worldview, in patriarchy life and its representatives become devalued only because they are the idealized features of the Goddess and her "religion." Many other details of the Bear festival attest to the shift towards the master imaginary and the exchange economy. It is, for example, a reflection of the master imaginary to ascribe ownership relations only or primarily to men (the hunters). In many studies of the bear hunt, there are references to hunters becoming "owners of the dead," once the bear has been shot. Scholars may have projected on the materials notions of heroic and economic victory reflecting the taken-for-granted property-related values that are at the core of the exchange economy and the master imaginary on which it is psychically grounded. The notion of private ownership is present even in the context of immaterial "possessions," according to J. Hakulinen. "In the birth charms of a medieval peasant society, the bear has been passed over to saints who now *own* it" (qtd. in Hallowell 1926: 152 [my emphasis]). N. W. Thomas for his part provides the most obvious projection of the exchange gaze as a strictly utilitarian/economic stance when he claims that "the propitiation of animals is in proportion to their usefulness" (qtd. in Hallowell 1926: 152). As this remark reveals, animals end up being seen as objects of exploitation, not as beings with their own inalienable and inherent rights to exist. This property-related interpretation needs revisiting in light of the protests of Indigenous scholars who state that their past and present cultures have not looked upon animals, particularly the most respected ones, through the exchange paradigm. Sami scholar Rauna Kuokkanen (2007) echoes my views:

> In Indigenous worldviews that foreground multilayered and multidimensional relationships with the land, the gift is the means through which the socio-cosmic order is renewed and secured. In this system, one does not give primarily in order to receive but rather in order to ensure the balance of the world on which the well-being of the entire social order is contingent. Thanks are given in the forms of gifts to the land's guardians, who sustain human beings; but the gifts are also given for continued goodwill. According to this worldview, human beings are only one aspect of the creation; that is why

their view of the world is marked by a clear sense of responsibility toward other aspects with which the socio-cosmic order is shared and inhabited. As Deloria notes, this "view of life was grounded in the knowledge of these responsibilities…. The human ceremonial life confirmed the existence of this equality and gave it sustenance." (33)

What used to be regarded as attributes of women's divinity are now reversed. Just as women could not at particular historical moments touch the sacred vessels on the altar of Christian sacrifice, neither could they touch the weapons of war. Both sets of artifacts were designed to create and sustain a "spiritual" world, which contact with women would threaten. As in religious sacrifice, the blood of women shed at birth defiles, but the blood of men shed in war (or as part of holy hunts?) takes on mythic and sacramental proportions, making possible and regenerating the political "graces" necessary for the mythic life of the state (Condren 2002: 193). Childbearing and war-making are both powerful acts, but childbirth, according to patriarchal ideology now becomes something "weakening," whereas war is regenerative. Inevitably as new centralized social structures arose, religious power began to taken on an elite quality. "The Goddess was no longer to be found in the bushes, trees, and holy wells" (Condren 2002: 17). Furthermore, the "people would no longer 'participate' in the cosmos but would submit to their divine Father or his representatives, who could be counted on to know his will at all times. Gods may well be described as being above and beyond sexuality, but his representatives on earth would be firmly male" (Condren 2002: 93). Instead of the gift imaginary enhancing nature's cycles of growth, the new reproductive consciousness, expressed in institutionalized religions, focuses on developing the transcendent spirit, at the expense of the Earth and the denigrated "matter" or carnality. It seems to me that where the growth cycle of nature with its gynocentric mysteries marginalized men within the central creative activities (although not through any strict and hierarchical politics of spiritual othering), gradually the male elite appropriated the imaginary of growth and the fertility calendar, attaching it to male spiritual processes and its milestones. Today, of course, "growth" has become the economic obsession linked with an ecosocially questionable value of competitiveness and endless productivity in a world of dwindling resources. Women's menstrual calendar has been replaced by the quarterly time measurement of the neoliberal corpocracy and its economic priorities.

Anything that hindered men's spiritual growth—nature, women, or sexuality— would now have to be controlled and kept in its place. Under polytheism with its co-presence of one and of many gods or goddesses, a great deal of energy was expended in spiritual ceremonies that kept the people in tune with the rhythms of the universe (Eisler 1987). The gods/goddesses could be approached by both women and men. Originally there was very little conflict between lay and official priesthood. Even when there was a distinction made between "high" religion and "folk" or domestic religion, the gods could still be approached in the temples by both sexes. The question then becomes: would not such a democratic version of spirituality better guarantee respect for the dwindling planetary resources, rather than the attitude glorifying life in the beyond, and denigrating matter, the feminine, the earth, and notions of human/animal interdependency? Is such a notion of ecospirituality not beyond the reason/intuition, mind/body dualisms that take us down a misleading path of artificial distinctions?

Makilam (1999) describes woman-centered customs in modern Algeria that echo the Irish-Celtic and Finno-Ugric fertility calendars and sense of cyclical time. She points out that among the Kabyle, a woman in the different stages of her life, and in her daily activities from birth to death, is transformed in the same way as the seasons. In her changing nature, she adapts the rhythms of the year to the annual ritual of her work.[33] For example, in the spring she begins the cycle of pottery in accordance with the prohibitions of the earth, and she roughcasts the interior of her walls before covering them with magic paintings (Makilam 1999: 9). The seasonal work and women's activities with its attendant restrictions are surprisingly similar also in the Finnish context (see Enäjärvi-Haavio 1954 on Finnish Shrovetide traditions). Finally, feminist theologian Carol P. Christ (2004) analyzes the pre-Christian holiday knowns as Imbolc: "...the legends of St. Brigid connect her to the nourishment provided by the milk of ewes and cows. The Abbess Brigid's cows miracuously gave milk three times in one day, creating a veritable lake of milk. Milk was poured on the ground on St. Brigid's day. At St. Brigid's shrine in county Louth at Faughart, on July 12, 1986, six young girls were seen dressed in white, the color of milk" (13). Even the meanings of virginity and the colour white are reverted by patriarchy into signifiers of sexuality and purity—defined from the point of view of male sexual desire and property entitlements.

Edsman (1956) suggests that Bera and Bear of bygone Finnish-Swedish customs are mysteriously connected with milk and blood offerings. The milk that is replaced by blood on the day preceding the hunting and killing of the bear might well symbolize the valued, life-centred liquid of gift economies (milk). Also, as mentioned above, non-violent menstrual blood offerings (Grahn 1982) are known to have preceded or offered alternatives to the patriarchal sacrifices where, in contrast, violent blood shedding has come to fully replace the more peaceful give-back rites (i.e., Heikkilä 2004) which may have preceded them, or existed side by side with them. To quote Condren (2002): "Milk was so sacred that the Irish continued to baptize their children with it until the twelfth century, when the practice was banned" (228). Makilam (1999) refers to similar evidence in Kabyla society, where spiritual midwifery, healing, baptism, and many other typically male-appropriated religious functions were in women's hands and part of women's woman-exclusive mysteries (69).[34]

There is solid evidence that the emerging Catholic and other Christian Churches in Europe appropriated and transformed the rituals and the very imaginary of their rival—matricentric gift economies. Pentikäinen (2007) notes that "St. Margaret's day was possibly in the whole Baltic Finnic area celebrated as the bear's birthday, when the song of the bear's birth was sung and a mid-summer festival was held.

The Catholic church strove to fight against the bear by moving St. Margaret's day to 13 July—elsewhere its celebration takes place a week later" (109). A clear policy of the early church was thus to appropriate the symbols and feast days of the old religion and convert them to Christian celebrations. Another example is the day dedicated to the "Purification of the Blessed Virgin Mary," held annually on February 2nd (Condren 2002: 74). This is the time when the bear was known to turn in its den, marking the arrival of spring. Not surprisingly, this date has been linked with Bear cults across many cultures, including Greece and Crete: "The German Classicist Bachofen (1863: 11) is the first to point out the tension that exists between the maternal figure of Kallisto, the bear, and the virginal figure of Artemis, the huntress. He supports the caring qualities he imagines for Kallisto as Bear by adducing other realizations of female Bears in Greek culture: the ursine transformation of the nurses of Zeus, Atalante's adoptive Bear-mother, the She-bears at Brauron, and the feminine gender of Greek *arktos*, 'bear.'" To these may be added the Panagia Arkoudiotissa, "Virgin Mary of the Bear" whose festival is celebrated in the cave of Acrotiri, near ancient Kydonia in western Crete, on February 2nd, also known as "Candlemas." Many scholars have traced Candlemas to the combined celebration of regeneration embodied by mothers and bears or other paradigms of rebirth (cf. Makilam 1999). The bear-shaped stalagmite found at the Arkoudia ("Bear") Cave near Akrotiri is the site where offerings were made to Artemis Kourotropos (i.e., Nursing Artemis) from the Classical through the Roman ages. By the sixteenth century CE, however, Nursing Artemis had been transformed under the Christianized cover of Panagia Arkoudiotissa, the "Holy Virgin of the Bear," whose rituals clearly follow bears' annual cycle (cf. Reischl 2004). The celebration of the "Virgin's Purification" also links with the ritual sauna for young mothers in eastern Lithuania, celebrated at the time of Candlemas, February 2nd, when, in the European tradition, "bears are said to emerge from their winter dens" (Gimbutas 1989: 116). Menstruating and birthing women were, in many cultures from the North American Indians to nineteenth century Latvians, believed to be closer to Bear-ness than usual, and it was commonly believed that women change into bears (Gimbutas 1989: 116).[35] In Greek, Northern Athabaskan, and Siberian versions of women and bears, women's maternal bearness is conceived as a temporary state, a state into which they enter and from which they return (Reischl 2004). Candlemas is also the period of time during which carnival bear-hunts are mimicked in Armenia, Austria, Germany, and the Basque country (Reischl 2004: 72) Ó Catháin (1995) shows in *The Festival of Brigit* that even Santa Lucia, an important symbol of light for Scandinavians during the Winter Equinox harkens back to the Goddess as the Bringer of Light, the harbinger of spring and renewal (16). These signifiers of rebirth, light, and the promise of new life are intimately connected with the gift imaginary in which the human norm for women as well as men is enhancement of the energies of growth, linked with sustainability and balanced, respectful relations.

I will now focus on the forbidden gaze between women and Bear, to which the Finnish and Sami materials make ample reference.

The Unbearable Gaze and Taboos on Women and Bear

> Do not devote your attention to the beauty of women.... For women are
> evil, my children ... they scheme treacherously how they might entice man
> to themselves by means of their looks.... By a look they implant their poison,
> and finally they take them captive (*The Testament of Reuben*, written in the
> second century before the Christian era, 4:1; 5:1, 3). (Phipps 1976: 40).

Hallowell's (1926) summary of the cross-cultural Bear ceremonial, noted earlier
in this paper, refers to the central meaning of a communal, often eat-all feast of
bear meat governed by numerous prescriptions and taboos and emphasizing *sexual
differences* (41-43). In this section I show how the Bear feast reflects dimensions
of a male reproductive consciousness and the exchange economy including appropriation of the feminine Sacred and an increasing demonization of Bear, the
feminine forms of creativity, and the very notion of inclusive interconnectedness
in which world renewal rituals most likely were grounded.

Cross-cultural research and other evidence on Bear ceremonials contain a wide
range of depictions of women's marginalized role ranging from her total exclusion
in male-only religious activities to the explicit misogyny of labelling her as a "polluting" influence. The taboos placed on women can be summed up as avoidance of
"matter out of place" (Douglas 1996)—i.e., the exclusion and banning of women's
touch, look, or presence in realms considered holy for men. In her classic book,
Purity and Danger: An Analysis of the Concepts of Pollution and Taboos (1996),
Mary Douglas notes that any deviation from the categorical ideal, including the
mixing of any one kind, physical blemishes, or the discharge of bodily fluids, is
tantamount to pollution, a loss of holiness, integrity, and strength (51-53). This
tends to apply to all socially powerless or marginalized groups. It goes without
saying that sexual relations between humans and animals are strictly taboo. Hence
the forbidden gaze between women and Bears can be seen as desirable now and
in the past. However, the women and Bear narratives should not be reduced to
such literalism but rather seen as part of a socio-cosmic imaginary.

Women were considered sources of pollution in areas of male activity such as fishing, hunting, cooking holy foods, and moving about in the woods. It is interesting
though that previously, under the era of the Goddess, the very wells and sacred sites
that are out of bounds for women were the very realm of her Divine influence. In
the land-based spiritual imaginary of the polytheistic era, all entities had their spirits,
guardians, and powers, but there were also goddesses presiding over various social
functions, as we have seen, without any strict hierarchies. Since research materials
are historically multilayered, they contain different, even mutually exclusive reasons
for the sexual politics of the unbearable gaze (i.e., the diverse ways of wresting
power from women and undermining the gift imaginary). Nevertheless, some of
the reasons given for women's exclusion also contain more "positive" explanations,
evoking the gift gaze between women and Bears. According to Rockwell (1991),
men of the North American Indigenous Kiowa Bear woman society were not

allowed to watch women's ceremonies (105) so gendered segregation need not have always reflected male supremacy. Since scholars of the Bear ceremonial have mostly been men, with the gender-blindness male research has often involved, we may indeed have more evidence of the exclusion of women from communal rituals and feasts than of woman-exclusive festivals and events—something that is bound to distort the objectivity of historical truth. Still, we have seen that the Festival of Brigit allows us to trace women-only rituals that involved none of the misogynous evaluations of women's spirituality or creativity present in the male exclusive rites of more recent eras (Condren 2002).

Hallowell (1926) provides references to some of the most demeaning and degrading interpretations of women's exclusion from the communal feast:

The carcass of a bear was always carried into a wigwam by a special entrance made to the right or left of the regular one. This was explained by saying that women did not *deserve* to pass through the same place by which the bear had entrace to the dwelling [my emphasis]. Childless women and girls had to leave the wigwam while the animal was being eaten. (68)

Frank Speck (Speck and Moses 1945) claims that "the Mistassini Cree in Quebec require[d] young unmarried women to cover their faces at the bear feast because looking at the bear would signify an insult to the bear and provoke disease" (95-96). There are numerous examples from Indigenous North American and Finno-Ugric contexts that women must not look at the dead bear in the Bear ritual (see, for example, Tanner 1979, among the Cree) and that they must keep to the women's side of the house. Although many interpretations of Indigenous practices have subsequently come under more careful scrutiny and cannot be accepted at face value, much evidence of the same calibre can be found in Sami texts by the Sami themselves (see Bäckman 1982, 1981). Comparative perspectives on the taboos regarding women's eating restrictions likewise do not suggest any logical motivation but rather show that a number of different excuses justified women's exclusion from the "ursine eucharist."

The taboos we find among the Sami people regarding the Bear ceremonials echo those found more generally among Eurasian hunting peoples. According to Louise Bäckman (1982), "Women were not allowed to come even close to sites of sacrifice and holy sites. Women may not touch shaman drums. Women were forced to take complicated roundabout paths to avoid holy places" (143-144). Both Finnish and Sami women were forbidden to fish in lakes that were considered holy, *pyhä, passe/basse, bissie*. Furthermore, the holy places were considered dangerous for women as they could make a woman ill but she was also "dangerous herself" (Bäckman 1982: 143-159). Sami women were not permitted to touch or eat those parts of bear associated with Bear's power, or as some argue, the parts of the body that women would have touched when being carried into the den by the bear. As Rafael Karsten (1955) states, "No woman is allowed to enter the house where the men are cooking the flesh. When afterwards the meat is eaten, the women are allowed to consume only certain parts of the body of the bear, no doubt those parts in which the dangerous power of the bear is supposed to be concentrated in a lesser degree and therefore can be eaten by them with impunity"(121). According to Kaarle Krohn (1914), in the Finnish Karelian context bear had himself forbidden his former partner to eat his meat (51). Krohn suggests that men would eat the soup but left a little for the women (qtd. in Edsman 1994: 104). Bäckman (1981) suggests Sami women were restricted to eating only from the bear's hind legs. Women were also not allowed "to eat of the noble brains, heart—sacred meat" (Edsman 1994: 104). The role of women was to serve men beer—a far cry from the power of the Finnish bear goddess Osmotar, who was able to create ale—another element in the chain of signifiers denoting generativity and nature's powers of growth (Krohn cited in Edsman 1994: 104). According to Pentikäinen (2007): "Women's participation in certain parts of the festival was limited: for example, they had to be veiled, as *the bear could not stand the sight of female flesh, and some songs were too sacred to be heard by women.* But women would embrace and wake the bear to partake of the festal meal, and the bear's interest in the female sex is emphasized in the dramas" (36-37 [my emphasis]).

A special taboo is attached to the "unbearable" gaze between the woman and the killed bear, her symbolic former partner. According to Hallowell (1926) "Women are forbidden to look at the dead bear (Mistassini, Ostyak) or are required to leave the dwelling into which it is taken (Montagnais, Micmac, Finns)" (147). Bäckman (1982) notes that during Bear ceremonials, Sami women would gaze at the bear and hunters through a small brass ring meant to neutralize the danger presented by such a "look." They were even expected to cover their faces while looking through the ring. One reason given for the exclusion of women and their separation from the Bear has to do with the mysterious, even telepathic connection that women and Bears are believed to have, which could, at worst, lead to the Bear seeking an opportunity for rebirth through the woman's womb, implying that the primal bond was only acceptable in the mythic origins (Kuusi and Honko 1963: 42; cf. Paproth 1976). Rockwell (1991) provides an example of the supposedly contaminating female gaze from Ojibway culture, which I suggest reflects the patriarchal, possibly Christian-influenced interpretation of female power, transmitted through the eyes, the pathway of the soul: "During her [menstrual] seclusion, [a Tlingit girl] … observed a number of taboos. The Ojibwa believed her powers to be so great that her glance or touch could bring paralysis to another, death to a child, or the destruction of the year's berry crop.… During her seclusion, the girl's relatives called her *mukowe*—literally 'she is bear'" (16). If a woman's gaze or powers now protect, now destroy in Ojibway, Cree, and Finnish Carelian contexts, is this not a clear instance of the whore/madonna split so central to patriarchal religious projections on women's "essence"?

Clearly, the power of the female gaze is not by itself good or bad; it is the way it is incorporated into the dominant imaginary, its gender and animal relations, and to other cultural protocols that it acquires meaning. Rockwell notes that the bear was "not only a symbol of initiation but also a symbol of the *maleficent* [my emphasis] powers of the menstruating woman" (17). For many scholars, in the case of Finno-Ugric peoples, it is the totemistic myth of origin that explains the taboos. However, the prescriptions imposed on women appear to have changed as patriarchy got stronger, only to reflect a less noble and practical reason: misogyny pure and simple—and behind it, the appropriation of the role of reproduction. How else can one explain Edsman's (1994) statement that "the bear does not feel at home among women at the bear ceremonial" (110)? This argument sounds as contrived as the claim that women simply did not "like" bear soup (Uusitalo 1997: 27). It is likely then that "the forbidden gaze," which is a recurring element in the Bear hunting rituals, is a reversal of the life-oriented female ways of being and seeing (cf. Kallio 1997: 40). Rockwell's study (1991) provides an apt example of the way in which bears and women come both to connote "evil" in a combined historic, patriarchal assault on the kind of power that previously represented the core of a life-centred worldview and socio-cosmic order (time-reckoning, menses, rebirth, nature's abundance and the other elements described above).[36]

The concept of rebirth is still present in more recent Bear festivals although it is now associated with the reproduction of a masculated social order. The positive associations of the hibernation period of the bear, and the 40-day healing period for women after childbirth has been reversed into a "quarantine," with its clearly negative clinical associations of pathology rather than the wonder of birth. As Condren (2002) reports in her research, soldiers appropriate the healing period as a "couvade," a symbolic male hibernation ritual (41), a time of retreat imitating the menstrual period, necessary to prepare for battle.[36] While holding women in contempt, elite men in patriarchal societies began to imitate women's creativity in an attempt to draw upon its power, the same way that the hunters sought to incorporate the bear's power and strength by removing the organs where its power was believed to have its seat (the eyes, the claws and the paws, for example). Celebrating the overthrow of the Great Mother in childbirth, through the reproductive consciousness the male elite thus appropriated the Goddess power/culture of life for the culture of death. Ultimately the disdain for women's creativity beyond reproductive labour extends to generalized male attitudes toward the socially-constructed realm labelled as "feminine."

The reasons invented to justify the claim of women's "unbearable gaze" are also resonant with those listed by Condren (2002) in the Irish-Celtic context, in more recent Christianity: "Contact with women would weaken men's potency when engaging in their two most powerful activities—hearing the word of God or going to war. In this we can see a very clear connection between the development of a militaristic culture and the development of a new male identity independent of women or the world that women had represented" (18).[37] With the denigration of women and the very act of giving birth (leading to the necessity of women being "purified" by priests after delivery) came the denigration of the other signifiers of regeneration. They became patriarchy's rivals in the imaginary of reproduction which now places male creator gods in the center.

Numerous references to taboos on women's participation and behaviour in ancient Bear festivals are present in the primary materials and are not just a reflection of the researcher's "imaginary;" still this exclusion, even denigration of, women has been accepted at face value. It suggests that the male reproductive consciousness and master imaginary have been so internalized as "natural" that women's exclusion and misogynist labelling does not command special attention. What is obvious in the implied valorization of scholars' and perhaps ancient hunters' worldview is that "collective" economico-religious interests supersede in importance the nurturing and reproductive labours of women and nature. In this sense, the attitude toward women and nature is the same today as in the patriarchal past.[38] Although why the central woman-positive rebirth symbolism of matricentric societies was transformed is apparent, it is also important to examine historical views on how this change was justified and legitimated. Merchant (1989) describes in detail, with examples taken from the sixteenth century, how the organic worldview of cultures (of life) changed with the adoption of a mechanical view of nature as dead matter. Complementing such views, Condren (2002) points out that that with the gradual strengthening of Christianity, male cultural birthing came to be considered infinitely superior to anything women could hope to achieve. It is a matter of debate at what point the male reproductive consciousness came to invade the Bear religion, particularly since the Bear religion is believed to precede Christianity by tens of thousands of years. The Bear rituals, however, that have come to us from the Christian era bear convincing evidence of the shift away from holy female to holy male blood rituals.[39] Condren (2002) comments that for the elite men wishing to turn women's attributes of divinity into the opposite, the "Blood Covenant" was a perfect solution, a voluntary act that they could control, allowing them to decide to whom they would be affiliated in the political, religious, and military realms:

> By forging covenants of blood, men were no longer at the mercy of biological accident or change. Mothers could give birth biologically but only the voluntary union of men in some form of covenant could bring about rebirth into culture, a birth infinitely superior to the birthing by ordinary mothers. Indeed in some cultures blood brothers were known as "blood-lickers," as distinct from "milk-lickers," and the distinction signified a much greater degree of unity between them. (116).

The unbearable gaze can be understood in yet another dimension:

> Those responsible for the control of sexuality in society had better show evidence that they could control themselves. Indeed the holiness of men has become inextricable from the sensuality of women. As was said of Magnenn of Kilmainham, "He never looked a woman in the face" (for fear that he should see the guardian devil of her). Maintaining women in their roles as "guardian devils" became a vital part of male spirituality. Holiness in some male saints'

lives is almost synonymous with avoidance of women. For instance, we are told of St. Ciaran that "the holy Claran of Cluain, owes humility, from which he did not rashly swerve. He never uttered a word that was false, *nor looked upon woman* from his birth" (Condren 2002: 96).

It would seem that woman's "maleficiant gaze," quoted by Rockwell (1991), was invented to allow men to appear more holy and beneficial in contrast, and that this is the ultimate purpose of the reversal of the originally positive associations of the feminine in cultures of life. For Freud, "looking" means possessing the tools of knowledge, knowing how to manipulate knowledge (see Mulvey 1989), an idea that Michel Foucault (1980) also explores as the root of power. For Freud, at the root of knowledge is desire; if truth is always in excess of what we can know, ideologies are bound to creep into the gap between assumptions and reality (Kailo 1990). "Looking," in the context of women and Bears, is connected to relations other than to mere knowledge; it relates to establishment of power and the consolidation of a particular worldview: male reproductive consciousness. Making such developments visible is not a matter of essentializing the sexes, but of revealing how the imaginary body is coded through fantasies, fears, and desires that take the male or female body as the object of their socio-political projections (Gatens 1991).

Across the Christian world, the former realms of female authority and specialization are thus taken over by male priests. The sacrifice of Christ in the Christian Mass also helped accord new prestige to male blood. Cultures focused on the imaginary of death/domination thus came to attribute higher value to blood linked with violence than the menstrual blood associated with female reproductive power. Even today, the media is immersed in blood from violence, but the female menstrual blood, evident in ads, is taboo: the pads are sold in "hygiene" sections of shops and the blood is represented as a mark of dysfunction, illness, or lack of hygiene. The subconscious notion of polluting, female blood (not red, but a clinical blue evoking a modern version of "market churching") is perpetuated in more subtle forms in contemporary times. The female life-cycle mysteries are finally also medicalized, becoming objects of medical interventions as though they were pathologies. Likewise, if harvesting and creating food in harmony with the fertility calendar was formerly women's special responsibility, in male sacred rituals men become the holy "cooks"—and, indeed, today gourmet cooks are generally men. Complementary or parallel gender-segregated activities have been replaced by a devaluation of women's naturalized domestic labour and the more highly-valued ritual roles of men. The long, richly decorated dresses worn by priests and pastors are telling remnants of the religions of the Goddess, carrying unrecognized traces of former histories. Women are sacred enough to be imitated, but they must not be allowed to preach. The male lineage must be kept unpolluted and male-exclusive, despite many advances regarding the rights of women to act as pastors, or priests.

We now witness around the world how far the patriarchal appropriation of birth as essentially a cultural, religious act has taken us, in contrast to the "merely natural" culture of reproduction that based its social order, imaginary, and understanding of creativity on biological *and* cultural motherhood. Eugene Wolfenstein (1993) points out in his study of Freud and the "Ratman" (Freud 1905, 1918, 193; Freud and Oppenheim 1911), that "Freud and Marx each view money as embodying concealed social meanings. For Marx, it signifies the alienation of labour and the brutal exploitation of workers in the process of producing surplus value." For Wolfenstein, in both instances, "the analysis of money reveals failures of mutual recognition, which are the failures of the gift. These failures of recognition, and likewise the meaning of money, originate," according to Wolfenstein, "in the interplay between capitalist social relationships and the psycho-dynamics of the paranoid-schizoid position" (279). Not only is it unwarranted to universalize the kinds of dysfunctional relationships characterized by the master imaginary/ exchange economy at their worst, but violent sacrifices are also historically and culturally contingent. For the Adivasi in India, sacrifice consists even today in offering food and other culturally meaningful items to the dead, to spirits, or special places, like wells or caves (*Adivasi Justice is to Live in the Forest* 2007; see also Makilam 1999).

Conclusion

The church may well have begun by protecting women from the power of the male warriors, but who would now protect women from the power of the male church? (Condren 2002: 112)

In a gift cycle the gift is given without contract or agreement about return. And yet it does return: a circulation is set up and can be counted upon. (Hyde 1983: 114)

How, then, is all of the above of relevance to our contemporary social and ecological dilemmas? Why should we familiarize ourselves with the gift imaginary and the societies that in the past, and even in the present, express their values of interdependency and balanced human/animal, male/female relations? If one cannot provide exhaustive proof of a truly egalitarian, peaceful, matriarchal era (the very term meaning different things to different people), there is sufficiently convincing evidence from past and still existing societies that the master imaginary, the exchange economy, and the male or elite reproductive consciousness have not been unchallenged universals. In fact, patriarchy may well be a fairly recent historical development out of the give-back worldview of Indigenous peoples and other societies that placed ecological and collective balance and stability at the center of their episteme. As mentioned above, there are still gatherer-hunter societies or gift-based egalitarian communities in India (*Adivasi Justice is to Live in the Forest* 2007), China, Sumatra, North America, and Africa and many other parts of the world.[40] This fact exposes the groundless claims also of the scholars who dismiss matriarchal research as hopelessly deluded, utopian, and misguided (Binford 1979; Eller 2000).

The argument that ecofeminism and ecocritical studies have much to offer in terms of much-needed ecological wisdom and a grounded politics thus deserves attention. While there is no guarantee that a sustainable society would automatically enhance women's political power and general well-being, a collective sense of human/animal and male/female interconnectedness, linked with rituals of birth, death, and renewal appears to have discouraged the kinds of hierarchical structures that characterize "cultures of death" and that have incorporated gendered and other forms of violence at the core of their praxis. I have also suggested that the gift gaze and imaginary, as well as attendant symbolic systems of ritual social arrangements and festivities, might well provide that politically engaged and emancipatory "non-binary worldview" that transcends simplistic, essentialist beliefs regarding gender and other relations/roles, and the universality of sharply segregated male and female cultures. It is no doubt true that patriarchal societies do not always denigrate nature, or that nature-identified societies do not necessarily treat women with respect. What I hope to have brought out, however, is that such complexity within human social order and arrangements from the cultures of life to the cultures of death should also not make us close our eyes regarding worldviews that provide radical challenges to the dominant eurocentric epistemic assumptions.

Solely for the purpose of doing something serious about global climate change, deforestation, and the short-sighted plunder of the Earth's dwindling resources, we should consider openly the implications of privileging and naturalizing the master rather than the gift imaginary. There is simply too much evidence that patriarchy and its kinship systems provide the psychological foundations for the denigration and emotional rejection of the natural world (denial of forms of dependence, the cult of autonomy and individualism, emotional detachment, disembodied research). There are different stakes for men than women to embrace their connection with the natural world, such as having to resist the various aspects of hegemonic masculinity that provide men with power and entitlements within particular societies. There are gains with identifying with the exchange economy and the master identity or imaginary. But without a healthy planet, the privileges are beginning to appear illusory and superficial, for men as well as women, across the spectrum of privilege involving also ethnicity, sexual orientation, age, religion, and many other variables. To allow/encourage women to take pride in their (her)historic contributions and a gynocentric life-oriented past—however romantic such a Golden Past appears to some—may also promote the agenda of enhancing ecosocial sustainability. In the same way, bringing values and ways associated with the socially-constructed female gender into the academic world means colluding with its concealed masculated and eurocentric norms. Feminists themselves often collaborate in the denigration of the "feminine," of mothering logic and the like—whether the reasons are internalized misogyny, mother phobia, or a more conscious desire to possess the epistemic phallus and make it in the world of male "gods" and authorities. Scholars include many women that Plumwood (1993) calls "Artemis"-identified, i.e., epistemically motherless.

Alternative cosmo-visions may provide hope—if nothing else. For both men and women, "traditional" peoples assimilated into the western worldview of mastery over nature, environmental action, and a radical shift in worldview, means collective resistance against the power structures of capitalist patriarchy. The master imaginary and the exchange system it supports presents a threat to women, nature, and the remaining "few" grizzlies and polar bears; a socio-cosmic mythology in which men and women—whatever the precise sex/gender/species system—respect the female principle in the bosom of goddess festivals cannot undo all that. But we do need eco-socially sustainable narratives as compasses toward a recognition of the mutual dependency between humans and the environment which has now been turned into the market's monocultural field of profit.

Condren (2002) states: "at first Christianity merely claimed that its power was superior to that of the old religion; then it asserted that women only used these powers for evil ends; lastly, it denied that they possessed any sacred powers in the first place" (80-81). All of these excuses for excluding women from the Bear feast can be found in texts and fragments from different cultures. Condren (2002) traces how matricentric ethics were given the final blow

when the ties to one's children as extension of one's lifeblood were replaced by an imaginary where immortality would finally be located in the sacred sphere, in obedience to God the Father, rather than in the Chain of Being between parent and child. The ultimate test of patriarchal ethics was obedience to the point of death, or the willingness to sacrifice even one's own son in response to the demands of Yahweh, no matter how arbitrary. (21-22)

Essentially, in this process of the transformation of women's symbols of power, the gods and goddesses of the old religion became the demons of the next, and a new system of values came to the fore based on might with the male reproductive consciousness taken to its logical conclusion. The development of patriarchy (in its varieties and different levels or manifestations) has depended on several factors that Condren (2002) sums up: "the male discovery of his role in reproduction; the male realization of the insecurity of his position in the reproductive universe; his attempt to build a more secure basis for 'fatherhood'; the creation of a specifically transcendent or 'spiritual' culture achieved through death or death defiance" (41). As Sarmela has demonstrated (1991), in the agricultural era Bear becomes a mere enemy of cattle and humans, and finally, in more recent periods, bears are reduced to targets for elite shooting parties. In the end, the mindset naturalizing violence dominates and sexual politics continues to be a battle fought in the realms of law, mythology, and religion. Annis Pratt (1994) shows that the general role of patriarchal narratives, not just of the women and Bear stories but of many other stories as well, is a way to keep women in their place:

When the invading Achaeans needed to enforce more patriarchal control than Indigenous Old Europeans might be willing to accept, they used narratives about gods and heroes raping local divinities and their priestesses and worshippers to suggest the kind of punishment a sexually self-determining woman might expect. It is interesting that when threatened with rape, women heroes often turned themselves (or were helpfully metamorphosed) into natural objects: Daphne turned into a laurel tree to escape Apollo, Syrinz into a reed to avoid Pan, and Arethusa into a spring to elude Alpheus. Sometimes this metamorphosis is described as a punishment visited upon the hero by a patriarchalized goddess, as in the case of Athena turning Medusa into a snake-haired Gorgon. (353)

Based on her study of the woman/Bear theme in literature, Pratt (1994) believes that "Women take sanctuary in the green world to renounce excessive gender demands and to renew and re-empower themselves" (300). Christine Downing (1989) likewise believes that to be fed only male images of the divine is to be badly malnourished; many women are starved for images that recognize also the sacredness of the feminine and the complexity, richness, and nurturing power of female energy. For gift-identified women, nature could thus refer to "culture"—that of their own mythic traditions rather than evoking anatomy as destiny. Men, too, have increasingly come to grasp the need for new mythologies beyond the master narratives that have impacted also on their anguish (cf. Korten 2005). I believe that the importance of the Goddess in her various guises lies in the worldview and imaginary that legitimated her high status. Only Goddess imagery and ecomythologies rooted in a worldview of gender-symmetrical collective responsibilities promise improvement of the status of both wo(men) and the environment, or rather, the nature, of which we are part. Gynocentric activities and research have also an intrinsic value beyond any utilitarian, political demands—they are Gifts. The research into taboo areas of western culture are their own excuse for being. If exposing another logic and coding of the body politic, now a "feminine" one, is a spiritual need for women abused by patriarchy, the gift paradigm means also providing for such needs beyond the more purely academic motivation of bear research. To demonize such research with intentionally unfounded claims of essentialism or male hatred is denying the gift, denying women and Indigenous peoples their past—both real and imaginary. Nineteenth century nationalism meant the elites researched the past as a means to redeem the present, or claimed the distant past as a charter for future social change. This desire can be viewed as historical dualism (the horrible present, the wonderful past), but also as a much-needed Golden Future.[41]

Bearwomen like myself—whatever this intentionally ambivalent term means to the reader—are perhaps not unlike the women excluded in the Bear feasts—they are perceived as matter out of place (research invisibly threatening patriarchal master narratives and power bases) as well as a "polluting" influence. Perhaps we can look upon modern ecofeminists or scholars identifying with ecocritical literary politics also as modern-day Bearwomen taking on the role of "women marrying the Bear," whose mythic and historical role was to transmit and circulate the archaic cosmo-visions, gift-based social contracts obligating hunters and other members of clans and groups to honour and respect the animals they hunted. Ecofeminists and scholars like Kremer, Heiskanen, Paper, and Helander-Renvall in this volume, who heed the "strange" messages they hear in their dreams, are not unlike the mythic guides and partners of bears, who remind their fellow-citizens about the importance of ecologically more responsible attitudes, the basis of the sustainable worldview of balance. Numerous scholars that have dared to study matriarchies, matrilinear, or matrilocal societies as alternatives to hierarchical and domination-based patriarchies have also experienced serious harassment and subtle, or less subtle, academic sanctions (von Wehrlhof et al. 2003). Such work is one of today's dominant taboos. The veil must not be lifted. The perpetuation of the naturalized aggressive and competitive norm of *homo economicus*, the exchange economy, and the master imaginary is evident in how the gift is also perceived by scholars through that imaginary or lens. I read the bond of wo(men) and Bear/s then as metaphorical, supernatural, metaphysical, and real to the extent that it has spiritual as well as practical, ecosocial effects. On one level, the veiling of the matricentric past is an example of what Gayatri Spivak considers a form of "sanctioned ignorance" (cited in Kuokkanen 2007: 24). This ignorance and use of epistemic power denies the complicity of colonizers—male and female—in the historical process leading to current ecological crises. But most importantly, we need to recognize the extent to which today we need the ecological wisdom wherever it can be found:

> In practical terms, hunter-gatherers would have to be the affluent societies *par excellence*. They are self-sufficient and thus genuinely autonomous. They have a stable interchange with their habitat, they use low-impact technologies—they work only a few hours a day, and give energies to social bonds, ceremony and art. Ecologists taking a lesson from Aboriginal cultures might discover how to devise low-demand, low-impact economies where sustainability and social equity can go together. (Salleh 1997: 130)

An overly sharp boundary drawn between Indigenous and non-Indigenous women also needs to be revisited.[42] In *The Eros of Everyday Life: Essays on Ecology, Gender and Society*, Susan Griffin (1995) links the gift with women's daily practices, affirming implicitly Vaughan's (1997) theory of the gift paradigm:

> Everything I encounter permeates me, washes in and out, leaving a tracery, placing me in that beautiful paradox of being by which I am both a solitary creature and everyone, everything. Isn't this what shapes our days? The paradox accounts for gravity, which is a kind of eros ... There is an eros present at every meeting, and this is also sacred. One only has to listen inwardly to the histories and resonances of the word we use for religious experience. In Sanskrit the word *satsand* which translates into English as "eating" means "godly gathering." In the English language the word "Common" is linked through the word "communicate" to "communioni." And earlier meanings

of "common" point to levels of meaning that have been obscured in our idea of the sacred. Gary Snyder gives us the etymology for "*collon*" as "*ko*, gether,' with (Greek) *moin*, 'held in common." And he also traces the word back to the Indo-European root *mei*, meaning "to move, to go, to change." This "... had an archaic special meaning of "exchange of goods and services within a society as regulated by custom or law," he writes, as in "the principle of gift economies: 'the gift must always move '...." And the gift does move. To exist in a state of communion is to be aware of the nature of existence. This is where ecology and social justice come together, with the knowledge that life is held in common. Whether we know it not, we exist because we exchange, because we move the gift. And the knowledge of this is as crucial to the condition of soul as its practice is to the body. (Griffn 1995: 150-151)

Vaughan (1997) for her part believes that by understanding and dismantling the social process of masculation: "we can restore the nourishing model for all, providing a nurturing economy (a social cornucopia), which will abundantly satisfy all needs. A nurturing economy would not require any changes in male or female physical bodies. No castration or adding on organs where they originally were not. Only a change in our interpretations of these differences would be necessary, together with the dismantling of their psychological, economic and social projections. How can we provide abundance for all?" Vaughan asks, and then proposes her solution: "Follow the life-giving and nurturing mother model" (385).

In this age of deconstruction, it may be necessary to stress that this performance, citational mothering is something radically different from what we fear in the Mother (goddess?) and the logic based on her socially-constructed attributes. We need to underline that it is also a care-oriented masculine subject position, a logic, not an essence—that men and women, the traditional, assimilated, resisting and rebelling Indigenous people and wo(men) can all identify with and adopt—if they share a desire for bear-adise, "bear-*archy*," the *arch*-aic worldview of balanced, ecosocially sustainable human/animal relations. An age before and beyond our world of "dog-eat-dog" and of questionable anthropocentric metaphors.

I would like to conclude with Genevieve Vaughan's (1997) interpretation of the primal symbol of the gift, which echoes my references to Pandora as "the first mother"—the "ALL-GIVER":

The Holy grail is the free source of abundance, the Grail, the cup, is symbolically also the cornucopia or womb.... The Grail is not a material thing but a logic, a way of organizing our economic behavior. The Grail is the gift paradigm. It is not a physical object—not womb, vagina, breast or penis, not horn nor sword, chalice nor blade—but a refusal to mis-align the microcosm and the macrocosm, a refusal to create the shift into the artificial structure of exchange and its ego, where abundance and nurturing should be. The Holy Grail is the gift that gives, the gift of the gift paradigm which we all receive from our mothers—we only have to overcome our childhood complexes and our masculated misunderstanding of language and life in order to be able to receive it at last…. Rather, the answer lies in changing planes from the physical, and metaphysical, to the social and psychological. (110)

The modern variations of the Holy Grail as the alchemical vase for creating life epitomize the shifts from "bear-archy" and life-oriented cultures towards the culture of death and violence. Apart from the Christian Eucharist, the Grail is perhaps manifest on a more secular level as the *Coupe du monde*, the great cup of male sports where the notions of eros and rebirth have been replaced by "scoring" and "homecoming," with bonding giving way more narrowly to more or less violent sports and competition. Decolonizing wo(men) and bears requires nothing less than rewriting masculated mythologies and replacing their most ecophobic variants with modern *arch*-aic ecomythologies. Ecosocially powerful and sustainable symbols of interspecies and intergenerational ties, based on affectual forms of rationality and serving as means of socialization, are as important as environmental laws and taxes in turning around current ecologically disastrous developments. Without both affective and economic interventions against the abuse of women and bears, the future may well turn out unbearable, for us all. An ecological ethic of responsibility needs to be grounded in an ethic of ecojustice that recognizes the interconnection of both social and cultural domination and the mastery over nature.

I wish to express my thanks to the scholars, colleagues, and friends who have taken the time to comment on various drafts of this article or have otherwise influenced it: Sima Aprahamian, Åke Hultkrantz, Matti Sarmela, Inger Birkelund, Pauliina Kainulainen, Raija Warkentin, Irma Heiskanen, and more recently, Heide Goettner-Abendroth, Mary Condren, and Genevieve Vaughan. I also thank the students in my Women and Culture classes at Simone de Beauvoir Institute, Montreal, where the topic was highlighted from many ethnocultural perspectives between 1991-1999. Thanks are due also to the students and research assistants who helped me with research-related tasks: in Canada, Ella Saganash; in Finland, Marjo Stenius, Mari Kivilahti, and Marjo Taivalantti. Finally, several members of Feminists for a Gift Economy network have given me valuable feedback particularly with respect to the gift economy aspects of my research. I thank Genevieve Vaughan and Rauna Kuokkanen in particular for comments regarding this particular text. Helga Reischl also provided useful comments in the context of completing this manuscript. Special thanks go to Mary Condren for organizing the conference, "Challenging Cultures of Death and Sacrifice," November 2-4, 2007, at the Centre for Gender and Women's studies, Trinity College, Dublin. The conference gave me the chance to present my ongoing research on women and Bear/s and a rich opportunity to discuss my work with experts in the field of feminism, psychoanalysis, and religion (Genevieve Vaughan, Peggy Reeves Sanday, Bracha Ettinger, Griselda Pollock, to mention just a few). Thanks to Mary Condren also for introducing me to Seamus Ó Catháin's work on Brigit and the Bear festival and for her very helpful comments. On a different note, I am grateful to the Finnish Academy for funding my position as Senior Research Fellow (2006-2008), which made it possible for me to concentrate on the project "Hemispheric Cross-Talk on Trauma and Healing. Comparative Perspectives on Northern Native and non-Native Women Writers" (Project 118461), and thus explore more deeply topics such as mythic and religious violence, which are reflected in the final version of this anthology. Finally, I thank Luciana Ricciutelli for her stimulating thoughts on Bear, for her patience, and her excellent comments on various drafts of this article. Dr. Michael Branch needs to be recognized as the Finno-Ugric studies scholar (University of London) who first triggered my interest in Bear feasts in the late 1980s when I helped him read through and provide comments on a section of The Great Bear: A Thematic Anthology of Oral Poetry in the Finno-Ugric Languages *(1993). I also thank the anonymous Indigenous reviewers who recommended that this anthology be published, and who thus implicitly gave me a mandate—beyond any politics of appropriation of voice and another's culture—to publish these stories and their analyses. Juha Pentikäinen gave permission to use Clive Tolley's translation of some Finnish folk poetry to which I refer in this paper. I thank both Clive Tolley and Juha Pentikäinen for giving Inanna Publications these rights.*

[1]In this article, I distinguish Bear as spirit/deity and animal by capitalizing the former and not the latter. I use the phrase "wo(men) and Bears" to refer to the stories in general because, although the primary version of the story is about women and Bear/s, there are a few versions where it is a male figure that marries a She-bear. I use the phrase "women and Bear/s" to refer in these instances specifically to the role of women in the stories.

[2]Having lived in Toronto, Chicoutimi, and Montreal between 1984 and 1997, I witnessed the heated debates in Women's and Native Studies in Canada in the 1990s to do with the inappropriate, colonizing, appropriating, and in other ways ethnocentric/racist attitudes toward First Nations cultural practices and writings. Following the Oka Crisis in Montreal in 1991, Indigenous and non-Indigenous students and activists of Concordia University, where I held a position at the time, brought about a minirevolution to do with the necessity of integrating Indigenous perspectives in all academic fields on terms set by the First Nations communities themselves. I wrote about issues of appropriation and other political concerns voiced by Indigenous Canadians in Finland in 1994, pioneering also articles focused on power relations and postcolonialism within my Indigenous Finnish context regarding the treatment of the Indigenous Sami (e.g., Kailo 1994; Helander and Kailo 1998). Space does not allow me to elaborate here on these important issues to do with ethnosensitivity; however, I have reflected on my own cultural background and epistemic desire, as it impacts on this research and my relations with Indigenous communities. I lived for nine years in Montreal and became very close to a Cree family in a neighbourhood. I had the opportunity then to become familiar with First Nations ways of life, theory, and values. My academic vision has been greatly influenced by this experiences, as well as later

close collaborations with both Cree and Sami women, where I participated actively in their daily lives and rituals. As a result, I began to research my own cultural traditions in order to be able to "give back" the important ecological knowledge I was introduced to during those times. To avoid engaging in imperialist, neo-colonial research through sanctioned epistemic ignorance (Kuokkanen 2007), I have studied Finnish ecomythologies, pre-Christian rituals and worldviews, at the same time researching those of various Indigenous groups. Like Jürgen Kremer in this anthology, I am sensitive to the importance of egalitarian knowledge exchange, or rather, circulation, even while recognizing that asymmetrical academic relations are structural, historical, institutional, and thus beyond my control. Self-reflection about issues of power relations is necessary to avoid perpetuating the processes of epistemic violence and research that benefits only mainstream scholars. Giving back to my Cree friends in Montreal consists, among other things, in circulating and making thus available this anthology in the communities where I gained much personal and academic wisdom.

[3]The goal of "gift-based" societies is to consolidate the human/nature relationships on which the socio-cosmic order is premised, instead of being an expression of economic interest, obligation to exchange, and even less, the substitution of peace for war through a sacrificial contract. What characterizes gift-giving societies is their ecological ethics, the attempts to enhance and ensure the cycles of growth, of plants, animal, and human life through various seasonal festivals and rituals (see Kailo 2006a, 2006b, 2005a, 2005b, 2004a, 2004b; Kuokkanen 2007; Vaughan 2007, 2004a, 2004b, 1997).

[4]I use the term "gift gaze" as an ecofeminist alternative to the "male gaze" that might also be applied to ecosocially sustainable societies today and in the past. It also refers to the values and the imaginary prevailing in gift economies. With this concept I seek to do justice to the ancient/modern practice of giving back or returning to nature what it bestows. In contrast, I use the male gaze to refer to a hegemonic (patriarchal) gaze that blocks or renders invisible an alternative (matriarchal or matricentric) outlook on gendered issues.

[5]Hodder (2004), for example, has contributed to the debate about the reliability of Gimbutas's (1982) theories of the Goddess and Old Europe. Binford (1979) has challenged the studies on matriarchies with arguments that merely reveal she has not familiarized herself with this vast field. Eller (2000) has likewise presented questionable criticisms against matriarchal studies (for example, that matriarchal studies promote population growth and divert feminists from more serious pur-suits!) (see Dashu 2000). I will not address these criticisms in more detail as they do not, in my view, challenge my theses but merely attest to the partly ideological nature of any and all research.

[6]My primary materials include the archival collections at the Finnish Literature Society in Helsinki, Finland. There are hundreds of notations about folk beliefs concerning women and Bears in the card catalogues. I wish to thank Juha Nirkko among others for help in locating the materials that I have also used for my com-parative study of the Finnish sauna and the First Nations sweatlodge (Warkentin,

Kailo and Halonen, 2005). I have compared some 70 stories of women and Bears found in books, journals, scholarly treatises in Canadian and Finnish libraries, and as part of my previous research projects in Canada to do with self-help and healing. To avoid appropriating and misreading First Nations cultural materials, I had several students (foremost Ella Saganash of Waswanipi, Quebec, and Montreal) gather information and stories in their own communities. Some of these materials were published in the local Cree papers and in Montreal's *The Nation*.

[7]The male gaze was first described by Laura Mulvey (1989) when she challenged the foundational myths behind the pleasures of cinematic "looking" and more generally, of the male gaze. Drawing on Lacanian psychoanalysis, Mulvey argued that cinema is structured around three explicitly male gazes: the "look"/gaze of the camera filming the scene, which is voyeuristic since most films are made by men; the gaze of men within the film narrative, which is structured so as to make women objects of their gaze; and, finally, there is the gaze of the male spectator, each of which turns women into mere objects and stereotypes.

[8]Ecofeminist Ariel Salleh (1997) sums up the (masculated) hegemonic perspective of science also by referring to the overprivileged Sight: "Since Newton's optic, the image of the lens has guided men in focusing on discrete objects. The art of aiming the canon in war, perspectival drawing, and causal argument in philosophy are each guided by this linear mastery. The discipline of philosophy also serves the thought police of modernity by keeping debate locked into the synchronic grid and its either/or, theory/praxis, fact/value. The argument by Reason always proceeds by 'drawing a clear line between.' When it comes to envisaging complex, weblike patterns, where each part resonates information from the whole, nonsequentially, the holograph is a more useful metaphor than the lens. Even so, the way we have come to talk about it still favours the patriarchal organ of sight" (159).

[9]I refer to the English original paper presented by Val Plumwood at the Mujeres y ecologia—Historia, Pensamiento, Sociedad—symposium at the Universidad Complutense de Madrid, March 23-24th, 2001.

[10]See Leahy (1998) for a very thorough and useful description and critique of the various ecofeminist positions, their contradictions as well as their insights.

[11]The constructionist ecofeminist position differs from the essentialist one in the following way: its advocates claim that women are culturally constructed to be more in tune with the natural world. It can hardly be refuted that some humans and cultures have a more benevolent attitude toward non-human nature than others—the key thesis of ecofeminism in its variety. Likewise, even if we find convincing evidence of gender-equal societies, we cannot automatically assume that they did not experience of violence.

[12]Lacan's use of the symbolic, the imaginary, and what is real, is of course quite specific. While I am aware of the complex philosophical and psychoanalytic ramifications, I refer to the imaginary not only as a psychic phenomenon, but as including material and power-related gender relations.

[13]According to Bhaya (1982) O'Brien "argues that changes in reproductive labor

have played a large and previously unexamined role in creating political theory and the political order. Since men and women participate in reproductive labor in different ways, one can talk about a male and a female reproductive consciousness. According to O'Brien, the first major event in this history was the discovery of paternity, a transformation in the male reproductive consciousness which made it possible for men to appropriate 'their' children, thereby appropriating the prior reproductive labor of women accumulated in the child. This discovery, she claims, occurred in European history shortly before the emergence of the Greek *polis*. Men could steal the products and value of women's labor only if the actual process of reproduction were banished to a private realm ruled by exclusively male public institutions. Male reproductive consciousness has been expressed through what O'Brien calls the 'potency principle': principles of continuity, such as hereditary monarchy, primogeniture, eternity, and claims about the stabilizing role of the political community. O'Brien's evidence here is a revisionary reading of Engel's discussion of the 'world historic defeat of the female sex,' anthropological studies and an analysis of the underlying themes of Aeschylus's Oresteia and several of Plato's Dialogues" (361).

[14]The category of nature is a field of multiple exclusion not just of non-humans, but of various groups of humans and dimensions of life which are cast as nature. Sexism, ageism, speciesism, colonialism, and racism have drawn their conceptual strength from the master imaginary which projects racial, sexual and ethnic differ-ence as somehow closer to the material realm, the body and animals, construed at the same time as realms beyond the ideals of the human and beyond "rationality" and "culture."

[15]Plumwood (1993) exposed the rationalistic legacy of western philosophy not as a universal ordering of reality but as a particular mode of dualism and hierarchy. "…Reason in the western tradition has been constructed as the privileged domain of the master, who has conceived nature as a wife or subordinate other encom-passing and representing the sphere of materiality, subsistence and the feminine which the master has split off and constructed as beneath him. The continual and cumulative overcoming of the domain of nature by reason engenders the western concept of progress and development. But as in other patriarchal reproductive contexts, it is the father who takes credits for and possession of this misbegotten child, and who guides its subsequent development in ways which continue to deny and devalue the maternal role" (8).

[16]It is often also characterized by an either/or rather than both/and way of ap-proaching phenomena, involving an increasingly atomistic, fragmented, compart-mentalized and dissociated stance and form of relatedness to the world.

[17]According to Alan D. Schrift (1997), the theme of the gift can be located at the centre of current discussions of deconstruction, gender, ethics, philosophy and economics (see also Wyschogrod, Goux and Boynton 2002). The theme of the gift has emerged also within the humanities from literature to Indigenous studies (Kuokkanen 2007), within sociology (Komter 2005) and women's stud-ies or theories recognizing gender (Berking 1999; Cheal 1988). See also Jacques

Godbout's *The World of the Gift* (1998) which spans a number of fields in an interdisciplinary social science and anthropology perspective.

[18]Vaughan's theories of the gift economy as well as research by members of the network she initiated, Feminists for a Gift Economy, provide gender-sensitive correctives to the Maussian theories that I find useful for making visible the other imaginary that likely accompanied the Bear rituals with its focus on gift circulation. I also belong to the research and activist group Vaughan set up at the Norwegian Women's University, Kvinnouniversitet at Løten in 2001. Since then a group of women from around the world have taken turns gift giving in academe and at the grassroots level, a practice we share as a value and way of challenging the near-naturalized neo-liberal worldview.

[19]The model of exchange-related object relations is rooted particularly in the eurocentric context of boys' different (socialized) relationship with their mother, and their categorization as the non-giving, non-mother identified "exemplar" of the human. Vaughan (1997) is talking about the mental and identificatory frame—a kind of metaform or imaginary—to which the different models of socialization lead. It is the very fact of humans called boys, named in opposition to humans called girls, that provides the gendered logics with their different implications. Vaughan feels that this explains the projection of masculated thought patterns or "metaforms" into everything today from linguistics, economics, religion (monotheism) to legal and penal policies, and academic research.

[20]Among other comparative approaches, Goettner-Abendroth has also studied modern egalitarian or peaceful societies. Her writings (i.e., 2007), which may not in each case present the "hard" proof for past and present matriarchal societies, has given some people an excuse to try to discredit her. Her vast body of collected information on peaceful societies and matriarchies should be read before projecting assumptions of an idealizing stance.

[21]See the video produced of the Societies in Balance: World Congress on Matriarchal Studies, Luxembourg 2003, and the film documentary of the World Congress on Matriarchal Studies by Uschi Madeisky and Gudrun Frank-Wissmann, 84 min., Germay, 2005. Aavailable at <www.akademiahagia.com>.

[22]Peggy Reeves Sanday (1998) has argued for a reconfiguration of the term matriarchy not as a construct based on the gendered division of political power but one based on gendered divisions in the sociocultural and cosmological orders. Aware of the disdain that the term matriarchy evokes in the minds of many anthropologists, she suggests that matriarchy has never been theorized in and of itself. From the start its meaning was fashioned by analogy with "patriarchy" or "father right." Because patriarchy developed as a code word for male tribal leadership, matriarchy was restricted to female-oriented social rule. In the nineteenth century, the term was mired in the conceptual swamp of evolutionary theorizing about a primordial matriarchy. In the twentieth century the term suffered from the fortunes of sexual politics in which matriarchy came to be associated with exclusive female rule in response to the definition of patriarchy in similarly exclusive terms. In reconfiguring the term matriarchy, Sanday excludes any consideration of universal stages of

cultural evolution. She also excludes the concept of female rule, "on the grounds that a more appropriate term exists, found in the ancient Greek sources, namely gyneocracy after the Greek *gyne,* woman + *kratos,* rule (Sanday 1998: 2). The key to my reconfiguration is in the meaning of the -archy stem [from the Greek *arché*] found in Liddell's *Greek-English Lexicon* 1961: 252). Under the first of two broad categories of meaning presented, *arché* is defined as: "beginning, origin; lay a foundation; source of action; from the beginning, from the first, from of old; the original argument; first principle, element; practical principle of conduct; principles of knowledge" (Sanday 1998: 1).… Combining these concepts with the matri- prefix (after Latin *mater,* mother [cf. *Oxford English Dictionary*]) suggests a different approach to the definition of matriarchy as compared with the one traditionally followed using the second category of meaning, which alludes to "sovereignty" or "empire" (Sanday 1998: 2).

[23]According to Makilam (1999), "The cave is in itself a sacred place and a sanctuary, no tomb is ever found there, and yet it participates in the same cults of fecundity, as the tomb because, like it, the cave is an open door to the world of the dead (70).

[24]The research of Gimbutas (1982, 1989), Walker (1983), Condren (2002), Sanday (1981) and Eisler (1987), among numerous others, lend credence to Goettner-Abendroth's thesis that societies based on her criteria have and continue to exist, even if any model as such is bound to fall short of an exact correlation.

[25]The source from Finnish Literature Society's card archives is (according to the Finnish notation system) Paulaharju 12401, (mp 1922, 1930, Hukka-Salkko, 60 years of age).

[26]Annis Pratt's writings on Bear (1994, 1987) are the most extensive cross-cultural analyses of the motif from the explicit feminist perspective. Christiane Sourvinou-Inwood (1988) also covers a vast body of classical mythic material on women and bears, showing how the dramatization of woman/animal affinities came to be replaced by a focus on the rape of bear-identified women. It is also worth mentioning the work of Kathleen Geminder (1984) and Kathleen Wall (1988), who traces the Callisto archetype as a structural motif in European narratives. See also the classic bear novel, *Bear,* by Marion Engel (1976) and John Irving's *The Hotel New Hampshire* (1981), which feature women marrying Bears.

[27]However, research is very rich, particularly when it comes to analyses of women's sexual power, female *väki* (a particular energy/power unifying women and bears) (Stark-Arola 1994, 1993; Apo 1999, 1998; Tarkka 1994), and Finnish women's relations with bears and other animals (Kailo 2005a, 2003, 1998, 1996a, 1996b, 1993; Korte 1988; Tarkka 1994).

[28]Rockwell's study, for all of its useful cross-cultural information, contains discrepancies between his interpretation and the actual sources. This itself might be a reflection of the unrecognized impact of the "male gaze" or imaginary.

[29]Timo Miettinen (2000) also refers to a recently found rock painting near a crevice in Jaala, Finland (Rakoluola) that likely depicts a woman (a goddess?) giving birth that he among others interprets as a possible evidence for a matriarchal era.

[30]Echoing the values of the gift, Plumwood (2003) notes that "one framework is arrogant, reductive and human-centred, assuming a hierarchy of value in which human lives are worth more than those of other species, while the other is compatible with a basically egalitarian framework of honesty, non-ranking, gratitude and reciprocal benefit—a benefit which does not accrue of course in liberal-individual terms (as Adams 1994: 103 insists it must) but through taking our turn in benefiting from and and sharing in the systems of flow and exchange that nurture all life (Cheney 1997)" (9).

[31]Edsman (1956) has also indicated that certain Sami, Finnish, and Swedish wedding customs have their origins in the Bear festival itself. In the "liminal" period between engagement and wedding, the bridegroom has been referred to as "the bear." This and related customs survived up to the latter part of the nineteenth century (35).

[32]For Goettner-Abendroth, this concept is the basis of the matriarchal view of life and is confirmed by Makilam (1999) in the research to which I have referred above (see also Condren 2002; Ó Catháin 1995). At the root of this belief is matriarchal societies' relatedness to the natural world they live in, where they witness that every plant that withers in fall is reborn in the following spring. The belief in rebirth explains the respect for Mother Earth and the Goddess of Cosmos, the divinity of the entire world; the absence of a dualistic worldview and morality, and the view that everything in life is part of the symbolic system of sacral societies as cultures of the Goddess (Goettner-Abendroth 2005: 5; cf. Adivasi people recently living as hunter-gatherers [*Adivasi Justice is to Live in the Forest* 2007]). Finally, an element that can be linked to matriarchies, including Finno-Ugric peoples, and more specifically, the Finns, is the practice of honouring the dead. The cult of ancestors meant that bonds were sustained with the dead even after their passing away, involving food and drink offerings, and providing them opportunities for rebirth by regiving the names of the dead to newlyborns. Perhaps we can look upon the gifts to the dead as a further element of the gift imaginary and an element of the circular worldview of no beginning, no end. It also expresses the non-binary logic of a socio-cosmic ethos and imaginary where the distinctions between humans and animals, the dead and the living are not as sharp as they are under patriarchal religions and philosophies.

[33]Effectively, through its hibernating habits, the bear also acts as a time indicator with respect to the seasons, its biocosmic rhythms subtly responding to changes in light and darkness. The hibernation of the bear was thus seen as a stable, reliable sign of the limits of the seasons and became a dominant symbol of the entire transition from summer to winter and back again (Bäckman 1982: 38), and those activities associated with those periods of time throughout the year.

[34]Gimbutas (1989) finds this for Greece, Lithuania and Bulgaria (116). See also Rockwell (1991) for Indigenous American cultures. A Norse example can be found in the story of Bjørn and Bera in the *Hrolfs Saga Kraka*.

[35]Finnish scholar Veikko Anttonen (1993), in his discussion of "pyhä" (Finnish for "sacred"), refers back to times when women were not embodiments of impurity

(or the "impure" and the sacred coincided) and he reminds us that it is not that women's blood is dirty; it is the way in which it threatens the (male-defined) social order that it is taboo (72).

[36]"The warriors would take it upon themselves to ensure the fertility of their endeavours by undertaking a period of hibernation when they would perform the birth mimes and other forms of *couvade* in imitation of those activities that had been so successful on behalf of the Goddess. Celebrating the overthrow of the Great Mother in childbirth, they could appropriate her power for their warrior enterprises. At the same time, they could initiate the young warriors into the full life of the tribe. this is probably the meaning of the period of hibernation mentioned in the CURSE, which has proved such an enigma to Celtic scholars" (Condren 2002: 41).

[37]Finnish folk-poetry archives yield this "explanation" of the dangers of a female gaze: "Certain parts of a man's body [that] one mustn't let women see. One must especially guard against onlookers which there certainly are among women. If a woman happens to see [a man's genitals], they lose their 'accuracy'" (Ranta, Kaarlo, and Vihti qtd. by Stark-Arola 1994: 324). Reporting on the Christian church's views on the demonized gender, Condren (2002) writes: "women, according to the fully fledged theology of the church, were by nature incapable of mediating with the divine and should not be so arrogant as to assume these functions" (28).

[38]Condren (2002) provides a thought-provoking analysis of the new meaning also of sacrifice within cultures of death: "biological links were no longer important; really important life lay beyond the world. Committing the ultimate act of transgression enabled men to enter or create sacred space, implicitly denigrating the world of women and children" (196). She further surmises that in the institution of the Blood Covenant, unity among the male members seems to have become anchored in their willingness to avenge each other's deaths. In light of my own research on "shameful femicides," this for its part may well have given the motivation to sex/gender systems based on gendered notions of honor and shame still operating in many countries (Kailo 2004c). Condren notes that as more sophisticated versions of the Blood Covenant arose, those established as "brothers" were prepared to die on behalf of God the Father. This bond among "brothers" echoes also the Bear's sacrifice according to which it willingly gave up its life so humans could live (Honko 1993a). But in contemporary politics it is the collective fatherhood of the state that is being established (cf. Freud 1950). This explains why the role of the mother of the Bear-son, like the mother and grandmother of Jesus, take second place in the socio-religious imaginary.

[39]Although she does not deal with Bear festivals, Condren (2002) sums up the general shifts within communal rituals that may help us retrace our steps back towards a better understanding of the gender politics present also in the Bear religion, or worldview: "More importantly, the eradication of female values, based on women's experience of care, nurturance, the ethics of responsibility, and the preservation of life above all else, proceeded simultaneously, although this elimination would be successfully disguised for centuries to come" (127). Condren concludes that

quite a different sacrifice had also taken place in the course of history; that of the rights, blood, and power of women to the new patriarchal order.

[40]Visit <www.gifteconomy.com> and <www.hagia@aol.com> for examples.

[41]Ethnographic research and feminist anthropology today have shifted the focus from women to gender. See, for example, Micaela Di Leonardo's (1991) collection of essays in feminist anthropology, intended as an update on the classic woman, culture, and society focus, titled *Gender at the Crossroads of Knowledge*. Michelle Rosaldo's often cited *The Use and Abuse of Anthropology* (1980) includes a section on the search for origins and universals (390-96; see also O'Brien 1983), but Rosaldo frowns upon "at origins" theories, on the grounds that they depict gender systems as essentially unchanging (392-93). As I hope to have made clear, to study different types of gender-related imaginaries is not to claim anything unchanging about gender but to apply new lenses. As Amy Richlin (1993) laments: "to reconstruct Greek or Roman women's separate culture requires years of painstaking research and putting together tiny fragments; we long to know more; and yet almost everything we get is filtered through male texts and a culture that favored the male. A combined model would take into account the male nature of the sources while keeping a firm grip on the women hidden behind them. Those who seek evidence of matriarchal cultures and societies in the past have come under attack by historians (Lerner 1986), archeologists (see Bron, Passman, Zweig in this volume) and historians of religion (Fiorenza 1989). Yet, in turn, all these are themselves seeking validation in the past. Lerner's history is a search for a charter; if patriarchy has a historical beginning, it can have a historical ending. The archeologists substitute woman the gatherer for the Goddess. Church historians are looking for church mothers. The mythmaking function of history seems inescapable" (284-285). Richlin reminds us that we need to interrogate not only the received epistemology of mainstream disciplines, but the epistemology within which mainstream women have been working on topics such as women in antiquity. Indeed, the "ethnographer's dilemma" has hardly touched feminist writing in classics and matriarchal studies where class and other variables of difference are wished away (perhaps because too difficult to account for?). I conclude that much more needs to be considered than gender and species systems. I leave that focus for the future.

[42]It is also worth quoting Ojibway Winona LaDuke's (1997) view of what the differences are between capitalistic societies and the life-oriented, gift-circulating Indigenous cultures she represents: "Industrial language has changed things from being animate, alive, and having spirit to being inanimate, mere objects and commodities of society. When things are inanimate, "man" can view them as his God-given right. He can take them, commodify them, and manipulate them in society. This behavior is also related to the linear way of thinking.... In this country we are taught that capitalism is a system that combines labor, capital, and resources for the purpose of accumulation. The capitalist goal is to use the least labour, capital, and resources to accumulate the most profit. The intent of capitalism is accumulation. So the capitalist's method is always to take

more than is needed. Therefore, from an Indigenous point of view capitalism is inherently out of harmony with natural law. Based on this goal of accumulation, industrial society practices conspicuous consumption. Indigenous societies, on the other hand, practice what I would call "conspicuous distribution." We focus on the potlatch, the giveaway, an event that carries much more honor than accumulation does. In fact, the more you give away, the greater your honor. We make a great deal of these giveaways, and industrial society has something to learn from them" (28).

References

Abercromby, John. 1898. *Pre- and Proto-historic Finns Both Eastern and Western. With the Magic Songs of the West Finns.* London: David Nutt., Vol i-ii, 1898.

Adams, Carol. 1994. *Neither Man Nor Beast: Feminism and the Defense of Animals.* New York, Continuum.

Adivasi Justice is to Live in the Forest. 2007. Documentary. Producer: Ville-Veikko Hirvelä. 55 min.

Anttonen, Veikko. 1993. "Interpreting Ethnic Categories Denoting 'Sacred' in a Finnish and an Ob-Ugrian Context." *Temenos* 28: 55-80.

Althusser, Louis. 1984. *Ideologiset valtiokoneistot (Ideological State Apparatuses).* Trans. Leevi Lehto and Hannu Sivenius. Tampere: Vastapaino.

Apo, Satu. 1999. "The Mythic Woman: *Women in Finland.* Keuruu: Otava.

Apo, Satu. 1998. "Ex Cunno Come the Folk and Force: Concepts of Women's Dynamistic Power in Finnish/Karelian Tradition." *Gender and Folklore: Perspectives on Finnish and Karelian Culture.* Eds. Satu Apo, Aili Nenola, and Laura Stark-Arola. Studia Fennica Folkloristica 4. Helsinki: Finnish Literature Society. 9-27.

Aristotle. *The Works of Aristotle.* 1908-31. Trans. and ed. W. D. Ross. Oxford: Clarendon Press.

Armstrong, Jeannette. 2007. "Indigenous Knowledge and Gift Giving: Living in Community." *Women and the Gift Economy: A Radically Different Worldview is Possible.* Toronto, Inanna Publications and Education Inc. 41-50.

Bachofen, Johann Jacob. 1863. *Der Bäer in den Religionen des Alterthums?* Basel.

Bäckman, Louise. 1982. "Female–Divine and Human: a Study of the Position of the Woman in Religion and Society in Northern Eurasia." *The Hunters.* Eds. Åke Hultkrantz and Örnulv Vorren. Tromsø: Universitetsforlaget. 143-162.

Bäckman, Louise. 1981. *Kort berättelse om lapparnas björnafänge (A Brief Account of the Lapps' Bear Hunt).* Facsimile based on original 1755 edition. Umeå. Pehr Fjellström.

Berking, Helmuth. 1999. *Sociology of Giving.* Trans. Patrick Camiller. London: Sage.

Bhaya, Shakuntla. 1982. "The Politics of Reproduction." *Signs* 8 (2): 361-63.

Biehl, Janet. 1990. *Rethinking Eco-Feminist Politics.* Boston: South End Press.

Binford, Sally R. 1979. "Are Goddesses and Matriarchies Merely Figments of

Feminist Imagination?" *Human Behavior* 6 (121) (May): 11-12.

Bourdieu, Pierre. 1997. "Selections from the Logic of Practice." *The Logic of the Gift. Toward an Ethic of Generosity.* Ed. Alan D. Schrift. New York: Routledge. 30-50.

Campbell, Joseph. 1959. *The Masks of God.* New York: Viking.

Cheal, David. 1988. *The Gift Economy.* New York: Routledge.

Christ, Carol. 2004. "The Feast Day of St. Brigid." *Women's Journal* (Spring): 13-14. Cixous, Hélène. 1980. "The Laugh of the Medusa." *New French Feminisms.* Eds. Elaine Marks and Isabelle de Cortivron. Brighton: Harvester. 245-64.

Cixous, Hélène and Catherine Clément. 1986. *The Newly Born Woman.* Trans. Betsy Wing. Minneapolis: University of Minnesota Press, 1986.

Columbia Electronic Encyclopedia, The. 6th Ed. 2001-2005. "Pandora, in Greek Mythology." Online: < http://www.bartleby.com/65/pa/Pandora.html>.

Condren, Mary. 2002. *The Serpent and the Goddess: Women, Religion and Power in Celtic Ireland.* 1989. Dublin: New Island Books.

Dashu, Max. 2000. "Knocking Down Straw Dolls: A Critique of Cynthia Eller's *The Myth of Matriarchal Prehistory: Why An Invented Past Won't Give Women a Future.*" Online: <http://www.suppressedhistories.net/articles/eller.html>.

Derrida, Jacques. 1981. *Dissemination.* Transl. Barbara Johnson. Chicago: University of Chicago Press.

Di Leonardo, Micaela. 1991. *Gender at the Crossroads of Knowledge: Feminist Anthropology in the Postmodern Era.* Berkeley: University of California Press.

Douglas, Mary. 1996. *Purity and Danger. An Analysis of the Concepts of Pollution and Taboo.* 1966. London: Routledge.

Downing, Christine. 1989. "Artemis: The Goddess Who Comes from Afar." *Weaving the Visions. New Patterns in Feminist Spirituality.* Eds. Judith Plaskow and Carol P. Christ. San Francisco: Harper. 119-127.

Edsman, Carl-Martin. 1994. *Jägaren och makterna. Samiska och finska björncer-emonier (The Hunter and the Powers: Lappish and Finnish Bear Rites).* 1965. Uppsala: Skrifter utgivna genom Dialekt-och folksminnesarkivet.

Edsman, Carl-Martin. 1965. "The Hunter, the Games and the Unseen Powers: Lappish and Finnish Bear Rites." *Nordic Symposium on Life in a Traditional Hunting and Fishing Milieu from Prehistoric Times to the Present.* Ed. Harald Hvarfner. Luleå. 159-88.

Edsman, Carl-Martin. 1960. "Bear Rites Among the Scandinavian Lapps." *Proceedings of the Ninth International Congress for the International Congress of the History of Religions,* 27 August-9 September 1958, Tokyo/Kyoto. 25-32.

Edsman, Carl-Martin. 1956. "The Story of the Bear Wife in Nordic Tradition." *Ethnos* 21: 36-56.

Eisler, Riane. 1987. *The Chalice and the Blade.* San Francisco: Harper and Row.

Eller, Cynthia. 2000. *The Myth of Matriarchal Prehistory: Why An Invented Past Won't Give Women a Future.* Boston: Beacon Press.

Enäjärvi-Haavio, Elsa. 1954. "The Finnish Shrovetide." *FF Communications* 146, Helsinki.

Engel, Marian. 1976. *Bear*. Toronto: McClelland and Stewart.

Foucault, Michel. 1980. *Power/Knowledge: Selected Interviews and Other Writings 1972-1977*. New York: Pantheon.

Frazer, James George. 1890. *The Golden Bough: The Roots of Religion and Folklore*. London: Macmillan.

Freud, Sigmund. 1953-74. *The Standard Edition of the Complete Psychological Works of Sigmund Freud*. 24 vols. Trans. and ed. James Strachey. London: Hogarth Press.

Freud, Sigmund. 1950. *Totem and Taboo*. London: Routledge and Kegan Paul.

Freud, Sigmund. 1933. "New Introductory Lectures on Psychoanalysis." *The Standard Edition of the Complete Psychological Works of Sigmund Freud*. Vol. 22. Trans. and ed. James Strachey. London: Hogarth Press. 1-182.

Freud, Sigmund. 1918. "From the History of an Infantile Neurosis." *The Standard Edition of the Complete Psychological Works of Sigmund Freud*. Vol. 17. Trans. and ed. James Strachey. London: Hogarth Press. 1-122.

Freud, Sigmund. 1905. "Three Essays on the Theory of Sexuality." *The Standard Edition of the Complete Psychological Works of Sigmund Freud*. Vol. 7. Trans. and ed. James Strachey. London: Hogarth Press. 130-243.

Freud, Sigmund and David Oppenheim. 1911. "Dreams in Folklore." *The Standard Edition of the Complete Psychological Works of Sigmund Freud*. Vol. 12. Trans. and ed. James Strachey. London: Hogarth Press. 175-204.

Ganander, Christfrid. 1984. *Mythologia Fennica (Finnish Mythology)*. 1789. Åbo Facsimile. Jyväskylä: Suomalaisen kirjallisuuden seura.

Gamman, Lorraine and Margaret Marshment. 1989. *The Female Gaze. Women as Viewers of Popular Culture*. Seattle: The Real Comet Press.

Gatens, Moira. 1991. "A Critique of the Sex/Gender Distinction." *A Reader in Feminist Knowledge*. Ed. Sneja Gunew. London: Routledge. 139-157.

Geminder, Kathleen Elaine. 1984. *Callisto: the Recurrence and Variations of her Myth from Ovid to Atwood*. Unpublished disseration, University of Manitoba.

Gimbutas, Marija. 1989. *The Language of the Goddess*. San Francisco: Harper and Row.

Gimbutas, Marija. 1982. *The Goddesses and Gods of Old Europe, 7000 to 3500 B.C.: Myths and Cult Images*. Berkeley: University of California Press.

Glotfelty, Cheryl and Harold Fromm. 1996. *The Ecocriticism Reader: Landmarks in Literary Ecology*. Athens: University of Georgia Press.

Godbout, Jacques T. in collaboration with Alain Caillé. 1998. *The World of the Gift*. Tr. by Donald Winkler. Montreal: McGill-Queen's University Press, 1998.

Goettner-Abendroth, Heide. 2007. "Matriarchal Society and the Gift Paradigm: Motherliness as an Ethical Principle." *Women and the Gift Economy: A Radically Different Worldview is Possible*. Ed. Genevieve Vaughan. Toronto: Inanna Publications. 99-107.

Goetttner-Abedroth, Heide. 2005. "The Relationship between Modern Matriarchal Studies and the Gift Paradigm." Conference Proceedings. Another World View is Possible Conference, November 14-17, 2004. Online: <http://www.

gift-economy.com/athanor/5.html>. Accessed February 7, 2005.

Goettner-Abedroth, Heide. 2004. "The Relationship between Modern Matriarchal Studies and the Gift Paradigm." *Another Worldview is Possible: Conference Proceedings*. Ed. Genevieve Vaughan. Las Vegas County Library. Nov. 14-17, 2004.

Goettner-Abendroth, Heide. 2000. *Das Matriarchat II,2: Stammesgesellschaften in Amerika, Indien, Afrika*. Stuttgart: Kohlhammer-Verlag.

Goettner-Abendroth, Heide. 1995. *The Goddess and Her Heros: Matriarchal Religion in Mythology, Fairytales and Literature*. Trans. Lillian Friedberg. Stow, MA: Anthony Publishing Company.

Goettner-Abendroth. Heide. 1991. *Das Matriarchat II, 1: Stammesgesellschaften in Ostasien, Indonesien, Ozeanien*. Stuttgart: Kohlhammer-Verlag.

Goettner-Abendroth. Heide. 1988. *Das Matriarchat I: Geschichte seiner Erforschung*. Stuttgart: Kohlhammer-Verlag.

Grahn, Judy. 1982. "From Sacred Blood to the Curse and Beyond." *The Politics of Women's Spirituality: Essays on the Rise of Spiritual Power Within the Feminist Movement*. Ed. Charlene Spretnak. New York: Anchor. 265-280.

Griffin, Susan. 1995. *The Eros of Everyday Life. Essays on Ecology, Gender and Society*. Anchor Books: New York.

Haavio, Martti. 1968. "Karhu, kantaisä (Bear, Forefather)." *Kalevalaseuran vuosikirja* 48: 61-89.

Haavio, Martti. 1967. *Suomalainen mytologia (Finnish Mythology)*. Porvoo: n.p.

Hallowell, Irving, A. 1926. "Bear Ceremonialism in the Northern Hemisphere." *American Anthropologist*. 28 (1): 1-175.

Hammarstedt, N. E. 1929. "Vår och bröllopsbjörn (Spring and the Bear Bride)." *Budkavlen* 8: 7-11.

Harrison, Jane E. 1955. *Prolegomena to the Study of Greek Religion*. 1903. New York: Meridian Books.

Hakulinen, J. Tohmajärvi. 1891. *Suomen Kansan Vanhat Runot* VII, 5: 3942.

Heikkilä, Timo. 2004. *Aurinkolaiva, Lemminkäisen myyti ja Ritvalan kultti (Solar Boat: The Myth of Lemminkäinen and the Cult of Ritvala)*. Helsinki: Basam Books.

Helander, Elina and Kaarina Kailo. 1998. *No Beginning, No End: The Sami Speak Up*. Alberta: Canadian Circumpolar Institute.

Hodder, Ian. 2004. "Women and Men at Çatal Hhöyük. *Scientific American*. Jan.

Honko, Lauri. 1993a. "Belief and Ritual: The Phenomenological Context." *The Great Bear: A Thematic Anthology of Oral Poetry in the Finno-Ugric Languages*. Eds. Lauri Honko, Senni Timonen, Michael Branch, and Keith Bosley. Pieksämäki: Suomen Kirjallisuuden Seura. 63-75.

Honko, Lauri. 1993b. "Festivities." *The Great Bear: A Thematic Anthology of Oral Poetry in the Finno-Ugric Languages*. Eds. Lauri Honko, Senni Timonen, Michael Branch, and Keith Bosley. Pieksämäki: Suomen Kirjallisuuden Seura. 259-287.

Honko, Lauri. 1993c. "Hunting." *The Great Bear: A Thematic Anthology of Oral Poetry in the Finno-Ugric Languages*. Eds. Lauri Honko, Senni Timonen, Michael

Branch, and Keith Bosley. Pieksämäki: Suomen Kirjallisuuden Seura. 117-186.

Honko, Lauri, Senni Timonen, Michael Branch, and Keith Bosley, eds. 1993. *The Great Bear: A Thematic Anthology of Oral Poetry in the Finno-Ugric Languages.* Pieksämäki: Suomen Kirjallisuuden Seura.

Hultkrantz, Åke. 1965. "Type of Religion in the Arctic Hunting Cultures: A Religio-Ecological Approach." *Hunting and Fishing. Nordic Symposium on Life in a Traditional Hunting and Fishing Milieu in Prehistoric Times and Up to the Present Day.* Ed. H. Hvarfner. Lulea, Sweden: Norrbottens Museum.

Hyde, Lewis. 1983. *The Gift. Imagination and the Erotic Life of Property.* 1979. New York: Vintage Books.

Irigaray, Luce. 1985. *Speculum of the Other Woman.* 1974. Trans. Gillian Gill. Ithaca, NY: Cornell University Press.

Irving, John. 1981. *The Hotel New Hampshire.* New York: Elsevier-Dutton Publishing Co.

Kailo, Kaarina. 2008. "The Helka Festival: Traces of a Finno-Ugric Matriarchy or Worldview?" *Societies of Peaces: Matriarchies Past, Present and Future.* Ed. Heide Goettner-Abendroth. Toronto: Inanna Publications and Education.

Kailo, Kaarina. 2007. "Pan Dora Revisited: From Patriarchal Woman-Blaming to a Feminist Gift Imaginary." *Women and the Gift Economy: A Radically Different Worldview is Possible.* Ed. Genevieve Vaughan. Toronto: Inanna Publication and Education. 50-71.

Kailo, Kaarina 2006a. "Cyber/Ecofeminism." *Encyclopedia of Gender and Information Technology.* Ed. Ellen Moore Trauth. Hershey, PA: Idea Group Reference. 172-176.

Kailo, Kaarina. 2006b. "Kave, Louhi ja Pandoran lipas—miesnäkökulmaisen mytologian uudelleenarviointia." *Myyttien Hyrinässä.* TAIDA, Oulun yliopistopaino. 79-111.

Kailo, Kaarina. 2005a. "Archaic Aspects of the Finnish Sauna and the Sweat Lodge: The Gift of Bare Being." *Sweating with the Finns: Sauna Stories from North America.* Eds. Raija Warkentin, Kaarina Kailo and Jorma Halonen. Thunder Bay, ON: Lakehead University, Centre for Northern Studies. 45-76.

Kailo Kaarina. 2005b. "Mythic Women of the North: Between Reality and Fantasy." *Northern Dimensions and Environments.* Eds. Lassi Heininen, Kari Strand and Kari Taulavuori. *Northern Sciences Review.* Thule Institute, University of Oulu. 173-223.

Kailo, Kaarina. 2004a. "Desde el di-curso viril a los con-cursos fértiles: El ecofeminismo y las mujeres nordicas (From Virile Dis-Course to Fertile Concourses: Globalization, Ecofeminism and Northern Women)." *Mujeres y Ecologia: Historia, Pensamiento, Sociedad.* Coords. Mária Luisa Cavana, Alicia Puleo, Cristina Segura. Madrid: Asociacion Cultural, Al-mudayna, Colección LAYA 25. 129-153.

Kailo, Kaarina. 2004b. "Giving Back to the Gift Paradigm: Another Worldview is Possible." *Dono The Gift: A Feminist Analysis.* Ed. Genevieve Vaughan. *Athanor* 15 (8): 39-69.

Kailo, Kaarina. 2004c. "Honour-Related Violence and/or Shameful Femicides within Patriarchal Sex/Gender Systems." Paper presented at *Aware II*. Increasing Teacher Trainees' Awareness of Sexualized and Gendered Violence, Oulu University, 4 February. Online: <http://wwwedu.oulu.fi/aware>.

Kailo, Kaarina. 2003. "Baring our Beeing: Sauna and Sweatlodge as Ritual Spaces." *Sauna Wellness Weltweit: Dokumentation des XII. Internationalen Sauna-Kongresses 5-9 Mai 1999*. Ed. Conradi Eberhard. Bielefeld, Deutschland: Deutscher Sauna-Bund e.V. 33-64.

Kailo, Kaarina. 1998. "Indigenous Women, Ecopolitics and Healing:'Women who Marry Bears.'" *Minorities and Women*. Ed. Robert Jansson. Mariehamn: Åland Fredsinstitut, Åland Peace Institut. 85-121.

Kailo, Kaarina. 1996a. "The She-Bear: Circumpolar Mother of Spiritual Feminism." *Canadian Woman Studies/ les cahiers de la femme* 17 (1) (Winter): 48-52.

Kailo, Kaarina. 1994. "Trance-cultural Travel: Indigenous Women and Mainstream Feminisms." Ed. Mari Peepre. *Trans-Cultural Travels: Essays in Canadian Literature and Society.* 19-36.

Kailo, Kaarina. 1993. "Furry Tales of the North: a Feminist Interpretation." *Simone de Beauvoir Institute Bulletin/Bulletin de l'Institut Simone de Beauvoir* 12 (2): 104-133.

Kailo, Kaarina. 1990. *The Short Fiction of Nathaniel Hawthorne and Gérard de Nerval-A Study in Post-Jungian Aesthetics*. Diss., University of Toronto.

Kallio, Biret Maret. 1997. "Noaidi: The One Who Sees." *ReVision* 19 (3) (Winter): 37-41.

Karsten, Rafael. 1955. *The Religion of the Samek: Ancient beliefs and Cults of the Scandinavian and Finnish Lapps*. Leiden, Netherlands: E. J. Brill.

Kheel, Marti. 1995. "Licence to Kill: An Ecofeminist Critique of the Hunter's Discourse." *Women and Animals*. Eds. Carol Adams and Josephine Donovan. Durham, NC: Duke University Press. 85-126.

Klemettinen, Pasi. 2002. "Kurkistuksia karhun kulttuurihistoriaan. (A Glance at the Cultural History of the Bear)." *Eläin ihmisen mielenmaisemassa (Animals Within Humans' Mental Environment)*. Eds. Henni Ilomäki and Outi Lauhakangas. Helsinki: Suomen Kirjallisuuden Seura. 134-173.

Komter, Aafke E. 2005. *Social Solidarity and the Gift*. Oxford: Oxbow Books.

Korte, Irma. 1988. *Nainen ja myyttinen nainen (Woman and Mythic Woman)*. Helsinki:, Yyliopistopaino.

Korten David C. 2005. *The Great Turning from Empire to Earth Community*. San Francisco: Kumarian Press.

Kovalainen, Ritva and Sanni Seppo. 1997. *Puiden Kansa (People of the Trees)*. Hämeenlinna: Kariston kirjapaino.

Krohn, Kaarle. 1914. *Suomalaisten runojen uskonto: Suomensuvun uskonnot (Finnish Folk Poetry: The Religions of Finnish Peoples)*. Helsinki: Suomalaisen kirjallisuudenseuran tutkimuksia.

Kuokkanen, Rauna. 2007. *Reshaping the University: Responsibility, Indigenous Epistemes, and the Logic of the Gift*. Vancouver: University of British Columbia Press.

Kuokkanen, Rauna. 2004a. *Towards the Hospitality of the Academy: The (Im)possible Gift of Indigenous Epistemes.* Unpublished dissertation. University of British Columbia, Vancouver.

Kuokkanen, Rauna. 2004b. "The Gift as a Worldview in Indigenous Thought." *Il Dono/The Gift: A Feminist Analysis.* Ed. Genevieve Vaughan. *Athanor* 15 (8): 81-97.

Kuusi, Matti. 1963. "Karhun peijaiset (The Bear Feast)." *Suomen Kirjallisuus. I.* Helsinki: Otava.

Kuusi, Matti and Honko, Lauri. 1963. "Sejd och saga. Den finskan forndiktens historia (Heritage and Poetry: The History of Ancient Finnish Poetry)." *Suomen Kirjallisuus. I.* Helsinki: Otava.

Lacan, Jacques. 1977. *Ecrits: A Selection.* 1966. Trans. Alan Sheridan. New York: W. W. Norton.

LaDuke, Winona. 1997. "Voices from White Earth: Gaa-waabaabiganikaag." *People, Land and Community.* Ed. Hildegarde Hannum. New Haven: Yale University Press. 22-38.

Lang, Andrew. 1899. *Myth, Ritual and Religion.* New Edition. London: Longmans.

Leahy, Terry. 1998. "What is Ecofeminism? Different Positions within Ecofeminism." Online: <http://www.octapod.org:8000/gifteconomy//content/zedgendone.html>.

Lönnrot, Elias. 1847. *Kalevala.* Helsinki: Otava.

Loucks, Georgina. 1985. "The Girls and the Bear Facts: A Cross Cultural Comparison." *The Canadian Journal of Native Studies* 5 (2): 218-239.

MacCormack, Carol and Strathern, Marilyn, eds. 1980. *Nature, Culture and Gender.* Cambridge: Cambridge University Press.

Makilam. 1999. *Symbols and Magic in the Arts of Kabyle Women.* Tr. Elizabeth Corp. New York: Peter Lang.

Mauss, Marcel. 1969. *The Gift: Forms and Functions of Exchange in Archaic Societies.* Trans. Ian Cunnison. London: Cohen and West.

Mauss, Marcel. 1923/1924. "Essai sur le don: Forme et raison de l'échange dans les sociétés archaïques." *L'Annee Sociologique* 30-186.

McClellan, Catharine. 1975. *My Old People Say: An Ethnographic Survey of the Southern Yukon Territory.* 2 Vols. Ottawa: National Museums of Canada, Publications in Ethnology, Number 6 (1 and 2).

McClellan, Catharine. 1970. *The Girl Who Married the Bear. A Masterpiece of Indian Oral Tradition.* Ottawa: National Museum of Man, Publications in Ethnology, No. 2.

Melchiori, Paula. 2007. "From Forced Gifts to Free Gifts." *Women and the Gift Economy. A Radically Different Worldview is Possible.* Ed. Genevieve Vaughan. Toronto: Inanna Publications and Education Inc. 318-327.

Merchant, Carolyn. 1989. *The Death of Nature: Women, Ecology and the Scientific Revolution.* c1980. New York: Harper and Row.

Meyer, Leroy N. and Tony Ramirez. 1996. "'Wakinyan Hotan': The Thunderbeings Call Out. The Inscrutability of Lakota/Dakota Metaphysics." *From Our Eyes. Learning from Indigenous Peoples*. Ed. Sylvia O'Meara and Douglas A. West. Toronto: Garamond Press. 89-105.

Miedzien, Myriam. 1991. *Boys Will Be Boys: Breaking the Link Between Masculinity and Violence*. New York: Double Day.

Miettinen, Timo. 2000. *Kymenlaakson kalliomaalaukset (Rock Paintings in Kymenlaakso)*. Kotka: Kymenlaakson maakuntamuseo.

Moore, Henrietta L. 1988. *Feminism and Anthropology*. Oxford: Polity Press.

Mulvey, Laura. 1989. "Visual Pleasure and Narrative Cinema." *Visual and Other Pleasures*. Bloomington: Indiana University Press. 14-26.

Nagl-Docekal, Herta. 2000. *Continental Philosophy in Feminist Perspective: Re-Reading the Canon in German*. University Park: Pennsylvania State University Press.

O'Brien, Mary. 1983. *The Politics of Reproduction*. 1981. Boston: Routledge and Kegan Paul.

Ó Catháin, Séamas. 1995. *The Festival of Brigit. Celtic Goddess and Holy Woman*. Dublin: Dundalgan Press.

Owen, Lara. 1998. *Honoring Menstruation: A Time of Self-Renewal*. Freedom, California: The Crossing Press, 1998.

Paproth, Hans-Joachim. 1976. *Studien über das Bären Zeresischen Völkern (Studies on the Bear Ceremonial)*. Uppsala: Skrifter utgivna av Religionshistoriska institutionen i Uppsala 15.

Pentikäinen, Juha. 2007. *Golden King of the Forest: The Lore of the Northern Bear*. Trans. and ed. Clive Tolley. Helsinki: Etnika, Saarijärven Offset Ltd.

Pentikäinen, Juha and Timo Miettinen. 2006. *Pyhän merkkejä kivessä (Signs of the Sacred in Rocks)*. Helsinki: Etnika, Atena.

Phipps. W. E. 1976. "Eve and Pandora Contrasted." *Theology Today* 45 (11): 34-48.

Plumwood, Val. 2003. "Feminisma y ecología—¿Artemisa versus Gaia? (Feminism and Ecology—Artemis vs. Gaia?)." *Mujeres y Ecología: Historia, Pensamiento, Sociedad*. Proceedings of the Women and Ecology Symposium, Madrid, March 23-24th, 2001. Coords. Maria Luisa Cavana, Alicia Puleo, Cristina Segura. Madrid: Asociación Cultural Al-Mudayna, Colección LAYA. 53-107.

Plumwood, Val. 2001. *Environmental Culture: The Ecological Crisis of Reason*. London: Routledge.

Plumwood, Val. 1993. *Feminism and the Mastery of Nature*. New York: Routledge.

Pratt, Annis. 1994. *Dancing with the Goddesses*. Bloomington: Indiana University Press.

Pratt, Annis. 1987. "Affairs with Bears: Some Notes Towards Feminist Archetypal Hypotheses for Canadian Literature." *Gynocritics/la Gynocritique*. Ed. Barbara Godard. Toronto: ECW Press. 167-179.

Quick-to-see Smith. 1993. *First Nations Perspectives On Cultural Practice: Essays*. Ed. Caffyn Kelley. North Vancouver: Gallerie Women Artists' Monographs Gallerie Publications. 64-69.

Reischl, Helga. 2004. "Who is Kallisto? Semiotic and Discursive Comparisons of Texts about Bears, Women, and Wolves." Diss. Humboldt University, 2004.

Richlin, Amy. 1993. "The Ethnographer's Dilemma and the Dream of a Lost Golden Age." *Feminist Theory and the Classics.* Eds. Nancy Sorkin Rabinowitz and Amy Richlin. New York: Routledge. 272-303.

Rockwell, David. 1991. *Giving Voice to Bear.* Toronto: Roberts Rinehart.

Rosaldo, Michelle Zimbalist. 1980. "The Use and Abuse of Anthropology: Reflections on Feminism and Cross-Cultural Understanding." *Signs* 5(3): 389-417.

Ruether, Rosemary Radford. 1992. *Gaia and God: An Ecofeminist Theology of Earth Healing.* San Francisco: Harper.

Salleh, Ariel. 1997. *Ecofeminism as Politics: Nature, Marx and the Postmodern.* London: Zed Books.

Sanday, Peggy Reeves. 1998. "Matriarchy as a Socio-Cultural Form. An Old Debate in New Form." Paper presented at the 16th Congress of the Indo-Pacific Association, Melaka, Malaysia, July 1-7. Online < http://www.sas.upenn. edu/~psanday/matri.html>.

Sanday, Peggy Reeves. 1981. *Female Power and Male Dominance: On the Origins of Sexual Inequality.* Cambridge: Cambridge University Press.

Sarmela, Matti. 1994. *Suomen perinneatlas (Traditional Finnish Cartography).* Helsinki: Soumalaisen Kirjallisuuden Seura.

Sarmela, Matti. 1993. "Minkälainen on kulttuurimme tausta? (What is the Background of our Culture Like?" *Mitä on suomalaisuus? (What is Finnishness?).* Ed. Teppo Korhonen. Helsinki: Suomen Antropologinen Seura.

Sarmela, Matti. 1991. "Karhu ihmisen ymparistössä (Bear in the Human Environment)." *Kolme on Kovaa Sanaa. Kirjoituksia Kansanperinteestä (Three Tough Words: Writings on Folk Tradition).* Eds. Pekka Laaksonen; Sirkka-Lisa Mettomäkki. Jyväskylä: Suomen Kirjallisuuden Seura. 209-250. Online: <www.kolumbus. fi/matti.sarmela/karhu.htm>.

Sarmela, Matti. 1984a. "Metsän kuninkaan kuolema (The Death of the King of the Forest." Ed. Heikki Kirkinen. *Sukupolvien perintö. 1. Talonpoikaiskulttuurin juuret (The Legacy of Generations: The Roots of Peasant Culture).* Eds. Heikki Kirkinen, Toivo Hakamäki, Martti Linkola, Arno Rautavaara. Helsinki: Kirjayhtymnä. 155-261.

Sarmela, Matti. 1984b. *Eräkauden henkinen perintö. Sukupolvien perintö I (The Spiritual Heritage of the Early Period: The Roots of Peasant Culture).* Helsinki: Kirjayhtymnä.

Sarmela, Matti. 1983. "The Finnish Bear-Hunting Drama." *Suomalais-ugrilaisen seuran toimituksia* 83: 283-296.

Schmidt, Eva. 1989. "Bear Cult and Mythology of the Northern Ob-Ugrians." *Uralic Mythology and Folklore.* Eds. M. Hoppál and Juha Pentikäinen. Budapest/Helsinki: Ethnological Uralica 1.

Schrift, Alan D., ed. 1997. *The Logic of the Gift: Toward and Ethic of Generosity.* New York: Routledge.

Shepard, Paul and Barry Sanders. 1985. *The Sacred Paw: The Bear in Nature, Myth and Literature.* New York: Viking Penguin, 1985.

Simma, Paul-Anders, dir. *Guovza* (Bear) [Film]. Prod. Tuomainen, Hannu. Somerniemi, Finland: Cinemaker Oy, 1994.

Sjöö, Monica. 1992. *Return of the Dark/Light Mother or New Age Armageddon? Towards a Feminist Vision of the Future.* London: The Women's Press.

Suomen Kansan Vanhat Runot (SKVR) (*Ancient Poems of the Finnish People*). *I–XIVII.* 1908-48. Suomalaisen Kirjallisuuden Seuran kansanrunousarkiston kokoelmat. Suomalaisen karhuperinteen primaarilähteet. Suomen Kirjallisuuden Seura (Finnish Literature Society's Folklore Archives).

Sourvinou-Inwood, Christiane. 1988. *Studies in Girls' Transitions: Aspects of the Arkteia and Age Representation in Attic Iconography.* Athens: Kardamitsa.

Speck, Frank, and Jesse Moses. 1945. *The Celestial Bear Comes Down To Earth: The Bear Sacrifice Ceremony of the Munsee-Mahican in Canada as Related by Nekatcit.* Scientific Publication no. 7. Reading, PA: Reading Public Museum and Art Gallery.

Stark-Arola, Laura. 1994. *Magic, Body and Social Order: The Construction of Gender Through Women's Private Rituals in Traditional Finland.* Helsinki: Studia Fennica Folkloristica 5, Finnish Literature Society.

Stark-Arola, Laura. 1993. "Minä olen suuri susi, kaikki muut lampahaita: sudet ja karhut yhteiskunnan ulkopuolisten ihmisten symboleina (I Am a Great Wolf, Everyone Else a Lamb: Wolves and Bears as Symbols of Humans Outside of Society)." *Metsä ja Metsän Viljaa. Kalevalaseuran Vuosikirja* 73 (1993): 103-110.

Tacitus, Cornelius. 1942. "Germany and its Tribes." *Complete Works of Tacitus.* Trans. Alfred John Church and William Jackson Brodribb. Ed. Moses Hadas. New York: Random House, Inc. Chapter 46.

Tanner, Adrian. 1979. *Bringing Home Animals: Religious Ideology and Mode of Production of the Mistassini Cree Hunters.* London: C. Hurst.

Tarkka, Lotte. 1994. "Other Worlds: Symbolism, Dialogue and Gender in Karelian Oral Poetry." *Songs Beyond the Kaleval.* Eds. Anna-Leena Siikala and Sinikka Vakimo. *Songs Beyond the Kalevala.* Helsinki: Suomen Kirjallisuuden seura. 250-301.

Uusitalo, Leena. 1997. *Björnceremonialismen i Finland. Fortsättningskurs i religionshistoria. Höstterminen.* Stockholm: Religionshistoriska Institutionen. Stockholms universitet, 1997.

Vaughan, Genevieve. 2007. *Women and the Gift Economy: A Radically Different Worldview is Possible.* Toronto: Inanna Publications and Education Inc.

Vaughan, Genevieve. 2006. "Epistemology and Gender: Knowledge as Gratitude." *Homo Donans.* Online: <www.gift-economy.com>.

Vaughan, Genevieve, ed. 2004a. *Il Dono/The Gift: A Feminist Analysis.* Special issue of *Athanor: Semiotica, Filosofia, Arte, Letteratura* 15 (8).

Vaughan, Genevieve. 2004b. "The Exemplar and the Gift." *Semiotica* 148 (4): 93-118.

Vaughan, Genevieve. 2000. *36 Steps to the Gift Economy.* Austin, TX: Anomaly Press.

Vaughan, Genevieve. 1997. *For-Giving: A Feminist Criticism of Exchange.* Texas:

Plainview/Anomaly Press, 1997.

von Werlhof, Claudia, et al. 2003. *Die Diskriminierung der Matriarchatsforschung. Eine moderne Hexenjagd.* Bern: Amalia.

Walker, Barbara. 1983. *The Woman's Encyclopaedia of Myths and Secrets.* New York: Harper and Row.

Wall, Kathleen. 1988. *The Callisto Myth from Ovid to Atwood Initiation and Rape in Literature.* Montreal/Kingston: McGill-Queen's University Press.

Warkentin, Raija, Kaarina Kailo, Kaarina and Jorma Halonen, eds. 2005. *Sweating with the Finns: Sauna Stories from Canada.* Thunder Bay: Lakehead University, Centre for Northern Studies.

Winant, H. 1990. "Gayatri Spivak on the Politics of the Subaltern." *Socialist Review* 20: 81-97.

Wolfenstein, Eugen Victor. 1993. "Mr. Moneybags Meets the Rat Man: Marx and Freud on the Meaning of Money." *International Society of Political Psychology, Special Issue: Political Theory and Political Psychology* 14 (2): 279-308.

Wyschogrod, Edith, Jean-Joseph Goux and Eric Boynton, eds. 2002. *The Enigma of Gift and Sacrifice.* New York: Fordham University Press.

Elina Helander-Renvall, "The Bear," acrylic on paper, 21 x 14.8 cm, 2007.

ELINA HELANDER-RENVALL

"Váisi," the Sacred Wild

Transformation and Dreaming in the Sami Cultural Context

The Sami regard humans, animals, and spirits as equal partners of a relationship. They extend their notions of equality and respect to all aspects of nature, including the spiritual and metaphysical aspects (Rochon 1993: 58). The Sami culture is thus animistic in the sense that there is no clear border between spirit and matter, and that all beings and things in nature are considered to have a soul or spirit. Animism credits natural phenomena with spirit and soul, and attributes life to such phenomena as trees, thunder, or celestial bodies (Bird-David 2002: 74). It has been defined as "as an ontology that postulates a social character to relations between humans and non-humans: the space between nature and society is itself social" (de Castro 2004: 481). More recently, animism has become a term to describe "a style of worldview that recognizes the personhood of many beings with whom humans share this world" (Harvey 2006: 205).[1] As one Sami reindeer herder in Sweden explained to researcher Tim Rochon (1993) "I am part of the forests and the mountains" (46). The Sami, therefore, do not stand apart from nature; instead, they regard themselves as an inherent part of her. As we shall see in this article, the Sami anthropomorphize animals and nature, regarding other (non-human) life forms as part of a global "we" (Bird-David 2002: 77). In the broadest sense, then, the Sami ascribe human characteristics to nonhumans, natural and supernatural phenomena and events (Guthrie 1997: 493). The Sami word, *ealli* (animal, game) means "alive, living." For the Sami, animals are beings who are "alive" (Ingold 2000: 134) and deities, stars, planets, rocks, and even sickness can manifest as persons. As Sami artist and shaman, Nils-Aslak Valkeapää (1994) explains in a poem[2]: "we have lived here from generation to generation ... when they come they will find this land, us, and *we are* stones, plants, animals, fish, water, wind, earth, sky..." (n.p. [my emphasis]). Jeannette Armstrong (2007) gives expression to similar thinking from the point of view of the Okanagan people in British Columbia. "Our word for people, for humanity, for human beings, is difficult to say without talking about connection to nature. When we say the Okanagan word for ourselves, we are actually saying 'the ones who are dream and land together'" (35).[3]

The Sami culture is also closely connected to the practice of shamanism. Many modern definitions of shamanism are based on the ideas forwarded by Mircéa

Eliade (1972) who describes shamanism as "one of the archaic techniques of ec-stacy—at once mysticism, magic, and "religion" in the broadest sense of the term" (xix). Sami shamanism can be defined as an ecstatic religious complex with trance, drum, song, and help from spirits as its main elements (Bäckman and Hultkrantz 1978). The Sami shaman is a visionary, a healer, a seer, and an expert on ecstasy. Furthermore, the shaman is an individual who personally seeks sources of the sacred (Beck and Walters 1977: 104). This may take place while soul-journey-ing in "non-ordinary reality" (Harner 1990). The Sami shaman, *noaidi*, is also nomadic "knower" aware that coming-to-knowing takes place in many different ways and situations (Helander 2004: 555). In addition to all of the above, I sug-gest that knowing how to perceive other realities and how to gain power from the earth and other natural elements, Sami shamans, as members of society, give service to others (Helander 1997: 87).[4] Similar thoughts are forwarded by Alberto Villoldo and Stanley Krippner (1986) who state that shamanism "is an attitude, a discipline, and a state of mind that emphasizes the loving care and concern of oneself, one's family, one's community, and one's environment" (85).

Dreaming is an integral aspect of Sami shamanism and therefore an important element in the articulation of Sami sacred and daily life (Siri 1998; Nergård 2006). Dreams, in the Sami context, are embedded in daily life, similar to the practices of the Aborigines of Australia, where "there seems to be a grand circulation of activity between the waking world and the Dreaming ... [and where] even the dreams of animals are made manifest" (Smoley 1992: 16). Thus, the dream dimension is as real as life when awake (Deloria 2006). It is common in Sami society to share dreams, *niehku*, with family members, close friends, and others.[5] My parents, for instance, used to discuss their dreams while drinking their morning coffee. Sami shaman, Aslakka Siiversen Siiri from Kautokeino, Northern Norway, believed that all people move in the realm of spirits but not all people know that they do. As soon as they fall asleep, he said, "they belong to the world of spirits and they can move around and talk to all beings they want to talk to"[6] (qtd. in Therman 1940: 240). If it is true, as explained by Fred Alan Wolf (1991, 1992), that the life humans live arises from the realm where dreams and shamanic experiences dwell, then it is important to attend to what lies beyond our waking life. By nar-rowing the spaces for cultural knowledge, the ability to know and learn things about the world we live in is hindered. In this sense, knowledge is limited and, therefore, subjected to power in general, which may discount alternate ways of knowing the world.[7]

In this article, I will elaborate on the Sami belief system and worldview that is based on an understanding of the world as a complex web of life, in which we meet animated beings and share intersubjective, reciprocal relations that sustain all life on earth. I will also show the way in which awareness of messages from other beings in altered states can significantly impact our lives in the postmodern world. However, as May-Lisbeth Myrhaug (1997) states, "all knowledge of Sami belief and world picture has been mediated from men to men" (116). Denying Indigenous, and female spirituality is a colonial act intended to disempower minorities and other oppressed groups (Smith 1999; Porsanger 2004). Assertions of (colonial) power systems are not limited to the political realm; the denial of cultural practices and knowledge systems are also linked to "power-over" strategies of domination and oppression (Foucault 1980). Indigenous female spirituality, with its expanded and inward ways of knowing, has an important role to play here (Noble 1993; Bäckman 2000). Following Jorunn Eikjok and Inger Birkeland (2004), I believe it is important to bring forth the views of both women and men with respect to our natural environment in order to avoid attitudes that subordinate nature. It is within these contexts that I will explore a bear dream that belongs to a series of dreams I had during 1999-2001, aiming with this paper to contribute to discussions relating to Indigenous and western ways of knowing and being.

Mythic Discourse

The Sami believe that land, animals, and humans, and the spirits that govern them have a connection to each other. According to the Sami worldview, humans and non-humans are interrelated through intersubjective co-existence in life. This interrelationship is seen as having an impact on one's character and actions. Nils Oskal (1995) describes, for example, the Sami concept of "reindeer luck." He argues that for a Sami reindeer herder to be successful in his herding activities, he must honour the powers of nature, especially the grazing lands, and the spirits dwelling there (132-149). There are certain rules to follow. For example, it is important for herders to negotiate with spirits for permission to use a particular location for herding. The resting and dwelling places of reindeer, *livvasadji*, are sacred, and it is not permitted to swear or curse when situated there (Eira Buljo 2002: 14). Through talking to and listening to the lands and the spirits who protect the reindeer, the herder acknowledges them as social agents. Paul-Anders Simma, member of a reindeer herding family, says that offerings are also an important element in the acquisition of "reindeer luck," as they are linked to a deep respect for, and humble attitude toward all of nature (qtd. in Eriksson 1987).[8]

The underground spirits of the Sami tradition that dwell everywhere are called *Gufihtar*. These spirits live a similar life to humans. They are regarded by Sami as friends and, in addition, as "small gods" (Outakoski 1991: 161) who have the power to command humans. Nilla Outakoski (1991) has researched underground spirits in the modern religious context. He argues that *Gufihtar* have helped the Sami in many ways: they "offered advice, helped, gave warnings, protected and comforted" (160). Sometimes underground spirits share their wealth with people. In a 2004 interview, an elderly Sami woman living in Utsjoki, Northern Finland, told me that she made an agreement with the underground spirits "to live in a proper way and not to disturb these spirits." In return, the *Gufihtar* promised to protect and increase her reindeer.

In the Sami context, communication with spirits governs the relationships between herders and spirits, animals, and land, and this communication takes place through dreams, rituals, stories, prayers, and discussions with spirits and animals (Rochon 1993; Oskal 1995; Myrhaug 1997). These and other similar relationships are reciprocal. For instance, humans give protection to reindeer and reindeer take care of humans (Turi and Turi 1920). Nature "speaks" (Abram 1997: 116). In Jokkmokk, Sweden, a well-known Sami shaman, Nila Pirak (still living at the beginning of the twentieth century), used to talk to wolves and was said to be able to keep a wolf pack away from reindeer (Eriksson 1987: 9; see also Pirak 1983; Turi 1978: 84). When wolves threaten reindeer, a herder can calm the reindeer down by talking to them (Itkonen 1948: 95). It is believed that reindeer like people who communicate with them (Itkonen 1948: 105). Aslakka Siiversen Siiri, also a Sami shaman, used to discuss matters with the dead (Therman 1940: 237), but if spirits were evil he had to use "rough language" to communicate with them (238). In the Southern Sami language there is a specific verb, *soedattet* (to talk, to discuss with the dead), which is used when talking about people who have the ability to talk to the dead in a such a way that the dead answer (Sjulsson 1979: 95). *Hålet* (to speak) refers to talking with living beings (92). Nils-Aslak Valkeapää was famous for being able to talk to birds. Referring to his childhood, he explains: "I understood the language of the birds better than I understood the language of the human being" (qtd. in Helander and Kailo 1998: 93). Thus, as Graham Harvey (2006) claims, "Animist relationality is an all-round, all encompassing sociality" (210).

Robin Ridington (1988) writes that mythic beings of the Ojibwa culture are as much causal agents as are the physical instruments of causality (see also Hallowell 2002). He notes that "in native theory, an individual's power is believed to reflect his or her reciprocity, both with supernatural creatures, and with other humans" (104). The relationship of a hunter with the game is thus interpersonal (101). Naskapi hunters experience a powerful transformation in their contact with animals. This communication or sharing of an experience of transformation takes place in a dream-state (Speck cited in Ridington 1988: 99).

Communication between humans and spirits/animals can be referred to as "mythic discourse." According to Lee Irwin (1994), mythic discourse, which involves processes of interpersonal communication, is based on a religious worldview. Mythic discourse uses stories, memories, intuition, dreams, and performance to "recreate memorable, foundational events in a context of social solidarity for the purpose of explicating similar or related events" (185). Mythic discourse is open-ended and multi-voiced (Siikala 1994: 49). In Sami storytelling tradition, there are two levels of mythic discourse: the first level is at the everyday level and is easily understood by all listeners. The second, deeper level is a location that is understood by those who have a personal relationship with spirits and/or animals (Gaski 1997: 15). These levels are dimensions without reference to the "conscious" or the "unconcious." The deeper, inward, expanding level of mythic discourse is something that shamans in particular make use of in their learning, and the method through which shamans acquire knowledge (Siikala 1994: 49-51). During earlier periods of colonization, Sami directed messages of resistance to each other by using these deeper levels of communication (Gaski 1997).

Mythic discourse includes manifestation of personal empowerment and its public expression deeply affects people and other beings (Irvin 1994: 186; Hallowell 2002: 21). The shamanic articulation and performance, however, may take different paths in modern contexts (Eriksson 2002). For instance, Nils-Aslak Valkeapää has shared his experiences as a shaman and his shamanic wisdom with wide circles of people in his book *The Sun, My Father* (1997) and enhanced cultural awareness and dynamics among the Sami people, helping them to reach collective cultural consciousness (Helander 2004). Moreover, Rane Willerslev (2007) has shown that the Siberian hunters communicate even today with spirits in the same way as shamans. Mythic discourse thus helps people in their daily activities. Sami hunter Aslak Aikio explains that a hunter has a way of knowing things that some may call instinct but might be something else: "I don't know what it is. At night I get this feeling that now I must go fast to this place and when I get there, there is an otter of course" (qtd. in Mustonen and Salin 2004: 312).

Dreaming

As indicated earlier, according to the Sami tradition, it is important to pay attention to dreams. For instance, the name of a child was, and in many cases is still, received through dreams (Thomassen 1999: 151). Dreams also may provide motivation for the dreamer to follow a spiritual path. Even today, some Sami healers become aware of their abilities, knowledge, and calling through dream states (Sande and Winterfeldt 1993; Helander 2000; Nergård 2006). Sami hunters and fishermen receive relevant information through their dreams (Helander 2004), learning in dreams which fishhook should be used, where the fish will bite, or where the moose will travel during hunting season. For the Sami, the altered dreaming state and the waking state are contained in one and the same cosmic wholeness. A Sea Sami woman, Vigdis Siri (1998), known for her handicrafts, dreamt about a wooden eagle with a human carved on it, and a sun made of wood. The dream was based on an ancient Sami folktale but it took her on a modern journey. She read many books and did lots of research and thinking until she understood the dream's contents and meaning. The knowledge she needed to apply to her life appeared to her through the teachings of this shamanic dream (Helander 2004: 556).

Dreams therefore also function as keys to the possibilities in one's own life (Rinpoche 1998: 66). Through dreams, a person can discover who they are and what they should be doing (Irwin 1994: 18), future possibilities, and any obstacles they might face. In dreams this happens because there are none of the conceptual limitations that a person is hindered by when awake (Irwin 1994: 9). "In dreams, everything is allowed" (Khariditi 2001: 168). In Sami tradition, dreams are also messages from the ancestors and spirits.

Dreaming shapes and is shaped by mythic discourse (Thomassen 1999: 151). In the Sami context, a dreamer must structure their dream before revealing it to others. The dream is transformed into a conceptual form. The dreamer exploits the reality of the dream and places its contents in a story that will be told to other members of the local community, in their storytelling tradition. Sami writer Kerttu Vuolab states, "All the things that we were taught were through a story" (qtd. in Helander and Kailo 1988: 50). According to D. Jean Collins (1992), "Early societies emphasized collective dreamwork; the dreamer's experiences in the dream world were to enhance and sustain the harmonious operation of the collective" (57), leading to a higher level of social integration because the gifts of the dream tend to unify the group. The Sami dreamer brings the self, and her/his experience, into a "public"[9] view. Such an approach helps the individual Sami enter a collective dream state in which they may receive help for personal and community-related problems. Writing in Sami tradition is also a form of (dream) "storytelling" (Damm 1993: 106). Valkeapää (1997) was very conscious of the power of language, symbols, and images as expressions and mediators of cultural traditions (Helander and Kailo 1988: 87-102).

Inside Sami circles, in some cases, the processing of a dream can take many years, therefore, dreams are not always shared with the community members immediately after the dreaming occurs. In addition to its private aspects, a dream has general aspects that are familiar for a dreamer from local storytelling traditions. Sami that are conscious of their traditions are able to link their dream symbols to core elements (Nergård 2006) within their traditions by listening to and telling stories. Stories have a cultural form or manifestation that a listener of the same cultural circle will understand. What dreams and stories tell the Sami is usually already part of their cultural system and worldview. Many times, Sami listeners will add something to a dreamer's or a storyteller's statement (Demant Hatt 1922; Pirak 1983: 62; Nergård 2006: 222). By doing so, they take part in the patterning of a story and in the interpretation of its contents (cf. Helander 1997: 86; Helander 2004: 554). For me, this openness to epistemic labouring makes dreamwork dynamic and reflexive. Some Sami analyze dreams with the aid of symbols as well, whereby the meaning of a dream can sometimes be linked to its opposite. For instance, if one is afraid in a dream, once awake the dream may point to success in life (Bongo 1998: 7).

Dreams appear to each person in different ways. Sami believe dreams have a private component, a message, a solution to a problem, and/or some sort of practical wisdom. These parts of the dream are normally kept secret (Nergård 2006: 209) as overt activity in relation to dreams can duplicate problems (if there are any) of a person or a local society, or can spoil the mythic discourse that is taking place. Here, Christianity also has an impact and may disturb such discourses (Eriksson 1987: 17-26).

Bear in Sami Tradition: The Place of Grounding

For the Sami, bear, *guovža*, is an animal that according to Louise Bäckman (2000) belongs to the realm of the sacred, in Southern Sami, *bissie* (217). Bear thus has strong connections to the realm of gods (Bäckman 2000; Pentikäinen 2007). All animals have their own inherent dignity that must be respected (Oskal 1995, 166-167). Many Sami honour bears and are inspired by the bear. For instance, the whistling of bear is included in some traditional Sami songs, bear teeth are used as amulets and healing items, and a Sami female singer, Tiina Aikio, uses a bearskin as clothing in public song performances. The bear also stimulates human erotic fantasies (Bäckman 2000: 225). *Runtamaš* is a bear-shaped female spirit who provides sexual teachings to humans in the forests; at the same time, however, she does not approve of sexual promiscuity.

The bear is a symbol of strength, wisdom, and courage. Juha Pentikäinen (2007) writes that "the bear was the most powerful feature of the natural world, with whom men wished to be in a good relationship, but whose powers they at the same time wished to share; in ritual this power of the bear became part of the Samis' own power" (48). Sami researcher Harald Gaski (1985) claims that the bear has some understanding of Sami family bonds. The bear thus prefers to fight with several men from unrelated families instead of fighting with two brothers (Turi 1987). Inherent in this animistic attitude is a person's desire to acquire superhuman powers, or at the least, extraordinary human strength in order to be able to have an impact on what happens in one's life (Drake 1979: 264). Bear blood and parts of bear were traditionally used as medicine in order to gain the powers of the bear. In the contemporary Sami society, there are still some individuals who, in order to acquire bear power, use bear medicine such as chewing on bear penis bones (Bornstein 2002).

Southern Sami professor Louise Bäckman (2000) argues that the she-bear is a symbol of woman as an independent individual. In many Arctic areas, the she-bear's role is also that of Mother Earth, the representation of spiritual womanhood. Traditionally Sami used to organize Bear ceremonials after a bear hunt to honour the bear and to convince bear that s/he can return safely from the realm of the dead. Detailed information about ancient Bear ceremonials can be found in descriptions of Bear feasts by Pehr Fjellström (1755; see also Schefferus 1674). These descriptions, by male scholars and writers, tend to be focused on role of men, including male shamans, in the ceremonials. We know that women and female spirits assisted male shamans in their roles as *shjarak* and *rudok* (Myrhaug 1997: 71), although there is no evidence to suggest they participated in Bear ceremonials. *Shjarak* were Sami women who had shamanic knowledge. They attended other Sami shaman ceremonials dressed in their finest clothing. *Rudok* were female spirits visible only to the shaman, and possibly also to the *shjarak* (Myrhaug 1997: 71). *Rudok* were often in the company of *årja*, also a female spirit. Louise Bäckman (2000) indicates that the Bear ceremonial was originally about the marriage between a bear and a human (see Kaarina Kailo's close examination of the role of women in bear ceremonials in this volume).

Many cultures bear witness to acts of human/animal transformation, through which humans transform themselves into a bear, or a bear into a human (Rock-

Elina Helander-Renvall, "Wolverine and Reindeer," acrylic on paper, 21 x 14.8 cm, 2007.

well 1991: 71-73; Pentikäinen 2007: 110-112). According to Sami traditions, a shaman, *noaidi*, or even an ordinary person, *olmmoš*, can transform her/himself into a bear (Itkonen 1948: 364). Further, Western Sami believed that Eastern Sami and bears belong to the same family-group. According to Itkonen (1948), the female ancestor of the Skolt Sami[10] was thought to be a Sami woman who wintered with a he-bear (364). Sami believe one has to be careful when in contact with a bear or when transformation takes place. There is a Sami story (Turi 1987: 93) according to which a human female once lived the whole winter with a male bear. The underground spirits provided her with food. She became pregnant and gave birth to a baby boy who had one bear paw in addition to one human hand. There is another story about an Eastern Sami couple who transformed themselves into bears because they thought that if they did so, their family would not need so much to eat. Their sons, however, came to their den before they managed to transform themselves back. Something went wrong and the husband was killed and one of the women's feet remained a bear paw (see Aikio and Aikio 1978: 108). The single bear paw gives expression to the arbitrary status of humans vis-à-vis animals and vice-versa, and as I see it, it signifies intersubjectivity between humans and non-humans.

According to Sami beliefs, the bear knows everything and can understand Sami language. Bears have a soul that makes them living, thinking, perceiving beings (Bäckman 1981: 47). This is one of the reasons why the Sami had a special linguistic code or collection of words that were used when talking about the bear. Indeed, uttering the word *guovža* (bear) was to be avoided. Instead, words such as grandfather, sacred game, and hill-manure were used when talking about the bear. These alternate words for bear are used in everyday life (a practice that continues today) and not only in the context of Bear ceremonials (Gaski 1985: 21). The names that are given to the bear are often associated with land, forest, and even an old fur coat. These descriptions refer to common interests and ways of interacting between humans and bears. Specific names also acknowledge the particular status of the bear in nature (Drake 1979: 329). *Váisi* means the "sacred wild." Furthermore, certain names signify intimacy and esteem. Traditionally, the Sami have held their elders in high esteem. Sami words such as *muodda-áddjá, muedd-aja*, and *muoddak* refer to a bear wearing an old fur coat. *Áddjá (Aja, grandfather)* is used for older men when one wishes to acknowledge them with honour (Tomasson 1988: 42), thus linking them to the highly regarded and respected bear. The word *muoddá* (fur coat), in combination with other words, refers to Sami elders.

For Sami, language is the lifeline of their culture. Thus, certain terms or names are avoided if deemed disrespectful or dangerous. For example, wolves can be dangerous if the wrong word is used to refer to them (Drake 1979: 329). Southern Sami used to say that they aim to "eat" reindeer rather than saying that they are going to slaughter a reindeer (Drake 1979: 55). My mother also used to talk about "big meat" and "big reindeer" when referring to moose during hunting season. The intentions of humans (to hunt) were not voiced. To

Elina Helander-Renvall, "Night Wanderer," acrylic on paper, 21 x 14.8 cm, 2007.

emphasize that reindeer are as valued as they are, is regarded as important (Oskal 1995). This esteem is shown by keeping reindeer in a reindeer herd that are not needed for food or that have no economic value. On the other hand, one also cherishes those animals that are productive, such as female reindeer with calves (Fjellström 1985: 169).

Northern Sami also have many names for reindeer that describe their nature such as, among others, *láikkan* (lazy), *gieris* (loving), *siivu* (quiet), and *duhkoraddi* (playful) (Itkonen 1948). The same descriptions can, in many instances, be used for people! Other animals are described in similar ways. For example, in Southern Sami a wolverine is referred to as *saurak vaisje*, a persistent beast (Drake 1979: 345) because they never tire. A bear may be called *suokok*, the fat one. Land too shares human characteristics. Johan Turi (1987) writes that lands are so beautiful that they laugh. And when people are sad all land, all stones and trees, cry with them (80). As social beings (de Castro 2004: 466), animals have conscious ways of doing things. Tomasson (1988) provides examples of reindeer who sacrifice themselves for humans, meeting humans' need for sustenance. Furthermore, Turi (1987) believes that animals have the capacity to shamanize humans (56-58). He argues, for instance, that a wolf can make a herder drowsy when she/he is watching reindeer (99). Bears can also influence humans in similar ways (Drake 1979; Sjulsson 1979).

The Sami considered the bear a wise animal. They believe that animals are teachers and for humans, they are models of how to survive. Johan Turi (1987) explains, for example, that Sami have learned much about the weather from reindeer (46). Siv Norlander-Unsgaard (1985) argues that the ancient Sami considered the bear as "a central point of life-giving force for flora, fauna and homo sapiens" (198) and concluded that Bear ceremonials were therefore joyful gatherings where people became "wise and healthy" (199). Sami also believed that bears have conscious-ness (Turi 1987: 94). If a bear happened to kill a person, it was believed that the bear was restless during the winter sleep. The Sami, however, did not generally expect bears to be dangerous (Norlander-Unsgaard 1985: 196). For Sami, there are at least three kinds of bears: an ordinary bear, a transformed human in a bear shape, and a bewitched bear. The bear is regarded as strong and fierce, but not necessarily dangerous (Thomassen 1999: 132). A bewitched bear, though, is to be treated with caution. Sami believe a bear is aware if the child inside a pregnant woman is a boy or a girl. A pregnant woman carrying a son was believed to be in danger (Åhrén 1963: 140) as bears percieve men not just as prey, but also as predators. Southern Sami people believed that the sudden appearance of a bear might frighten a pregnant woman so much that the child in her womb may be injured (Drake 1979: 251).

Bruce Cushing's research suggests that bears are attracted to women during their menstrual cycle (as they are to the blood of seals and other animals) (cited in Mys-terud 1985). Interestingly, in the Sami language, *leaibi* or *leipe* refers to menstrual blood, bear blood, and alder (chewed alder juice) (see Pirak 1933: 70; Collinder 1993: 159). For the Sami, there is no doubt about the connection between women and bears. But are women a prey for bears as has been suggested (Mysterud 1985: 61)? Or are the bears attracted to women for other reasons? According to Sami beliefs, in certain situations bears are afraid of women and even ashamed before women (Pirak 1933: 71). Generally, it is believed that the bear is very cautious regarding women and does not like to hurt them (Pirak 1933: 71).

There are many stories of humans cohabitating or collaborating with wild animals. During a series of interviews I conducted in Northern Norway during 1998-2000 inquiring about Sami customs, a former Sami reindeer herder from Sirma told me that once, when he stayed overnight in a Sami tent, a wolf suddenly showed up and remained with him in the tent throughout that night. This took place before the 1950s when there were still many wolves in the Sami north. This man believed the wolf needed protection because she/he was excluded from a wolf pack. In this context, it is important to take into account that the bear, in Sami tradition, has also an important role as *gázzi*, a helping spirit. Louise Bäckman (1975) has researched Sami assisting and guardian spirits. One of the tasks of these spirits is to bring messages to shamans and other people (116). Many believe, that *gázzi* are normally invisible but can make themselves visible in dreams (Itkonen 1948: 349).

The Sami also believe that the human soul is similar to an animal's soul (Gjessing 1953: 94). I suggest that it is the soul/spirit that unites a human to an animal (de Castro 2004: 475; Wolf 1992). Souls are perceived to continue to live long after the human/animal body dies (Bäckman 1983, 1975). Per Simma, a Sami healer, believes that "when we sleep our soul travels" (qtd. in Eriksson 2001: 68; see also Therman 1940: 240). According to a Sami shaman Aslakka Siiversen Siiri, only half of the soul/spirit can be sent on travels (Therman 1940: 239). A soul/spirit or mind of a person during sleep can be involved in discourses with other souls/spirits. By using the terms "soul," "spirit," and "mind," I mean that we have a wise self that knows the complete pattern of our lives (cf. Gerber 2000). Studies show that humans have an innate drive to seek altered states of consciousness (see Winkelman 1997: 421). During these altered states of consciousness humans can interconnect with animals and share perceptions and knowledge.

Sami believe in the existence of two souls: a body soul and a free-soul. The free soul is an immortal element, called by some "shadow" (Bäckman 1975: 160). The body-soul dies when a Sami dies, but her/his free-soul continues to live (Bäckman 1983: 32; Pentikäinen 1995: 194). The free-soul also moves when a person is asleep, in a trance, or in another altered state. The soul travels as an "out-of-body being" (Bäckman 1975: 160). According to Harald Grundström (1942) the "shadow" is lasting and independent (*"i sig självt bestående"*) and is very roughly materialized (*"mycket grovt materialiserad"*) (8). Shaman Nila Pirak soul-travelled to the Land of Death where he met his relatives, and saw the lands where he himself one day "would be reborn and work with reindeer" (Pirak 1983: 62). We can ask with Olga Khariditi (2001: 180): "how many people know their souls during their lives?"

Elina Helander-Renvall, "Center of the World," acrylic on paper, 14.8 x 10.5 cm, 1999.

My Bear Dream

While going to pick cloudberries, I approach a swamp, and see a bear eating berries. I know that a bear enjoys eating berries around autumn to prepare itself for winter. Bear eats cloudberries, blueberries, and other berries. In my dream, I am not afraid of the bear, but I ponder whether or not I should be.

Then it becomes dark, and I stand still to watch the bear, and start seeing my surroundings through the bear's eyes. I transform myself into a bear in the sense that I perceive things from the perspective of the bear. Colours become suddenly hard and harsh; the swamp crimson fire. The ground becomes dark red and reminds me of the juice of alder bark. The dusk sky shines with shades of blue and northern lights dance as in a cold winter's sky, and I realize that a bear's sight is both clear and beautiful.

I remember the bear telling me, at some other point, in another dream, about her/his connection to the northern lights and of her/his contact to stars. Now, in my dream, I stop to talk to the bear, and as I draw near her/him, I see how big and strong s/he is. In that situation, bear power seems very concrete. The bear has, of course, been eating delicacies all summer—reindeer, ants, hay, and berries. While I stand there, I see other bears high up in the sky. They are coming down.

The bear talks with me for a while and then gives me a sign to continue my walk in a specific direction. So, I leave and follow a path until I come to a market place located near a river. There I meet people who show me paintings, books for artists, artist tools, and colours. They give me advice on how to paint, shape, and colour my pictures. They show me motifs to paint. And they point to some helpful books on the table. While looking around and glancing at the paintings and other items on tables of the market place I realize that I feel empowered and I know what I have to do.

Empowerment Through Mythic Discourse

Dreams are, to a certain extent, experiences of the soul. In my dream, my spirit/ mind was transformed into the bear's mind and I was able to see, or perceive, nature in the same way as the bear of the dream. Animals may perceive humans in many ways (de Castro 1998: 470), and it is thus difficult to say with certainty how bears see their environment. Jürgen Kremer's article in this volume refers to "participatory consciousness." Kremer talks about bear and tells his story as raven and as subject of his own history, "celebrating with the bear again." An ancient Sami song, which was sung by bears after their long winter sleep, suggests some of the ways in which bears might perceive the world around them:

Awaken, my brother, na na nan-nan naa,
the sun now shines upon mountains,
the bird-song now rings upon our ears,
ants now run on the trees,
grandmothers mend seine nets,
grandfathers already store the sleds, and
boys play with arrows

According to Eduardo Viveiros de Castro (2004), shamanism refers to "the capacity evinced by some individuals to cross ontological boundaries deliberately and adopt the perspective of nonhuman subjectivities in order to administer the relations between humans and non-humans" (468). Shamanism seeks to view the world, and all the beings that are part of the world, from the perspective of that which must be known. This kind of knowledge, as related to animism, focuses primarily on relatedness, from a related point of view (Bird-David 2002: 77). Knowing turns attention to "we-ness," which absorbs differences, rather than to "otherness," which highlights differences and eclipses commonalities (96).

In my dream, I was transformed and thus able to understand the way bears perceive their surroundings. This took place through mythic discourse by which an exchange of thoughts led me to comprehend the importance of art and its potential as an agent for change. In this sense, my dream has a connection to Sami shamanism and animistic beliefs. I think that Christian de Quincey's (2008) thoughts about true intersubjectivity may shed light on the communication between myself and the bear. According to de Quincey, strong intersubjectivity "is direct subject-to-subject sharing of presence-when both (or more) subjects either mutually condition each other's sense of self, or, more strongly, mutually co-create each others's sense of self." From my point of view, the spirit/soul and mind integrate while bodies can transform themselves (de Castro 2004). At this level, it is possible to experience the abundance of knowledge and creativity.

It is important to also analyze my dream from a perspective of power as well as exploring its cultural significance. Nancy Hartsock (1983) points out that power can be understood as "energy and competence rather than dominance" (224). According to Hartsock, power can be conceptualized from a woman's perspective: for women, drawing on their own life experiences and values is a form of empowerment. My bear dream reminds me of transformative power as "the human ability not just to act but to act in concert" (Arendt 1970: 44). Furthermore, the dream affirms that power can be analyzed from the perspective of the sacredness and interconnectedness of all life. Indigenous traditions are of great importance in this context.

In my dream, I walked along the path and came to a place where different images, symbols, and items were shown to me. The Bear, the sacred being, as a *gázzi* and an acting subject, shared images and colours with me. The co-creating presence of Bear is what helped me to start painting. The artwork I have created is now public and I believe has an impact on how people understand the connection between and interrelatedness of culture and nature. My paintings speak to our traditional relationship to nature, to animals, to the earth, as one that is integral to the sustenance of all life on the planet, and that is respectful of all living beings on earth. For me, to use the words of Gabrielle Roth (1989), art is "a path in itself" and "a map to self-discovery" (9). Art also gives back to people something they have lost. Art has an integrative role in society (Radcliffe-Brown 1948: 330-341), and it is in this sense that my art hopefully contributes to reintegrating Sami belief systems and worldviews into current Sami society.

Concluding Remarks

It has taken time for me to analyze my bear dream. One reason is that I recognize that the dream comes from the realm of the sacred. As a consequence, I have nurtured my dream with care. I know that I have been given the miracle of subject-to-subject sharing of presence with Bear. The intriguing element of my dream is its focus on transformation. It is tempting for me to believe that I became the bear in order to see through the eyes of Bear. I was able, then, to view things from the perspective that I needed to "see" with and know. My dream shows that traditional Sami knowledge arises out of closeness to the land. My dream and its possible messages are, however, not intended to idealize Sami culture, nor to essentialize it through the myth of authenticity and harmony with nature (see Vadén and Tuusvuori 2007: 8). I also do not wish to portray Sami women as wise women with extraordinary powers, removed from contemporary life. What concerns me is that western society, and some parts of Indigenous societies, are in a "state of materialistic hypertrophy" (Kalweit 1988; Mander and Tauli Corpuz 2007). In this state it is easy to become subjected to an ontology and epistemology that does not understand the ways in which Sami perceive their environment and the world they live in and cohabit with others, including animals and non-human beings. As discussed by Graham Harvey (2007), western categories are not self-evident. For instance Tim Ingold (1988, 1995, 2000) and de Castro (1998) have shown that the concepts "human" and "animal" are very complex. The Sami shamanic and animistic concepts tend to blur many western (modern) concepts and they are expressed in everyday behaviours as this article bears witness to.

It is obvious, that there are differences between western and Indigenous ways of knowing, not as an us/them category, but as part of a diversity of cultures and truths. The reality of diversity creates transformative possibilities for oppressed groups in society. The western research community tends to analyze nature and society/culture as separate and autonomous entities. Recent research in anthropology, psychology, and religion shows that there is a new ontology emerging that breaks down barriers between humans/animals and culture/nature. The Sami understanding of nature constitutes a counter-example to the dichotomization of nature/culture. But Sami concepts and views have been marginalized in the educational system and in literature, and by Christian religion and western knowledge traditions. I have argued, however, that Sami reindeer herders and other Sami subsistence groups still live within a frame that can be called "animism." Nature is animated, and the human soul is believed to be similar to an animal's soul (Gjessing 1953: 94). Furthermore, animals and other beings are perceived as subjects, persons, and partners by the Sami. There is a social space between nature and society (de Castro 2004: 481). In this "borderland" (Willerslev 2007: 190), humans and non-humans articulate mutual communication and coexistence, and the differences between these two groups can be very small. Thus, absolute boundaries between humans and non-humans are non-existent.

Leroy N. Meyer and Tony Ramirez (1996) have stated that the belief system of one culture or worldview cannot be subject to truth or falsehood within another worldview (91). Understanding the nature of dissociation between a modern academic worldview and the traditional worldview of an Indigenous culture requires commitment to the integrity of Indigenous knowledge (Meyer and Ramirez 1996: 105). It is in this spirit that I have discussed here the belief systems of Sami culture, both traditional and contemporary, and the ways in which these may shape the lives of Sami today.

Paula Gunn Allen (1986) further exposes the biases of western observers who in her opinion do not understand "psychic travel," our soul-journeys, as follows:

> Western sophisticates presume that the experiences—sights, sounds, and beings encountered on psychic journeys—are imaginary and hallucinatory.... Nowhere in the literature on ceremonialism have I encountered a Western writer willing to suggest that the "spiritual and the commonplace are one." Many argue that these "hallucinations" are good, others that they are the

product of diseased minds, but none suggests that one may actually be "seated amid the rainbow." (qtd. in Kailo 1994: 71)

One reason for what Allen brings forth may be that materialist attitudes have caused westerners to "pour out the baby with the bath water" (Kalweit 1984: xiii). This can be seen as part of the colonial use of power against minorities and other oppressed groups. As Amilcar Cabral (1994) puts it: "with a strong indigenous cultural life, foreign domination cannot be sure of its perpetuation" (53). Power is thus not limited to the political realms: cultural practices and knowledge systems are linked to the accrual and maintenance of power as well (Foucalt 1980; Smith 1999).

It is also true that people often perceive a huge difference between "inner" and "outer" experiences (Kharitidi 2001: 205). Many times, only the outer events are regarded as "objective" and thus much attention is paid to them. Kharitidi suggests that people pay attention to the focus of other people's attentions. By doing so they join other people's reality. She writes, however, that the significance of reality and experience does not depend on other people supporting it, but is rather "connected with experience's ability to touch and activate the deepest patterns of transformation..." (205). The most fruitful dialogue between the mainstream science and traditional knowledge may take place individually and internally, through personal transformation, and without the need for any final proof or conquest of one particular knowledge system over the other (Knudtson and Susuki 1993: 185). This statement, however, does not exclude the need to describe and analyze things from the point of view of Indigenous people. Scholarly work needs also to relate to Indigenous women's worlds and their own interpretations of their experiences. Especially in Sami contexts, this would yield many new insights.

This paper is about one single dream, and what that dream meant to me and to the direction of my life trajectory. I have described the cultural conditions within which my dream has taken place because this approach, as I see it, has value for understanding the different knowledge/power systems that are operating here. It is not easy to produce a text about dreaming in the Sami context due to the lack of previous data. Yet, this is one research area that needs more attention. In my article, there are no definite answers given to what the relatedness of humans and non-humans in relation to the soul/spirit of all beings can mean for individual persons or societies, or for the planet as a whole. These issues demand ongoing dialogue. When I think of my bear dream, it seems quite ordinary to me. The dream is an invitation to realization of and participation in reality as it is. The waking state and the dream state are parts of the same reality. It does not matter who dreams or what the dream is about: "The 'physical' reality of the everyday life verifies what has taken place in dreams" (Deloria Jr. 2006: xxv). What works by the way of truth of my dream, is passed to others through my paintings. The Bear of my dream can also be seen as a metaphor for revealing oppression, where ever it exists, and giving voice to critical issues in Indigenous research and politics.

[1]Note that the Actor-Network Theory (ANT) assumes that the construction of reality is achieved through the interplay of different actors with equal constitutive character (Law 1999). ANT deals with "persons, things, artefacts, and events all in the same breath" (Strathern 1999: 156). These entities or actors "take their form and acquire their attributes as a result of their relations with other entities" (Law 1999: 3). Furthermore, social networks (human relations to each other) have neither "privilege nor prominence" (Latour 1998). Thus, both human and non-human actors are treated as equal partners in the network of a culture; this is integral to Sami culture. In the Sami culture, however, there are animals and spirits who at least in some situations are more powerful than humans.

[2]This translation from the Sami is made by the author of this article.

[3]The word "dream" means here "the unseen part of our existence as human beings" (Amstrong 2007: 36).

[4]It is important, nevertheless, to be aware that in the Sami society there are many kinds of shamans (Itkonen 1948; Bäckman and Hultkratz 1978; Myrhaug 1997).

[5]During 1999-2001, a period when I dreamed a lot, I had the privilege to share my dreams and paintings with a Sami woman of knowledge, Biret-Marét Kallio. I acknowledge and give thanks to her. I also honour and give thanks to my parents, Áibmijot-Jovnna and Ovllá-Per-Márgget, who are now in the spirit world. Thanks are due as well to my family, friends and colleaques.

[6]In Swedish: "*I sömnen tillhör de själva andarnas värld, och då kan man bege sig vart man vill och tala med vilka varelser man önskar.*"

[7]When Tere Vadén and Jarkko S. Tuusvuori (2007) interviewed me for the *Niin and Näin* journal of philosophy we discussed these issues. My concern with research on Sami culture is that this research has often been conducted using western methods shaped by strictly western concepts. Therefore, the truth remains outside the collected research material, and thus subjected to power. I argue that the Sami knowledge expressed in the form of storytelling (sharing of dreams) must also be taken into account.

[8]The Sami have a *šiella*-tradition, a sort of institutionalized way of sharing and giving gifts. These gifts are offered to persons, animals, land, sacred places, and nature spirits, among other things, as a gift or protective charm (Itkonen 1948).

[9]Though, not everything is told. Inga Juuso explained to me in an interview that "there are many things of which people do not want to talk about" (qtd. in Helander and Kailo 1998: 146).

[10]Skolt Sami are part of the Eastern Sami.

References

Abram, David. 1997. *The Spell of the Sensuous. Perception and Language in a More-Than-Human World.* New York: Vintage Books.

Aikio, Annukka and Samuli Aikio. 1978. *Girdinoaiddi bárdni. Sápmelaš máidnasat (The Son of the Flying Shaman: Sami Stories).* Porvoo: Werner Söderström Osakeyhtiö.

Åhrén, Jonas. 1963. *En same berättar. Sant, saga och sägen av Jonas Åhrén* (*A Sami Speaks: Truth, Story and Legend*). Östersund: Bokmalens förlag.

Allen, Paula Gunn. 1986. *The Sacred Hoop: Recovering the Feminism in American Indian Traditions.* Boston: Beacon Press.

Armstrong, Jeannette. 2007. "Community: 'Sharing One Skin'." *Paradigm Wars: Indigenous Peoples' Resistance to Globalization.* Eds. Jerry Mander and Victoria Tauli-Corpuz. San Francisco: Sierra Club Books. 35-39.

Arendt, Hannah. 1970. *On Violence.* New York: Harcourt Brace and Co.

Bäckman, Louise. 2000. "Björnen i Samisk Tradition (The Bear in the Sami Tradition)." *Samisk Etnobiologi. Människor, djur och växter i norr* (*Sami Ethnobiology: Humans, Animals and Plants in the North*). Eds. Ingvar Svanberg and Håkan Túnon. Falun: Nya Doxa. 216-226.

Bäckman, Louise. 1983. "Förfäderskult. En studie i samernas förhållande till sina avlidna (Ancestor Cults: A Study on the Relationship of the Sami to Their Deceased Ones)." *Lasta.* Ed. Elina Helander. Umeå: SáDS áigečála. 11-48.

Bäckman, Louise. 1975. *Sájva. Föreställningar om hjälp-och skyddsväsen i heliga fjäll bland samerna* (*Sájva: Conceptions of Guardian Spirits Among the Lapps*). Stockholm: Almqvist and Wiksell International.

Bäckman, Louise and Åke Hultkrantz. 1978. *Studies in Lapp Shamanism.* Stockholm: Almqvist and Wiksell International.

Beck, Peggy V. and Anna Lee Walters. 1977. *The Sacred: Ways of Knowledge, Sources of Life.* Tsaile (Navaho Nation), AZ: Navaho Community College Press.

Bird-David, Nurit. 2002. (1999) "'Animism' Revisited: Personhood, Environment, and Relational Epistemology." *Readings in Indigenous Religions.* Ed. Graham Harvey. London: Continuum. 72-105.

Bongo, Mikkel P. A. 1998. *Niegut ja nieguid čilgehusat* (*Dreams and Their Explanations*). Kárášjohka: Davvi Girji OS.

Bornstein, Anna. 2002. *Den Samiska Vandringsrösten: jag är kunskapen* (*The Sami Wanderer's Voice: I Am the Knowledge*). Stockholm: Svenska Förlaget.

Cabral, Amilcar. 1994. "National Liberation and Culture." *Colonial Discourse and Post-Colonial Theory: A Reader.* Eds. Patrick Williams and Laura Chrisman. New York: Ellis Horwood Limited and Tavistock Publications. 53-65.

Collinder, Björn. 1993. *The Lapps.* New York: Princeton University Press.

Collins, Jean D. 1992. "The Weighing of the Heart: What's the Right Use for Dreamwork Today?" *Gnosis Magazine* 92 (Winter): 56-59.

Damm, Kateri. 1993. "Dispelling and Telling: Speaking Native Realities in Maria Campbell's *Halfbreed* and Beatrice Culleton's *In Search of April Raintree.*" *Looking at the Words of Our People: First Nations Analysis of Literature.* Ed. Jeannette Amstrong. Pentincton, BC: Theytus Books Ltd. 93-114.

de Castro, Eduardo Viveiros. 2004. "Exchanging Perspectives: The Transformation of Objects into Subjects in Amerindian Ontologies." *Common Knowledge* 10 (3): 463-484.

de Castro, Eduardo Viveiros. 1998. "Cosmological Deixis and Amerindian Perspectivism." *Journal of the Royal Anthropological Institute* 4: 469-488.

de Quincey, Christian. 2008. "Wilber's Intersubjectivity." Online: <http://integralvi-sioning.org/article/php?story=cq-wilber-subjectivity>. Accessed 8 Feb. 2008.

Deloria Jr., Vine. 2006. *The World We Used to Live In: Remembering the Powers of the Medicine Men.* Golden, CO: Fulcrum Publishing.

Demant Hatt, Emilie. 1922. *Ved Ilden. Eventyr og Historier fra Lapland (At the Fireplace. Tales and Stories from Lapland).* Köbenhavn and Stockholm: J. H. Schultz Forlag A/S. A.-B. Nordiska Bokhandeln.

Drake, Sigrid. 1979. *Västerbottens Lapparna (The Lapps in Västerbotten).* Umeå: Två Bokförläggare Bokförlag.

Eikjok, Jorunn and Inger Birkeland. 2004. "Natur, kjönn og kultur: om behovet for dokumentasjon av samisk naturforståelse i et kjönnsperspektiv (Nature, Gender and Culture: Regarding the Need for the Documentation of Sami Understanding of Nature in Relation to Gender)." *Samiska landskapsstudier (Sami Landscape Studies).* Ed. Lars Magne Andreasson. Diedut 5. Guovdageaidnu: Sámi Instituhtta. 58-71.

Eira Buljo, Karen Marie. 2002. "Mu kultureanadagat (My Cultural Landscapes)." *Samisk landskap og Agenda 21. Kultur, naering, miljövern og demokrati (Sami Landscape and Agenda 21: Culture, Economy, the Protection of Nature and Democracy).* Ed. Svanhild Andersen. Diedut 1. Guovdageaidnu: Sámi Instituhtta. 136-149.

Eliade, Mircéa. 1972. *Shamanism: Archaic Techniques of Ecstacy.* Princeton: Bollingen Series.

Eriksson, Jörgen I. 2002. *Samisk Shamanism (Sami Shamanism).* Köpenhamn: h:strön-Text & Kultur.

Eriksson, Jörgen I. 2001. *Blodstämmare, handpåläggare. Folklig läkekosnt och magi i Tornedalen och Lappland (Bloodstaunchers, Healers with Hands: Folk Healing and Magic in Tornevalley and Lapland).* Umeå: h:strön-Text and Kultur.

Eriksson, Jörgen I. 1987. *Samisk Shamanism (Sami Shamanism).* Stockholm: Gimle.

Fjellström, Pehr. 1755. *Kort Berättelse om Lapparnas Björna-fänge samt Deras der wid brukade widskepelser (A Short Account of the Bear Hunt of the Lapps and their Superstitions).* Stockholm: Wildiska Tryckeriet.

Fjellström, Phebe. 1985. *Samernas samhälle i tradition och nutid (Sami Traditional and Contemporary Society.)* Stockholm: Nordstedts.

Foucault, Michel. 1980. *Power/Knowledge: Selected Interviews and Other Writings 1972-1977.* New York: Pantheon.

Gaski, Harald. 1997. *In the Shadow of the Midnight Sun.* Seattle: University of Washington.

Gaski, Harald. 1985. "Björnen förstår ikke metaforer (The Bear Does Not Understand Metaphors)." *Tidsskrift for nordnorsk natur og kultur* 5 (156): 20-23.

Gerber, Richard. 2000. *Vibrational Medicine for the 21st Century: The Complete Guide to Energy Healing and Spiritual Transformation.* New York: HarperCollins.

Gjessing, Gutorm. 1953. *Sjamanistisk og laestadiansk ekstase hos samene (Shamanic and Laestadian Ecstasy Among the Sami).* Oslo: Studia Septentrionalia.

Grundström, Harald. 1942. "Tro och övertro bland lapparna (Belief and Superstition Among the Lapps)." *Svenska Landsmål och Svenskt Folkliv* 1 (2): 5-30.

Guthrie, Stewart Elliott. 1997. "The Origin of an Illusion." *Anthropology of Religion: A Handbook.* Ed. Stephen D. Glazier. Westport, Connecticut: Greenwood Press. 489-504.

Hallowell, A. Irving. 2002. (1960). "Ojibwa Ontology, Behaviour, and Worldview." *Readings in Indigenous Religions.* Ed. Graham Harvey. London: Continuum. 17-49.

Hartsock, Nancy. 1983. *Money, Sex, and Power: Toward a Feminist Historical Materialism.* Boston: Northeastern University Press.

Harvey, Graham. 2006. *Animism: Respecting the Living World.* New York: Columbia University Press.

Harvey, Graham. Ed. 2002. *Readings in Indigenous Religions.* London: Continuum.

Helander-Renvall, Elina. 2006. *Beyond the Pale: Locating Sea Sami Women Outside the Official Fisheries Discourse in Northern Norway.* Ottawa: The Canadian Circumpolar Institute.

Helander, Elina. 2004. "Myths, Shamans and Epistemologies from an Indigenous Vantage Point." *Snowscapes, Dreamscapes. Snowchange Book on Community Voices of Change.* Eds. Elina Helander and Tero Mustonen. Vaasa: Tampere Polytechnic Publications. 552-562.

Helander, Elina. 2000. "Noidat ja parantajat ennen ja nyt: saamelaisista parannusmenetelmistä (Shamans and Healers Now and Then: Sami Healing Methods)." *Siiddastallan. Siidoista kyliin (To Live in Communities: From Communities to Villages).* Eds. Jukka Pennanen and Klemetti Näkkäläjärvi. Oulu: Pohjoinen. 238-245.

Helander, Elina. 1997. "Sami Medical Concepts and Healing Methods." *Simone de Beauvoir Review* 17: 81-87.

Helander, Elina and Kaarina Kailo, eds. 1998. *No Beginning, No End: The Sami Speak Up.* Ottawa: The Canadian Circumpolar Institute/Nordic Sami Institute.

Ingold, Tim. 2000. The Perception of the Environment. Essays in Livelihood, Dwelling and Skill. London: Routledge.

Ingold, Tim. 1995. "People Like Us: The Concept of Anatomically Modern Human." *Cultural Dynamics* 7 (2): 187-214.

Ingold, Tim. 1988. *What is an Animal?* London: Unwin Hyman.

Irwin, Lee. 1994. *The Dream Seekers: Native American Visionary Traditions of the Great Plains.* Norman: University of Oklahoma Press.

Itkonen T. I. 1948. *Suomen lappalaiset vuoteen 1945 (The Lapps of Finland to 1945).* II. Porvoo: Werner Söderström Osakeyhtiö.

Kailo, Kaarina. 1994. "Trance Cultural Travel: Indigenous Women and Mainstream Feminism." *Trans-Cultural Travels: Essays in Canadian Literature and Society.* Ed. Marie Peepre. NACS/ANEC (Text Series of the Nordic Association for Canadian Studies/L'association nordiques d'études canadiennes) 11: 19-36.

Kalweit, Holger. 1988. *Dreamtime, Inner Space: The World of the Shaman.* Boston and London: Shambhala.

Khariditi, Olga. 2001. *Master of Lucid Dreams.* Charlottesville, VA: Humpton Roads Publishing Company, Inc.

Knudtson, Peter and David Suzuki. 1992. *The Wisdom of the Elders.* Toronto: Stoddard.

Kremer, Jürgen. 1999. "*Bearing Obligations for Transgressing Nature/Culture: Women Bears and Desire.*" Unpublished paper.

Kuokkanen, Rauna. 2004. "Saamelaisnaiset, feministinen analyysi ja saamelais-yhteiskunnan dekolonisaatio (Sami Women, Feminist Analysis and Decolonization of the Sami Society)." *Tasa-Arvon Haasteita Globaalin ja Lokaalin Rajapinnoilla (Challenges of Gender Equalityat the Interface of the Local and the Global).* Eds. Kaarina Kailo, Vappu Sunnari and Heli Vuori. Oulu: Oulun yliopistopaino. 143-159.

Latour, Bruno. 1998. *An Actor Network Theory: A Few Clarifications 1/2.* Centre for Social Theory and Technology (CSTT). Online at: www.netline.org.

Law, John. 1999. "After ANT: Complexity, Naming and Topology." *Actor Network Theory and After.* Eds. John Law and John Hassard. Oxford: Blackwell. 1-14.

Mander, Jerry and Victoria Tauli-Corpuz. Eds. 2007. *Paradigm Wars. Indigenous Peoples' Resistance to Globalization.* San Francisco: Sierra Club Books.

Meyer, Leroy N. and Tony Ramirez. 1996. "'Wakinyan Horan'–The Thunderbeings Call Out: The Inscrutability of Lakota/Dakota Metaphysics." *From Our Eyes: Learning from Indigenous Peoples.* Eds. Sylvia O'Meara and Douglas A. West. Toronto: Garamond Press. 89-105.

Mustonen, Tero and Tiina Salin. 2004. "In Memory of Aslak Aikio [1931-2004]. A Hunter, Elder, Father, Friend, A Person of Knowledge." *Snowscapes, Dreamscapes: Snowchange Book on Community Voices of Change.* Eds. Elina Helander and Tero Mustonen. Vaasa: Tampere Polytechnic Publications. 310-317.

Myrhaug, May-Lisbeth. 1997. *I Modergudinnens Fotspor. Samisk religion med vekt på kvinnelige kultutövere og gudinnekult (Following the Mothergoddess: Sami Religion with Particular Relation to the Female Bear and Goddess Cults).* Oslo: Pax Forlag A/S.

Mysterud, Ivar. 1985. "Er björnen farlig (Is Bear Dangerous)?" *Tidsskrift for nordnorsk natur og kultur* 5 (156): 53-62.

Nergård, Jens-Ivar. 2006. *Den levande erfaring. En studie i samisk kunskapstradisjon (The Living Experience: A Study on Sami Knowledge Tradition).* Oslo: Cappelen Akademisk Forlag.

Noble, Vicki, ed. 1993. *Uncoiling the Snake: Ancient Patterns in Contemporary Women's Lives.* San Francisco: Harper.

Norlander Unsgaard, Siv. 1985. "On Gesture and Posture, Movements and Motion in Saami Bear Ceremonialism." *Saami Pre-Christian Religion: Studies on the Oldest Traces of Religion Among the Saamis.* Eds. Louise Bäckman and Åke Hultkrantz. Stockholm: Almqvist and Wiksell International. 189-199.

Oskal, Nils. 1995. *Det rette, det gode og reinlykken. Avhandling til dr.art.-graden i filosofi (Good, Bad and Reindeer Luck).* Ph.D. Dissertation. Institutt for Samfunnsvitenskap. Universitetet i Tromsö.

Outakoski, Nilla. 1991. *Lars Levi Laestadiuksen saarnojen maahiskuva (Picture of the Underground Spirits in the Sermons of Lars Levi Laestadius)*. Oulu: Oulun historiaseuran julkaisuja.

Pentikäinen, Juha. 2007. *Golden King of the Forest: The Lore of the Northern Bear*. Saarijärvi: Etnika Oy.

Pirak, Anta. 1933. *En nomad och hans liv (A Nomad and His Life)*. Uppsala: Almqvist and Wiksell.

Pirak, Lars. 1983. "Nåjden Pirak (Pirak: A Shaman)." *Norrländsk kulturtidskrift* 5: 59-62.

Porsanger, Jelena. 2004. "An Essay About Indigenous Methodology." *NORDLIT. Working Papers in Literature*. University of Tromsö. 115-118.

Radcliffe-Brown, Alfred R. 1948. *The Andaman Islanders: A Study in Social Anthropology*. Glencou, IL: The Free Press.

Ridington, Robin. 1988. "Knowledge, Power, and the Individual in Subarctic Hunting Societies." *American Anthropologist* 90: 98-110.

Rinpoche, Tenzin Wangyal. 1998. *The Tibetan Yogas of Dream and Sleep*. Ithaca. New York: Snow Lion Publications.

Rochon, Tim. 1993. *Saami and Dene Concepts of Nature*. Umeå: Center for Arctic Research, Umeå University.

Rockwell, David. 1991. *Giving Voice to Bear: North American Indian Rituals, Myths, and Images of the Bear*. Toronto: Roberts Rinehart Publishers.

Roth, Gabrielle. 1989. *Maps of Ecstasy: Teachings of an Urban Shaman*. Novato, CA: Nataraj Publishing.

Sande, Hans and Sigrun Winterfelt. 1993. "Four Sámi Healers. A Preliminary Interview Study." *Nordic Journal of Psychiatry* 47 (1): 41-51.

Schefferus Johannes. 1674. *Lapponia (Lappland)*. Francofurti: Christian Wolff.

Siikala, Anna-Liisa. 1994. *Suomalainen Šamanismi (Finnish Shamanism)*. Hämeenlinna: Karisto Oy.

Sjulsson, Kristoffer. 1979. *Minnen om Vapstenslapparna i början af 1800-talet (Memories of Vapstenlapps at the Beginning of the 19th Century)*. Acta Lapponica 20. Lund: Berlings.

Siri, Vigdis. 1998. "Dreaming with the First Shaman (Noaidi)." *ReVision: A Journal of Consciousness and Transformation* 21 (1): 34-39).

Smith, Linda Tuhiwai. 1999. *Decolonizing Methodologies: Research and Indigenous Peoples*. London: Zed Books Ltd.

Smoley, Richard. 1992. "Are Dreams for Real?" *Gnosis Magazine* (Winter): 14-16.

Strathern, Marilyn. 1999. "What is Intellectual Property After?" *Actor Network Theory and After*. Eds. John Law and John Hassard. Oxford: Blackwell Publishers. 156-180.

Therman, Erik. 1940. *Bland noider och nomader (Among Shamans and Nomads)*. Stockholm: Bokförlaget Natur och Kultur.

Thomassen, Ole. 1999. *Lappenes forhold (Lappish conditions)*. Kåfjord Kommune: Samisk Språksenter.

Tomasson, Torkel. 1988. *Några sägner, seder och bruk, upptecknade efter lapparna i Åsele- och Lycksele lappmark samt Herjedalen sommaren 1917* (Legends, Customs and Traditions of Lapps in Åsele and Lycksele Lappmark and in Herjedalen During the Summer of 1917). Uppsala: Dialekt-och folkminnesarkivet.

Turi, Johan. 1987 [1910]. *Muitalus sámiid birra* (*Book of Lapland*). Jokkmokk: Sámi Girjjit.

Turi, Johan and Per Turi. 1920. *Lappish Texts 1918-1919. Det Kgl. Danske Videnskabernes Selskabs Skrifter.* Köbenhavn: Historisk og filosofisk Afd.

Vadén, Tere and Jarkko Tuusvuori. 2007. "Lappi paljastaa Suomen. n and n-haastattelussa Elina Helander-Renvall (Lappland Reveals Finland: Interview of Elina Helander-Renvall by n and n)." *Niin and Näin. Filosofinen aikakauslehti* 55 (4): 6-10.

Valkeapää, Nils-Aslak. 1997. *The Sun, My Father.* Guovdageaidnu: DAT.

Valkeapää, Nils-Aslak. 1994. *Nu guhkkin dat mii lahka. Så fjernt det naere (So Near the Far).* Guovdageaidnu: DAT.

Villoldo, Alberto and Stanley Krippner. 1986. *Healing States.* New York: Simon and Schuster, inc.

Willerslev, Rane. 2007. *Soul Hunters. Hunting, Animism, And Personhood Among The Siberian Yukaghirs.* Berkeley: University of California Press.

Winkelman, Michael. 1997. "Altered States of Consciousness and Religious Behaviour." *Anthropology of Religion: A Handbook.* Ed. Stephen D. Glazier. Westport, CT: Greenwood Press. 394-428.

Wolf, Fred Allan. 1992. "The Dreaming Universe: Investigations into the Middle Realm of Consciousness." *Gnosis Magazine* 92 (Winter): 30-35.

Wolf, Fred Allan. 1991. *The Eagles Quest: A Physicist Finds Scientific Truth at the Heart of the Shamanic World.* New York: Simon and Schuster.

Bare on Bear

Her curves
hip and shoulder nestled
into thick musky fur
Her skin
prickling with bear sensations
Her mind
dreamy in thick slumber
cumbersome woolen dream
of Ursus

Helena Junttila, "Encounter," watercolour, 30.5 x 38 cm, 2000.
The Aine Art Museum, Finland.

IRMA HEISKANEN

Dreaming, Bear Spirit, and Finno-Ugric Women's Handicrafts

In the early 1980s, I was taking a course on cross-cultural psychiatry at Berlin's Free University in Germany that challenged my way of thinking in significant ways. I was completing my Master's degree in psychology in my home country, Finland, and had to make a decision whether to stay in Finland or move to Berlin on a more permanent basis. Shortly after completing the course, and while hesitating about where to take up residence, I had a dream about a swarm of mosquitoes dancing in the sunlight. The mosquitoes "told" me to "go North." The next thing I knew, I was flying above the fields in what resembled the landscape near my parents' summer cottage. Upon waking, with the guidance of my "power animal," the mosquito, I decided to "go North" and return to Finland, without realizing what a journey I was embarking on.

Several years later in a seminar where two researchers mentioned their "power animals"—wolf and bear—I had to confess that mine was a mosquito. Of course, everyone in the seminar burst out laughing! I knew then that my relatedness to nature, which since childhood had been so important to me, had been suffering and shrinking in the urban environment in which I lived, and that the theories of academic psychology that I had been studying had interfered with my connection to the earth. I felt a disharmony, an imbalance between the intellectual and the more sense-oriented "way of being," of dreaming and of being awake. I became aware of a thin thread inside me that called on me to "weave" myself into a sensuous relationship with the forces of life and death and knew I had to start seeking ways to gain balance.

In this paper, I will explore the significance of ornamental decorations on women's handicrafts, particularly women's spun cloth and woven mittens, and the ways in which these ornaments give expression to ancient life-centered worldviews of cultures in harmony with nature and the cycles of renewal and rebirth.

The Spirit of Bear

Around 1989 I was living in Northern Finland near the city of Oulu. I was desperate because I was in the process of divorcing after a brief marriage, and I was trying to learn to cope in a compassionate way with the psychic wounds of the father of my two children, and my own wounds, caused by his use of alcohol as "medicine"—something that later resulted in his death. I was also trying to cope with the wounds of my clients in psychiatric counseling and to function well in my important task as a single mother. In the evenings, I used to comfort myself by browsing through books of art. One night I came across a German book on the *Native Art of Indians and the Eskimos* (Haberland 1979) and was entranced by the image of a Dakota pipe head made of Catlinit (red pipestone), decorated with lead ornaments that depicted a man and a bear sitting on the pipe. Later that night, when going to sleep, I detected a soft whisper: "*The spirit of bear awakens, the heart hears with strange ears.*" Since that night, something opened up deeper in my senses. I could, for example, "hear" from a distance if my children had problems when playing out in the yard. I was able to trust what I was sensing and understanding, and I was able to transmit something about that to my clients. I received very beautiful and musical dreams that helped me to overcome the hard times, and pointed to ways that I might help my clients. I was astonished and grateful to the Spirit of the Bear who had shown me how to listen and hear deep inside myself.

I tried to talk to the head of the psychiatric institution where I worked at the time about this kind of sensing and how a spiritual connection to nature could teach us. Academic psychology and psychiatry, however, often do not accept the "gift of native teachings" (see Kuokkanen 2007). Fortunately, I heard about a course on "the spiritual values of the woods" that was being held in central Finland, near Jyväskylä, and decided to enroll. During the course we visited an old forest, home to a very rare spruce tree, over 130 years old, the tallest spruce tree in Finland (its rarity a testament to the extent to which our forests are commercially exploited). While walking in the forest by myself, overcome by feelings of sadness and loneliness, I wept against that spruce tree, and asked its spirit, if possible, to help me with my problems as a single mother. When I returned to meet up with the hosts of the course, our driver, one of the participants, got lost as we left the forest. Looking for somewhere to ask for directions, we happened by chance upon a dairy farm that was run by a bachelor—a place where I have now lived for 14 years. And so it was that years after my mosquito dream, I had finally found my way to the geological as well mythical North. Since then I have been developing a theory and practice of ecopsychology based on Finno-Ugric cultural traditions.

My research into Finno-Urgic cultural traditions began with my introduction to ancient Finnish folk poetry and laments, and through visits to the area where most of the poems for our national epic, *Kalevala,* and its "sister" counterpart, *Kanteletar,* were archived, the now Russian Carelia, in the region of Viena. My interest in Finnish/Sami poetry led me to the study of symbols and mythology which I later applied to my study of Finno-Ugric[1] women's handicrafts.

The Old Woman, Permian Casts, and Ornaments on Women's Handicrafts

About ten years ago I visited part-Finnish, part-Sami teacher and journalist Biret

Irma Heiskanen, "Sky Dance," 2005.

Marét Kallio in Sirma, Norway, because I felt I needed to go further North, attracted by the mosquito dream of years before. Sirma is thought to be the ancient dwelling of the early Sami (Samiland) and Permian people in the northern part of Norway near the Finnish border. In Biret Marét's backyard there was an *arrán*, a fireplace that dates back some 7,000 years, a testament to the ancient civilization that made its home there.

I journeyed with Biret to the Varanger fjord where I met Siri Vigdis, a professional *duojár*/Sámi handicraft-artist with an atelier and a shop in Nesseby. While speaking about her work and her interests, Siri referred to the rhombus (figure of a diamond) often depicted on Sami drums. "Usually in publications describing Sámi drums, we are told that the rhombus stands for the sun," I commented.

"No," she said. "The rhombus has to do with the opening in a tree through which the spirit of a tree teaches a shaman."[2]

Earlier in the day, I had gone to *Tana, Deatnu* or, "Grandmother River," driven there by mosquitoes of the Sirma countryside. The Sami consider mosquitoes to be helpers who drive the reindeer in herds up to the *tunturi*, the arctic fells. It is thought that without mosquitoes the reindeer would be scattered throughout the limitless wilderness and would, therefore, be difficult to hunt. While at the river I decided to collect a few river stones to take back with me as souvenirs. Remembering that it would be polite to ask the spirits for permission, I asked for a sign. I immediately had the impression that the stones nearest to me said "no" and thus decided to walk further along and look elsewhere. It wasn't long before I felt a strong attraction to some beautiful black stones just a few meters away. I took one of those stones in my hand and realized I was holding an ancient tool. It fit my hand nicely and bore marks of having been used for something. There were several of these stones along the riverbank and I felt intuitively that it would okay to bring some of them back to the house, to Biret Marét's spouse, Torgeir, an historian and ethnologist who at that time was making maps of the old dwelling places of Sami people on the arctic hills. He immediately recognized the stones as *Knochenbrecher*, or bone-breakers, used to get marrow from bones for food, among other functions. He told me that he had never thought to search along the riverbank for ancient artifacts assuming that the floods would have driven everything to the Arctic Ocean long ago. I left the stones/ancient tools with him for conservation in a Sami museum (except for the one which the spirits gave me permission to take with me).

Later, while Biret Marét and I were drumming in her backyard in Sirma, I had a vision. I saw in my drum journey an old woman from a distance, standing in front of a cottage made of peat moss. Before her lay several handcrafted ornamental bands and bronze casts that were half-hidden in the earth. I eventually learned that Permian casts are closely connected with women and while generally assumed that they were made for "keeping the souls of the deceased" (Autio 2001: 173), it has been shown that they were likely also used by women as fertility calendars (see Shutova cited in Autio 2001: 182). On Permian casts (from the sixth to the ninth century), bear, wolf, and elk motifs, as well as strong female figures with feet resembling the paws of a bear, often with what has been interpreted as a lizard underfoot, are common. This vision during the drumming session is what led me to examine ornaments depicting similar motifs on northern women's handicraft works, particularly women's spun cloth and woven mittens, and Permian casts more deeply. Prior to that I knew little of how ancient worldviews of life-centered cultures might be expressed in women's handicrafts. After finding the black stones along the river, and the vision of the old woman (Old Goddess?) in front of her cottage, I had the strange feeling of having accomplished something, maybe of finding a "calling," which was connected to my first dream of mosquitoes long before visiting Sirma.

Women-Bear-Bird-Spinning: A Chain of Life-Oriented Connections

Max Dashu (2006) argues that "the earliest known sources show the Old Goddess as a spinner. She is Fate, whose spinning has immense creative force in time and space. A Finnish kenning for the sun—'God's Spindle'—reflects her power (*Kalevala* 32, 30, in Grimm 1500). The Goddesses's 'spinning and weaving also symbolize the creation of matter, especially of human flesh' (Matossian 120)."

The "fateful Spinner" was worshipped as myriad goddesses (Srecha by the Serbs, Holle or Perchta by the Germans, Mari by the Basques, Laima by the Lithuanians and Latvians, the Befana in Italy, Mokosh or Kostroma in Russia to name a few) around the world. "[I]n the far north … the spinning wheel was sacred to the spring goddess of the Saami. She is the spirit maiden Rana Nedie, who makes the mountains green and feeds the reindeer. When sacrifices were made to her, they rubbed the blood on a spinning wheel and leaned it against her altar" (Dashu 2006).

The Old Goddess of ancient times was integral to rituals for well-being, abundance, protection, and healing. Reverance was made to the Old Goddess in planting and harvesting, baking, and of course, in spinning and weaving. In her research on Baltic folklore, Mary Matossian points to an ancient Estonian belief that Vana-ema (Old Mother) will spin all night if you leave out a distaff and thread (cited in Dashu 2006). In some districts Estonians called this spinner the "Grandmother" or the "Night Mother." She was connected to the dead and the underworld "spinning women" (*maa-aluste naised*) (Matossian 1973: 121).

In Finnish folk poetry (see SKVR 2002-2003) there are several variations of the "Old Woman" or the "Old Woman of the Dark North": Louhi, Loviatar, Luon-notar, Wife of Nature, Wife of Creator, even Maiden of North, Woman under the Earth. The Finnish words for "old woman" (*akka/eukko*) or "Earth mother" (*maan emäntä*) or the spirit under the Earth (*maan haltia*) are linguistically connected with the Sami words *ahkku* or *ahkka* (old woman, grandmother), also reflected in the names of the "sisters of hope": "Máttaráhkká, Sáráhkká, Uksáhkká, and Juoksáhkká." Dashu (2006) refers to her as

> Old Goddess because she was commonly pictured as an aged woman, and her veneration was ancient, as well.… Old Goddess is like the weathered Earth, ancestor of all, an immanent presence in forests, grottos and fountains. In her infinitude she manifests in countless forms, as females of various ages, and shapeshifting to tree, serpent, frog, bird, deer, mare and other creatures.

In Finnish mythology, *Mannun eukko* gives birth to different kinds of diseases that bring death, but as Woman of the Earth, *Mannun eukko* or *akka* is asked to "boost" the growth of crops. The dark of the year, the winter solstice, was seen as sacred to Old Goddess, as it is central to life's cycle renewal and rebirth. It is possible to suggest, therefore, that before the influence of Christianity, the Old Woman of the North/Maiden of the North represented the Creative Force of the Northern Night Sky or the dark fertile forces under the Earth.

According to Odd Mathis Haetta (1994) the "sister" goddesses "of hope" played key roles in the conception and birth of a human being. "Máttaráhkká was the ancestress, who as 'the leading woman' played a vital role in the procreation of a human being. She created the body for the soul and then handed it over to her daughter, Sáráhkká who allowed the soul in the womb to grow into a fetus. Sáráhkká resided in the *árran*, the open hearth in the turf hut, and was also called

Irma Heiskanen, "The Old Swamp Woman," colour pencils, 21 x 30 cm, 2007.

the mother of fire" (18). Her second daughter, Uksáhkká (the door wife), resided beneath the threshold and guarded the entrance, maintaining watch over those going in and out. The third daughter, Juoksáhkká, exerted her influence over the sex of the child and was able to transform a girl into a boy, as the ancient beliefs held that all children were created to become girls:

> The four sisters of hope spin a golden web
> of protection
> strong steady and vulnerable
> the four sisters of hope in the shape of gods
> ...
> the four sisters of hope
> were all there
> to bring me back to life
> singing in happiness
> in rhythm with the drums
> while the shawl's threads softly caress
> the green, the red, the yellow....
> ("Sisters of Hope" qtd. in Haetta 1994)

The four "sisters" are often depicted on Sami drums holding wooden sticks in their hands with two or three branches at the top of the stick,[3] evocative of the hunter's rod in Finnish mythology. In 1939, Samuli Paulaharju explained that hunters in the Sompio wilderness in Lapland used to leave a *torikko*, or rod of the *metsän emäntä* ("Good Mother of the Forest") in a tree stump after they had cut down a tree for a campfire. Leaving the rod guaranteed that the Good Mother of the Woods would protect the hunters and provide them with plenty of game (cited in Karjalainen 1994: 148). Having compared a number of different tools used for spinning in ancient times, I posit that the "rod" of the four sisters, or the *torrikko* of the Good Mother of the Forest, represents the principal tool of spinning, and creation itself. As a result, I have also come to associate the pre-historical rod and spike distaff, the helical movement of fingers caused by threading, the helical force of the sun during seasons, and the helical spinning of stars in the nightly sky, with the weaving principle of Mother Nature.

A close look at the way the needles of a young spruce tree are organized along the stem reveals a spiral arrangement. The beautiful cones of spruce trees in the spring give evidence as well of a similar spiral order. The leaves of many different plants likewise reflect a spiral order in their growth. When thinking of the red "thread" of the menstrual cycle, its connection to the phases and cycles of the moon, the creation of human life in a mother's womb and the helical thread of the umbilical cord, we can experience in our body and soul how women long ago connected the principle of "weaving" with the principle of "creating the web of life."

Linguist Toby D. Griffen (2007), in identifying and deciphering the ancient Vinca script,[4] was able to reconstruct the first sentence (found to date) ever written. Griffen was also able to reconstruct this sentence by identifying the Vincan signs/words for "bear," "bird," and "goddess" on ancient spinning whorls. The whorl inscriptions read "bear–goddess–bird–goddess–bear–goddess-goddess," which he interprets as "bear goddess and bird goddess: bear goddess indeed" (21). Griffen concludes that the Bear Goddess and Bird Goddess had coalesced into one. He compares the goddess figure on the spinning whorls with bear-like and bird-like attributes to the Greek goddess, Artemis. In Greek mythology, Artemis is usually depicted as the maiden goddess of the hunt, bearing a bow and arrows, and connected to different wild animals of the forest.

The Old European Bear Goddess, Bird Goddess and the Weaving Goddess of the sprindle whorls can be rediscovered in the stories and images that surround her, and the kind of festivals that were held in her honour. Spindles and loom weights were found in many of her shrines, and on Corinthian vases she holds the spindle of destiny as the weaver of the interlocking web of animals and human life. (Baring and Cashford qtd. in Griffen 2007: 22)

Early Permian casts depict a similar relationship between the female/goddess figure and Bear, birds, and other animals, the key motifs on Vinca artefacts. In Permian "animal style bronze casts" made by women (deduced on the basis of the remnants in burial findings where there were also bones of women and casting molds and bronze casts) there are often, among other figures, spirits of trees and other female figures in the center, elk-human figures on the side with bird-heads on the top, and the female figure with its strong "bear-feet" standing on a beaver, lizard or an a sturgeon/big fish (see Autio 2000; 2001). Sometimes, the female figure is partly merged with two other female figures standing on top of a beaver. Birds, bears, elks, lizards (perhaps sturgeons?), trees, and other fauna are commonly depicted on and around the female figure on the bronze casts of this period. Udmurtian archaeologist Nadezhda Shutova suggests the Permian casts are clear depictions of a goddess figure[5]—"a healthy and strong woman who was the beginning of everything created with the world, giving life to plants, animals and humans, and determining their fate. In this, birth, growing, death and rebirth became personified" (qtd. in Autio 2001: 175-176).

For me, the golden, sunny, or moonlike colour of the casts, and the tight positioning of the animal figures around the central female goddess, point to the intimate inter-dependence of totemic animals and their role in the nourishing and food-making-providing functions of women. This life-sustaining bond speaks to the physical nourishing role of women's bodies and their eggs, the spawns of animals, and humans, and their sacred spirits. The positioning of animals around the central figure also points to the whirling power of creation—the movement of the sun, the moon, and the constellations in the sky, the eternal return of migrating birds, the calving of elks, the spawning of fishes, and sexual heat and pregnancy.

German psychoanalyst and theologist Jutta Voss (2006) claims that the social imaginary at the beginning of "civilization" is rooted in representations of fe-

Aleksandr Suvorov, "Udmurtia 1996," Bronze Cast.
Courtesy of the Gallen-Kallela Museum, Pasi Mäkinen.

male cycles. According to Voss, many ancient traditions are based on the observation that all life in the universe runs in shorter or longer cycles and that women themselves, with their observable menstrual cycles, represent this cycle. Voss suggests this life-and-death cycle links sexuality and fertility to animal husbandry, agriculture, gardening, to celebrations of the cycles of the sun and the moon, to poetry, singing and music, to modes of honouring, to culture and civilization.

The research conducted by Shutova (1998) and Voss (2006) on Permian casts thus supports the perception that Permian bronze casts express the cyclical connection and symbolic affinities of women's cosmic and earthly fertilization cycles of life, and the motifs depicted speak powerfully to women's role in pre-patriarchal life and reverance for the Goddess that is the source of all life.

Ob-Ugrians etched ornamental black grouse on the birch bark of children's cradles. Black grouse are large birds with strong noses and feet that remain in the North throughout the long arctic winter and Polar night. Tyyni Vahter (1953: 113) states the black grouse was seen as a protecting spirit by the Ob-Ugrians. During sleep the soul of a child can escape in the form of a bird and this bird is at risk of being shot by a hunter. The black grouse is thus the guardian of the child's soul. Interestingly, the shape of a black grouse resembles the shape of a spindle, and their wings "spindle" the air when they are flying with a kind of spinning-like up-and-down

349

movement. They too thus represent the spinning movement of the creative life force and can also be seen as perhaps having the ability "to spin" the soul back to earth if it gets lost.

The work of the Russian researcher V. N. Tšhernetsov (1948, 1939) helps us to better understand why the bear has been so important in connection to the spinning force of life. He comes to the conclusion that the Mansi and Hanti god, *numi torum*, the spirit of upper air, "in spite of his/her high position is nothing but a bear and as birth giver to the *phratrias* (clans) is not a male but a female bear" (qtd. in Vahter 1953: 96). According to Tšhernetsov, this understanding is in harmony with the concepts of matriarchy and Goddess worship. Tšhernetsov also comments on how the beautiful bear ornaments on the bags of Finno-Ugric Mansi women's *por* family (families whose totem animal is a bear) are connected with their totemistic family names (cited in Vahter 1953: 100). There are many poems and songs about Bear feasts among the Finno-Ugric peoples that refer to the importance of Bear among those who consider themselves "people under the Big Bear," and Bear ornaments are commonly etched onto Ugrian Mansi baskets made of birch bark. It is here that I began to consider that the ornaments and motifs depicted on Finno-Ugric women's handicrafts are not only respectful expressions of our connection to nature, but might have also been intended to attract guardian spirits.

The Constellation of Great Bear

German archeologist Michael A. Rappenglück (2002) has described the ways in which

> Across cultures and throughout the ages[,] people's imaginations and rituals have been peaked by concepts of the centre of the world, the celestial pole(s) and the Zenith, the circumpolar rotation of the stars, the axis of the world, and the realms skewered around it. Around the globe, it was important for ancient people to create a habitable personal and social environment by organizing the world's landscape. Since Paleolithic times man [sic] recognized a deep connection between himself and his culture to nature.... Organizing the world's landscape is to recognize a center, a top and a bottom, an edge, particular directions and strata, and periods of change, to relate these to one's own culture and to give them a concrete shape, for example in images and buildings. (58)

Similar to Rappenglück's view of the ways in which ancient cultures may have created and organized their social and cultural relationship to nature, Finno-Ugric women's handicrafts, ornaments, and Permian casts can be seen as both personal and cultural "maps" that helped women and family members to orientate, to find "a right time and place" for everything they did, with a deep awareness of connection to the "order of life."

In Arctic conditions, winter is the time for hunting and killing animals, necessary for survival. Several months afterwards, a new spring arrives that brings with it newborn calves. The autumn ritual of ancient Samis was performed to give back to nature in order to sustain the balance between birth and death. Neglecting the act of giving back to the living force of Creation means breaking down the nourishing cycle of existence. Birth and death and rebirth are like the process of inhaling, of nurturing the body and soul with breath, which is then exhaled in a continuous cycle. This is the way creation works and expresses itself in and around us, now in a visible, now in an invisible, back and forth motion.

It is important to send the spirits of animals back to their Cosmic Mother, to her black womb of the Arctic night, so that they will be reborn. This is a time when the "tail" of the Big Dipper, the Great Bear—or Elk according to some ancient Sami views, as well as some other Finno-Ugric people—begins to rise upwards, "sending" the spirits toward the Polar North Star. It is common knowledge in the countryside that plants need the darkness of the night in order to ripen. Seeds also need darkness—and sometimes the cold—in order to germinate. Even modern science confirms that cells need the power of nocturnal energies or forces in order to "grow." It is no surprise then that the great Creative Power of the Arctic Night and the cold are represented as female. Winter is a necessary phase of death and an element of renewal. What is new is born in the spring out of the transformed remains of that which is old, and dead, in the winter—and comes back to those who took care of the souls of the dead animals by sending them back to the to their Cosmic Mother so that they will be reborn.

Uno Holmberg (later Uno Harva) wrote in his book *Der Baum des Lebens, Göttinnen und Baumkult* (1996) (*The Tree of Life, Goddesses and the Tree Cult*) about the mythical "tree of life," a motif shared by many different cultures. The roots of the tree are described as lying deep inside the earth in a hole—sometimes on a mountain, or in the navel of the earth, sometimes between "clattering" stones—its top shown as reaching up to the heavens. Holmberg states that the world axis or "tree of life" in Finno-Ugric cultures is sometimes held up by a frog—its Asian counterpart being a turtle.[6] The tree of life is thus a kind of path that connects the navel of the earth and the spiritual realm of the sky through *Pohjan tähti*, or the North Star. In Finnish, the word *Pohja* is connected with the words "bottom" and "North," although in the latter case only through mythic associations.

Holmberg (1996) refers to writings by missionaries that indicate every autumn pagan people of Lapland offer a male reindeer or some other animal to *Maylmen radien*, the highest god, to prevent the sky from falling down (24-25). Part of this ritual consists in smearing a tree, planted top down in a hole in the earth, and the nearby stones with blood. In some Finno-Ugric cultures there are also wooden birds situated on the "arms" of the "tree of life." The tree of life with an eagle sitting on top is often depicted on Finno-Ugric shaman drums.

According to the anthropologist Zelia Nuttal (1901), the observation that the Seven Stars of Big Dipper—in Finno-Ugric culture the Great Bear or Otava (older form Otama)—turn around the Northern Pole Star, *Pohjantähti*—a word which holds within it the Finnish word for the North, *Pohjoinen*—is of fundamental value to "primitive people" (as Nuttal calls the life-oriented peoples of bygone eras). This rotation, charted during the four seasons of the year, forms the pattern of a swastika. This swastika is a common ornament used all over the world. On Ob-Ugrian women's dresses or mittens, the swastika depicting the Big Dipper's seasonal positions is referred to as the "rasp" or "bunch of berries."

I agree with Nuttal's perception of the Big Dipper's connection to, and reflection of, seasonal cycles of life. Watching the Big Dipper, Otava, or Great Bear every winter morning and evening from our own yard far from city lights, I see its "tail" holding different positions in the night sky. In the spring the tail points downwards and the entire constellation looks like a "golden cradle with silvery chains" with which, according to Finnish folk poetry and mythology, the Bear was sent to the Earth from Heaven. The Constellation of the Great Bear or Otava/Otama also contains implicit references to a fishnet or fish-trap over a river. This may be connected to the belief that in the spring, when the ice is melting and the Great Bear is high in the eastern sky, it is time for the ancestors to start fishing the spawning pike and other fish with their nourishing roes. About the same time begins the migration of birds along the "milky way," *linnunrata* (bird's track), as well their nesting. The eggs of the mythical Goldeneye have represented a much-appreciated form of nutrition for thousands of years. In Finnish mythology the world, or *maailma* (literally "earth-air"), is created from the egg of the waterbird Goldeneye that lays its egg on the knee of Water-maiden, Mother of Water (Veen emo, later turned into a male god, Väinämöinen), which peeks out of the "primordial sea." When the Mother of Water moves her knee, the egg falls into the sea and a pike catches and swallows it. Then a *kokko* bird, which can refer to an eagle as well to Goldeneye, fights with the pike over the egg, which finally leads to the creation of the earth, the heaven, the sun, and the moon and the stars out of the pieces of the eggshell, the egg yolk, and the egg white.

The image of the Great Cosmic Mother with the earth as its body, the cosmic sky as its womb, and Pole star as its navel, positions us as living in a huge "tent" or womb of the Cosmic Mother throughout our lives. In this tent of Creation, Bear is the first to be born after the "cosmic pregnancy of the Arctic Winter." That is why Bear-Mother is so important. Bear is the "Mother of mothers" who starts the season of new births on Earth. Bear, often referred to as *Mesikämmen* (honeypaw), seems linked to the following fact: when the Bear mother wakes up from its hibernation and brings her newborn cubs out, it is time for the "trees of life" also to begin to raise their sweet sap. In ancient Finno-Ugric poetry there are hints, folk-beliefs, that suggest the Bear sucks on its honey-covered paws during its hibernation (Paulaharju cited in SKVR 2000-2003). It is common knowledge that bears like to eat wild honey and berries but referring to Bear as "Honeypaw" points to Bear's role as "Mother of the Spring," bringing to the earth the sweet sap of the "great Oak of the sky."

In Finnish folklore there are variations of the story of the Great Oak that grows so big it prevents the sun from shining. A small man comes from the sea to chop the Oak down, which falls with its top pointing to south/summer and its roots toward north/winter. Ancient Finnish folk poems describe the healing force of the sap of the Great Oak (SKVR VII 3 *loitsut* 326). Holmberg (1996) has researched the many folk tales around the world that connect the Milky Way with the Tree of Life and the Nurturing/Nourishing Sky Mother. In many legends the tree brings people milk and honey. The yearly movement of the sun in relation to the Milky Way reaches in the spring a point at which it starts to "fall," having moved over its "top" in the winter. Therefore it may seem to an observer that when bears wake up from their hibernation, they also bring with them the spring rains, which are soaked up and transformed to sap in trees, the meady nectar in the modest flowers of willows, for example. Therefore, the She-bear, the totemic ancient mother, creates the cyclical movement and enrichment of the nourishing and erotic arousal of healing properties between the sky and the earth.

In the spring the whole world warms up, gets wet and meady, joyfully and erotically aroused. The miracle of the Bear mother among all others is its ability to give birth to its cubs during winter and to nurse them under the conditions of the Polar night. Therefore celebrating Bear mother, as is enacted in Lithuanian rituals for example (Esser et al. 2001), is a celebration of the Creative Force of Life itself. When a woman can identify with the Bear's honeypaw, her role as mother, something spiritual, gentle, as well strong, she can both protect her children in the most difficult conditions and nurse them psychically and physically with the honey-sweet love she represents. Laime Kiskunaite writes that in Eastern Lithuania a woman was called "Bear" immediately after the birth of a child (qtd. in Esser et al. 2001). "'The Bear is coming,' women would shout as she approached the sauna for a ritual bath about five weeks after giving birth. After bathing the new mother would make offerings to the Birth Goddess Laima." (21).

The Bear thus opens up a cycle of mothers of different species giving birth and nourishing the earth. From autumn through the winter to the next spring the spirits of animals, and humans, are sent on their spiritual path along the sacred tree of life to the womb of the Arctic night sky. This cycle of life and rebirth is a central element of Finno-Ugric women's handicrafts and ornamental decorations, which I consider intimate expressions of power and a magical relationship to the creative forces of life/nature and the Cosmos.

Ornaments as Paths of Power

Finnish Carelian and Ob-Ugrian ornaments found on headscarves, tablecloths, woven mittens, socks, and containers as well as cradles are a reflection of the strong relationship of the creative forces and fertility of Nature to *haltia*, spirits or guardians. In Finnish, the ancient word for the leading-cord is *haltija-lanka*. *Haltija-lanka* is the piece of yarn that keeps the skeins separate when they are woven together (*pasmalanka*). The Constellation of The Great Bear and its connection to the fertile forces of spring is represented at all levels of weaving beginning from the *haltija-lanka* to the intricate pattern of swastikas with its

Ob-Ugrian ornaments: top row, mittens depicting she-bears; lower row, mittens depicting male bears.

rhythmic continuity. Ob-Ugrian Mansi women's womb-like, small leather bags and Carelian embroidery often depict Bear, suggesting ways in which women renew and strengthen their relationship to the creative forces of Nature. A she-bear with "paws up" might represent the strong, oncoming, erotic and nourishing power of spring, giving the woman who wears a decorated bag or woven mittens a powerful feeling of being an integral part of the cycle of life. A she-bear might also represent the life-force which makes everything grow, like fetuses grow in the womb of their mothers, or like trees, flowers, and grass grow in nature. This force is also connected to the way in which I feel myself to be a branch of the life-tree of my ancestors. A traditional Finnish-Carelian ornament, the tree of life, with with its branches pointing upwards, reflects the generations, the joys of life, the upstreaming force of life "juice." Some of the ornaments depict sacred groves, showing the guardian spirits of trees placed in the four cardinal directions around an abstracted vagina in the form of a rhombus in the middle. The "naked" poles on Ob-Ugrian headscarves with "soul-birds"—like those depicted on children's cradles (Vahter 1953: 113)—and vagina-like rhombus figures, in turn, may rep-

Ob-Ugrian ornaments: woman's dress decorated with swastika and rhombus ornaments.

resent the nakedness of the autumn forest, the transformation of death during the "cosmic pregnancy" of dark winter.

Writing about traditional Belarusian ornamental towels Vol'ha Labacheuskaia (2002) states:

> Linens, made by women's hands, didn't have strictly utilitarian function. They served, perhaps, as the first textbooks, visual aids for understanding the methods of comprehension of the World, realizing the notions of infinity and measure. From times immemorial linens that were woven during winter were whitened during the early summer dues in wet meadows, at the riverbank. The linens spread on the young grass under delicate rays of the morning sun, always evoked the image of the Way that calls you, leads you over the horizon into unknown World.
>
> The notions of cloth as a Path have been a part of the mythical World imagery since ancient times. They are embodied in rituals, folklore images, and works of folk art. The image of a towel-road originates from the process of thread spinning. The thread appears from the chaos of fiber, extends, and lengthens in hands of spinner—a mythical and poetic symbol of fate, personified in different cultures....
>
> The archetype symbolism of the towel is determined by stable ritual, ceremonial and decorative functions of that thing, peculiarities of its form, nature of decor and composition, quality of towel cloth itself.... The cloth was a kind of mark of a traversed path, and a woman's thoughts were reflected in its patterns.

Ob-Ugrian women's blouses are often decorated with swastikas, suggesting the position of the Otava, Great Bear's four seasonal positions as discussed above. To understand the swastika as the representation of the seasonal position of the Great Bear, and as a Cosmic Womb/pregnant woman's womb, we must return to neolithic Vincan signs. In the pregnant figurines of the Bird goddess of Vinca culture there are decorative labyrinths or swastikas, with whirling and creative elements and "forces" of nature—seen also in whirls of water, whirls of winds (in Ob-Ugrian ornaments, waves of wind), in the multitude of the spiral arrangements of Nature discussed earlier. A cyclical worldview represented as a spiral, evident even in human fingerprints, reflects the principle of creation found in nature. Spirals also characterize water, the "mouths" of rivers where fish rise to the surface to spawn. The spring winds raise spirals that spread the pollen of trees and the seeds formed earlier in the fall. When even the starry sky seems to move around the North Star, it makes sense to conceive of the creative forces as taking the form of a spiral.

I believe that ornamental decorations in Finno-Ugric women's handicrafts speak to the ways in which the depiction of key motifs were intended to strenghten women's relationship to the nourishing forces of life and, finally, their connection to the transformational forces of death, winter, and dreamtime. The Finno-Ugric ornaments in their "lay out" also represent and express in a rhythmic way how all creatures and creative forces of life are intertwined and belong together. It is as if the emotional and music-like experience of "all my relations" is transferred through the figures, colours, and patterns to protect and to strengthen the nurturing ties between all forms of creation. In Finnish and Ob-Ugrian handicrafts we also find ornaments that are connected to the fertility of Nature, with their gifts to the community, and with their deep meaning mediated through mythological knowledge. These ornaments express the intimate and intensive relationship between people and their environment. In old Finnish and Finno-Ugric cultures everything that "exists" was considered as "living." In this cultural context, every ornament has the power to "bear on," to relate to, to connect, to sustain the "being in being," *olemassaoloa,* as we say in Finnish.

Conclusion

In 2005, I was fortunate to meet the psychologist Patricia Vickers (of Haida, Tshimshian, Heiltsuk/British origin) during her visit to Finland. As she put it: "creating beauty from the beauty of Nature is nurturing." I remain grateful to her for her teachings on transforming suffering (see Vickers 2005). I deeply believe that a nurturing way of living, that honouring the teachings of ancestors and ancestral law as Vickers taught, building up nurturing and responsible relationships with "all relatives" is a way to balance the earth and ourselves.

In this paper I have brought together various elements in Finno-Ugric women's handicrafts and ornamental decorations that epitomize the matrix of the related forces of regeneration and procreation to which women and bears, birds, frogs, and fish also belong in a worldview of spirals that reflect the ongoing renewal of life and cycles of death and rebirth. Last autumn I was asked by a friend to meet the Native artist and teacher Jim Poitras who was visiting Finland from Germany where he has lived for several years. It was very touching to hear his story and his teachings. Because we were able to meet for only a short time, I sent him an email when he returned to Germany. I asked him if he would be able to go the Linden-Museum in Stuttgart where the Dakota pipe is conserved, and displayed, and thank for me the Spirit of the Pipe, the Spirit of the Bear, and the Carver of that pipe. He answered, "Will do." I feel now a new cycle is reaching its beginning. Thank you!

I thank Kaarina Kailo and Luciana Ricciutelli for turning the rough draft of my paper into a digestible form. My Bear-relationship with Kaarina goes back to the year 1999 when we met and founded the Finnish Ecopsychology Association (Metsänpeitto), through which we now seek to raise the Finns' awareness of their own Indigenous cultural roots and traditions before modernization and Europeanization. We both believe that changes are needed in people's attitudes towards nature and the broader cosmos. Kaarina introduced me the Gift Economy and as a result we co-edited a book applying the insights of a Gift-related worldview in the Finnish context (Heiskanen and Kailo 2006).

[1]Finno-Ugric peoples live west of the Urals—Zyrian Komis, Permian Komis, and Udmurts—with connection to the disputed Biarmians and Biarmialand at the entry of Viena River.

[2]See Biret Marét Kallio's (1997) article on her visions and drumming journeys.

[3]See, for example, Dragonfly Farms Spindles and Distaffs <pweb.jps.net/~gaustad/naturaldis1.jpg>.

[4]Vinca script got its name from the present-day village of Vinca, 14 kilometers downstream of Belgrade on the Danube River. The script was first used in the Balkans in the fifth millennium BCE and represents the first attested writing, well before the developments in Sumer, commonly perceived to be the source of the first writing discovered on the planet.

[5]"According to Udmurtian heritage records, the higher gods Inmar, Kvasia, and Kyldysin were male. The latter was the god of the earth and of the harvest as well as the protector of women and children. The word *kyldys* means in Permian "creative," "fertilizing," and *kyldysin* means "woman," "female (animal)," "mother," "mother-in-law." Kyldysin used to live on the Earth, but took offence by people's behaviour and went to heaven, or according to other records, underground. Kyldysin in heaven became mixed with Inmar and the underground god became Mu-Kyldysin, the god of fertility, who gave children a soul and protected young mothers as well as the welfare of the kinsfolk. The corresponding god for Komis was Zarni-an, or golden woman, for Maris it was Shun-Shochynava, or the mother of everything in existence, and for Mansis, it was Kaltash-*ekva*, the wife and sister

of the highest god" (Autio 2001: 175). "The goddess became a male god at the beginning of the second millennium, maintaining the same functions. Shutova elaborates on this process of change in her 1998 article, where she also claims that the time Kyldysin spent on the Earth symbolizes the happy times. Once the male god took over, this led to wars and much suffering in the sixteenth century" (Autio 2001: 176).

[6]Many North American Native peoples also refer to the continent on which they live as Turtle Island.

References

Autio, Eero. 2001. "The Permian Animal Style." *Folklore* 18,19: 162-186. Online: <www.folklore.ee/Folklore/vol18/permian.pdf>.

Autio, Eero. 2000. *Kotkat, hirvet, karhut, permiläistä pronssitaidetta (Eagles, Elk, Bears, and Permian Bronze Art)*. Jyväskylä: Atena, 2000.

Dashu, Max. 2006. "The Old Goddess." *MatriFocus: Cross-Quarterly for the Goddess Woman* 15 (3). Online: <www.matrifocus.com/BEL06/scholar.htm>.

Esser, Annette, Coletta Damm, Thalia Gur-Klein, Katerina Karkala-Zorba, Laime Kiskunaite, Asphodel Long, Caroline Mackenzie, and Susan K. Roll. 2001. "A Dialogue on Woman, Ritual and Liturgy." *Women, Ritual and Liturgy: Yearbook of European Society of Women in Theological Research*. Eds. Susan, K. Roll, Annette Esser, Brigitte Enzner-Probst, Charlotte Methuen, and Angela Berlis. Peeters: Leuven.

Griffen, Tony D. 2007. *Deciphering the Vinca Script*. Online: <http://www.geocities.com/~dubricius>.

Grimm, Jakob. 2004. *Teutonic Mythology, Vols. I-IV*. 4th ed. 1883. Trans. James Steven Stallybrass. London: George Bell and Sons.

Haberland, Wolfgang, ed. 1979. *Kunst der Welt, Holle, Nordamerika, Indianer, Eskimo (Native Art of Indians and the Eskimos)*. 3rd ed. Baden-Baden: Holle Verlag.

Haetta, Odd Mathis. 1994. *The Ancient Religion and Folk-Beliefs of the Sámi*. Árran Poetry Archive, Alta Museum. Online: <http://home.earthlink.net/~arran2/archive/sister.htm>.

Heiskanen, Irma and Kaarina Kailo, eds. 2006. *Ekopsykologia ja perinnetieto. Polkuja eheyteen (Ecopsychology and Traditional Ecological Knowledge: Paths Towards Wholeness)*. Helsinki: Greenspot.

Holmberg, Uno, ed. 1996 [1922]. *Derungs, Kurt, Der Baum des Lebens, Göttingen und Baumkult (The Tree of Life, Goddesses and the Tree Cult)*. Bern: Animalia.

Kallio, Biret Máret. 1997. "Noaidi: The One Who Sees." *ReVision* 19 (3) (Winter): 37-41.

Karjalainen, Annamari. 1994. "Runtâmâs on raju akka (Runtâmâs is a Fierce Crone)." Eds. Pekka Laaksonen and Sirkka-Liisa Mettomäki. *Metsä ja metsän viljaa (Forests and Everything They Give Us)*. Helsinki: SKS.

Kuokkanen, Rauna. 2007. *Reshaping the University: Responsibility, Indigenous*

Epistemes and the Logic of the Gift. Vancouver: University of British Columbia Press.

Labacheuskaia, Vol'ha. 2002. *Link of Times – Belaruski Ruchnik.* Trans. by A.L. Vasil'evaMinsk: Belarus. Online: <http://www.belarusguide.com/culture1/visual_arts/Belarusian_rushnik.htm>. Accessed 2 March 2008.

Matossian, Mary Kilbourne. 1973. "Vestiges of the Cult of the Mother Goddess in Baltic Folklore." *Baltic Literature and Linguistics.* Eds. Arvids Ziedonis et al. Columbus OH: Association for the Advancement of Baltic Studies.

Nuttal, Zelia. 1901. *The Fundamental Principles of Old and New World Civilizations.* Salem, MA: Salem Press, 1901.

Paulaharju, Samuli. 1939. *Sompio.* Helsinki: WSOY.

Paulaharju, Samuli and Jenni Paulaharju. 1946. SKVR, Digital Archive XIII 3, 9545. Online: <http://dbgw.finlit.fi/skvr/skvr.phtml>. Accessed 2 March 2008.

Pentikäinen, Juhani. 1990. *Suomalaisen lähtö. Kirjoituksia pohjoisesta kuolemankulttuurista (Silent as Water We Live – Old Believers and Abroad: Cultural Encounters with Finno-Ugrians).* Studia Fennica Folkloristica, no. 6. Helsinki: SKS.

Poitras, Jim. Online: <http://www.sicc.sk.ca/faces/mpoitji.htm>. Accessed 2 March 2008.

Rappenglück, Michael A. 2002. "The Pivot of the Cosmos: The Concepts of the World Axis Across Cultures." Cultural Context from the Archaeoastronomical Data and the Echoes of Cosmic Catastrophic Events: Papers presented at the SEAC 2002 Tenth Annual Conference, 27-30 August in Tartu, Estonia. Eds. Mare Koiva, Harry Mïrk and Izold Pustolnik. Online: <http://www.folklore. ee/SEAC/SEAC_teesid.pdf>. Accessed 2 March 2008.

Shutova, Nadezhda I. 1998. *Zhenskoe bozhestvo plodorodia v dukhovoi zhizni, Finno-ugrov Priuralia. Ob etnicheskoi psikhologii udmurtov.* Izhevsk.

Suomen kansan vanhat runot (SKVR). 2002-2003. *Ancient Finnish Poetry.* Helsinki: Suomen kirjallisuuden seura. Digital archive. Online: <http://dbgw.finlit. fi/skvr/skvr.phtml>.

Vahter, Tyyni. 1953. *Obinugrilaisten kansojen koristekuosit. Ornamentik der Ob-Ugrier (The Ornamental Textiles of Ob-Ugrian Peoples).* Kansatieteellisiä julkaisuja IX-Travaux ethnographiques de la Société Finno-Ougrienne. Helsinki: Suomalais-ugrilainen seura.

Valkeapää, Nils-Aslak. 1997. *The Sun, My Father.* Trans. Ralph Salisbury, Lars Nordström, and Harald Gaski. Guovdageaidnu, Norway: DAT.

Valkeapää, Nils-Aslak. 1994. *Nu guhkkin dat mii lahka/Så fjernt dat naere.* Trans. Ralph Salisbury, Lars Nordström, and Harald Gaski. Guovdageaidnu, Norway: DAT.

Vickers, Patricia J. 2005. "*Sayt k'ilim goot* (Of One Heart): Transforming Suffering?" *The American Indian Quarterly* 29 (3,4): 691-706.

Voss, Jutta. 2006. *Das Schwarzmond – Tabu. Die kulturelle Bedeutung des weiblichen Zyklus (The Black Moon – Taboo: The Cultural Significance of the Female Cycle).* Stuttgart: Kreuz Verlag.

Satu Maarit Natunen, "Bear Energy. The Woman Inside Me,"
gouache on handmade paper, 8" x 9", 1999. Private collection.

"Baiki" ... The Place Where Your Heart Is

This conversation took place initially at the Arctic Hysteria Gallery in Helsinki, in the summer of 1999 where the Sami artist, Satu Maarit Natunen then held her art gallery and studio, and where she had an exhibition of her artwork dealing with Sami mythology. Most importantly for my research, the exhibition focused on bears, wolves, and other mythic Sami animals, prompting me to converse with the artist on our shared interests. I wanted to hear her views on Bear because I knew that in Sami culture, art is considered at least as important as the sciences for expressing and transmitting intergenerational knowledge.

Kaarina Kailo (KK): I would like to start our conversation about women, bears, and other mythic animals by asking you to tell me something about yourself.

Satu Maarit Natunen (SN): My complete name is Satu Maarit Natunen and my Sami background is reflected in the name Maarit.

KK: I recognize that in Sami culture names are very important. Do you know anything about the naming process or the meaning of your name?

SN: Not really about this name; I have a Sami name, too. It is a bit different. It tells you about my family and relatives. The name Satu Maarit Natunen is my Finnish name. What I do know (from my mother) is that my grandmother wanted me to be called Satu, which means a "fairy tale."

KK: They say that a name is an omen. You are a storyteller in addition to being an artist.

SN: Yes, I am. For some reason, I am attracted to fairy tales. They are part of my work.

KK: What part of Samiland do you come from?

SN: Today I would say that my roots are from Karigasniemi, but mainly I am a city Sami. I have studied in big cities around the world—the art of textiles in France, and Native Studies in Washington, DC, at Georgetown University—and I have lived in Helsinki for a long time. I have moved around a lot, like the Sami did traditionally. We have a name for the place where your heart is and it is called *baiki*. We didn't use to have a name for "home," but now in the Sami language we do. It was important when somebody left their home that the person could survive wherever they went. Surviving, making a home, is still a very physical thing.

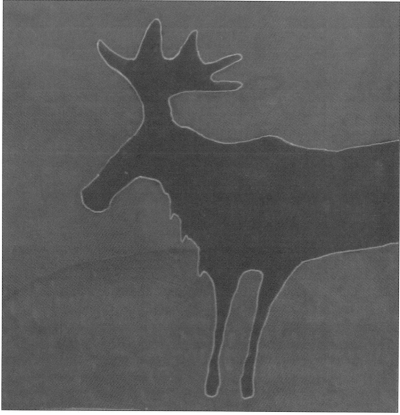

Satu Maarit Natunen, "Elk," gouache on handmade paper, 20 cm x 20 cm, 2007.

KK: Apart from your art representing a political stance with regard to Sami self-expression, are you involved with the Native peoples' movement?

SN: Yes, although I try not to be an overtly political person because I am an artist. It is not easy to be a politician and an artist. We have a movement for young Indigenous people. I participated in a few meetings and follow their news and events.

KK: As an artist, what do you think are the most important issues that need to be resolved in Sami culture today?

SN: That we should let ourselves be modern people, that we should develop. We have to keep our culture, and our language, but we also have to find new words and new things and also develop culturally in that context and live in these times. Many times I meet people who expect me, as a Sami, to come from the caves, to be dirty and eat raw meat. We need the strength to update ourselves.

KK: When I came by your studio, I was struck not only by the vibrant colours in your artwork that exude so much energy and have recurring nature motifs, but by their particular thematic focus, animals. Are you particularly attracted to animals artistically?

SN: I paint birds, wolves, and other animals a lot. I have a special relationship with animals because Sami culture is very much related to nature. All our stories, beliefs, and lives relate to nature and also to animals. All peoples have a creation story about themselves. Our creation story includes animals. We do not put ourselves in a different category. We do not separate or compare ourselves with animals. We are on the same level. We think we are a mixture of all animals: foxes, wolves, bears, and humans. Some Finns might have a strange understanding about that. Some come here and ask me what kind of a tail I have! In our traditional dress we have a lot of fabric at the back of the outfit, so it looks like you might have something there, which could be a tail. They think that if we consider ourselves half human/half animal then we should have a tail. However, not all Sami think the same way, today. Many don't even know the old stories. Not all the Sami today are friends of nature, unfortunately. Even though we have always been closely related to nature, we are normal human beings with normal needs. Sometimes all the "outside" impulses are much more interesting than our own.

KK: I have been researching the theme of women and bears around the world. The Finns also believed that they were related to and originated from Bear. In the bear hunting culture thousands of years before Christ, they believed also that the differences between humans and animals—particularly humans and bears—were not as sharp as they are today. That is all a matter of degrees. Are these people who used to worship Bear the same Finns to whom you refer as the ones who view the relationship to nature so differently?

SN: I think so. I do not feel angry or disappointed. I feel a little bit sorry for them for all they have lost by no longer following Sami or Finnish traditions and culture. We have our problems, but we still must respect all things: nature and its relationships. That is what I do. It is a way of living, and the traditional stories one hears make it possible to see things differently.

KK: Why have the Sami not been able to retain closer ties to the oral tradition? Or, is a vibrant storytelling tradition still alive in some Sami communities where the stories continue to be told and passed down to successive generations?

SN: Maybe it is because the Sami language was not a written language. It is recent historically for us to have our language in written form. It is a also relatively new for us to have newspapers and/or books written in Sami. Conditions of life in Sami communities were harder than in Southern Finland, for example. And our people were not so-called "educated" in the global way. They did not have newspapers in the Sami language, and they did not read other papers either to get outside information. So there was not a lot of information coming into Sami communities, even though there had been a lot of research conducted among the Samis. But researchers did not give us information from the outside world. Only the priests started to tell us that it was bad to think about this and that. It was then that some strong people started to hide Sami cultural traditions, to be able to hold on to them.

KK: It has always amazed me that the Sami have managed to retain their na-ture narratives in a more "authentic" or traditional form. Finns also have stories

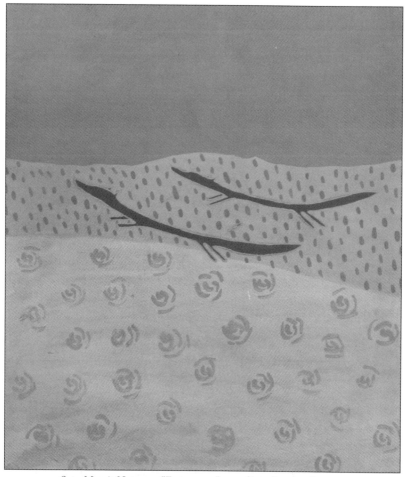

Satu Maarit Natunen, "Encounters," gouache on handmade paper,
20 cm x 20 cm, 2007.

about nature, but usually these stories reflect Finns' increasing distance from an ecosocially participatory way of life. Have stories about women and animals been central in the Sami oral tradition?

SN: Yes, mainly bear stories. These stories are about energies that exist in the world. And for some reason, I do not know why, people, mostly men, think these "energies" are dangerous for women. I think men are afraid of women, how women can use their strong energy. I am also talking about sexual energy. That is the strongest energy. But men think that women have too much energy. If we think we are a mixture of a bear and a human being, the woman is connected, still, through an umbilical cord to the bear. And women can access the energy that comes from that and be stronger than men, for instance. And I am not saying this in a symbolic feminist sense, I mean this literally.

KK: The Sami taboos of women not participating in Bear rituals and Bear ceremonials, of having to look at the bear through a brass or metal ring [thought to neutralize the danger that the bear represented to women], were therefore invented by men to keep women from getting too powerful, from having too much power? Could this be connected with the reproductive processes? The life energy women embody?

SN: Yes, that could be it, but it is not so straightforward or obvious. It is not necessarily related to reproduction but, somehow, the bear is an immediate power animal with strength and power. We think of sexual energy as the strongest of energies. I know many people who would deny what I am saying now. This includes even some Sami because today Sami are close to the [Christian] religion so that for them, too, sexuality has come to be seen as a bad thing.

KK: Have you formed your own opinion about the link between women and bears on the basis of your readings, from stories you have heard, what people have said in your communities, or is it intuitive?

SN: I think it is a mixture of everything, and a mixture of my thoughts and experiences. When I am working I need to think about Sami issues, and other issues to do with art, nature, culture. I am living with these things all the time. Even if I know how to use a computer, and have a driver's licence, I am working with these things. And the truth is that we no longer have the entire stories anymore. We have bits and pieces here and there. For me, it has been very important to talk to other people who have found another piece of the stories, different than the ones I have found and experienced. And somehow, when you have enough pieces, you can see the whole thing.

KK: One interpretation I have heard why bears are dangerous to women is because it is seen as the coming together of two powerful beings, beings that may cancel each other out, neutralize each other. Is that what gave rise to taboos that are used to women away from the power of the bear?

SN: Maybe it is because people are trying to survive. All of life is about surviving. That is in the background when we think of the bear and the woman that stayed together in the same cave during the winter. In the stories, where the woman came from, no one says. After the winter hibernation, the woman gives birth to a new, stronger human being [a combination of bear and human]. We think the strongest people are the Sami people. But even so, these stories point to an opportunity to create a new, and stronger human by living with the bear, and mating with the bear. When a woman and a bear put their powerful energies together they can create something that is perceived as being able to destroy human people of former times.

KK: Why would that be threatening?

SN: It would mean the death of the now-living people. It is all about survival. This is what I have in my mind now. I know that men in particular have tried to keep women away from the bear. We think that we are able to change into animals. Nothing can keep women from transforming into bears; we have no exceptions. I would say to women who feel weak, who are not self-confident, to transform themselves into a bear in order to find themselves. And then to find the power, and also the sexual power, within. You need the bear if your "doors" are closed.

KK: Scholars say that there is nothing more fierce than a mother bear defending her cubs. This is "love" with very strong boundaries. This is an image of femininity where the love is so strong that the female turns into a ferocious animal, which goes against the Christian ideal of meek, obedient, passive mothers. Maybe there is something in this motif that really appeals to women, even subliminally. This very strong, adamant, fierce mother is able to fight and does not need a man to do the fighting for her (although she is not against partner help). A male bear is never as fierce as a mother bear.

SN: Yes, that is true. But, I have friends who have children and they are all ferocious when it comes to protecting their children, but they no longer compare themselves to the bear. Today, they are trying to find their counterparts, for example, in tigers, which are not really from our culture. I find that today even people who are not related to the Sami culture, or are not really interested in these things, have started comparing themselves to animals.

KK: Bears have always been linked with the rebirth of cyclic life. The bear stays in its den throughout the entire winter and manages to feed itself by sucking its paws. For me, as a woman, there is something about that self-reliance; the ability to survive and come back to life in its richness after hibernation. What are the common elements that bears and women share that might explain the metaphysical, spiritual, and mythic attraction? Men relate to bears in a positive way as well, but often the hunting perspective restricts this relationship.

SN: I think that men also want to be important but, somehow, they are always fighting, trying to make us believe that is just as important as giving life. In real life, in the past and today, women in Sami villages have to be twice as strong as men because they have to know how to do men's work and women's work. After a couple of months of men's absences from the villages, men return and realize that everything is working without them; it may be frightening to them. So, why do we need men? Nobody says out loud, but everybody understands it. It *is* frightening.

KK: Why are men so threatened by women when they are the ones with all the power? This has always been a mystery to me. Society continues to tell us that men are the leaders, men are the ones who are prominent in the public sphere. Men have most of the social and political power, so why do they feel threatened?

SN: This is a difficult question. I think men need to feel safer than women. Women are, in a sense, wilder and we have the power to give life and to survive. I am always saying, "Hey, this life is about surviving! We can make it really nice, we can laugh, and we do not have to suffer." That is what women do, we survive.

KK: The bear is also the healer of the animal kingdom. (It is interesting that in the English language we talk about animal "kingdom," why not *queendom*?) The bear is, among animals, the one who seeks out herbs and roots and is thus related to symbolic healing.

SN: If I remember right, in former times, all healers used to follow a bear to discover which herbs and plants the bears were collecting and using, so they could use those herbs for healing.

KK: I think of a bear in its den as withdrawing from the world into a private place to heal and to renew the energies. Perhaps we do not always know, or do not even need to know, what it is—this mysterious something—that is speaking to us through the body and the senses, that we feel on many levels intuitively, in our bodies. What does the bear mean to you personally?

SN: The bear is part of my culture's legends and beliefs. The bear gives me strength. The bear awakens me. S/he opens my eyes. Even if I am not a shaman, and just an artist, I can say to some people "Find the bear and go into the bear and then find yourself."

KK: Does this mean that you have found the bear in yourself, you have found its strength yourself?

SN: Yes. The bear has helped me. When I found the bear, and all of these other animals, I had an awakening, or as Buddhists would put it, I found enlightenment. It made me strong.

KK: I was seriously ill at one point and I started to dream about the bear. The bear was literally "getting in touch" with me. I had many dreams in which the bear was holding me, holding my hands with its paws, and then forcing me to dance when I did not want to dance. Once, I spent the night during a storm in a tent with Elina Helander. We were in Samiland, on a mountain, where we were working on a project together. In the morning she asked me to tell her what I had dreamt. The bear has a wonderful sense of humour. In the dream there was what looked like a closed-down weather station, a broadcast station. Nobody lived inside it but the doors were open so I went in. There was a kitchen and although there was nothing in the kitchen, I knew something was "cooking." Then brown bears appeared and began circling the house, looking in and waving at me. They were not threatening; they were very friendly bears. They had big smiles on their faces and I could sense their mirth and sense of humour. They brought me medicine, some positive energy. At the time, I did not understand why they brought me this medicine/positive energy, but I had this when I started to do research on the bear. This research was becoming much more than simply an academic project. Later, I wondered: why did the bears contact me? What were they trying to tell me? Why did they come to my kitchen and why was my kitchen empty? The kitchen is where you cook, where you find food and nourishment. The bears were bringing me some other kind of nourishment—a type of "soul" food. The broadcast station suggested I would need to do outreach and "call out," to spread awareness of ecomythologies (my last name, Kailo, *kailottaa*, means "to call out," and it is also related to healing).

I am the daughter of a nurse and a pastor, but I do not get much nourishment from the patriarchal side of Christian Lutheran traditions. I am disillusioned with institutionalized religions' hierarchical, dominating approach and the way the Christian Church gave rise to, and continues to reinforce, patriarchal, hierarchical gender relations. I cannot accept the spiritual monopolies and religious capitalism that places women below men as both practitioners and authorities in the realm of the spiritual life. Despite some changes in attitude, there is, in the dogma, no interconnectedness with nature and gender relations are asymmetrical, based on an unequal distribution of resources and power. I find that the Bear is a figure of connection. It is a mediator between humans and animals. The bears in my dream came to give me the nourishment I needed at the time, and to point me to pre-patriarchal, pre-Christian life-oriented ways of life. The bear gave me strength, "awakened" me, as it did you.

SN: In your dream, the bear was a kind of guide.

KK: Why do women have look at the bear through a brass ring in bear rituals or festivals instead of looking at the bear directly, as I did in my dream?

SN: Because it is too powerful. It is felt that their energies combined would be too much for women. But really, it was the men who were afraid of what would happen. For some reason women obeyed. The men like them to obey. The men told them stories like, "This might be dangerous, the bear will harm you." I believe somehow that it was finally women's curiosity that led them to access that Bear power. It led them to not always obey.

KK: Do you think women pretended to comply with the requirement to use the brass ring? Maybe the brass ring is a symbol of socialization or social regulation; a social taboo according to which women must neither peek, nor see (i.e., partake of the establishment of the social and socio-cosmic order).

SN: Yes, I think so. I feel that women were saying "yes, we do what you say so that there will not be any argument." When I trust my own femininity, however, I do look. And if it happens that you do look, you get more energy. Men have tried, and still do to some degree, control everything. Today women can change things. It is usually the women, the mothers, who pass on traditions and culture to children. We need to change those traditions, and bring women, and women's issues, to the forefront.

KK: Sami women would throw or spit alder juice on men when they came back from a bear hunt. Alder juice red, a powerful colour. The colour red evokes the power of blood—female blood, menstruation, childbirth, a special energy that in Finnish we call *väki*. *Väki* is very powerful. I read that women spat this red blood on men to neutralize the dangerous power of a bear. When a dangerous bear had been killed and women's blood came into contact with it, the woman's blood neutralized the danger. I have also read that alder juice is used to draw symbols on Sami drums.

SN: Blood has traditionally been used for a number of "sacrifices" offered to the gods. Sami used to put blood from a reindeer on a wooden hammer, which they then offered to the gods.

KK: Is this a give-back ritual? A ritual, where you give back to nature what you take from it?

SN: Yes, and the Sami also believed that if you make a special kill, then you must take the bones, the entire skeleton, and bury them underneath the earth to

Satu Maarit Natunen, "The Legend," gouache on handmade paper,
20 cm x 20 cm, 2007.

give them back to the land.

KK: How have people reacted to your paintings about women and bears?

SN: Some people, I feel, immediately understand what I am doing. Men and women. But then there are those who think I am a little bit crazy; that it is childish to make women and bears the focus of some of my art, and that I even think about these things rooted in our past. But mostly, I think people are interested. Some people ask if I have something in writing about the women and my bears in my art. I have brief explanations, but it is very general information because you cannot tell everybody everything. If people are not open, they will not be able to listen. For example in Savo, Finland, they say that when a Savo person talks, the responsibility goes to the listener. You need to know that the other person is able first to understand and then to be able to listen before you can pass on the knowledge, the gift of that knowledge.

KK: You have said that sometimes you feel intuitively that a woman buying a piece of your art needed something, that she needed the energy that is in your paintings. Do people comment on the energy of your artwork?

SN: Yes, sometimes. That is why I always feel a little bit sad to sell a piece during an exhibition when I am not there. I like to give really good explanations. I like to see the people who buy my work. When I paint, for instance when I use silver, I am connecting to, and depicting, the underground people, the *väki*, of Sami legends. You canmay not be able to see them directly, but if you are open you can sense that they are there, somewhere. If you met them, a man or a woman or their reindeer, you would need to throw some silver or some other metal over them. Then they would remain visible. In my mind I paint (even if my paintings look really modern), I paint this *väki* to be part of this world, and to be part of the underground world. First I paint them for the underground world because there is no silver there, then I make them stay in this world by painting them with silver.

KK: So you are painting both the *maahinen*, what we Finns call the little spirit people, and the people of the middle world?

SN: We called them *kufitars*.

KK: Is the silver the energy?

SN: Yes, it is an energy line in the painting so the *kufitars* will stay in this world.

KK: You also paint foxes and wolves. But would you say that the bear motif is one of the most popular?

SN: Yes, bear is the most popular but I do not paint that many of them. I find I could sell bear paintings all the time but I do not want to. So the bear is just kind of inside me. The thing about the bear is that with bears you are not breaking the law, and any transformation is permanent and has to be done the proper way.

KK: What do you mean when you say "not breaking the law"?

SN: The wolf is another really strong animal. But when you change into a wolf you want to come back to you former life. And if I tell somebody: "Why don't you change into a wolf?" then I mean, "Do something strange or maybe have a lover for a while but then you go back to the former state." But when you transform into a bear, it is permanent. It will change you so much.

KK: Wolf represents an adventure but bear is a spouse. You marry a bear, but you flirt with wolves and foxes in order to get another kind of a perspective? So you can have flings with other animals but with a bear you actually have to make a commitment.

SN: Yes, and you need to be able to change completely, not only for a while. I tell people to change into a wolf when they want to experience new facets of their being. We have too many rigid, strict "rules" in this world and that's why it is important to be a wolf for a while.

KK: I can hear many people laughing at us, but I understand exactly what you mean. The negative aspects of globalization and monoculture include the eurocentered refusal to accept, or to even try to understand, foreign cultures and worldviews, one example of which is the inability of many to understand the concept of "shapeshifting." It is acceptable only as a commercially-exploitable element of "exotic" fiction. We need to spend and buy, purchase and kill nature, because we have lost our moorings in and with nature. Have you thought about the link between women and bears, ecology, and the environment? Are those kinds of issues present in your art in general?

SN: Yes, it all has to do with respect. If you believe that you can transform yourself into a wolf, then you are also as vulnerable as the wolf. If somebody kills you as a wolf, you will die, but there is a special respect accorded to you as wolf. What I mean by this is that if a hunter kills you as wolf, the hunter will notice the signs there that tell him you were human. But he cannot do anything and you cannot come back. You need to respect the danger and the freedom that comes with transformation. The main point is that you are as weak or as strong as the animals you transform into.

KK: Do you regard the creation of art as a way to deal with the consumerist obsession of our modern society? I am trying to look for solutions for how humans can find a way back to sustainable modes of living so that they do not have to go along with the fast food and short-sighted junk culture. There is not much real spiritual nourishment anymore. Storytelling has been replaced by television soap operas, which are consumerist, based on stereotypes, repetitive, and which do not bring out creativity in people. They render you passive.

SN: My artwork demands that the viewer think. One thing I always say is that I want to I want to present the bear in symbols—even though I could paint a realistic looking bear, what you see in nature. While I have my own ideas about what the painting, the colours, and everything else in a given piece of art means, I want to give the person looking at my art some work for the brain too, and in this way create more. I do not always place everything in a painting on the same level. There are people who come to my studio who do not see anything. They do not see the symbols; instead they are enjoying the colours. I feel sorry that it is popular now to have art that depicts terrible things and that makes people sad. Horrible things are a part of life, but as an artist that I want to give the viewer something positive.

KK: Do you see your art as medicine?

SN: In a way, yes. I went to see a Tibetan exhibition. I felt really comfortable with the mandalas because they are made for healing and helping people. That is in a way what I am doing too. This is not to say that I am a healer, but in a way that is what I aim to do through my art.

KK: Do you agree that the dominant gender relations as far as women are concerned are limiting and asymmetrical, leaving us with a deficit that somehow we compensate for with mythic narratives. Mythic narratives help women expand their being, which is restricted by Christian gender scripts, for example. Do you think this might explain women's attraction to the bear and the wolf and so on?

SN: These legends, or mythic narratives, are from the time before Christianity. I think somehow it is women's strength and awakening that draws women to these

Satu Maarit Natunen, "Sun," gouache on handmade paper, 20 cm x 20 cm, 2007.

stories. I think of it as an awakening because it gives a sense of relations.

KK: Are bears a kind of a shaman figure in a modern sense that takes you to another realm?

SN: Yes, it is the same thing with wolves and other animals. The only difference is what happens to you as a particular animal then. You must perform a special ritual in order to transform yourself to another being.

KK: Probably many women would like to know how they can transform into an animal.

SN: What I tell you is for everybody. It is not sacred in that way, it is not secret. It is like telling you to concentrate on something. Like finding things. Then you start to wonder, "Why did I not find this earlier?" It is not very easy to tell someone how to do this. I think there is always a time when you can do these things. For different people, there are different traditions or rituals to access the energy and transform. And, there is not only one way of doing it. It is unique to every individual and takes a great deal of willpower as well as an open, and receptive, mind.

KK: A European, westernized woman who does not feel that she gets spiritual nourishment from Christian imagery or rituals, might feel intuitively that the bear can give her something. What would you recommend that she do? Paint the bear, write the bear, imagine the bear?

SN: I would tell her to go to the forest, for example, to touch the earth, because the bear is related to the earth. Try to breathe the same air that the bear is breathing. But you do not need to go to a forest where you know there is a bear. You just need to think like a bear. When you are in touch with the bear, it is like electrical current running through your body.

KK: Some people may also find it through meditation.

SN: Yes, but the way to start is to touch the earth and just to breathe. Because it is your own power that you need to tap into. I would be a little bit afraid to give the power to somebody else to be a bear.

KK: Yes, you have to discover your own power?

SN: Yes. If you give it to the other person, it is not the same thing. You have to find your own bear. You can talk to the people and you can get the different aspects of the thing, but you cannot give it. Other people cannot do it for you.

KK: What about the other important spiritual powers, the goddesses of Sami culture, Maderakka, Sarakka, Juksakka, Uksakka? Do you paint them as well?

SN: I do not paint them; I put them on my t-shirts. Young Sami people are not used to using symbols. And I was bothered about how about how other people, non-Samis, are using them, for example, putting them on t-shirts. I decided to start using the goddess symbols and put them on my own t-shirts. We believe that wearing symbols can heal you. We wear the symbol of the sun on our clothing. As I said earlier, we need to be in this world and communicate in this world. I decided to make my own t-shirts because think I can reach more people by doing something they understand. It is kind of a modern thing. I am telling them what it really is: not only that it is female gods, but divine females. I am telling them about their background, about where they live, and I know and see people start to think about these things. Many people ask about why I use the colour blue. It is a very sacred colour because we have what we call the "blue moment"—the daily moments when gods are flying across the sky. It is when the blue of the sky becomes concentrated, when we are inside the colour blue.

KK: In Finland the colour blue is part of our flag and very much in our mythology. So what we have here are some overlapping notions: the importance of the colour blue in Finnish and Sami culture. In my research I am very interested in ethnic "overlap/p" in all its dimensions. I play with the word "Lapp," with Finns and Samis. The further back you go, the more connections there are, the more similarities in terms of mythologies, ideas, and relatedness. One thing is certain, the motif of the woman and the bear unites us, at least in some ways. And perhaps the Sami concept you mentioned earlier, *baiki*, also captures that sense of trance-cultural desire, of mythic, psychic, dream-time home-coming, the shared space of wo(men) and bears. Thank you Satu for this discussion.

The Cunning Woman and the Bear

A Finnish Bear Story

"Ahaa" the bear says, "now that you have stumbled upon me, we must have a little wrestling match. If I topple you," he says, "then I will eat you on the spot, but if you topple me, then you eat me!"

The woman takes a fright, does not know what will happen now—already looks death in the eyes. She says: "Oh well, bear, so it shall be, so we will do, but," she says, "let us not inflict a wound, let us not wound each other, so neither one of us gets wounded."

But the bear says: "I won't wound you, don't you wound me either."

When they grabbed each other, the woman shouts, "AIYEEEE ... I am wounded!"

"Where?" asks the bear.

The woman lifts her leg, and says, "Look, a wound."

Well, the bear takes a peak and off he goes, takes off on the spot.

From Helmi and Pertti Virtaranta, Karjalan kieltä ja kansankulttuuria I (On Karelian Language and Folk Culture), *Tverinkarjalaisia kielennäytteitä (Tver Karelian Linguistic Samples). Helsinki: Suomalaisugrilainen Seura, 1990. Reprinted in "Furry Tales of the North: A Feminist Interpretation," Special issue of* Folktales/ Contes et legendes, Simone de Beauvoir Institute Bulletin/de l'institut Simone de Beauvoir, *edited by Kaarina Kailo, 1993. 104-127. Translated from Karelian by Kaarina Kailo.*

KAARINA KAILO

Honeypaws in Heaven

Honeypaws, in Heaven
Sacred is your name
Wake up, sweety
get up, and leave
your hot and steamy lair
Honeypaws in Heaven
Holy is your name
May you keep on sending
our daily, sacred bread
may you keep on sending
our daily soulful being
Grandmother, sweetypie
time is up, to wake up
Time to Raise Your Nature, Go to your Being
Go Beserk, raise your feet, prepare for battle
Bear this no more, sweet sister,
Mother in Heaven,
our bearings are weak
can't we see this loss of soul
McHunters are coming
McCutters of your Trees
Please forgive us
Meady Mighty Mother
Mother of Mountains, Mother of Streams and Sacred Trees
For the plunder
and the rape, of
Your Mother Earth
Your sap is bleeding
Your skin is scarred
and your soil sore, eroded
Please send us healing
Mother Earth, Queen of Heaven

KAARINA KAILO

Please restore
the growth, grow back
Your meady, furry,
grassy skin
Give us back
our sense, and self,
Our tender Teddy Bear
Mchunters are coming
to round you up, to
rape your land
Wake up, Mother, Sister, Brother Earth,
Grandmother, Grandfather, Woolly ear
Help us restore the Balance
The skyworld full of hot air
Amen
Awomen
Little cubs of the future.

Dreaming

As autumn ends and the leaves form a blanket over the earth, the rhythm of life slows, and all creatures spend more time sleeping. Even the woman turns within, replenishing her energy and communing with the deeper levels of her being. She dreams along with the bear, learning from her the craft of entering the "dream-time." Nearby, squirrels scuffle about, preparing their food stores for winter, and sleeping in their cosy nests. The woman has reclaimed her animal nature, and is therefore accepted in the winter den of the animals. She enters the communal dream of all living things, and emerges with a sense of belonging to the Earth, of flowing with the Lifestream.

Maureen Enns, "Retreat," mixed media, paper, drawing and painting, 36 x 62", 1993

Maureen Enns, "Blondie – Divide Pass," mixed media, paper, drawing and painting, 30 x 42", 1991

MAUREEN ENNS

Artist Statement: A Testament

In 2002, for the invitation to my art exhibition and book launch at Masters Gallery, Calgary, I wrote the following: *I believe there is a small window of time left whereby man can get it right about what is possible for coexisting on this planet with a summit predator like the bear.*

In 2003, Charlie Russell and I were on the verge of concluding the eighth year of a ground-breaking study on human/bear coexistence in Kambalnoye Lake, South Kamchatka Sancturary, an International Biosphere Reserve in the Russian Far East. May found us looking forward to focusing on our six-year-old orphan-bear, Biscuit's birth of her first cubs: a benchmark for successful reintroduction to the wild.

No bears greeted us this year, as was usual within the first day or two of our annual return. Instead, nailed to the wall of our tiny cabin, which we had built at the base of the Kambalnoye volcano in 1996, was the bladder of a two-year-old cub (Lemon's age!). Too swiftly, it became apparent that our study bears had been brutally slaughtered sometime before spring arrival. The bladder was a clear and cruel message to us that some individuals did not appreciate our efforts to halt the poaching of salmon and grizzlies. We estimated that between 20 and 40 bears had been killed, including Biscuit, Brandy and her cubs, Lemon and Lime. We were devastated.

While the sadness and grief are still fresh, I have created an exhibition in tribute to the bears' lives that were. I pay special tribute to Biscuit who taught me about the possibility of inter-species love with a large wild carnivore. I thank Brandy and her two generations of cubs that demonstrated to me that a mother grizzly with cubs is predictable and peaceful enough to join in a walk, as with any other bear. The series titled, *A Testament*, is of paintings and drawings to celebrate our bears' love of life, their sensitive nature, and their suprising tolerance of me, quite often hovering two feet away from their faces with my camera!

On the darker side, I examine in my paintings, the nature of betrayal, killing, and consumption. What is the difference between a gruseome torture of a fish as a bear peels it alive to eat the tender bits, and a human stalking an animal for the family larder? I have always justified killing for food as acceptable, both in the animal and human world. What is unconscionable and hideous, is killing for purposes of ego-building, greed, or the pleasure of torture—these motives are the ultimate betrayal of nature.

Additionally, this series of work is a culmination of all the different materials, techniques, and ideas that I have been exploring for the past eight years. Each canvas contains aspects of drawing, casting, found objects, and painting with the emotional state of the bear being captured. These new paintings give one a haunting feeling of the bear being torn from its environment and the balance —life-tearing.

I mourn the deaths of the bears of Kambalnoye Lake and I am grateful for what they taught us. They are life-long lessons to be interpreted to endure and teach humanity for generations to come.

—Maureen Enns, August 2003

Contributor Notes

Sima Aprahamian completed her Ph.D. at McGill University in Anthropology. Currently, she is a Fellow at the Simone de Beauvoir Institute, Concordia University in Ottawa, where she teaches anthropology and occasionally women's studies. Her research interests include cross-cultural gender and ethnic identities, community studies, gender/race/class/sexuality, women and development, social inequality, ideologies, literary criticism, the politics of representation, literary responses to genocide, genocide studies, theories of inclusion and exclusion. Her interest in the bear developed while doing fieldwork research in Armenia.

Susan Bright is the author of 19 books of poetry. She is the editor of Plain View Press (plainviewpress.net), which since 1975 has published 220 books. Her work as a poet, publisher, activist and educator has taken her all over the United States and abroad. Her most recent book, *The Layers of Our Seeing*, is a collection of poetry, photographs, and essays about peace done in collaboration with photographer Alan Pogue and Middle Eastern journalist, Muna Hamzeh. Her poetry and essays appear regularly on the blog: earthfamilyalpha.

Isabella Colallilo-Katz is a writer, poet, editor, storyteller, psychotherapist, and holistic educator. She leads workshops on personal creativity and writing and has presented at many international conferences. She is the co-creator and producer of the award-winning audiotape for children, *Crocket, Carob and Crystals: The C3 Trilogy*. Isabella is the author of two books of poetry, *Tasting Fire* (Guernica, 1999) *And Light Remains* (Guernica, 2006). She is a co-editor and author *of Holistic Learning and Spirituality* (SUNY, 2005). Her poetry, articles, and short stories have appeared in magazines, journals, and anthologies. She has given numerous storytelling and poetry performances in Canada and internationally. Isabella teaches Creativity and Creative Writing at Centennial College and Humanistic Psychology at The University of Western Ontario, King's College.

Maureen Enns is an internationally celebrated artist/photographer and co-author of the national best-selling books, *Grizzly Heart* and *Grizzly Seasons*. She is best known for her groundbreaking experimental research concerning human co-existence with grizzly bears in Russia's Far East. She and former research partner, Charlie Russell, were the subject of the documentary *Walking With Giants*; according to PBS, the most popular documentary produced on human/animal interaction. In 2001, Maureen left her tenured teaching position at the Alberta College of Art and Design to take on, full-time, the presidency of the Kamchatka Grizzly Bear Research. She and her Russian Associate, Tatiana Gordienko, negotiated an unprecedented agreement with the head of the equivalent of Parks Canada in Moscow to set aside the southern end of the Kamchatka Peninsula for the research of Enns and Russell. She has also been the subject of two CBC television documentaries; *Games End* (1990); *Grizzly Kingdom* (1993). Maureen has garnered numerous national and international awards in the visual arts and writing. Currently, she is focusing on the creation of the first wild horse preserve in Alberta to not only preserve an important part of Alberta Heritage but the pristine land these horses occupy. Her new painting, drawing and photography, *Wild and Free*, was exhibited at Masters Gallery in the fall of 2007. Pyramid Productions Inc. is developing a documentary based on Maureen's study and art on the wild horses of the Alberta Ghost Forest, titled, "Wild Horses of the Canadian Rockies," to be released in 2008.

Edwina Goldstone was born and grew up in England, but commuted between Finland and her home country while studying the arts. She fell in love with Finland and moved there in the 1990s. She has just completed an Masters in Fine Arts at the Norwich University of the Arts in England. Her art has been exhibited, among other places, in Finland and Egypt, and will soon be shown in London. As a child, she preferred teddybears to dolls and has always been close to nature and animals—a topic she has focused on in many of her illustrations. She works as a teacher, illustrator and painter in Finland.

Marie-Françoise Guédon is an ethnographer and an Associate Professor of Religious Studies at the University of Ottawa. With a Master in Anthropology from the University of Montréal, and a Ph.D. on Anthropology from Bryn Mawr College in Pennsylvania, she has lived with and done research with the Dene (also known as Athapaskan) peoples of Canada and Alaska, Mz'abite communities in Southern Algeria, Inuit communities in New Quebec, and Gitksan people in Northern British Columbia. She is presently working with people of the Northern Pacific Coast in Alaska and with ethnic minority communities in China. She is the Director of InterCulture, a centre for intercultural research and training, at the University of Ottawa. She heads the Frederica de Laguna Northern Books, a press dedicated to the preservation and dissemination of information on Aboriginal populations and ethnic minorities of the Northern and circumpolar regions. Her interests include spirituality and shamanic tradition, as well as Canadian and world Indigenous cultures, and the preservation of Indigenous cultural heritage and Indigenous philosophies. She has published extensively on these topics, and brought to them a woman's point of view. Her last book, *Le rêve et la forêt*, published by Les Presses de l'Université Laval, earned the Luc Lacourcière Medal, and a nomination for the Governor General Literary Award.

Karen Guilbault graduated from the University of Victoria. She has lived in Nelson, British Columbia since 1991, where she works as a teaching assistant in the senior high school. In the summer she also teaches drama and mask-making classes. She began her artistic career painting Tibetan-style mandalas in gouache and watercolour. From there she began painting the human figure in mystical contexts, surrounded by birds, flowers, and animals. Often, the animals in her paintings have a symbolic significance. Today, she paints similar themes in oil, acrylics, and watercolour, as well as landscapes and still lifes. She shows her paintings locally and sells her work a number of different venues.

A Cree poet who originally hails from Saddle Lake First Nations Reserve, **Sky Dancer Louise Bernice Halfe** currently lives in a straw-bale house in Saskatchewan. She has published three poetry books: *Bear Bones & Feathers* was published by Coteau Books in 1994. It received the Canadian Peoples Poet Award, and was a finalist for the Spirit of Saskatchewan Award. *Blue Marrow* was originally published by McLelland and Stewart in 1998; its revised edition was released by Coteau Books in September 2004. *Blue Marrow* was a finalist for both the Governor General's Award for Poetry and the Pat Lowther Award, and for the 1998 Saskatchewan Book of the Year Award and the Saskatchewan Poetry Award. Her latest publication, *The Crooked Good,* was released by Coteau Books in late fall, 2007. In 2005-2006, she was Saskatchewan's Poet Laureate.

Irma Heiskanen graduated with a Masters in Psychology from the University of Turku, Finland 1984, and has been practicing as a psychologist ever since. Her special interests include the ancient Finnish song-poetry, Finnish culture, and worldview. For the past ten years, she has been developing and practicing Finnish ecopsychology based on Finno-Ugric tradition. She lives with her husband on a dairy farm in the Finnish countryside, next to a Conservation Area and one mile from her closest neighbours. She has been drawing and painting since childhood. She creates her artwork in a "related way" that attends to the needs of those for whom she is making the painting. Her artwork, based on the Finno-Ugric tradition of ornaments and casted bronze figures, will be featured in an upcoming book, *Naisten sampo (Female Sampo)*.

Elina Helander-Renvall was born and lives in Utsjoki, Northern Finland. She is a reindeer owner and artist. She also works at the Arctic Centre, University of Lapland in Rovaniemi as senior scientist and as director for the Arctic Indigenous and Sami peoples research office. In addition to research on the Sami language and culture, she has investigated biological diversity, reindeer herding, Indigenous knowledge, and customary law among the Indigenous peoples of the Arctic. Before coming to the Arctic Centre, she has worked among others, as director for the Nordic Sami Institute in Kautokeino, Norway.

Helena Junttila lives and works in a little village called Aska in Finland, Lapland. She graduated from the Free Art School in Helsinki in 1989. She is one of the best-known artists in Lapland, especially renowned for her artwork on bears, men with horns, and women in the wilderness, symbols for the human mind, strengths, and emotions. Helena Junttila's work has been shown in several countries, including Sweden, Norway, Iceland, Germany, Spain, Russia, the United States, Australia, and Japan. Visit her website at: <www.helenajunttila.net>.

Kaarina Kailo holds a Ph.D. in comparative literature (University of Toronto, 1991) and has since held positions in French and in literary and women's studies (Simone de Beauvoir Insitute 1991-1999); professor of women's studies, University of Oulu, Finland (1999-2004), senior researcher of the Finnish Academy (2006-2008). She has published over 70 articles on a wide range of topics from feminism and neoliberalism, Indigenous women and anti-racism, the gift imaginary, gendered violence (shameful femicides), peaceful societies to cyber/ecofeminism and women's spirituality. She has published a book on economic violence, neoliberalism, and healing from violence, *Irti talousväkivallasta—reseptejä solidaariseen hyvinvointiin (Emancipating from Economic Violence: Recipes Towards a Solidarity-Based Well-being)* (2007), and has co-edited books on postcolonialism and Sami Indigenous people, *No Beginning, No End: The Sami Speak Up* (in Finnish and English), with Elina Helander (CCI/Sami Nordic Institute, 1998, 1999); on ecopsychology and healing, *Ekopsykologia ja perinnetieto—polkuja eheyteen (Ecopsychology and Traditional Ecological Knowledge: Paths to Wholeness)*, with Irma Heiskanen (2006); on North-American sauna stories and the sweat-lodge, *Sweating with the Finns, North American Sauna Stories*, with Raija Warkentin and Jorma Halonen (Centre for Northern Studies, Lakehead University, 2006); as well as on cyber/ecofeminism and feminist perspectives on folklore and Northern Native women's issues. Currently she is working on Northern Native and Nordic women's writings on trauma and healing, and on "Arctic Mysteria." She is also a grassroots activist in the women's and peace movement, believing with the "Feminists for a Gift Economy" network that "a radically different world is possible" provided women of all backgrounds form this pro-democracy sisterhood.

Jenny Kangasvuo currently lives in Oulu, in northern Finland. She wrote her doctoral dissertation about Finnish bisexuality at the Department of Art Studies and Cultural Anthropology of the University of Oulu. She draws, writes speculative fiction, and trains aikido and astanga yoga. Visit her website at: <www.iki.fi/jek>.

A central theme of **Ritva Kovalainen's** photography and poetry is the relationship between humans and nature. She has collaborated with Sanni Seppo for the past fifteen years, photographing trees and forests. Their collaborative work explores the spiritual and cultural connotations of mythology associated with the forest as well as modern-day people's relationship with the forest. Together they have published books, created and exhibited multimedia art, and produced a short film. Visit their website: <www.puidenkansa.net>.

Jürgen Werner Kremer, Ph.D., is a clinical psychologist by training and teaches at the Santa Rosa Junior College as well as Saybrook Institute Graduate School and Sonoma State University. He is the editor of the journal *ReVision*. He has published on decolonization, Nordic mythology, ethnoautobiography, shamanism, and various issues in transpersonal psychology.

Celine Leduc graduated with a Masters in Religious Studies from Concordia University, Montreal, Canada, with a particular focus on women and religion. For five years she hosted, researched, and produced a weekly radio show dealing with women's issues for the past five years on CKUT, Radio McGill. She is a published writer and poet, and has performed at Black Theatre Workshop, and Ethnic Origins.

Satu Marit Natunen is a Sami artist living and working in both Inari, Samiland and Helsinki, Finland. She describes her art as "modern ethnic naivism." Apart from being a Bear woman, she describes herself as Sagittarius. She has worked and at the Atelier de Tissage in the South of France, at Muurla Opisto in Finland, and in Washington, D.C. at Georgetown University. She has also studied in her native Samiland, at the Education Centre (SAAK) of Inary (1995-1996) where she received her Sami Duoddji-patent. She has held numerous art exhibitions in cities around the world, and has worked in Mexico, Guatemala, El Salvador, Equador, India, Malaysia, and Bali, familiarizing herself particularly with the arts traditions and practices of other Native artists. In 1997, she organized an art exhibition in Argentina for the World Council of Indigenous Peoples.

Kirsti Paltto is from and lives in Utsjoki/Ohcejohka, the Finnish side of Samiland. She has written and published in the Sami language since the late 1960s. She has published 19 books including novels, short story and poetry collections, as well as children's books. She has also written plays and newspaper columns. Her most recent books are *Násttis muohtagierragis*, the last part of her historical trilogy of Sami life, and *Ája*, a collection of short stories for youth, both published in 2007 by the Sami publishing house Davvi Girji.

Jordan Paper is Professor Emeritus (Religious Studies) at York University (Toronto) and a Fellow at the Centre for Studies in Religion and Society at the University of Victoria (British Columbia). Raised as an Orthodox Jew, his spiritual understanding radically changed when coming out of a lodge, on completing a traditional four-day fast, an Anishnaabe elder informed him of the sex of Bear, with whom he had had a relationship for several decades, as female. That epiphany not only brought to fruition his functional spiritual life, but led to his later writing the book, *Through the Earth Darkly: Female Spirituality in Comparative Perspective* (Continuum 1997). His father would not have realized how prescient he was in choosing Dov (Bear) as Jordan's second Hebrew name.

Mari Redkin is studying to become a teacher at the Faculty of Educational Sciences at Oulu University in northern Finland. Her ecologically-oriented artwork takes various forms, relies on many kinds of artistic mediums, and consists in portrayals of animals, humans, and fantasy figures. She has held several art exhibitions in Oulu and her work is also displayed at <www.undefinedart.net>.

Ulla Ryum is an Inuit storyteller and playwright from Greenland. She has worked in theatre, in politics, and has taught in several universities. She loves to travel and share the knowledge she acquires from visiting other countries. When she is not visiting Canada, or living in Winnipeg, she lives near the Baltic Sea, south of Copenhagen. She first wrote her play "Annanatsiat" as a short story, which was published in Greenland. In 2007, the play was translated into Kalatlisut, the Greenlandic language. It was presented as a stage-reading in Winnipeg and is currently being developed for a performance in Nuuk, Greenland in the summer of 2008.

Kari Sallamaa is a professor of literature at the University of Oulu, Finland. He has held several academic positions at the universities of Oulu, Helsinki, Tromsoe (Norway) and Vienna since 1980. His research interests include ethnic minority literatures, particularly among Finno-Ugric (Uralic) peoples; northern literatures of the Barents region; Uralic folklore and mythology. He is one of the leading developers and philosophers of ethnofuturism, a cultural and political program aimed at preserving and restoring the national and ethnic consciousness of Uralic peoples. He has published two collections of poems, among them *House of the Black Elk* (2001).

Sanni Seppo is a photographer whose work has a documentary quality that focuses on society and depicts individuals leading in various social situations. His collaborative work with Ritva Kovalainen explores the spiritual and cultural connotations of mythology associated with the forest as well as modern-day people's relationship with the forest. Visit their website: <www.puidenkansa.net>.

Aleksandr Suvorov was born Uvinskoje, Udmurtia. He has worked as senior instructor in drawing and painting at the Department of Design of the University of the Republic of Udmurtia and has held numerous local exhibitions of his art. The bronze cast "Udmurtia 1996" included in this anthology is from the Ugriculture Exhibition 2000, Contemporary Art of the Finno-Ugrian Peoples, Karelia-Komi-Mari-Mordvinia-Udmurt-Hungary-Estonia held at the Gallen-Kallela Museum from May 2000 to January 2002. Suvorov's bronze works were also exhibited in Finland in 2001 at Lönnström Art Museum and Riihimäki Art Museum.

Christopher G. Trott is an Assistant Professor in Native Studies at St. John's College, University of Manitoba. He has worked with the Inuit communities of Arctic Bay and Pangnirtung since 1979.

Kira Van Deusen is a professional storyteller and cellist based in Vancouver, Canada. She travelled extensively in Siberia's forests, tundra, and steppes over 15 years beginning shortly after the fall of the Soviet Union, and connected with indigenous traditions, stories, and people. In 2004, Kira travelled in all three regions of Nunavut with filmmaker John Houston recording the legend of Kiviuq from Inuit elders. She performs widely in Canada and beyond and has published several books on Siberian and Inuit culture. <www.kiravan.com>.

Patricia June Vickers is a doctoral candidate at the University of Victoria, British Columbia. Her feast hall status comes from the Gitxaala nation, Laxsgyiik from the House of Gilaskamax. She also has ancestry in the Heiltsuk, Haida, and British nations. She currently resides in Ts'msyen territory in Terrace, British Columbia. <pjvickers@mac.com>.

In January, 2002, **Wacoquaakmik (A. Rodney Bobiwash)** passed from our human world to the Spirit world, but the memory of his spirit and courage lives on. At only 42, he lost his battle with that great enemy of Indian people—diabetes. The Bear Clan philosophy guided his life in every way, and in his brief but full life he accomplished more than one might in several lifetimes. He gave his time and knowledge and skills, sometimes even jeopardizing his own safety, for the greater good of all Native people. He spent the majority of his life fighting for Native rights in many roles: as a teacher, advisor, director and speaker. In the mid 1990s, he was one of only two non-lawyers appointed by the Ontario government as an Adjudicator with the Ontario Human Rights Commission. He was the key figure in two successful human right proceedings against hate crimes, resulting in the silencing of the Heritage Front (a neo-nazi hate group) in Toronto. He also served as a member of the Toronto Mayor's Committee on Race Relations, co-chaired the Ontario Joint Aboriginal Anti-Racism Task force, and wrote extensively on issues related to human rights and anti-racist organizing. He was the founder of the Toronto Native Community History Project, and taught in Aboriginal Studies programs at the University of Manitoba, Trent University, and the University of Toronto. He served as Director of First Nations House at the University of Toronto, and Executive Director of the Native Canadian Centre of Toronto. He worked with Indigenous peoples in Siberia, Indonesia, Vanuatu, Columbia and Mexico and participated in the United Nations Human Rights Commission-Working Group on Indigenous People.

Photo: Kirsti Laurinolli

Kaarina Kailo has published over 70 articles on a wide range of topics from feminism and neoliberalism, Indigenous women and anti-racism, the gift imaginary, gendered violence (shameful femicides), peaceful societies to cyber/ecofeminism and women's spirituality. She has published a book on economic violence, neoliberalism, and healing from violence, *Irti talousväkivallasta—reseptejä solidaariseen hyvinvointiin (Emancipating from Economic Violence: Recipes Towards a Solidarity-Based Well-Being)* (2007), and has co-edited books on postcolonialism and Sami Indigenous people, *No Beginning, No End: The Sami Speak Up* (in Finnish and English), with Elina Helander (1998, 1999); on ecopsychology and healing, *Ekopsykologia ja perinnetieto—polkuja eheyteen (Ecopsychology and Traditional Ecological Knowledge: Paths to Wholeness)*, with Irma Heiskanen (2006); and also on North-American sauna stories and the sweat-lodge, *Sweating with the Finns, North American Sauna Stories*, with Raija Warkentin and Jorma Halonen (2006).